Praise for

ARE YOU WITH ME?
KEVIN BOYLE AND THE RISE OF
THE HUMAN RIGHTS MOVEMENT

'Kevin Boyle contributed to the building of modern Ireland, and the wider world, as a place of universal human rights. Practitioner, law teacher, activist and global champion of human rights, Boyle deserves this splendid biography. It explains his place in the pantheon of human rights champions.'

MICHAEL KIRBY, *former Justice of the High Court of Australia and past President of the International Commission of Jurists*

'An eloquent account of the life and work of one of the greatest heroes who has ever worked in the sphere of human rights ... The world was made a better place because of Kevin Boyle – a charismatic, generous and ebullient figure – and I am delighted that Mike Chinoy has written this book.'

ZEINAB BADAWI, *broadcaster and former Chair of Article 19*

'Brilliant and charismatic in equal measure, Kevin Boyle ... showed how scholarship could be done with an eye to real change. What a pleasure it is to have a book that brings his fully-lived life back into view.'

CONOR GEARTY, *Professor*
Lon(

D1354231

'Mike Chinoy has written an engaging portrait of Boyle the lawyer and Boyle the man, and anyone interested in Ireland, justice, or international law should read this book.'

HURST HANNUM, *Professor of International Law at Fletcher School of Law and Diplomacy, Tufts University*

'Part of the problem in remembering the past in Northern Ireland is that the people who were most demonstrative and aggressive are given their place in history while the more effectively assertive and tactically intelligent are bypassed. Mike Chinoy has placed Kevin Boyle back at the heart of the story, where he belongs, as a civil rights activist and lawyer who went on to gain global importance. He shows Boyle to have been a man of thoughtful conscience and immense personal courage who was concerned with the rights of all and who – along with allies like Tom Hadden – has bequeathed us an impartial emphasis on rights untainted by prejudice or allegiance. Chinoy brings the necessary journalistic thoroughness to this story of a world-shaker whose moves were quiet, deliberate and compassionate.'

MALACHI O'DOHERTY, *Gerry Adams: An Unauthorised Life*

ARE YOU WITH ME?

KEVIN BOYLE AND THE RISE OF THE HUMAN RIGHTS MOVEMENT

MIKE CHINOY

THE LILLIPUT PRESS
DUBLIN

For Inez

First published 2020 by
THE LILLIPUT PRESS
62–63 Sitric Road, Arbour Hill
Dublin 7, Ireland
www.lilliputpress.ie

Paperback ISBN 9781843517726

1 3 5 7 9 10 8 6 4 2

The Lilliput Press gratefully acknowledges
the financial support of the Arts Council/
An Chomhairle Ealaíon.

Set in 11pt on 15pt Caslon by Marsha Swan
Printed in Poland by Drukarnia Skleniarz

Contents

Illustrations between pages 208 and 209.

Author's Note

FOR SOMEONE who spent most of his career in the public eye, Kevin Boyle was remarkably private. By nature unassuming and self-effacing, he was less interested in talking about himself than about the issues on which he was engaged, or the work of his colleagues or students. Many of his greatest achievements took place away from the glare of publicity. Boyle's prodigious intellectual and political output contains relatively little about his own personal emotions, motivations, decisions, or actions. While there are references to him in many books about the Troubles in Northern Ireland, or in analyses of broader questions related to the struggle for human rights, the role he actually played over more than four decades, let alone his compelling personal story, is barely known. Yet, arguably, he was one of the most influential figures in the Northern Ireland civil rights movement and in the search for a peace agreement. On the global stage, he was a pioneer in using international law on behalf of the victims of torture, unjust imprisonment and discrimination, and in defence of freedom of expression, belief and association. In the process, he helped create the intellectual foundation for an expansion of human rights protections around the word, and inspired generations of activists who have followed him. In short, as Mary Robinson, Ireland's one-time president and the former UN High Commissioner for Human Rights, said when I told her about this book, 'Kevin Boyle deserves to be remembered.'

I first met Kevin Boyle in Belfast in 1972. As a student at Yale University, influenced by the ferment of the anti-Vietnam war movement in the US, I had become interested in the struggle for civil rights in Northern Ireland. While visiting my college professor parents, who were on sabbatical leave in London, in December 1971 I flew to Dublin to learn more. Arriving at the office of Sinn Féin, the IRA's political wing, I asked if I could talk to someone. Moments later, I was ushered into a back room and told to 'have a wee word with Joe'. It turned out that 'Joe' was Joe Cahill, a legendary IRA gunman, then on the run from the authorities in Belfast. Balding, with hooded eyes and a cigarette between his lips, he apparently had nothing better to do than to spend an entire afternoon explaining the history and rationale for the IRA's campaign against the British in Northern Ireland to a nineteen-year-old American college student. As an aspiring journalist, it was my first scoop, which I duly published in the *Yale Daily News*.

Five months later my sociologist father was invited to give a talk at Queen's University Belfast, and, with my interest in Irish issues, I accompanied him. We arrived in Belfast as the Ulster Defence Association, the extreme loyalist paramilitary force, was setting up no-go zones in Protestant areas in protest at Catholic neighbourhoods having done the same thing. The city was in terrifying turmoil, with barricades on the streets, gangs of stone-throwing rioters rampaging through both communities, smoke from burning tyres darkening the summer skies, and nervous British troops struggling to maintain order.

Queen's University, however, was an oasis of calm. My father gave his talk, and at a reception afterwards I met Kevin Boyle. Puffing on his pipe, utterly without airs, he was as interested in hearing my thoughts as I was in learning more about him. When he told me that he was coming to Yale that September on a postgraduate fellowship, I asked if he would be willing to supervise me in an independent study course on Irish history. He readily agreed, and almost every week during the following academic year we met to discuss the readings he had assigned. It was the beginning of both a close friendship and a deeper intellectual appreciation of the complexity of Irish history and politics.

With ambitions to be a foreign correspondent, after graduating from Yale I decided to freelance in Northern Ireland. Kevin generously offered to let me stay in the spare room of his house. I spent many weeks there in 1974, 1975, 1976 and 1977. During that time he became my invaluable source as I sought to understand the conflict in Northern Ireland and the many issues it raised. After moving to Hong Kong to work as a journalist covering China and Asia in the mid-1970s (I had majored in Chinese Studies at Yale), I maintained my interest in the Troubles. In 1983 I became the fourth foreign correspondent hired by CNN, based in London, and resumed reporting on Irish issues. Boyle's perspective was again instrumental in helping me make sense of what was going on. In the years that followed, as I moved to Beijing and Hong Kong for CNN, and then joined a think tank at the University of Southern California, Kevin and I stayed in touch.

My own experiences and insights, which Kevin Boyle played a significant role in shaping, provided an initial framework for this project. However, I discovered that, although we were friends for nearly forty years, the same modest and unassuming qualities that characterized his dealings with so many others meant that I actually knew relatively little about the range, scope and influence of his many activities. In seeking to understand and depict his remarkable life and work, I have therefore used the tools of the investigative journalist and historian – documents and interviews. I have relied first and foremost on the extraordinary archive of his papers at the James Hardiman Library at the National University of Ireland, Galway, where Boyle taught from 1978 to 1986. Donated by his wife Joan after Kevin's untimely death in 2010, and archived by Barry Houlihan and colleagues, the letters, papers, diaries, journals, emails, manuscripts, press clippings, and audio and video recordings became the indispensable resource not only in reconstructing what he did, but also what he thought and felt.

I have also made extensive use of two long interviews with Boyle: the first, *Violence in Ulster*, an oral history published in 1975 by the late William Van Voris, contains Van Voris' verbatim transcripts from conversations with Boyle in 1972 and 1973; the second was a four-hour interview conducted in 2006 by British historian Simon Prince, author of *Northern Ireland's '68*. These interviews offer valuable insights and recollections about Boyle's youth, the evolution of his thinking, his role in the civil rights movement and the violence that followed.

In addition, I interviewed over 100 people – family, friends, colleagues, lawyers, scholars, journalists, activists and others who shared their own memories, providing letters, photographs and other documents, and offering guidance and suggestions. When quoted in the text, these interviews are not footnoted, although citations are provided for all other written sources.

Hong Kong
November 2019

Prologue

IT RAINED SO HARD on the day Kevin Boyle was buried that his widow Joan and their two sons barely made it to the funeral on time.

On a grey and stormy morning in January 2011, they arrived at the quaint, non-denominational Victorian chapel at Colchester cemetery, Essex, squeezed into a local taxi secured at the last minute, just as the hearse carrying the body drew up. In the churchyard, Joan, Mark and Stephen were met by a sea of sombre faces. They were of all ages and nationalities: current and former students from Britain, Ireland, the rest of Europe, the Middle East, Africa and Asia, fellow academics and lawyers, friends and relatives, luminaries from the world of politics, the media, and the law. A former doctoral student from Turkey was there, her infant son strapped to her chest. The Boyles' next-door neighbour, a dentist, had closed his surgery to attend.

The chapel sat on the edge of a tree-lined 57-acre cemetery, where birds, deer, badgers and foxes wandered among the thousands of gravestones. The chapel could accommodate nearly 200 people, including standing room in the aisles. But on this raw day, so many had come that dozens were forced to stand outside, seeking shelter from the wet weather under the chapel's portico.

Joan was astonished. She had expected a substantial turnout – indeed, the funeral home had been alerted and had set up loudspeakers to broadcast the service to anyone who could not find a seat – but nothing had prepared her for the size of the assembled mourners. The University of Essex, where Kevin had taught for twenty years, had laid on a coach to bring staff and students. So many expressed a desire to attend, however, that when the university offered to arrange additional coaches, Boyle's closest colleagues, who were helping with the funeral arrangements, quietly discouraged the move, concerned that the modest venue would be unable to cope with the numbers.

Kevin Boyle was only sixty-seven when lung cancer claimed his life. Packed into the tiny church, or wet and shivering outside, the mourners heard him eulogized as a towering figure, one of the great human rights lawyers of his time

Among the mourners was Michael Farrell. Thin, bearded and intense, he had been Boyle's fellow student at Queen's. The two had marched together, confronted the Northern Ireland police, and argued over strategy while spearheading the struggle for civil rights at a time when the North's minority Catholic community faced systematic discrimination at the hands of the Protestants who dominated the government, the economy and the security forces. After learning of Kevin's death, Farrell had written to Joan, noting that Kevin was among the first activists who sought to use not just street protests but the law to push for change, playing a pioneering role in challenging state-sanctioned abuses in Northern Ireland before the European Commission of Human Rights.

Sitting nearby was Hurst Hannum, an American law professor from Tufts University in Boston and one of Boyle's closest friends. In the early 1970s they had brought a landmark case to the European Commission on behalf of seven Northern Irish men who had been interned without trial and beaten and tortured in detention. The legal battle was one of the earliest moves to draw attention to abuses perpetrated by the British army and Northern Ireland police in an international legal forum. Hannum remembered Boyle as a charismatic but exceptionally modest man who would joke that he had learned everything he knew about law from Hannum (as well as everything he knew about fine wine). Hannum, though, was clear that Boyle was a 'first-rate lawyer' in his own right, with a remarkable skill for building relationships and getting things done.

Tom Hadden was also at the funeral. On the face of it, Hadden – from a conservative, well-to-do Protestant family in one of Northern Ireland's most staunchly Protestant areas – was as different from Boyle as it was possible to be. Although they came from warring communities, he and Boyle, colleagues at the Queen's University law faculty during the worst days of the Troubles, had become friends and had forged a remarkable intellectual partnership. It was just one of many instances in which Boyle, despite his background, transcended Northern Ireland's sectarian divide in his professional, political and personal life – not least by marrying Joan, a Protestant from a small town outside Belfast. Hadden and Boyle had collaborated on several crucially important books and papers over two decades which offered practical proposals for resolving the Northern Irish conflict – proposals that helped provide the intellectual underpinning to the peace process that would end that conflict.

With all but one of seven surviving siblings looking on, Boyle's younger brother Louis talked about how Kevin had grown up as one of nine children, son of a taxi driver in a small town in Northern Ireland. Slight, white-haired and soft-spoken, Louis reminisced about how Kevin became one of the leaders of the Northern Ireland civil rights movement, where 'he brought a strong intellectual, strategic and moderating influence to its affairs'.[1]

Louis Boyle was followed by Sir Nigel Rodley. Since 1990, when Boyle had become the director of the University of Essex Human Rights Law Centre, Rodley had worked with him to turn it into the world's leading centre of human rights education – 'a multi-disciplinary powerhouse of research, teaching, and support for litigation'.[2] To Rodley, a child of refugees from Nazi Germany, who for many years was the top lawyer at Amnesty International, Kevin had two sides. He was a 'slightly dreamy' idealist and 'a really sharp, hard-headed lawyer'. Rodley spoke about Boyle's 'powerful commitment to the repair of damage and the righting of wrongs: redress and justice'.[3]

Kevin Boyle's career covered a sweeping range of human rights causes, from equality and social justice to censorship, discrimination and state-sanctioned torture and murder. It spanned decades – he had begun teaching law in 1966 – and continents. He dealt with freedom fighters, political prisoners, presidents and prime ministers, terrorists and the Secretary General of the United Nations. He was the lead lawyer in the case that decriminalized homosexuality in Northern Ireland. He played a key role in Amnesty International's campaign against apartheid in South Africa. He fought and won landmark cases at the European Court of Human Rights on freedom of expression, and he spearheaded the international effort to defend the writer Salman Rushdie after he was condemned to death by Iran's Ayatollah Khomeini. He became the chief legal advisor to the UN High Commissioner for Human Rights, and was an inspirational figure in the creation of human rights law centres at universities from Brazil to Japan.

As the rain poured down relentlessly, another Essex colleague, Françoise Hampson, delivered the final eulogy. Thin, intense, with a rapid-fire delivery, she was one of the world's leading experts on the law of war, but she was like a sister to Boyle. 'They were joined at the hip,' Joan Boyle recalled. 'He would bring her home to dinner. They would drink red wine, Kevin would smoke his pipe, Françoise would smoke cigarettes, and they would argue and argue, usually about points of law. They would go outside. Kevin would walk her home, but they would stop to continue arguing. Then they would get to her house and continue arguing.'

Hampson told the mourners about the dozens of cases she and Boyle had brought to the European Court of Human Rights in the 1990s on behalf of Kurdish villagers savagely treated by the Turkish state – cases that required difficult, often dangerous journeys to distant corners of Turkey, shadowed by government agents, as they met with grieving mothers and widows. After learning of Boyle's death, Kurdish activists had called Joan to say that they wanted to erect of statue of Kevin in the mainly Kurdish city of Diyarbakır to honour what he had done for them.

In her eulogy, Hampson observed that it was not simply what Boyle did that had attracted the overflowing crowd. 'It is who he was,' she said. 'For Kevin was loved at least as much as he was respected.'[4] Indeed, for a man who had spent much of his life engaged with some of the world's most divisive issues and bitter conflicts, the immense goodwill he generated – and his lack of enemies, even among those who had been his adversaries, was striking. 'I wouldn't say that about many people,' recalled Hurst Hannum, 'but everybody liked Kevin.' This view was endorsed by newspaper stories about his death. The *Belfast Telegraph* described him as 'an internationally respected inspirational figure',[5] while, to the *Irish Independent*, he was a 'truly good man who lived and breathed human rights'.[6] And just before the funeral, Joan had received a letter from a retired member of the Royal Ulster Constabulary, Northern Ireland's police force, an organization that had been the target of much of Boyle's early activism. The police officer wrote how, at the height of the Troubles, he would visit Kevin's home regularly for drinks and 'late night debates, where we constantly surprised each other by how much we agreed, the civil rights champion and the RUC man'.[7]

Hampson recalled how 'Kevin was the same with everyone, from cleaners to heads of state. You did not need to be a colleague or a student to be sucked up into his care and concern. Once taken under Kevin's wing, you stayed there.'[8] This view was endorsed by generations of his students, for whom Boyle was not simply a professor but a beloved teacher, mentor, colleague and guide. In the words of one colleague, Boyle 'spawned a global battalion of pragmatic optimists, all of whom contributed, in an infinite variety of ways, to the advancement of human rights'.[9]

So many of Boyle's students at the University of Essex had become important figures in the world of human rights that, within the field, they were known as the 'Essex mafia'. On this day, they included the chief legal advisor for Médecins Sans Frontières, officials from Human Rights Watch, Amnesty International, and former students working on human rights from Britain, Turkey and South Sudan. Messages from those who were unable to attend the funeral flooded Joan Boyle's inbox, coming from Jamaica, Japan, Uzbekistan, Uganda and Malawi. A Turkish student working at the European Commission on Human Rights wrote that what Boyle had 'done for the hundreds of victims of human rights violations in Turkey and elsewhere will never be forgotten'.[10] And from Malawi, former student Zolomphi Nkowani, now a human rights lawyer, wrote: 'His tremendous contribution to the cause is one of the greatest gifts he had left us all.'[11]

In the thirty-four years that Kevin and Joan Boyle were married, he often described his career as a combination of 'three 'A's: academic, advocate and activist'. Yet Joan, in her words, was 'astounded' by the outpouring of tributes from so many quarters. 'The same words came up again and again.' It wasn't that she and her sons were unaware of what Kevin had done. 'The boys and I knew all about the projects Kevin was involved with, as he talked non-stop about them at mealtimes, always enthusing about something – or in the case of some of the Kurdish cases, having to be silenced as the graphic details of some of the horrors were not suitable for mealtimes.'

Although Boyle's warmth and Irish charm were legendary – as were his consummate political skills – he was such a modest, unassuming person that it would never have occurred to him to describe the impact of his work, and of how people responded to him, in the way that so many were now doing. Joan recalled attending a freedom of expression conference with Boyle in Oslo not long before he was diagnosed with lung cancer. They spotted a booth for Article 19, the freedom of expression advocacy organization of which Kevin had served as director in the late 1980s:

> We went over. Kevin talked to them about the importance of their work and then moved on. I was really frustrated about this, as I thought they would have been very excited to meet the organization's founding director. So after Kevin had moved on, I told them. I then persuaded him to go back and talk some more about his work. But this was quite typical. I was left to do the bragging.

As Pia Jennings, a former student who had gone on to work for the Irish Human Rights Commission in Dublin, wrote to Joan, 'he was the most humble man I have ever met. He rarely spoke of his many achievements in life, preferring instead to hear about his students' interests and visions for the future.'[12]

Joan later recalled that 'we never saw the joined-up picture until people from every one of Kevin's projects and adventures all came upon us at once' at the funeral. 'That was what was astounding – the extent of what he had been involved with and what he had achieved.' Indeed, to Hannum, what was striking about Boyle was how he evolved from a civil rights leader in 'a little place' like Northern Ireland to being a leader on the global stage of international human rights. 'It was so much broader than anything else that anyone else from Northern Ireland ever did.' Of all the activists who came to prominence during the Troubles, Boyle was 'the only one who escaped or grew into anyone who had a much more global influence, that wasn't just about Northern Ireland'.

In his lectures, Boyle would stop at critical moments, look at the class and ask, 'Are you with me?' To the students, the double-edged meaning was clear. Did they understand the material? And were they with him in the fight for human rights, in which, through his teaching, he provided the weapons?

It was no accident that the first prayer chosen for the funeral service, composed by the great British hymnist John Dudley Smith, was for 'those whose freedom has been taken from them ... and in whose heart the lamp of hope burns low. God of mercy, give them hope.'

Kevin Boyle spent his life trying to kindle that hope.

[1]

The King

KEVIN BOYLE did not meet a Protestant until he was seventeen.

Born on 23 May 1943, he was the fourth of nine children in a devoutly Catholic family living in Newry, an overwhelmingly Catholic town just a few miles north of Northern Ireland's border with the Irish Republic. When Ireland was partitioned in July 1921, despite calls from local residents that Newry and its surrounding hinterland be incorporated into the newly established Republic, the town and County Down were made part of Northern Ireland, where Protestants outnumbered Catholics two to one.

Kevin's father, Louis, the youngest of six brothers, was born in 1910 in Whitecross, a village of a few hundred people, almost all Catholics, a few miles from Newry. In the late 1920s the family moved to Newry and established a 'Hackney cab' or taxi business. Kevin's mother, Elizabeth McArdle, born in 1911, also came from a rural background – the tiny settlement of Aughnamoira, south of Newry. Her family were farmers, so poor that the young Elizabeth had to walk to school in bare feet. Although a good student with ambitions to become a teacher, poverty kept her from continuing her education. In keeping with the priorities of the time, her parents used what little they had to ensure that her brother Desmond Leo would stay in school. He eventually opened a chemist's shop in Newry. For her part, Elizabeth followed her other brother Hugh John – and a long line of Irish people – to America at the age of sixteen, where she spent three years working as a barmaid in Boston. Returning home to help nurse her younger sister Bridget, who was dying of TB, Elizabeth met Louis Boyle. They were married in 1939.

Their nine children – Anne, Desmond, Finola, Kevin, Eugene, Bernadette, Louis, Jim and Damian – arrived in quick succession.

For the first few years of their married life, Louis and Elizabeth lived with their rapidly expanding family in a flat above the chemist's shop run by Elizabeth's brother in the centre of Newry. To keep his taxi company afloat, Louis worked long hours, seven days a week. He had two vehicles, an Austin 18 and, later, a black London taxi. It was a tough way to make a living, but Boyle's Taxis became well known in Newry, and Louis soon saved enough to purchase a three-storey terrace house with an adjoining garage at 37a Castle Street in one of Newry's oldest areas, next to McCann's, a well-known local bakery. It was here that Kevin and his siblings grew up.

The house was cosy, filled with a mixture of smells: bread baking next door, their father's pipe, and coal from the fire in the living room. With a family of eleven packed into five bedrooms, however, it was more than a little cramped. As the oldest, Anne was entitled to her own room, but the two other girls had to share, as did the boys: Kevin, Louis and Jim in one room, and Desmond, Eugene and Damian in another. There was only one toilet. With the raw Irish weather, the children often did their homework wrapped up in blankets. Hot water came from a back boiler behind the coal fire. One bath a week was the routine, and the water generally had to be shared.

Kevin described his father as a taciturn man who was always working. Eugene, a year younger than Kevin, remembered him as 'very strict, a hard man who took no nonsense'. Louis, two years younger than Eugene, recalled their father as withdrawn around visitors, and often volatile, with sharp mood swings and a temper. 'If you stepped out of line, a beating was in order. But when my father did beat you, he quickly calmed down and offered you a cup of tea.' His sister Finola, in a short autobiographical reminiscence published years later, wrote of her father: 'He hadn't had much of an education, but was a born leader, and reckoned a holy terror when you did wrong. Under it, though, he had a heart of pure gold and a great sense of humour. He could shake with great laughter for minutes at a time, the pipe dangling dangerously from his mouth.'[1]

Elizabeth – or Lilly, as her husband always called her – was more outgoing and 'kind in every way',[2] according to Finola, but the family largely kept itself to itself. 'The whole family was regarded as a wee bit eccentric,' Kevin recalled years later, 'because we didn't mix very well. We imitated our parents in having few outside contacts. All of us spent a lot of time at home. We were not encouraged to go out anywhere. We were not encouraged to make a lot of friends.'[3]

Kevin grew up a gentle child, his brother Eugene recalling him as 'quiet and thoughtful, with his own ideas'. He disliked arguing, bullying and any sort of conflict. Even when he was little, he played the role of family peace-maker, seeking to resolve the inevitable quarrels that erupted in a crowded house with so many children. As Eugene remembered, 'Kevin was the inter-mediary, always saying "calm down, calm down".' It was a role he continued to play as an adult. He was especially close to his mother. Years later, after he had become a prominent public figure, a friend of his mother's saw him on television and wrote to remind him that he had been 'a good little boy'.

For the Boyle family, life revolved around the Church. 'We were steeped in religion,' Kevin's brother Louis recalled. 'That was probably the most abiding theme throughout our early lives.' Newry Cathedral was just a few minutes' walk from their home, close enough to hear the bells for morning Mass and evening devotions. 'Our mother was a very holy woman,' wrote Finola. 'She cycled to Mass almost every day of the year, rising up early for the first one just after six.'[4] For the Boyle children, going to mass, commu-nion and confession every week was non-negotiable. During Lent, they were required to attend mass every morning before school, as well as to participate in a week-long mission held by one of the local religious orders. Every evening, each child had to say the Rosary. 'We had to recite it ten times,' said Louis. 'Father called on each child to lead.' Giggling or a lack of seriousness would produce a menacing glare from their father. At the St Patrick's and St Coleman's Cathedral on Hill Street, Louis was a choir boy, while Kevin served six years as an altar boy.

The intense Catholicism was reinforced at school. A hundred yards down the street from the Boyle home sat the Abbey Christian Brothers Grammar

School. Established in 1802 by the Irish businessman Edmund Rice, the Christian Brothers were a Catholic religious order whose mission was to educate the children of the poor. The first President of the Irish Republic, Éamon de Valera, attended a Brothers school, as did several subsequent Irish taoisigh (prime ministers), as well as important figures in Northern Ireland. The Christian Brothers later became enmeshed in scandal, with widespread reports of physical and sexual abuse in schools run by the order throughout Ireland, although the school the Boyle boys attended in Newry was never tainted with such allegations.[5]

The curriculum at the Christian Brothers school was explicitly Catholic, with a heavy dose of Irish nationalism for good measure, expressed in the promotion of the Irish language as well as Gaelic football and hurling. Soccer was derided as a 'foreign' game. Kevin's brother Louis described the curriculum as a form of indoctrination, reinforced by relentless pressure to study and harsh punishments for misbehaviour. The children's parents constantly encouraged them to consider vocations in the Church – priesthood for the boys, nuns for the girls.

Early on, Kevin displayed strong academic potential, excelling in Irish, Latin and history. At home, his early nickname was Big Head. 'It's all them brains in there, packed with promise,' one of his aunts said.[6] Later, according to Finola, 'he cleverly twisted the name to suit himself. First the "Big" was dropped, and for a while he was known as "Head", then by some further manoeuvring "Head" became "King", finally immortalized as "The King".[7] Stories of some younger classmate arriving at the Boyle home and announcing 'The King's forgotten his football boots. I'm here to fetch them' became part of family lore. While this reflected Kevin's emerging leadership skills, he treated the nickname as a joke. Indeed, most of the Boyle boys had nicknames. Jim was 'Bimmer' and Eugene, after an incident in which he killed a chicken, became 'Pierrepoint', named for the last hangman in Britain. Damian, last of the boys to attend the mixed Infants School run by the local nuns, was known as 'Baby Nun'.

Anne, Finola and Bernadette attended the Sacred Heart grammar and primary school, run by the Sisters of St Clare. Even in the conservative Catholic tradition, the nuns, called Poor Clares, were known for their austerity, with shaved heads and a demeanour the Boyle children remembered as 'very mysterious and bizarre'. As Finola wrote, 'The nuns were a terror.'[8]

Louis Boyle recalled that it was a struggle for each child to assert individuality and independence in such a big family. Desmond, Jim and Louis played on various Gaelic football teams run by the school. Kevin was brains not brawn, and showed little interest in, or aptitude for, sports, except swimming. Louis, in particular, looked up to his older brother and often sought his advice. 'Kevin and Louis were mates,' Eugene recalled. 'They had a special comradeship.'

Elizabeth Boyle pushed her children to become avid readers. 'She very much influenced us towards education,' Kevin recalled:

> Whenever she bought presents, she always bought books. She created an atmosphere. You did your homework, and then, along with everybody else, you sat around reading books. It was perfectly normal in our house for five or six people to be sitting around different parts of the living room reading books for hours on end.[9]

Kevin's favourite books were the classics like *Robinson Crusoe* and *Moby-Dick* – both of which depicted adventures in far-off places – or the novels of Dickens and Hardy, to which his mother introduced him. These were augmented by the cowboy stories his mother's brother Hugh John would send from America. Kevin devoured books, attaining a reading level well beyond his age and acquiring a manner so serious and studious, Joan would later tease him by asking if he had even *been* a child.

The family also listened regularly to the BBC Home Service on the radio, especially the news. Despite her initial scepticism about television, in 1957 the Boyles became one of the first families on Castle Street to acquire a TV set. Westerns were especially popular, and each week some of the teachers from the Christian Brothers school would come to the Boyle home to watch the Western series *Bonanza*. Kevin would later joke that this is what probably saved him from the worst of the punishments the Brothers inflicted at school.

Pretending to study also became the children's excuse for avoiding household tasks. According to Kevin, 'If you wanted to get out of some chore, you always said you were studying, and she [my mother] never challenged it, even though she knew it was a lie half the time.'[10]

The Boyles escaped the rigours of church and school by hanging out on the streets, which at the time had very few cars. 'Everyone knew one another,'

Louis said. 'The boys played handball, hide-and-seek, marbles and football. The girls played hopscotch, swing around the lamppost, and skipping.' In the autumn there were excursions to gather blackberries, which the more entrepreneurial kids sold to local grocers for half a crown a bucket. In the summer, they took turns visiting a farm outside Newry run by a cousin of their mother's, Sissie Bradley, and her husband John. They stayed in an old farmhouse and helped to care for the hens, turkeys, geese, horses, cows, pigs, goats and a donkey.[11] Even the non-athletic Kevin pitched in, milking the cows, cleaning out manure, collecting eggs from the hen house, cutting hay and harvesting the corn, making the most of any opportunity to spend time away from the city. 'From my memories,' Louis said, 'these were magical days.'

Beneath the veneer of small-town tranquillity and the daily routine of classes, mass, homework and reading, however, Northern Ireland remained a society in which political and sectarian tensions were never far from the surface. One evening in November 1956, as thirteen-year-old Kevin was climbing over one of his brothers to go to sleep in their shared bed, there was a loud explosion. 'A bomb shook the house,' he remembered. 'We were thrown out of bed, and I fell on top [of my brother].'[12]

The Irish Republican Army had blown up the local labour exchange just a hundred yards away. It was the start of what became known as the 'border campaign', an ultimately abortive assault on Northern Ireland's British connection. But even though the campaign petered out, it highlighted the tensions in the six counties that would soon shape the trajectory of Boyle's life, and on which he in turn would have a major influence.

When Kevin Boyle's parents were born, Ireland was still part of the United Kingdom, in effect a British colony. Three-quarters of its population of just under three million people were, like the Boyle family, Catholics, descended from the native Irish who had lived on the island for centuries and consistently resisted British attempts to exert control. For most Irish Catholics, Britain was an alien occupier who had forced them from their lands and denied them basic rights. The remaining inhabitants were Protestants, descendants of the Scottish and English settlers who, with the encouragement of successive British governments, had emigrated to Ireland in the sixteenth and seventeenth centuries. The Protestants were concentrated largely in parts of the north-east province of the island and its main city Belfast, where they built a prosperous industrial economy around linen, ship-building and engineering. The Protestants were committed to a union with Britain, finding more in common with great Victorian industrial cities like Manchester and Liverpool than with Dublin, and strongly opposed any efforts to weaken the link with the United Kingdom.

In April 1916 a group of radical Irish nationalists seized the centre of Dublin and declared an independent Irish Republic in what became known as the Easter Rising. After a week of fierce fighting, the Rising was crushed. The British captured and executed its leaders, among them socialist revolutionary James Connolly, who had been badly wounded after the surrender only to be transported from a prison hospital on a stretcher, propped up and shot dead.

Such treatment, not only of Connolly but of other leading figures in the revolt, fuelled popular anger and boosted support for the rebels' cause. In a general election of November 1918, the nationalist party, Sinn Féin, won a landslide victory in Ireland and, in defiance of London, formally declared independence. This sparked a savage guerrilla war in which the Irish Republican Army – Sinn Féin's military wing – fought to drive the British out. In the north of the island, however, the Protestant unionists wanted no part of an independent Ireland. While the twenty-six counties in the rest of Ireland became an independent nation under a negotiated settlement in 1921, six of the nine counties in Ulster – areas with a Protestant majority but a significant Catholic minority – were carved off and became the statelet of Northern Ireland, technically still part of the United Kingdom but with its own parliament at Stormont, just outside Belfast.

In what is now the Republic of Ireland, the settlement triggered a civil war between those prepared to accept a Treaty whereby the fledgling state would have 'dominion' status within the British empire, would acknowledge partition of the North, and would have members of its new parliament take an oath of allegiance to King George V, and those unwilling to do any of the above. After two years of bloody fighting, the pro-Treaty forces won, while many, on both sides, still did not accept the legitimacy of Northern Ireland.

From the beginning, the North was deeply divided, 'composed of two communities who shared the same area but owed their allegiance to two different nations'.[13] The half-a-million Catholics and million Protestants regarded themselves as beleaguered minorities – the Catholics in the North, and the Protestants in the entire island of Ireland.

For the Protestants, this sense of perpetual anxiety – the fear of being sold out by Britain and forced into a predominantly Catholic united Ireland – fuelled a deep suspicion of the largely nationalist Catholic community in their midst, and it became the defining feature of the newly created state. Convinced that the only way to prevent Irish unification was to maintain political power at all costs, unionist leaders built their new state on the basis of permanent Protestant majority rule, in which Catholics faced systematic discrimination, principally in housing, jobs and political rights – issues that became central to Kevin Boyle's political awakening.

Protestant supremacy was ensured by the flagrant gerrymandering of electoral districts to ensure perpetual unionist control, even in parts of the province where Catholics were a majority, and by control of law and order. A draconian piece of legislation called the Special Powers Act, introduced in 1922, gave the authorities sweeping powers of arrest; these included internment without trial, backed by an entirely Protestant armed auxiliary police force known as the B Specials, a body that 'enjoyed a reputation in Catholic Ulster that induced paranoid terror and hatred'.[14] Campaigning for the abolition of the Special Powers Act was one of the first causes Kevin embraced when he became an activist. Underpinning these measures was the Orange Order, an exclusively Protestant fraternal organization founded in the eighteenth century, which saw itself as the primary institution opposing Catholic influence; it staged regular parades to assert Protestant dominance. Orange Order members held nearly all senior government positions.

Sectarian divisions and institutionalized discrimination were woven into the DNA of Northern Ireland. They were underscored by a famous quote from Sir James Craig, Northern Ireland's Unionist Party prime minister in the 1930s: 'All I boast is that we are a Protestant Parliament and Protestant State.'[15]

The Catholic Church was allowed to go about its business running schools and hospitals, offering services and organizing social and recreational activities for the minority community. Indeed, the unionists were more than happy that the Catholic Church was itself not enthusiastic about integration and discouraged its flock from casual socializing with Protestants. But the ruling establishment and the Protestant population still clearly regarded the Catholics as second-class citizens.

As a child in what he would later describe as the 'small-town, inward-looking, narrow-minded puritan society'[16] of predominantly Catholic Newry, Kevin Boyle was largely oblivious of these larger issues. Indeed, because of the town's large Catholic majority, there was nothing like the overt sectarian discrimination that existed in other parts of Northern Ireland. In Newry, he recalled, 'the Catholics never felt themselves threatened. My family was not political. My father never talked about politics. One of the reasons was that … as a taxi driver he had an image of himself as serving everybody.'[17]

'There was absolutely no bigotry [against Protestants] in our house,' Louis Boyle recalled. 'My father had customers on both sides.' And Elizabeth Boyle had an almost exaggerated respect for the British royal family. Still, the sense of separateness remained. The Boyles, although not poor, were hardly well-to-do, and generally viewed the Protestants of Newry as different – people who lived in big, solid houses and led untroubled, orderly lives. Kevin's sister Anne claimed that she could always tell a Protestant by their 'sallow skin'. Ironically, Kevin's future wife, Joan, growing up in a rural Protestant community at the same time, had been taught to believe that Protestants could always identify a Catholics because it was they who were sallow.

Despite his Catholic surroundings, Kevin did not develop a strong Irish identity. 'I was never really happy with an exclusive identity. I was as happy to be part of both countries.'[18] And he did not share the same sense of burning resentment and anger towards Protestants or the political structure in Northern Ireland which motivated many Northern Catholics – resentment that fuelled the IRA campaign and produced the bomb blast that toppled Kevin from his bed, and that would surface even more dramatically at the end of the 1960s.

By the mid-1950s, as he entered his teens, Boyle began to have doubts about religion and the society around him. 'Religion was a big problem,' he would say years later. 'The thing didn't move me at all. My going to church was difficult for me because I felt it was wrong.'[19]

Despite these feelings, he continued to serve as head altar boy. A photo of Kevin aged twelve shows him dressed in religious robes, staring ahead with calm determination. But his heart wasn't in it:

> I had got to the point where I was playing a role. Those experiences allowed
> me to appear in public where one was extremely visible and yet not visible.
> You get to realize people cannot know what's going on in your mind. If you

stand up and appear to be confident, people will see you as that. In a way, confidence is your capacity to play roles consciously.[20]

As a teenager, Boyle experienced what he described as a 'very normal adolescent search for personal meaning'.[21] His reading evolved away from the family classics, and shifted to a new hero in the form of John Osborne, the English writer whose 1956 play *Look Back in Anger* depicted the disillusionment and alienation from conventional values of his post-war younger generation, and gave rise to the term 'angry young men'. Kevin saw something of himself in Jimmy Porter, Osborne's anti-hero, a young working-class man filled with fury at Britain's privileged classes, the oppressiveness of organized religion and the lack of social justice.[22]

In the summer of 1957, when he was fourteen, Boyle attended a month-long Church-run camp in County Donegal, across the border, to study the Irish language. Damien Daley, a close friend who also participated, recalled that 'Kevin was one of the few to take the experience seriously'. While Daley and others paid little attention to their language classes and 'lived life to the full in sporting events and social gatherings in the evening', Boyle wandered through the hills, stopping at the homes of local farmers to practise his Irish, a 'free spirit kicking against the trend'.[23]

Boyle also became friendly with Eamonn McCann, a young man from Northern Ireland's second-largest city Derry (which Protestants called Londonderry). 'The Derry boys', as Daley remembered, 'were years ahead of us Newry boys, spurning the edicts of the priests. Already politically aware and anti-church, they had a defiance that they clung to.'[24] Late one night, in what was then an act of rebellion, McCann and Boyle went swimming with some young women, and were discovered by a priest. 'This was not allowed, of course,' Boyle recalled, 'and the priests banished us. The young ladies were excused, because we had misled them.'[25]

Expelled from the camp three days before it was due to end, Kevin did not dare go home, fearing his mother's wrath. Instead, he went to stay with McCann in Derry. After seeing a film in the city centre one evening, the two were walking back to McCann's house in the Catholic working-class neighbourhood known as the Bogside, 'whooping it up for no reason, running about and trying to jump and hit street signs with our hands, and just generally being a nuisance'.[26] The two exuberant teenagers were stopped by a police officer who asked for their names. McCann, a city kid savvy about Northern Ireland's religious fault lines and suspicious of the predominantly Protestant police, gave a fake name. Kevin followed suit, giving his own name as John Smith.[27] A few years later, as leaders of the civil rights movement, Boyle and McCann would be involved in very different interactions.

Growing up in a Catholic home in a largely Catholic town, Kevin had almost nothing to do with Protestants. That changed when he was seventeen. One day he was sitting in a Newry café eyeing up an attractive young woman when another young man came over and said, 'Well, you fancy her too.' They began chatting and after leaving the café together, walked through the centre of town before the young man said goodbye and entered the local Protestant Social Club. He was the first Protestant Boyle had met:

> I had already picked up little clues from the fact that he was my age and wasn't in the same school as me. I discovered he was at the state school. The majority of the student population would not have come into contact in seventeen years with Protestant girls or boys, who were in a minority in the town. There were few opportunities for meeting.[28]

Despite their different backgrounds, the two boys discovered that they had enough in common to meet again. When they did, each found the other to be disenchanted with the narrow, parochial environment in which they'd been raised. 'I talked a little bit about my growing dissatisfaction with the whole situation of a separate education. He said the same, and said he was hoping quite soon to get to Queen's [University Belfast]. I said I was hoping to go there too.'[29]

Even before this chance encounter, Kevin 'was aware there was something wrong' with Northern Ireland,[30] but, looking back years later, he said he simply did not know enough to be clear in his own mind of just what the problem was. Already, however, he had soured on the educational system. He called it 'The Evil of the Three S's' – a system that was segregated, sectarian and selective. 'I opposed segregation in terms of the sexes, and sectarian divisions on religion, and the selective basis whereby there was only a proportion who got an opportunity at a better education. And I believed that a system had to develop which ended all those three.'[31]

Yet, even as Kevin's disillusionment with the education system grew, he was poised to benefit from one of the most important educational reforms ever enacted in Northern Ireland. In the aftermath of World War II, the Labour government in London passed a series of measures that created the modern British welfare state. The 1947 Education Act dramatically increased educational opportunities for lower-income families, and the number of Catholics able to attend university grew significantly. This, in turn, underpinned the growth of a Catholic middle class, some of whose members, like Kevin Boyle, were to play crucial roles in the political upheavals to come. 'There are two things for a Catholic to do to break out of the system here: either become educated or emigrate,' he noted.[32] Eventually, all nine Boyle children would receive university degrees or obtain professional/managerial qualifications. In the autumn of 1961, Kevin enrolled in Queen's University Belfast.

[2]

A Kind of Revolt

AT THE START of the 1960s, Belfast was still a mostly Victorian city, ringed by dark green hills, its streets lined by red-brick buildings dating back to the previous century. The skyline was dominated by the giant cranes of the Harland and Wolff shipyard, erected at the peak of the Industrial Revolution and used to build the *Titanic*. The damp air was rich with the smell of coal, and red and white double-decker buses and trams, cars and the occasional horse-drawn cart jostled for space on the roads. In the centre of the city was the majestic City Hall, built in 1906 to celebrate the city's industrial prowess at the height of empire.

Spreading out from the city centre were the slums where lived Belfast's working class, who had supplied labour for the mills and shipyards. These communities were similar in their crowded, damp and squalid Victorian houses, usually without a toilet or bathroom, though sharply divided along sectarian lines.

West Belfast, with the Falls Road winding through its heartland, was mainly Catholic. Adjacent to the Falls was the Protestant Shankill Road, the demarcation line for a heavily Protestant area running northwards. Across the river Lagan, east Belfast was overwhelmingly Protestant, except for a tiny Catholic enclave of 6000 citizens in the Short Strand. The two communities lived close together, yet had very little contact. When the Troubles erupted in the late 1960s, the Falls and the Shankill would become synonymous with violence. When Kevin Boyle arrived at Queen's University in 1961, communal clashes of earlier decades were largely a memory, and daily life was marked by an uneasy coexistence.

The Queen's campus was located in the southern part of the city, a middle-class and mixed area, insulated from the grime and sectarianism of other parts of the city. Michael Emmerson, an Englishman from Shakespeare's birthplace, Stratford-upon-Avon, who entered Queen's at the same time as Boyle, remembered the university as 'a really great oasis, a kind of sanctuary, and religious tolerance was sacrosanct'.

The university was a major centre of non-sectarian education, having accepted Catholics since its foundation in 1845. With post-war educational reforms, the number of students from poorer families increased. In the early sixties, Catholic students formed about a fifth of the student body. Its tree-lined campus provided a tranquil environment where students from different backgrounds could interact.

Like Boyle, most Catholic students had come from Church-run secondary schools. For many, the opportunity to break free of their narrow upbringing was a liberation. Nobel Prize-winning poet Seamus Heaney, a native of County Derry who had attended a Catholic boarding school and who would later become a friend of Boyle's, graduated with a degree in English the year Boyle arrived. 'Going to Queen's you met people from other schools,' Heaney told an interviewer. 'You met other accents, other mores. You met women, which was a new development. I would say sectarian differences mattered nil.'[1]

'I mixed with Protestants and Catholics,' Boyle recalled. 'There was no question of any religious consciousness at all except that Catholics would sometimes joke among themselves about the repressiveness of the Church.'[2]

Struggling to find himself, with no clear idea of what he wanted to do, Kevin decided to study law for the most unsubstantial of reasons: because his favourite footballer had become a lawyer.[3] He discovered that the vast majority of his fellow law students were the children of solicitors or came from people connected with the legal system or the government. According to Kevin, he and one or two other law students formed 'a disgruntled minority who were there to pursue law for no obvious reason'.[4] Boyle soon found himself 'bored to death' with the rote memorization of laws, regulations and other practical matters, but he struck up a particularly warm relationship with James Louis Montrose, who had been a professor and dean of the Queen's law faculty since the late 1930s.

J.L. Montrose was a towering figure at the university, but was also known for supporting an innovative approach to the teaching of law. In writings and speeches – often over the strong opposition of a highly conservative legal profession – he advocated what he called a 'joint adventure of ideas', the notion that law students should also be exposed to a broader liberal education. 'It is not true,' Montrose wrote,

> that the undergraduate is the passive recipient of facts ... The student must learn how to pursue facts and to evaluate them; the teacher must ever be humble before old and new truths ... At a university, the undergraduate ... acquires freedom to think for himself, rejecting subordination to mere authority, liberating himself from prejudice but accepting bondage to truth.[5]

Montrose was so intimidating that many students were afraid to engage with him, but he became an important influence as Boyle searched for an intellectual framework for his still-evolving world view. Montrose, Boyle recalled, had a tremendous intellect:

> I was very much the envy of the majority [of students] because I could handle this extraordinary man who didn't conform to the kind of image of teachers that they expected and who didn't talk about practical matters but more about abstract and general questions that also interested me. He encouraged my interests in jurisprudence or philosophical aspects of law against the more practical matters.[6]

This was just one way in which Boyle was moving away from the rigid Catholic values and limitations of his upbringing. 'I made a conscious effort when I was at Queen's to live with nobody from Newry,' he recalled. 'I still had a few Catholic school friends or nationalist background people, but I usually selected English or Protestant. It was a kind of revolt from a background which I then regarded as demeaning me.'[7]

One of those friends was John Phillips, a chemistry major from Plymouth, who met Boyle in the autumn of their first year when both became involved with the Queen's Drama Society. They would later share a flat on Eglantine Avenue near the campus. Phillips remembered Boyle as usually wearing jeans and an old sweater and 'sucking noisily on his pipe', an affectation Kevin picked up from his father while still in his teens, and one he continued throughout his life. His father had always believed that smoking a pipe was less hazardous to one's health than smoking cigarettes.

For Boyle, Phillips, Emmerson and many other Queen's students, the Drama Society or 'Dramsoc', became the centre of their life outside the classroom. It was a consciously non-sectarian club, although Protestant members vastly outnumbered the Catholics. 'Its parties, where sing-songs alternated between nationalist and loyalist tunes … drew students from around the university, including those who had nothing to do with productions'.[8]

The Drama Society became what Boyle called 'an alternative career', consuming much of his energy. 'My main undergraduate engagement was the theatre. Theatre was a much bigger part of my experience as a student than politics. I wasn't really very engaged politically. I was more interested in changing the world, excited by ideas, music – and theatre.'[9]

With no interest in acting, Boyle became Dramsoc's lighting expert. 'I remember him as being passionately technical', said Michael Emmerson, who ended up directing most of the Dramsoc productions and would in 1962 establish the Belfast Festival, which quickly became the largest arts festival in Ireland and was still going strong more than half a century later. 'Kevin was terrific. He always got things done and got things solved.' Friends like John Phillips wondered where he had acquired the technical skills. Boyle never explained his secret: that his father had taught his sons how to clean and fix cars, and how to undertake home repairs. 'All of us were involved in the enterprise of tearing down the house and rebuilding it. We became plumbers, electricians, carpenters.'[10] Still, as Phillips noted, 'Those were the days of heavy manual dimmers [rheostats] and hot tungsten filaments, so there were a lot of ampères available – rehearsals were accompanied by occasional flashes, bangs, and the smell of burning insulation.'

During his time at Queen's, Boyle lit numerous plays, but his favourite, 'the greatest', he called it, was Beckett's *Waiting for Godot*. The play, a classic of the Theatre of the Absurd, which became popular in the late 1950s and early 1960s, features two tramps waiting for a man, Godot, who never arrives. The attempt to make sense of a world that seemed incomprehensible resonated with Boyle and his friends. 'It reflected the existentialist/absurdist flavour that was in the air at that time,' Phillips said. 'Samuel Beckett became an icon.'

In 1961 the Drama Society had hoped to participate in the Edinburgh Fringe, an alternative theatre and arts festival held in August in conjunction with the more formal Edinburgh Festival. Unfortunately, the students could not raise the necessary funds, find accommodation, or secure a performance venue, and were unable to go. The following year Emmerson formed the Queen's Players, with members, including Boyle, drawn mostly from Dramsoc, and managed to make the necessary arrangements. For six weeks the group stayed in an empty Edinburgh University hall of residence with no furniture and no hot water, and put on one full-length play and three one-act productions, all written by Queen's students.

The Queen's Players were consciously irreverent and cheeky. Their Edinburgh programme flyer acknowledged 'Stage by McKee and Co. (Belfast) Ltd', 'Fabrics by Tibor' and then 'Stout by Guinness' and 'Spaghetti Bolognese by Heinz'. But they soon ran into serious trouble.

One of their short plays was called *The Jesus Revolution*, written by a well-respected student playwright, John Hamilton. As Emmerson recalled, the play was structured 'as an interview between a psychiatrist and his patient – God and Jesus Christ', with Jesus depicted as a rebellious son.

It was a daring move for the times, deliberately designed to court controversy because, as Boyle noted, 'not only did they have Christ on the stage, but he was black'.[11] Emmerson had cast Max Enchill, a Nigerian student at Queen's, to play the role of Jesus.

Even more controversial was the fact that the students suddenly found themselves accused of violating Britain's centuries-old blasphemy law. Even in the 1960s, all plays had to be licensed by the Lord Chamberlain before they could be presented to the public, and *The Jesus Revolution* was banned because, at that time, it was forbidden to represent either God or Christ on stage.

It was Boyle's first personal encounter with an issue to which he would devote much of his professional life – combating censorship – and it led him to publish his first article. In a piece entitled 'Queen's Christ Banned' for the student newspaper *The Gown*, he wrote that the banning of the play 'caused considerable furore'.[12]

There was, however, a way out. The law did allow such productions to be shown at a private 'theatre club', as long as everyone attending was a member and no one paid admission. So the students formed a 'club', got people to sign up, and did several performances of *The Jesus Revolution* at lunchtimes with restricted entry in the same venue where their other plays were being shown in the evenings. Every day 'we had CID [Criminal Investigation Department] and the police and all kinds of people checking that nobody was buying tickets at the door', said Emmerson. 'When public decency was at stake, officialdom became very officious.'

Despite his modest and often introspective nature, Boyle had been attracted to Dramsoc in part because it represented a challenge to conventional wisdom, and his willingness to speak out against the banning of the play was an important step for him. His openness to fresh thinking was reinforced when he and his friends would meet regularly at a number of favourite watering holes just off campus to argue and debate, while consuming copious amounts of alcohol. As John Phillips recalled: 'There was much drink taken, sometimes too much. On one occasion, I literally carried Kevin home on my shoulder.' In a journal Boyle kept as an undergraduate, he noted, 'My drinking habits are by now legendary among a group, yet cannot give me much satisfaction.'[13]

Indeed, for all his exposure to theatre, music and new ideas, Boyle was still struggling to come to terms with his alienation from Catholicism, and, as a result, from his parents. In keeping with the youthful fashion trends of the early sixties, he grew his hair long, eliciting a pained response from his mother: 'In your letter, you said your hair was longer than ever. I beg you don't come home in that condition, as I've suffered tortures with Bimmy [younger brother Jim] and Louis with fringes at their noses. So a nice clean haircut please.'[14] Because he knew his refusal to go to church would upset his parents, Boyle returned to Newry less and less frequently after he started at Queen's. On one visit, he ostentatiously shined his shoes so his father would think he was off to church, but instead he went into the centre of town.

In the autumn of 1964, as Boyle entered his final year at Queen's, his mother was diagnosed with incurable cancer. On 17 November 1964, she died. Elizabeth Boyle was only fifty-three. 'Just at the time when, having devoted many years to home-making and rearing all of us and could take things a bit easier and watch with satisfaction and pride how her children were progressing,' Kevin's brother Louis wrote years later, 'she was taken away. Life can be very unfair and cruel at times. It was a major blow for all of us.'[15] The oldest child, Anne, had just taken a teaching job in Belfast, but had to give it up and return to Newry to help look after her father and younger siblings.

Kevin was devastated by his mother's illness and death, his grief possibly mixed with guilt at his rejection of his parents' core religious beliefs. His mother's passing intensified his internal struggles and doubts. 'He was horribly affected,' his wife Joan would later say. 'And there were no psychologists to help.' A letter written to Boyle (which he kept) a week after his mother's death by a former girlfriend named Lesley gives some sense of his bleak emotional state. 'You are very depressed,' she wrote. 'You have started off the term rock bottom … with the desire to do nothing but drink.'[16]

In early 1965, musing about having been an altar boy before attending Queen's, he wrote in his journal: 'Here I am, four years later, at the opposite extreme, indifferent and atheistic.'[17] Indeed, his mother's death affected his studies, and in his diary he wrote of his 'lack of interest in the [academic] results'.[18]

At the same time, however, the sense of social injustice and the growing awareness of the contradictions of Northern Ireland, which had been stirring within him, began to crystallize. And it did so at a moment when the long-static situation in the North was beginning to change. As he described it: 'There was an initial period … when people were talking about change and something had to be done.' It couldn't be called a movement in those years, he observed, but was more 'a kind of fermentation'.[19]

In 1963, a liberal Unionist, Captain Terence O'Neill, became Northern Ireland's prime minister. Educated at Eton and a veteran of World War II with a plummy British accent, O'Neill was a former minister of finance who sought to attract foreign investment and to develop the North's economy. He knew success lay in bridging, even in a small way, the territory's deep sectarian divide and securing Catholic acquiescence to what he hoped to project as a modern Northern Irish state. He reached out to the Catholic community, visiting Catholic schools – something his predecessors had never done – and was photographed with priests and nuns. In a dramatic gesture to ease the long-standing chill between the two Irelands, O'Neill welcomed Irish taoiseach Seán Lemass to Belfast in January 1965, and reciprocated by visiting Dublin a few months later. These moves came at a time when the mood in the Catholic community was itself changing. The failure of the IRA's border campaign from 1956 to 1962, the benefits of the British welfare state, compared to the still-impoverished Republic, and the emergence of a Catholic middle class meant that the issue of partition was fading in importance. Growing numbers of Catholics cared less about the border and more about their status as second-class citizens in the North.

In 1964 Dr Conn McCluskey and his wife Patricia, who lived in the rural town of Dungannon, formed the Campaign for Social Justice. At the time, Dungannon had a Catholic majority, but the Unionists had long controlled the local council, a situation that existed elsewhere, particularly in Derry. Because Northern Ireland law stipulated that only householders could vote in local government elections, the Unionists, to ensure their hold on power, had for years allocated only a handful of houses to Catholics in Dungannon, while giving hundreds to Protestants. Publishing pamphlets that documented sectarian discrimination and lobbying British politicians in London, the McCluskeys sought to make the case that since Northern Ireland was part of the United Kingdom, its residents ought to have the same rights as other British citizens. It was the first stirring of what would become the Northern Ireland civil rights movement.

For all his symbolic gestures, however, Terence O'Neill's approach remained cautious when it came to making concrete progress, and he could not escape the province's long history of sectarianism. His efforts to build roads, clear slums, open a new university and attract foreign companies remained focused on the eastern, predominantly Protestant, part of Northern Ireland. Far fewer resources went into the more heavily Catholic western counties or the city of Derry. And O'Neill could not shake the prejudices of his background, patronizingly declaring that 'If you treat Roman Catholics with due consideration and kindness, they will live like Protestants.'[20]

Even these tentative moves of O'Neill's, however, sparked opposition from Unionist hardliners both within his party and outside. The sharpest criticism came from the Reverend Ian Paisley, a fundamentalist Protestant preacher with a booming voice and a deep hatred for all things Catholic, who launched an increasingly angry campaign against O'Neill's reforms. Accusing him of being a traitor to Northern Ireland, and declaring that Catholics 'breed like rabbits and multiply like vermin',[21] Paisley also regularly denounced the Pope, even staging a protest march when the Union

Jack was lowered at Belfast City Hall following the death of Pope John XXIII. Paisley's rowdy rallies periodically led to violence in the streets.

For Boyle and his friends, Paisley seemed such a crackpot religious bigot that it was initially hard to take him seriously:

> I remember a dozen of us going along to a Paisley rally in the Ulster Hall ... We had been drinking, and ... we regarded it all as a big joke, shades of Germany and all that ... We marched, Catholics and Protestants ... One of us grabbed the flag, and off we rushed with the Union Jack down to the car, disappeared, and put it up on the wall of the flat. It was a joke, a prank.[22]

In the same vein, Boyle wrote a series of satirical articles, one of them describing the province as 'Ulcer, 1984'. Yet he was also beginning to analyse the current situation more seriously, writing a long piece in his senior year about the contrast on Sundays in Belfast between the city's Catholic and Protestant neighbourhoods – both deeply religious yet markedly different in character. He noted the 'oppressiveness of the atmosphere' in working-class Protestant areas – 'no Sunday games, no Sunday parks, no anything but the bible'. In the Catholic Falls Road, however, he saw 'a sense of community with a culture significantly different from the rest of Belfast ... watching the crowds pour out of the churches, hundreds of children cleanly dressed, the fashion of the girls ... for Sunday is a day to be seen and enjoy'. And, despite his youth and lack of political experience, he detected worrying undercurrents, predicting 'a religious and political confusion that someday is going to burst'.[23] Following up on his interest in free expression sparked by the banning of *The Jesus Revolution*, in 1964 Boyle wrote an article in a student magazine – *New Ireland* – about the still-strict censorship regulations in the Irish Republic, blaming the restriction on the strong Catholic influence in the Republic's constitution.[24]

His political understanding was slowly evolving. While it was confined at this point to intellectual exploration, though, a few of his Queen's classmates – people who would later be his comrades in the struggle for civil rights – became involved in more direct political activity. Eamonn McCann was now studying psychology, and became president of Literific (Literary and Scientific Society), the university's debating society. Boyle declined to join, citing the fact that he didn't like formal debates, as he admitted to an interviewer a decade later. This was an interesting trait for someone who would soon become one of the most visible figures in the public debate about the future of Northern Ireland.[25]

In 1963 McCann had travelled to Britain to participate with thousands of others in a peace march organized by the Campaign for Nuclear Disarmament – part of a burgeoning peace movement that would become even more active with the intensification of the American war in Vietnam. The following year he joined a small group of Queen's students who worked on a report about anti-Catholic discrimination in the allocation of housing by the Derry Corporation, the city's Unionist-controlled local government.[26]

A classmate of McCann's, Nell McCafferty, who later became a prominent Irish journalist, playwright and feminist, described him as 'the most brilliant orator of his generation... [He] laid bare the sectarian, anti-Catholic, anti-Irish nature of the statelet. He was fearless, informed, young ... and breathtakingly beautiful.'[27] He also, by his own admission, 'drank far, far too much at Queen's'.[28] In 1965 McCann got drunk after a Literific dinner, broke into a closed hotel bar, and stole several bottles of champagne. For this episode of what he called 'alcoholic rascality', he was expelled from the university and moved to London, where he got involved with a group of Irish radicals who introduced him to Marxism.

As an undergraduate Boyle remained reserved and cerebral, but he found himself attracted to, and perhaps somewhat envious of, McCann's unconventional and freewheeling manner. Michael Farrell, in contrast, was austere, almost cold, with a calculating political mind. Farrell, who came from Magherafelt near Derry, a town with a much more bitter history of tension between Catholics and Protestants than even Newry, arrived at Queen's a year after Boyle, and also quickly plunged into politics, chairing the Labour Club, which was tiny at that time. Michael Emmerson remembered Farrell as 'always making speeches', while McCafferty recalled him as 'a fresher with a beard [who] stood by himself waving a bible and declaring himself an atheist'.[29] Farrell, like others of his generation, had been inspired in part by the struggle for black equality then unfolding in the US. Watching TV news reports of American blacks demanding the basic rights of American citizenship fuelled a similar sort of thinking among many Northern Catholics.

Farrell knew Boyle 'slightly but not well' during their undergraduate years, and described him 'as a sort of mild leftist [who] would have stuck out a little bit – really as someone who would be sympathetic to things that we would do in the Labour Group'. For his part, during his undergraduate years, Boyle did not feel particularly close to either McCann or Farrell: 'I had never got on very well with them. I always felt they were a bit distant.' But he respected them both. He viewed Farrell as 'tremendously able' but also 'cold and reserved. I always think about him as more theological. McCann is more like a leprechaun … a kind of carefree spirit.'[30]

In the spring of 1965 Boyle graduated from Queen's with a second-class honours degree in law. His academic work had suffered following his mother's death, and he failed to get the first for which he had hoped. Nonetheless, he went to Cambridge University to do a one-year graduate diploma course in criminology. It was an important turning point, giving him a fresh perspective on Northern Ireland. With the benefit of distance, Boyle realized 'just how bad the place was. I had begun to read about Northern Ireland when I was at Cambridge, and began to see the realities of discrimination and the whole political monolith that was Unionist Ulster.'[31]

The year in Cambridge also opened his eyes to a radical new way of thinking about the law known as critical criminology.[32] Spawned by the political ferment of the mid-1960s, the theory challenged conventional ideas about the criminal justice system and role of law in society. Instead of seeing crime simply as behaviour that violated the law, this approach argued that what was and was not deemed legal reflected the power structure in society, and that the criminal justice system all too often served the needs of the rich and powerful. The solution, therefore, was to use the law as a mechanism to promote change and create a more just and equitable society. It was a powerful ideal that would help shape Boyle's approach to his chosen profession for the rest of his life.

Boyle also resumed his acquaintance with Michael Farrell and Eamonn McCann, who were both also in Britain. The two men were deeply involved in the politics of the 'New Left', which centred on opposition to the war in Vietnam, support for the civil rights struggle in the US, and calls for broader political and economic change. They were also members of what Boyle described as a 'hazy organization called the Irish Workers' Group',[33] a collection of Irish radicals looking to build a broad anti-capitalist movement in both halves of Ireland. 'They had a newspaper and published pamphlets,' Kevin recalled. 'They were believers. They were socialists.'[34]

For his part, while Boyle occasionally came to meetings in London, he resisted making an ideological commitment, preferring instead to educate himself on the issues while wrestling in his own mind with how best to tackle them.[35]

Meanwhile, significant shifts were underway in the IRA and its political wing, Sinn Féin. The IRA's 1956–62 border campaign, whose opening salvo Boyle had experienced when the bomb went off near his home in Newry in 1956, had failed, due in large part to the absence of support from Northern Ireland's Catholic community. Consequently, the remnants of the movement began to adopt a new strategy of open political agitation in both parts of Ireland. The men behind the new approach were IRA Chief of Staff Cathal Goulding and Roy Johnston, a physicist with strong Marxist leanings. They sought to cloak their strategy in the legacy of James Connolly, the legendary Irish socialist, dropping the IRA's traditional emphasis on physical force to expel the British from Northern Ireland and, instead, embracing explicitly left-wing politics in the hope of generating wider public support. They 'saw the trench-coated gunman – the symbol of the IRA's ethos – as a prop that must be carried off the stage of Irish history and dumped.'[36]

As he pored over books and pamphlets, attended meetings in Cambridge and London and continued his political self-education, Boyle became aware of this development, which Michael Farrell described as Republicans in the North beginning 'to involve themselves in social agitation and [becoming] interested in cooperating with other groups to oppose repression and discrimination within the Northern state'.[37] And, after years of quiescence, other groups were also pushing for change in the North. The Campaign for Social Justice continued its efforts to publicize cases of discrimination against Catholics. Then, in May 1966, Gerry Fitt of the Republican Labour Party was elected to the British Parliament as the member from West Belfast. His victory, in a general election that brought the Labour Party to power in London, broke a long-standing Unionist monopoly on representation at Westminster. For the first time, Northern Ireland's Catholics had a voice in Parliament, and Fitt used his inaugural speech to outline their grievances. To startled MPs, he denounced Northern Ireland's 'anti-democratic electoral system', in which the unionists believed 'they rule by divine right. Discrimination is an everyday occurrence. People are denied jobs because of their religion.' It was time, Fitt said, for Parliament to get involved in 'bringing about a new political situation' in Northern Ireland.[38]

For decades, the British government had largely ignored Northern Ireland. The province had its own government, and as long as things were quiet, British politicians had little interest in getting involved in a place that could produce only headaches. Now, however, Boyle, Farrell and many others hoped that the new government of Labour prime minister Harold Wilson would prove more sympathetic to calls for change. 'When Wilson was elected,' Farrell recalled, 'there was a quite substantial backbench group in the British Labour Party who were calling for more pressure on the Northern Ireland government to end the Special Powers Act and to bring in anti-discrimination legislation. That raised a lot of hopes.'

The Special Powers Act, introduced by the Northern Ireland government in 1922, and applicable only to the North, was a source of particular bitterness for Catholics because it gave the authorities what one British journalist described as 'powers of search, arrest, and detention without trial almost unheard of outside a police state'.[39] Over the years the law had been used to ban newspapers, books, films and organizations, and had been invoked from 1938 to 1946, and again from 1956 to 1961, to intern without trial those the Unionist government viewed as a threat. As Boyle and two colleagues would write some years later, although the law was 'not formally directed against Roman Catholics and Republicans, it was common knowledge that it was against them and them alone that it was directed and used.'[40]

Now, though, there was a sense that the long-frozen political situation in Northern Ireland was on the cusp of change. 'In London,' Boyle remembered, 'we used to talk about what we could do and what could be done about Ireland and the fact that something had to be done.'[41]

As his year in Cambridge drew to an end, Boyle explored the possibility of studying for a doctorate in the US, but then decided to return to Northern Ireland where he applied for a teaching job at Queen's. Most of the university's faculty did not come from the North but from Britain or abroad. 'The university felt vulnerable in that they had few local employees,' Kevin said. 'And that helped me get a job.'[42] He was offered a position as an assistant lecturer in the Faculty of Law.

Equipped with a deeper and more discriminating sense of what was wrong in his native land, aware that the winds of change were now beginning to blow, and determined to play a role in the political drama he could sense was coming, Boyle arrived in Belfast in the summer of 1966. 'I was conscious I was coming back to do something. I didn't know what I was going to do, but I was coming back to get involved.'[43]

[3]

The Faceless Committee

THE NORTHERN IRELAND to which Kevin Boyle returned was a society beginning to smoulder. Prime Minister Terence O'Neill continued his cautious efforts at reform, promoting economic modernization and making tentative overtures to the Catholic community. At the same time, there was growing pressure from lobbying groups like the Campaign for Social Justice, continuing activity by a small but increasingly political republican movement, and calls for change from Labour MPs in Westminster.

However incremental, any prospect of change infuriated Protestant loyalist hardliners. Their fears were most vocally articulated by the fundamentalist preacher Ian Paisley. His unceasing rants against Catholicism and 'support for Britain while rejecting everything Britain tries to stand for'[1] made Paisley seem a throwback to the religious wars of previous centuries. It was easy to see why Boyle and his Queen's classmates had mocked him when he had first become prominent a couple of years earlier. Now, however, with his fiery speeches, and, during the summer of 1966, instigation of occasional street disturbances, Paisley had become a serious, and fearsome, political force. At a time of social, economic and political change, he was steadily gaining support, especially from rural and working-class Protestants anxious that their traditional standing was under threat.

By that autumn, however, when Boyle began his first term at Queen's, tensions had subsided, and Belfast had returned to its normal state of uneasy calm. Boyle was eager to make a success of his first academic job, confiding to a diary that the Queen's appointment 'was the momentous step of my life. New work – and plenty of it – new people.'[2] He threw himself into teaching and research, and into adjusting to being a member of a faculty in a deeply conservative institution with a reputation as the place where future Unionist lawyers and politicians went to be educated.

Boyle's main teaching responsibilities covered criminal law and juris-prudence. But he also developed a growing interest in the sociology of law – the study of the role of law in society. William Twining, who had grown up in a British colonial family in Uganda and had been teaching law in Khartoum and Dar es Salaam for the past decade, arrived in Queen's at the same time to take up the chair of jurisprudence. He and his wife Penelope, a Dublin-born Protestant, were much less conventional than the average Queen's faculty member, and soon became Boyle's close friends and confi-dants. In late 1967 Boyle wrote that his new friendship with Twining 'gave me the supportive environment I needed'.[3]

'Queen's was a very hierarchical place,' Twining said. 'Kevin found it difficult to settle in and adjust to academic life.' Assuming the role of mentor, Twining hosted Boyle for long conversations at his home on Deramore Drive, near the campus, advising him about his teaching and acting as a sounding board for his evolving political ideas. Boyle was frustrated by the rigidity of the system. 'He wanted to do something that was more experi-mental,' Twining said, but it was 'more than what Queen's would permit'. And the rigidity extended well beyond campus. Boyle developed a plan to study for a doctorate, based on empirical research, about law enforcement in Northern Ireland. He approached the Royal Ulster Constabulary for coop-eration, but the research was shelved when the RUC declined to participate.[4]

Kevin's awareness of sectarian discrimination and the broader inequities of Northern Irish society continued to grow. On 29 January 1967 he joined more than a hundred other people who had gathered at the International Hotel in the centre of Belfast to establish the Northern Ireland Civil Rights

Association (NICRA). Inside a conference room sat representatives of all Northern Ireland's leading political groups – the Unionists, Nationalists, Labour and the Communist Party, the trade union movement, the Campaign for Social Justice, assorted leftists and several people associated with the republican movement. They agreed on a series of sweeping demands for reform, including giving all adult citizens the right to vote, fairer electoral boundaries and housing allocation, anti-discrimination legislation, and the disbanding of the Protestant quasi-military reserve police known as the B Specials.

NICRA explicitly defined itself as non-sectarian, and was modelled on Britain's National Council for Civil Liberties. It was, in the words of Michael Farrell, 'a sober, moderate body' that hoped to coordinate Northern Ireland's rapidly diversifying civil rights effort.[5] Its structure was loose, and involved representatives from numerous different groups. For his part, Boyle was not interested in allying with any particular group. Rather, he was motivated by a broader commitment to promote human rights,[6] and volunteered to provide legal advice to NICRA activists.[7]

Boyle's decision to join NICRA reflected his determination 'to do something about the situation in the North'.[8] Years later, he told an interviewer: 'I was genuinely mobilized by the sense of injustice. It was an appalling situation that such a large section of the population was excluded from power in a British state. After all, we were calling for British rights.'[9]

For the Unionist system in Northern Ireland, NICRA's approach created a new and unusual challenge. As Anthony Coughlan, a Republican activist who attended the meeting, later wrote: 'The novelty of the new movement was that it was not going to raise the constitutional issue, the North's membership of the UK, and the Partition question. British rights for British citizens were to be its focus. This was deeply subversive of the sectarian political basis of the Northern statelet.'[10] This fact contributed enormously to the power of the argument the new movement was making, alerting a British public and political class to realize that rights they took for granted were being denied in what was supposed to be an integral part of the United Kingdom, and exposing the hypocrisy and contradictions at the heart of Unionist rule. 'The majority Unionist government at Stormont was used to dealing with the IRA,' Coughlan continued. 'It could handle the anti-Partition agitations that had been the focus of Nationalist minority politics since 1920. But the demand for equal treatment for Catholics and Protestants within the existing constitution was something quite different.'[11]

If Boyle's form of protest was to reject the Catholic Church and get involved in the emerging civil rights movement, his younger brother Louis took an entirely different path. After following Kevin to Queen's, Louis had joined the Ulster Unionist Party in 1966, being one of a very few Catholics to do so. It was, in an odd way, his own youthful rebellion against his rigid upbringing. While he never abandoned his Catholic faith, even in secondary school Louis had become fascinated by what he called 'the other side'. In an unpublished memoir, he wrote: 'I wonder was I becoming ashamed of my own roots, what was this fascination?'[12]

In any case, weeks after Kevin attended the inaugural meeting of NICRA, Louis became the first Catholic to be elected chair of the Queen's University Conservative and Unionist Association. However sharp their political differences, the two brothers remained close. Indeed, they shared a flat at 42 Mount Charles, a leafy street next to the campus. Louis didn't agree with his brother's politics, and he recalled that Kevin 'was embarrassed' by his own politics, but 'always respected my right and admired my courage'. Among hard-line Unionists, Louis' activities generated considerable suspicion, especially because he publicly supported the liberal reforms being promoted by Terence O'Neill. The previous year, he had been expelled from the Association, although he was then reinstated.

O'Neill was attempting a delicate balancing act, trying to push his reforms without further alienating his growing number of critics. One of them was the hard-line Minister of Home Affairs, William Craig. In March 1967 Craig invoked the Special Powers Act to ban the Republican Clubs, set up as a successor to the IRA's political wing, Sinn Féin, after that party was banned during the IRA border campaign the previous decade. NICRA denounced the move as a violation of freedom of speech, and Boyle wrote an open letter condemning the ban, while students immediately moved to establish such a club, in direct defiance of the ban. His letter got him into trouble with the university's authorities. 'After going to that [Civil Rights Association] meeting, and getting involved, my first political act was to write a letter on Queen's stationery on the Republican Clubs,' Boyle recalled years later.[13] 'My letter condemned the prohibition from a legal point of view, and the TV picked it up. Queen's then put out a general prohibition against lecturers using their university address [to raise sensitive political issues].'[14] Although the Stormont government viewed the Republican Clubs as subversive, Boyle believed they showed that the Republican movement was moving away from its history of violence:

> For me, the reason I wrote that letter [was] that it was a positive development that the Republican movement was engaging in politics ... One of the sparks which lit the whole place off was this kind of repression. It was an attempt to destroy political change, no matter what shape it would take.[15]

Opponents of the Republican Clubs ban tried to get it reversed in the courts. Eventually, the case went to the House of Lords, the upper chamber of the Westminster Parliament. The Lords upheld the legality of the ban, concluding that it was for Northern Ireland's Minister of Home Affairs alone to decide whether a particular organization was subversive. As Boyle and two colleagues later wrote:

> In the context of Northern Ireland, it was the final proof to the minority community that they could expect no aid from Britain in their struggle for what they regarded as their legitimate civil rights. There can be no doubt of its symbolic importance in showing the futility of pursuing the civil rights campaign through the courts.[16]

To many, the only recourse left was to take to the streets. 'In the absence of a Bill of Rights and some other statement of rights,' Boyle subsequently told a reporter, 'the courts, unlike the United States civil rights campaign, were not used at all. And so it was predictable, I think, that demonstrations became part of the claim for justice.'[17]

In June 1968 a Catholic family in Dungannon was evicted from a house where they had been squatting, which was then allocated by the town's Unionist-dominated Urban District Council to an unmarried nineteen-year-old Protestant who was the secretary to a Unionist politician. The incident fuelled widespread anger. In August the Civil Rights Association staged a march – its first – from the nearby village of Coalisland to Dungannon, to protest about discrimination in the allocation of housing; it attracted some 4000 people. 'When this demonstration was called in August '68, it was a big turnout,' recalled Michael Farrell, who had returned to Belfast from Britain a few months before and was now leading a small left-wing group called the Young Socialist Alliance. 'And [the reason] was clearly the bubbling indignation – the frustration.' A thousand supporters of Ian Paisley gathered to oppose the march. A few scuffles broke out, but a major clash was avoided. Still, a pattern had been established of loyalist counterdemonstrators turning out to challenge civil rights protestors – something that would before long become the catalyst for violence.

Soon after, a group of radicals from Derry, including Boyle's classmate Eamonn McCann, approached NICRA about holding a protest march in the city. Derry had long been an emotive flashpoint in Northern Ireland. In 1689 Protestants in the city had withstood a months-long siege by the army of Catholic James II. In more recent years, despite its large Catholic majority, manipulation of electoral district boundaries had given the Unionists continued political control. For many Catholics, the gerrymandering, high unemployment, wretched housing conditions and blatant discrimination meant that Derry 'epitomized the evils of Unionist rule'.[18]

The date of the Derry march was set for Saturday 5 October. Two days before, William Craig, the architect of the ban on the Republican Clubs, issued an order banning the march, ostensibly because a Protestant group, the Apprentice Boys, had announced at the last minute their intention to stage a parade at the same time and place. The civil rights organizers, some of whom were hoping to provoke the authorities into confrontation, decided to defy the ban.

On an overcast Saturday afternoon around 400 people assembled, among them dozens of students from Queen's as well as three Labour MPs who had flown over from London. Three hundred yards from the starting point, a cordon of police blocked their way. Those at the head of the march refused to stop. As Eamonn McCann wrote, 'We marched into the police cordon but failed to force a way through.'[19] The police then overreacted, wading into the crowd, clubbing people and drenching them with water cannon.

Bernadette McAliskey, then still known by her maiden name, Devlin, was a Catholic from the town of Cookstown, County Tyrone, and a third-year psychology student at Queen's. She found herself in the middle of everything. 'There were policemen to the right and the left, to the fore and aft, and they just moved in on all four sides, with truncheons and heels and boots, and beat everybody off the street.'[20] Police then chased the protestors into the predominantly Catholic Bogside neighbourhood, where sporadic rioting continued into the evening. Dozens of people were hurt, many with head injuries from police beatings. A cameraman from RTÉ, the Irish television network, recorded the scene, and made the film available to the BBC. That night, viewers in Ireland and Britain saw shocking images of the Northern Irish police clubbing peaceful protestors, including MP Gerry Fitt, whose face was covered in blood.

'We got beaten up,' said Michael Farrell; '[because] it was on the British television, it had an impact in Britain. It had a huge impact in the North.' As English journalist Max Hastings wrote:

> every household in England was reading the fantastic tale of what had been taking place across the Irish Sea, and they were staggered by what they saw. These things were unheard of in the relative tranquillity of modern Britain; many Englishmen had been unaware that the Northern Irish police carried guns, far less that they were equipped with water cannon.[21]

Kevin Boyle had not been at the demonstration in Derry. That night, he was in his flat in Belfast listening to classical music on BBC Radio 3 when the broadcast was interrupted for a news bulletin featuring an interview with William Craig. 'I can remember saying to myself, this must be quite serious, because there's never a news programme on Radio 3. And then of course my life was to change.'[22]

The violence in Derry penetrated the insulated walls of the Queen's campus. As Bernadette Devlin wrote: 'Derry was being talked about in the lecture rooms, in the tutorial rooms, in the snack bar at dinner, in the cloakrooms, in the showers, at the bar … People were talking and thinking about the society they were living in.'[23] The following Monday, Boyle was in his office at the law faculty on University Square when a student arrived and asked for help. Plans were being made to hold a march to the centre of Belfast. Since Boyle was a professor of law, the organizers wanted his assistance in negotiating the route with the police.

On 9 October Boyle joined nearly 2000 students, a third of the entire student body, who set off from Queen's for Belfast City Hall. One of them was eighteen-year old Eilis McDermott, who had grown up in West Belfast. She had been educated at a convent school and was that week starting her first year at Queen's. 'We were filled with outrage at the RUC attack on the 5 October march,' she wrote, 'but there was also a feeling of hope and energy, a feeling that, whatever was wrong, we were going to sort it out.'[24] Boyle was one of around twenty faculty members who participated. As he did at the first big civil rights march in Dungannon in August, Ian Paisley and a handful of hard-line loyalists staged a counterdemonstration, prompting the police to block the route to City Hall, which Boyle had secured agreement for the demonstrators to use. It was 'a classic case of the police restricting a legal civil rights demonstration because they had not been quick enough to prevent an illegal loyalist counterdemonstration'.[25]

Blocked by police, the students staged a three-hour sit-in on Linenhall Street near City Hall. 'There had been discussion on the way down that if the road was blocked, they would have a mass sit-down,' Boyle said. 'These were ideas they did not have from traditional Republican protests. I don't think there had ever been a sit-down. This was something new. It was a tactic which clearly puzzled the police. They were used to separating crowds of people trying to break through.'[26]

'I was genuinely mystified when we were not allowed to go any further than Linenhall Street,' Eilis McDermott wrote:

> We sat on the ground within sight of the City Hall. There was no question of violence. The demonstration was quite good-humoured [but] as it became clear that it was not a mistake and that the serried ranks of riot-helmeted police were going to stay there as long as we did, puzzlement gave way to indignation and determination.[27]

As one of the few professors who had joined the march, Boyle was asked to address the crowd. 'I talked about how we can't even walk through our own city.'[28] In a journal entry, Boyle later observed that this was the moment when he and the students 'discovered Northern Ireland society and how rotten it was'.[29]

Michael Farrell recalled: 'There was a sort of debate as to what to do, and I and some others proposed that we go back to Queen's and hold a meeting as to what to do. The students were very angry.' After sitting in the street for three hours in the rain, the students eventually did trudge back to Queen's. As Bernadette Devlin noted, 'Our behaviour that day earned us a great deal of respect in the community.'[30]

Boyle accompanied the crowd back to the campus, and found 'the whole place was in ferment, maybe two thousand students coming in and out, talking endlessly.'[31] The packed meeting at McMordie Hall in the university's student union building was, in Devlin's words, 'impassioned'[32] and unstructured. Anyone who wanted to was given the opportunity to speak.

The meeting went on until the early hours of the morning. It was chaired by Rory McShane, who had attended the same Christian Brothers school in Newry as the Boyle brothers, and had been a classmate of Louis Boyle. Arriving at Queen's in 1965, he had been active in protests against the ban on the Republican Clubs in 1967, and his left-wing views had already earned him the nickname 'Red Rory'.

'The mood was of anger and defiance,' McShane recalled. 'We were not going to be stopped. This was just plain wrong. We're going to continue. We're not going to allow a demagogue like Ian Paisley stop us from vindicating the rights of peaceful marching. That was the kind of mood.'

Out of the anger and passion emerged an organization that called itself People's Democracy, or PD. Eilis McDermott wrote:

> It was agreed that anyone could be a member of the People's Democracy as long as everyone thought they should have a vote, a job, and a house, that the Special Powers Act should be repealed and the B Specials should be disbanded. There were no membership cards or subscription fees. Everyone was welcome, and from the start it was taken for granted that marches and demonstrations would be non-violent.[33]

Boyle was inspired, convinced that 'this was an important movement that could make a difference'.[34] When a ten-person leadership committee was established in the wee hours of the morning, he offered to join. Michael Farrell, with his experience, political skills and forceful personality, had already emerged as a highly visible figure in the protests. But as the head of the Young Socialist Alliance, his views were much further to the left than the others who had marched that day. To make the movement as broadly based as possible, a majority at the meeting agreed that the main criteria for committee membership was to have no existing political affiliations.

'There was a bit of a backlash,' Farrell acknowledged, 'in that there were people who complained they were being manipulated by a small minority of left-wing socialists, which was me and a few others.' Kevin, who had deliberately avoided joining any of the numerous organizations making up the Northern Ireland Civil Rights Association, to maintain his political independence, was an ideal candidate. Nine of the ten members of what became known as the 'Faceless Committee' were students. Boyle was the only faculty member voted in. In a journal entry some weeks later, he noted 'after all the time standing in the wings, I emerged as a leader – prepared to give something back to this society, to change it'.[35]

Boyle was proposed, accepted, and never looked back. 'Sometimes you can point to a specific date in your life where you actually took a choice; maybe the reasons you took it are not clear, but it certainly changes every-thing.'[36]

Bernadette Devlin – tiny, spirited and bursting with energy, always puffing on a cigarette – was also elected. It was the first time she and Boyle had met, and was the beginning of a personal and political relationship of special warmth and depth. 'In many ways, our relationship grew out of the fact that we were very similar people,' Boyle said later. 'We had no coherent political positions, but were moving towards a radical position.'[37]

The first thing the Faceless Committee did, in Boyle's words,

> was to articulate a programme of demands. It was Michael Farrell who produced them; he had them all in a certain amount of leftish jargon and we dressed them up. I remember ringing up one of my lecturer friends to get exact figures about Derry, and that first poster was reproduced thou-sands of times later: "One man, one vote. Jobs on merit. Houses on need. End the Special Powers Act. End gerrymandering." PD coined slogans which later became general.[38]

Apart from Unionist hardliners, the initial public reaction to People's Democracy was surprisingly tolerant, even positive. The president of the Methodist Church praised the restraint the marchers had shown[39] – a restraint reflected in a decision the group took on the day after its formation to postpone a proposed march the following Saturday because Paisley had announced plans for a counterdemonstration. On Wednesday 16 October 2000 protestors did march to Belfast City Hall after again negotiating with police to avoid another planned counterdemonstration by Ian Paisley.

According to the law, police had to be given the name of an individual organizer for any approved demonstration. At the meeting to plan for the 16 October march, no one volunteered. And then, as one of the participants, Anne Devlin, recalled:

> All of a sudden, I remember this extraordinary voice with its amazing rhetorical ability came from one of the rows. The voice went out to the roof and came back again: 'Mr Chairman, I am an orphan. I have nothing to lose. I will give my name.' It was extraordinary because it made everyone go quiet in a meeting of extraordinary egos and extraordinary politics. Everyone turned to see who it was.[40]

The voice belonged to Bernadette Devlin. It was the moment when she began to emerge as one of the key figures in the burgeoning movement.

When the demonstrators reached City Hall, they encountered a small group of Paisleyites – 'mostly middle-aged housewives singing "God Save the Queen".' Dennis Kennedy, who covered the march for *The Irish Times*, wrote that the women 'kept up a chorus of hymns during the speeches, but, despite repeated invitations to participate in the People's Democracy, no member of the group would take the microphone'.[41]

Both Kevin and Louis Boyle, who had also joined the march, addressed the crowd, as did Bernadette Devlin. 'Let me tell you,' Kevin declared, 'there are many people in this city who feel that now the students have got to the City Hall, our marching is finished for Civil Rights. I would like to say from the platform today that they are very, very wrong.'[42] The crowd burst into cheers.

A photograph captured the moment. It shows Boyle standing in front of a line of police, his Trotsky-style beard obscured by the bullhorn he is holding with both hands, as three double-decker buses snake through the road behind. Most of the policemen have their arms crossed, with expressions ranging from befuddlement to exasperation to contempt, while the students sitting on the street in the foreground are either looking up at Boyle with interest or at the police with frustration. One student angrily points a finger at the police. The picture became one of the memorable images of Northern Ireland's early civil rights struggle, a depiction of peaceful but determined protestors facing off against the forces of the state.

By now, as a profile of the group in *The Irish Times* noted, People's Democracy had become 'the most extraordinary operation ever initiated at Queen's',[43] and was attracting students who had never participated in politics. The article quoted one, Suzanne Powell, a first-year student from a Protestant family: 'This is about basic human rights – we're fighting for houses and jobs for people, and this is just a matter of justice. I don't think there is anything terribly political about it – at least not political in the sense of the parties we have.'[44] Eilis McDermott told the reporter that People's Democracy 'is a completely new organization that is absolutely necessary in Northern Ireland'.[45]

Not a week went by without PD demonstrations or protests. 'It was several marches a week that the PD were organizing in all the rural towns,' according to Bernadette Devlin. 'And Kevin would have been at them.' Many of them were planned in Boyle's flat, still shared with his brother Louis. The apartment was larger and better furnished than the average undergraduate accommodation, and soon became what Kevin described as the 'unofficial house' of the Faceless Committee. Amid a haze of cigarette and pipe smoke – Boyle was rarely without his pipe – and what Michael Farrell remembered as his friend's 'inexhaustible supply of Bushmills' whiskey', the young activists would gather to debate strategy and plan new meetings, rallies and demonstrations, as an old Gestetner mimeograph machine in a corner churned out impassioned leaflets and calls to action. Occasionally, students living at home, whose activism had alienated their conservative parents, would seek refuge by sleeping on the floor or the couch.

'One of the bizarre memories I have is of the contradiction of it,' said Devlin. 'Kevin was a very quiet and gentle-spoken person. He was sitting in the middle of this madness, and then at points in between would be reminding people that they wouldn't be wanting to let their academic work fall behind. And there was a certain degree of incongruity within that.'

It was during this intense period that Boyle and Devlin developed a particularly close friendship and political partnership. 'She and I were quite close from an early stage,' he said years later. 'I had a kind of avuncular sense and worried about her because she was a vulnerable woman in many ways.'[46]

Devlin believed their relationship was based in large part on their similarities. 'We were both from working-class backgrounds, who, without free education, would not have been at the university,' she recalled.

> So in a way, we had ... more realism, more practical adaptation skills and more links with the world outside the university in terms of understanding how community or society or other people worked. And there was a certain ... intellectual affinity then that we could see, analyse, interpret, and identify the need for action almost quicker than anybody else I knew could.

An additional factor in their friendship was that, within the People's Democracy, they had become the counterweight to the radicals grouped around Michael Farrell. 'She and Kevin were outside our clique of hard-line lefties,' recalled Paul Arthur, a Derry native and Queen's graduate student who, like Farrell, was a member of the Young Socialist Alliance. 'That brought the two of them closer together.'

The rise of People's Democracy had generated a sense of possibility in a long-stagnant situation, the hope of change that could transcend Northern Ireland's divided history. Years later Boyle recalled that 'in the early stages [of PD], many students were not aware of any Protestant/Catholic divide or even a Nationalist/Unionist divide. The late 1960s was certainly an age of innocence as far as the fight for civil rights is concerned.' [47]

It was a heady period, and not just because of the cause. 'A lot of it was just the fun of coming together,' Boyle remembered, noting that in the intense atmosphere of the movement, there were 'quite a few courtships' as well. [48] Indeed, it was at some point that autumn that Kevin and Eilis McDermott, who was becoming an important figure in the People's Democracy herself, began a romance that would last for nearly five years.

Kevin had had a series of girlfriends as an undergraduate, none of them serious, and, during his year at Cambridge, he described his personal life as 'wrapped up in a love affair. Here is not the case to discuss it but just to record it was unsuccessful.' [49] His relationship with Eilis was somewhat unconventional. Boyle was twenty-five, a professor, and while politically radical still quite conservative on social matters, while she was eighteen and just starting at Queen's. Ed Moloney, half-Irish and half-Scottish, had started as an undergraduate at Queen's in 1966, later becoming one of the most distinguished journalists to cover the Troubles, and was friends with both. He felt Boyle was 'not just chronologically so much older than she was, but also in terms of attitudes. Kevin did not approve of everything Eilis did. Eilis and I – we'd have all sorts of adventures. I remember one time we took psychedelic drugs together and Kevin found out, and he was so disapproving of it. But this was the sixties, so what the hell?' The bond between Kevin and Eilis was deep, however, cemented by a shared commitment to the political movement erupting around them. They soon became inseparable. As Bernadette Devlin noted, 'they were very, very close'.

By this time, internal tensions within People's Democracy between reformists like Kevin, and more radical leftists, such as Michael Farrell, were also beginning to surface. According to Boyle, 'the [Faceless] Committee was mercilessly manipulated by two forces, by Bernadette and myself and by Michael Farrell from the outside. We saw ourselves as standing between the innocents – we were three parts innocence ourselves – and the politicos.'[50]

'Kevin was coherent,' Farrell said.

> He didn't have an ideological background, but he was quite determined. He would obviously put a bit more emphasis on using official channels and that sort of thing. And, to some extent, he was a person who would help to pull things together at the end of a debate. We worked closely together in drafting statements. I would have put in the more agitational bits and he would have put in the more legalistic bits.

However, the growing sense of militancy within PD was evident as the group planned another march to Belfast City Hall on 4 November. When police again decided to reroute the march to avoid a counterdemonstration announced by Ian Paisley, the protestors refused. 'We told the police there would be no rerouting,' Bernadette Devlin wrote. 'Since this was home territory, we felt we had the right to walk through it.'[51] Some tried to go around the edge of the police cordon, and scuffles broke out. Finally reaching City Hall, the protestors sat down in the street; some were assaulted by Paisleyite counter-demonstrators, while others were beaten and dragged away by the police. 'When the students were blocked by loyalists and the RUC,' Boyle recalled, 'it was a great shock to them. There was a great deal of innocence at the time.'[52]

The authorities at Queen's – conservative, heavily Unionist – were none too pleased to see so many students becoming politically active. And they were even less pleased that faculty members like Boyle were getting involved, although he did not face any formal sanction as long as he carried out his teaching responsibilities. Still, as Paul Arthur, a fellow PD member who also lived next to Boyle on Mount Charles Street, observed, he was taking a risk. 'He was at the start of a very promising career. And the Queen's authorities would not have approved of what he was doing. He was very courageous.'

On 22 November 1968, under pressure from the streets and from a frustrated British government concerned that local authorities were dragging their feet on addressing complaints raised by the civil rights movement,

O'Neill announced a package of planned reforms. It included the creation of a commission to replace the gerrymandered Derry City Council, changes in housing policy, voting reform and repeal of parts of the hated Special Powers Act. To many Catholics, the moves appeared to have been grudgingly conceded.

As journalist Max Hastings wrote, 'The Unionists made it clear they were throwing a crust to the wolves only because the animals were becoming dangerous.'[53] Yet among hard-line Protestants, there was a furious reaction, which became evident when Boyle and his PD colleagues announced plans for a civil rights march on 30 November in Armagh, the town that contained the residences of Northern Ireland's Roman Catholic and Protestant archbishops. Ian Paisley warned the Northern Ireland government 'that if they did not stop the Armagh march, he intended to do so himself'.[54] Paisley supporters distributed flyers the day before that declared: 'Ulster's Defenders. A friendly warning. Board up your windows. Remove all women and children from the city on Saturday, 30 November. O'Neill must go.'[55]

Boyle and Bernadette Devlin drove to Armagh to take part. 'There was a pattern to these things,' Devlin noted:

> You would organize a meeting, and you would go. If the Paisleyites were there first, they would almost have seized the town, as they did in Armagh. Then a debate would ensue with the police, and Kevin would usually be involved … and then either the police would charge us or the stone-throwing from the Paisleyites would start. Or we would be in the town first and the Paisleyites would arrive and attack. But the result was that we would usually be under attack from both the police and the Paisleyites and scatter, and then we'd we go home and organize the next one.

In this case, Boyle believed that 'the threat of violence where we had a lawful march was such that it would have been cowardice to accede to it and that we should parade on even though it might mean the risk of violence'.[56] That afternoon, 5000 demonstrators surged through Armagh's narrow streets, and the police set up barricades to separate them from about a thousand Union Jack-waving Paisley supporters, many of them carrying cudgels and sticks and spoiling for a fight.[57]

Amid chants of 'Freedom! Freedom! Freedom!' the demonstration approached the town centre, where police warned the marchers that it would be unsafe to proceed on their intended route. 'There was a tussle with the Paisleyites,' Kevin remembered. 'There were blockages.' Despite efforts by a few youthful marchers to breach the barricades, stewards managed to maintain order, serious violence was averted, and the frustrated civil rights protestors eventually dispersed peacefully. Yet again, however, a lawful march had been prevented by the threat of violence.[58]

It was against this backdrop of worsening tension that Terence O'Neill, on 9 December, made an impassioned television appeal for calm, as well as for support from the middle ground. 'Ulster stands at a crossroads,' he declared. 'What kind of Ulster do you want? A happy and respected province in good standing with the rest of the United Kingdom? Or a place continually torn apart by riots and demonstrations and regarded by the rest of Britain as a political outcast?'[59] The speech generated positive responses from moderates in both communities, and NICRA announced a temporary halt in demonstrations. Louis Boyle, a liberal Unionist, 'felt personally very moved by the broadcast, and had a strong urge to respond positively to O'Neill. He had answered some of my concerns, in that he was recognizing the need for reform and was prepared to face up to the extremists typified by Paisley.'[60]

Within PD, however, there were significant differences of opinion. Ed Moloney and some PD friends watched the broadcast in his flat. 'O'Neill comes on and gives his Ulster-at-the-crossroads speech, which most moderates welcome as being a positive development. Let's calm things down, let's cool things down. And we're all watching that, and the response is "fuck that".' Michael Farrell was equally sceptical. 'We felt that this was not going anywhere, that it was losing the momentum of the movement.'

But Boyle, Bernadette Devlin and many others in People's Democracy were willing to give the beleaguered prime minister a chance. 'We wanted to go with the pause,' Boyle recalled. 'We were sceptical about O'Neill, but the majority of the community wanted to see how these changes would pan out.'[61] As Ed Moloney acknowledged, 'O'Neill's speech for a while changed the mood.' Indeed, Eilis McDermott was so confident that 'the movement's demands were so basic that all the trouble would be over by Christmas'.[62] In a reflection of that, shortly afterwards, the PD decided to cancel a march to Belfast City Hall that had been planned for 14 December.

But the truce would not last. The New Year would begin with another march – one that would help propel Northern Ireland towards disaster.

[4]

The Long March

ON THE CHILLY morning of 1 January 1969, Kevin, Eilis McDermott, Bernadette Devlin, Michael Farrell and several dozen other members of People's Democracy set off from Belfast's City Hall. Their plan was to march to Derry, seventy-three miles away. They carried banners reading 'Civil Rights, 1969', 'Houses for All, Jobs for All' and 'Anti-Poverty March'. The aim was to keep up the pressure for reforms; the result was an outbreak of violence that would become a turning point in Northern Ireland's descent into war.

The idea for the march had emerged at a PD meeting in mid-December and was enthusiastically embraced by Michael Farrell. He saw it as a Northern Irish version of Martin Luther King's famous 1965 march from Selma to Montgomery, Alabama, in which non-violent demonstrators were attacked by police, reinvigorating the American civil rights movement and leading to the passage of a landmark voting rights act.

In the same way that Selma–Montgomery forced the federal government to get involved, the aim for the PD was to force the British government's hand and gain its engagement with the issues. 'We were aware that we would be blocked lots of times,' said Farrell. 'We didn't know whether we'd ever get through, but we felt that if we were continually blocked, then it would demonstrate the intractability of the situation and the fact that you could not rely on the Northern Ireland administration to allow free speech.'

Boyle and Bernadette Devlin, fearful of possible confrontations with the police or with Protestant extremists, had initially opposed staging the march, but were in the minority, and so, with considerable misgivings, agreed to participate. From the start, the march ran into trouble. A close Paisley associate, Major Ronald Bunting, and a few other hard-line loyalists jeered and shouted abuse as the group made its way out of Belfast. Ironically, Bunting's twenty-year-old son Ronnie, a Queen's student and PD member, was among the marchers. In the main, the day was uneventful until the late afternoon. 'On we trudged,' Devlin wrote, 'singing Orange songs, Green songs, red, black and white songs, and just general pub-crawling and rugby songs, to keep us marching, and the whole tone of the thing at this stage was very good-natured.'[1] But as the marchers neared the town of Antrim, Major Bunting and a group of Paisleyites, including someone with a Lambeg drum – an enormous instrument that produces a deafening sound, which can be heard and felt miles away – gathered on a bridge to block their way.

The two sides were separated by a line of police. A report by the police officer in charge, Inspector Cramsie, described the situation. 'The Marchers' attitude was that it was our job to put them through, and the attitude of the other side was rigid determination not to let them through.'[2] Uncertain of what to do, Cramsie telephoned a senior officer, who instructed him not to use force to get the few dozen marchers through. Instead, he was authorized to provide transport in police tenders for the protestors to the local hall where they planned to spend the night.[3]

After some debate, the marchers agreed. While Devlin made soup in the hall's kitchen, Inspector Cramsie and another colleague arrived and met Farrell and Boyle, who had taken on the role of negotiators with the police. Farrell was present as an organizer, Boyle acting to put their points into a legal framework. Cramsie told them that the police believed the Paisleyites would continue their attempts to block their progress the following day. 'We said we wanted to go back into Antrim and start from there,' Farrell recalled, 'and he said we can't let you do that.' While they had the right to continue, Cramsie suggested that they should consider calling off the march, or, at a minimum, use an alternative route.[4]

Since their march was legal, however, the PD members decided that they had the right to proceed on the original route, and early on the morning of 2 January they set off for Randalstown. Outside the town they were blocked by a group of some 300 Paisleyites, with the police again keeping the two sides apart. Devlin wrote that the Paisleyites 'were armed with pick-axes, scythes, saw-blades: the most brutal-looking weapons. The general impression was that any marcher who got into Randalstown wouldn't leave it with his head in place.'[5] According to Inspector Cramsie, around 10 am,

> District Inspector Hood appeared down the side road with Farrell and Boyle, who had asked to see me. They wanted to know if we were going to do our duty and put them through, and I told them that they could see the situation for themselves; that if they attempted to go through there would be violence, and that as far as I was concerned, there could be no question of their attempting to march through Randalstown.[6]

Cramsie again urged them to take another route, which the marchers eventually agreed to do, although they were becoming increasingly frustrated at the unwillingness of the police to take any action against the loyalist counterdemonstrators. Even the moderate *Belfast Telegraph* found this troubling, asking in an editorial, 'For how long would the police permit a Roman Catholic crowd to stand in the way of a parade of Protestants, militant or otherwise?'[7] Still, by late afternoon, they had reached the predominantly Catholic village of Gulladuff, where they were greeted as heroes. 'The whole village came out to meet us,' Devlin recalled, 'and brought us into the town hall where soup and sandwiches in vast quantities had been prepared.'[8]

Paul Bew, a native of Belfast and a Protestant, who later became a distinguished historian of the Troubles, remembered Boyle as 'an important guy on this march … a big bloke, always wearing an orangey-yellow sweater and always at the front. McCann and Farrell took him very seriously.' As the marchers rested in the Gulladuff town hall, Boyle gave them a powerful speech. He explained that their plan was to exploit the tensions between the Labour government in London and the Unionist government in Northern Ireland. 'It made me think the guy knows what he is doing,' Bew recalled. 'The speech was entirely rational. Why was he doing this march? Because [of] critical analysis of the facts.' It was, to Bew, a sharp contrast to the more ideological tone of the left-wing Farrell and McCann. 'It was not based on ideology. It wasn't the crazy Trotskyist fantasy of permanent revolution.'

The original plan for day two had been to pass through the town of Maghera and spend the night in a small Catholic village called Barackaghreilly. Because of the raucous protestors and the consequent rerouting, the group was well behind schedule. Darkness was now falling, and the marchers began to hear reports of large numbers of loyalists gathering in the centre of Maghera. With friendly locals offering transport, the group was driven on side roads to avoid Maghera, and in the middle of the evening safely reached the Gaelic Hall in Barackaghreilly. In Maghera the angry mob of Protestants, frustrated that the marchers had eluded them, went on a rampage, smashing the windows of homes and shops.

There were fears that the marchers who were spending the night at Barackaghreilly might also come under attack. However, unknown to the students, 'fifty armed men set up roadblocks at the approaches to the village. They were the local company of the IRA.'[9] Answering a call of nature, a student, Malachy Carey, went outside in the middle of the night. 'He felt something behind his ear, and a voice said "Who are you?"' wrote Devlin. '"I'm Malachy Carey, one of the marchers," said the student, not knowing whether to raise his hands or his trousers. "Oh, that's all right, son," came the voice. "Sorry I disturbed you."'[10]

'Had the IRA asked us if we wanted protection,' Farrell said years later, 'I am sure we'd have said no, because we didn't want to be that closely identified with them.'[11] But given the threat posed by loyalist opponents of the march, the few student protestors who knew of the IRA's help were grateful that it had been provided.

Early the following morning the students set out again, determined to pass through Maghera. At 7.30 am a police inspector sought out Boyle and warned him against doing so. He told him 'of the riot which had occurred in Maghera the previous night and the very real possibility of similar outrages should the students attempt to go back towards Maghera'.[12] After an animated debate, the marchers acquiesced and made their way up the Glenshane Pass, which cuts through the rugged Sperrin Mountains towards the predominantly Catholic town of Dungiven. They were met there by an enthusiastic crowd, including a man playing the bagpipes. 'They had been waiting for us to arrive,' Devlin wrote. 'Women had made sandwiches, local tradesmen had given food, the priest provided cigarettes, the doctor held open surgery for blistered feet, and the municipally owned castle supplied free washing facilities.'[13] 'It was almost like the troops coming home from war,' Boyle recalled. 'Only of course the war hadn't yet occurred.'[14]

Yet Boyle was depressed at the raw sectarian hatred that the march had triggered. 'I had a sinking feeling the whole way through that we were just opening up a wound which I didn't understand as greatly as I should have done.'[15] His feelings came into sharp focus as the marchers, walking into Dungiven, passed two schools at the top of a hill, one Protestant, the other Catholic. 'I can remember now my depression seeing the Catholic school children out all waving to us and the Protestant school not waving and how that, in effect, was the end of my innocence in the Northern Ireland conflict, and the real worries about sectarianism that I had kept down becoming clear.'[16]

After lunch at the Dungiven Gaelic Athletic Association Hall, the marchers, now numbering around 500, moved on, only to be blocked by the RUC once again. District Inspector Harrison told Boyle and Farrell that there were hostile crowds on the main road and ordered them to take a side road to their next destination, the village of Claudy. In a subsequent report to his superiors, Harrison wrote: 'They discussed what action they would take, and after several persons addressed the processionists a vote was taken and the decision made that they would press forward on the police cordon.'[17]

'We had already been rerouted several times at other points,' Boyle later told an interviewer. 'So we decided not to accept the reroute, and to push our way through this cordon. Eilis, my girlfriend, was behind me, and I was in the front line. In front of us were two lines of police officers. We were not going to be stopped. There was going to be a confrontation. They thought they could hold us back, but they couldn't.'[18]

Indeed, as Inspector Harrison recorded, 'The pressure was so great from local followers who were at the back of the crowd that the police were forced to give way after a few minutes and the Civil Rights Marchers came through.'[19] In the crush, Boyle fell on top of a large police officer, and McDermott, who was so small Boyle described her as 'ethereal', was sandwiched in between. 'He was pushed right back on the ditch and I fell on his chest, and she was right in the middle,' Boyle recalled. 'He had this enormous grin on his face, and I remember he was saying, "If I could only think of this, I might even enjoy it." I said, "You bastard." But I really liked him at that moment.'[20] The policeman then pulled McDermott out of the way of the surging crowd. As Boyle observed, 'It broke the stereotype that the police there were interested in beating up people. He clearly made an effort. Eilis was frightened; she wasn't frightened because she was a woman, she was frightened because she was slight.'[21]

The marchers quickly passed by the outnumbered police. Contrary to police warnings, there were no counterdemonstrators on the main road. The marchers stumbled into Claudy, in Devlin's words, 'feeling exhausted but modestly triumphant, for we were almost home. Derry was only ten miles away.'[22]

That night Ian Paisley organized a 'prayer meeting' – his usual device to rally his followers – at the Guildhall in the centre of Derry. Nearly a thousand people listened to him denounce the marchers, invoke the heroic Protestant defenders who had resisted the siege of Derry by forces loyal to the Catholic James II in 1689, and warn of 'capitulation' to the civil rights activists.[23]

Meanwhile a large crowd of hostile Catholics gathered outside in Guildhall Square, angry at the repeated harassment of the march. The mood was one of outrage, but speaker after speaker appealed to the crowd to disperse peacefully. Among them was Eamonn McCann, who had been on the march for the previous three days and had travelled into the city that evening. 'You know I am not a moderate,' he declared. 'I want to see a lot of radical changes in our society. But nothing, nothing whatsoever, can be gained by attacking or abusing the people in the Hall.'[24] While most of the anti-Paisley demonstrators eventually left, around 200 remained. Suddenly, about a hundred young men who had been attending Paisley's rally 'swarmed through the front door of the hall armed with pieces of furniture and chased the Civil Rights crowds who were still in Guildhall Square and the surrounding streets'.[25]

Back in Claudy, while the marchers tried to get some rest in the village hall, Boyle did not sleep. During the night he met John Hume, a Derry businessman and ex-school teacher who had been involved in civil rights activities from the beginning, and would soon become a leading figure in the moderate Social Democratic and Labour Party.[26] Cautious and moderate, Hume was a key member of the Derry Citizens' Action Committee (DCAC), a group composed of prominent figures largely from Derry's

Catholic community. In a sign of divisions that were to intensify and subsequently damage the civil rights movement, the radical Eamonn McCann had denounced the DCAC as 'middle-aged, middle class, and middle of the road'.[27] In any case, Hume, who had been sceptical of the PD march from the beginning, was, in Boyle's words, 'in tears about the riot in Derry and why the march shouldn't have begun ... That was a bad scene.'[28] Boyle understood Hume's concern. 'There had been a civil rights truce; the PD had broken it, and new emotions were appearing on the surface, sectarian demonstrations.'[29] However, while sympathetic, Boyle was not convinced the PD marchers should do anything different as they made their way into Derry the next day. 'For us, in a way, the fact that Ian Paisley was mobilizing this was not a good enough reason. It wasn't the people. It was Paisley who was stirring it up. We were not going to bow to him.'[30]

Very early in the morning, Boyle found District Inspector Harrison to discuss the situation before the march set out on day three. 'No problem, go straight through,' said the district inspector, making Boyle immediately suspicious.[31] Exhausted, Boyle climbed into a car to take a brief nap as the marchers set off. He had only dozed for a half an hour, he recalled, 'when my name was called. Farrell wanted me.'[32] Making his way to the front of the march, Boyle found Farrell talking with a police officer who had briefly ordered the marchers to halt.

According to Farrell, the officer said, 'I have to warn you that the crowd of people up on the hillside there – they may throw a few stones, but we think that you can get through. It's up to you.'

Grabbing a loudhailer, Farrell told the crowd: 'There is a good possibility of some stones being thrown. Some people may be hurt. However, the police have said they are quite prepared to get us through.'[33] To the PD activists, a small group of people throwing stones was nothing new.[34] Supported by Farrell and Boyle, they decided to go ahead. Neither man had any sense of the scale of what awaited them.[35]

'We set off', Devlin wrote, 'at a kind of weary, healthy trudge – pleased to be arriving, but feeling it was a bit of an anti-climax none the less.'[36] At the front of the march were several dozen police constables who had put on helmets and were carrying riot shields. The marchers moved forward, walking beside a hedge to their right, behind which the ground rose steeply. Neatly organized piles of stones and orderly rows of bottles were visible through gaps in the hedgerows.[37] Up on the hillside, several hundred had gathered, wearing white armbands for identification. Among them were off-duty members of the despised B Specials.

It was the perfect place for an ambush.

Boyle was at the front of the march, in the first row on the outside on the left. The inspector in charge, whom Boyle had met many times during the march, approached him and said, 'I wouldn't stand there if I were you.' Boyle, who by his own admission was 'shaking in my shoes', worried that 'if it's dangerous for me, it's dangerous for anybody'.[38]

It was at that point that the marchers reached Burntollet Bridge across the river Faughn. Suddenly, in Devlin's words, 'a curtain of bricks and boulders and bottles' rained down. 'From the lanes burst hordes of screaming people wielding planks of wood, bottles, lathes, iron bars, crowbars, cudgels studded with nails, and they waded into the march beating hell out of everybody.'[39]

'The ambush came down a lane and cut the march in two,' Boyle recalled. 'Eilis was the second row behind me – we were in the front part. A couple of people ran around us and tried to block us, but they couldn't stop us running away, which is your instinctive reaction. We got hit about the feet with sticks and stones, but nothing serious compared to what happened to that march in the middle and the end.'[40]

Reporter Michael Heney was covering the march for *The Irish Times*. 'Long gashes were made on the side of many marchers' heads by the falling stones,' he wrote. 'Girls fainted. Others fell to the ground in blood.'[41] Judith McGuffin, a close friend of both Boyle and McDermott, was in the middle of the march:

> A middle-aged man in a tweed coat, brandishing what seemed to be a chair leg, dashed from the left-hand side of the road, hit me on the back, then pulled down the hood of my anorak and struck me on the head. I then tried to crawl away, but, teeth bared, he hit me again on the same spot on my skull. I fell and a fellow marcher picked me up and dragged me up the road. I passed out.[42]

In the middle of the crowd, Bernadette Devlin froze with fear. 'As I stood there,' she wrote,

> I could see a great big lump of flat wood, like a plank out of an orange box, getting nearer and nearer my face, and there were two great nails sticking

out of it. By a quick reflex action, my hand reached my face before the wood did, and immediately two nails went into the back of my hand. Just after that I was struck on the back of the knees with this bit of wood which had failed to get me in the face, and fell to the ground.[43]

'The severity of the attack drove about a hundred of the marchers, who did not retaliate, over the hedge on the left and down a deep ten-foot drop, in some cases through barbed wire, to the field on the left,' Michael Heney wrote. 'I could see many of these, the majority of who [*sic*] appeared to be young girls, being chased and beaten by "loyalists" who had been hiding behind the hedges.'[44]

Boyle, McDermott, Farrell and the others who had been at the head of the march began to run. After about fifty yards, they stopped and turned around. 'You could see people scattered all over the place,' Boyle recalled.[45] 'There were a lot of people quite hysterical,' Farrell said, 'and they were saying to me, "we can't go on, we can't go on. There's people back there being beaten to death."'

Farrell went back towards the bridge to assess the situation. 'At the bridge, the police and a crowd of the attackers were just standing around chatting and smoking,' he recalled. The attackers had armbands and clubs, and then one policeman said to Farrell, 'For God's sake, get out of here. They'll kill you.' Having done nothing to impede the attackers, the police also made no attempt to arrest them, and did little to assist the wounded. Quickly coming back up the hill, Boyle and Farrell agreed the best and only thing to do was to continue to march towards Derry.

While the dozens of victims were ferried to a nearby hospital, the march re-formed and set off. Reaching the outskirts of Derry, their numbers swelled, as supporters from the city, who had heard about the attack at Burntollet, joined their ranks. By the time they neared the city centre, there were about 2,000 people – a far cry from the few dozen who had set off from Belfast four days earlier. But the number of loyalists had grown too and, as the march passed a predominantly Protestant housing estate, it came under attack again.

Boyle was at the front of the march with McDermott and Farrell. 'A stone came across which missed me and hit her,'[46] Farrell remembered, 'There was a very strong hail of stones and bottles and a couple of petrol bombs, and I got hit with a concrete block on the head.' A lawyer friend of Boyle's took both Farrell and McDermott to a nearby hospital.

Boyle was now effectively left in charge of the march. 'The march was a shambles at that point,' he recalled. 'Already there were two or three thousand Paisleyites gathered right inside the city walls'[47] and the police had banned the marchers from using a direct route to the city centre. The police officer in charge approached him. 'Well, Kevin, what are we going to do now?'

'What do you mean, what do we do?'

'Very soon,' the cop said,

you are going to have to make a choice. You're going to have to go one road or the other. Let me make it clear to you: if you want to take the route to the centre that is banned, I can't stop you. I haven't enough men. I've exhausted the ones I have, and there's more people here than I can control. It's up to you. The only point I'll make is that there are two thousand of the effer's supporters [meaning Paisley] stuck inside the city walls. And you want a shindig, there's how to get it.[48]

Just at the moment came yet another attack. 'That was really horrible. Huge rocks came hammering over,' Boyle said. 'Rocks came rolling down … and breaking windows on the other side of the road. And by the time the people had made their way close to the city centre, they were in a militant mood.'[49]

The police officer found Boyle again on the Craigavon Bridge heading to the city centre, and asked him what he intended to do. 'We want no conflict with the Protestant people,' Boyle answered, 'and I'm not interested in arousing sectarian warfare. We'll go to the Guildhall by the easiest route, the route that will avoid that.'[50]

'That's what I thought you'd decide,' said the police officer.[51] Coming off the bridge, Boyle led the march towards Guildhall Square, away from the angry Paisleyites. They entered the square to a rapturous reception from a crowd that had now grown to around four thousand. Boyle delivered what he remembered as a 'very dull'[52] speech. He was followed by Devlin, who coined what became a widely quoted phrase: Derry was 'the capital city of injustice'.[53] The rally concluded with an address by Farrell, who had come straight from being treated at the hospital and was greeted with loud applause.[54] He demanded that Terence O'Neill 'give us what we want – now

– or we will get out on the streets, stay on the streets, and throw him out'. Like the other speakers, Farrell appealed to the crowd to disperse peacefully. He described those who had staged the attacks as 'unfortunate, misguided people. They are our brothers, even though they are misguided. Do not retaliate, because we are winning!'[55]

The reality, however, was that, as Eilis McDermott noted, being attacked 'showed me for the first time the depth of hatred and fear that existed amongst a section of the Unionist population. It was slowly dawning on me that by demanding elementary reform we were – without meaning to be – a threat to the state.'[56] Indeed, the hostility and anger of militant Protestants at the marchers was shocking. Andrew Hamilton, another *Irish Times* reporter who had witnessed the attack at Burntollet, wrote, 'There were unbelievable scenes of fury among militant Protestants. I heard fanatical Protestants who had rushed down a hillside shout: We'll kill them, we'll kill them.'[57]

Shortly after most of those attending the rally at Guildhall Square had dispersed, clashes broke out between a few hundred supporters of the march and several hundred Paisley loyalists. Police used water cannon, and barricades were set up to keep the RUC out of the Catholic Bogside. The mood among the local people was angry. 'It's resentment against the attacks on the marchers today,' one woman told a reporter. 'It was a sectarian police force which permitted these attacks,' said another. 'People don't realize how much we have had stuffed down our necks from Paisleyites for so long.'[58] The rioting went on throughout the night, as the police surged through the area, in the eyes of both onlookers and a later government commission of inquiry, out of control.

'That night [the police] went mad in the Bogside,' Boyle remembered. 'They got drunk and displayed their essential view of life, which is that Catholics should be kept down.'[59] As the commission of inquiry later concluded, 'A number of policemen were guilty of misconduct which involved assault and battery, malicious damage to property, to streets, in the predominantly Catholic Bogside area.'[60] This included assaulting Catholics at random, trashing their homes, and breaking into a department store where they beat several customers with batons.

The reaction to the PD's march and the violence in Derry was immediate and dramatic, with many Catholics who had stood on the sidelines now joining the civil rights movement. Outraged by the behaviour of the police, civil rights leaders declared that the truce called after Prime Minister O'Neill's Crossroads speech in mid-December – the truce the People's Democracy had broken – was officially over. The PD announced plans for a big civil rights demonstration the following weekend in Boyle's home town, Newry.

For his part, a furious O'Neill denounced the march to Derry as 'foolhardy and irresponsible. Enough is enough,' the Prime Minister said. 'We have heard sufficient for now about civil rights; let us hear a little about civil responsibility.'[61] After a three-hour cabinet meeting, O'Neill announced plans for a large-scale call-up of the B Specials, the force Catholics most identified with the injustices of Unionist rule.

Journalist Max Hastings said O'Neill's speech was 'ill-considered. Whatever truth there might be in what he said, it served only to infuriate further the Catholics, without appeasing the Protestants.'[62]

The driving force for the Newry march on Saturday, 11 January 1969 was a local civil rights committee with connections to People's Democracy. Kevin's brother Damian, who still lived at home in Newry, was one of those involved. 'The emphasis in the Newry march should have been on non-violence,' Kevin recalled.

> The regime had been caught in the open with its rioting police and the militant unionists and then violence. The idea should have been to show that the civil rights movement could organize a peaceful march and therefore attention wouldn't be distracted from what had happened at Burntollet.[63]

'The Newry civil rights march should have been a straightforward affair,' Louis Boyle later wrote.

> Newry was a nationalist town. Community relationships were good, and the Unionist minority were fairly well treated. There were no 'no go' areas in Newry for a Civil Rights march. The local organizing committee saw it as an opportunity to give vent to the need on the part of local people to hold a large, peaceful civil rights demonstration in their own town. Given the high level of feeling in the nationalist community following the events of the previous weekend in Derry, there were also many people from outside who wanted to take part in the march.[64]

Given the lack of local inter-communal tensions, the police in Newry appeared content to let the march proceed. However, the day before it was due to take place, the O'Neill government ordered that it be rerouted in a way the organizers believed was designed to make it appear more like a purely Catholic march than a non-sectarian one. The activists faced a dilemma. If they agreed to the rerouting, they would appear to be acquiescing in a politically driven decision that would discredit them. If they resisted, it might lead to trouble on the streets. Late that Friday night, after hours of intense discussions in which Boyle was deeply involved, the decision was made not to accept the rerouting. To avoid violence, however, it was agreed to lead the march to the police barricades, make a token breach, and then stage a sit-down protest.[65]

Late the next afternoon, in a dense fog, about 5000 people – a much larger crowd than had been originally expected – set off to defy the police. The *Irish Times* correspondent Dennis Kennedy, who was there, wrote: 'It seemed the decision to re-route the march away from the northern end of the business sector of the town had given it a new sense of purpose.'[66] In the centre of town, the marchers' progress was blocked by scores of police standing behind barriers. The mood of the crowd was angry, reflected in the tone of Boyle's speech to them.

'This is a humiliating day,' he told the marchers through a loudhailer, denouncing what he called the

> unjust and tyrannical re-route imposed by the discredited Unionist government. They made that decision because they have capitulated to the right-wing extremists whom we know love power in this country. They have allowed these people – the same people who harassed and assaulted the young marchers to Derry – to dictate to them how they should act. These fascist groups have only to threaten opposition and the government gives in. Let me say it loud and clear to this discredited government and the thugs who now have power … We are fighting for civil rights and we are a non-political organization. We embrace all religions and none. We are fighting against injustice and demand the right to proceed where we like. [67]

Boyle concluded his remarks with a call for calm:

> People of Newry. I have tried to express my anger, and my frustration, and I know it expresses yours. [But the organizers] are asking you to protest in a peaceful manner and follow their plans. Anyone who takes action by himself – who offers violence – is going against his own people. I appeal to you to stand by your community's decision and offer no violence. Be peaceful, because in this way we *shall* overcome.[68]

Even as Boyle was speaking, however, some of the protestors, angry that the organizers were not calling for a full-scale assault on the barriers, rushed the police lines, throwing rocks and bottles, setting two police vehicles alight and pushing another into a nearby canal. At the same time, a small group of radicals broke away from the main crowd, ran to Newry's main post office, smashed the windows and occupied the building. Eventually, police cleared the streets with a series of baton charges. Boyle and his fellow moderates had lost control.

Boyle was extremely upset by the turn of events. 'The Newry march was generally recognized … as a disaster because it tended to take away from the pacifist civil rights image,' he said. 'It did bring bad publicity to civil rights, which were then painted as just as riotous as the Unionists. This was the point. It now looked like there were rioting factions on both sides.'[69]

The events of January 1969 turned out to be a watershed in Northern Ireland's spiral towards disaster, shaping and hardening attitudes on both sides that would fuel a cycle of violence and bloodshed for decades. As Eilis McDermott had sensed, the civil rights demonstrations did indeed appear to many Protestants to be an existential threat both to their privileged position and to their state. One result was the fragmentation of the Unionist monolith that had ruled Northern Ireland since 1920.

O'Neill's position was severely weakened as he struggled to respond to growing demands for civil rights while facing heightened pressure from Protestant hardliners to crack down on the campaigners. To placate the civil rights movement he announced the creation of a commission, headed by a Scottish judge, Lord Cameron, 'to examine the causes and nature of the violence and civil disturbances in Northern Ireland'.[70] Loyalist hardliners, however, viewed the move as capitulating to their enemies. Within the Unionist Party, O'Neill's rivals began a concerted campaign which, in a matter of months, would drive him from power.

In the Catholic community, however, O'Neill's decision was widely seen as a meaningless gesture. For many Catholics, the lesson was that the state was incapable of reforming itself. As Ed Moloney, then still a Queen's student and PD supporter, later observed, the importance of Burntollet is underplayed as a pivotal moment in the history of the Troubles. For him, the aspiration of creating common cause with the Protestants, only to meet a brick wall, affected the movement deeply. 'It's not just the fact that you are attacked by loyalists,' Moloney said. 'It's that it was colluded in by the cops. In other words, cops don't do things without the approval of the government, without the approval of the power structure. That leads you to certain logical conclusions about the nature of the state, and one of which is that it is totally unreformable.' Indeed, Moloney, who more than thirty years later would write the definitive history of the IRA,[71] argues that the events at Burntollet 'laid the ideological basis for the Provisional IRA' because 'if you conclude that the state is unreformable, then you are accepting the IRA's argument that the only way to solve this thing is to destroy the state'.

Surveying the political landscape in the wake of Burntollet and Newry, Boyle found himself profoundly discouraged. In notes drafted to deliver at a People's Democracy meeting following the Newry riot, he wrote:

> I will admit to you now that in the whole of this hectic three months' campaign for civil rights, I have never been so depressed about the situation in Ulster as I am today. Northern Ireland has hit an all-time low, the nadir of its history, so that we are all thinking, can it get any worse? We have a government that seems to have just given up – that has apparently no power to arrest and prosecute and punish offenders against its laws – the people who stormed and beat up many members of this room at Burntollet bridge, and further, a government that bends the knee at every threat of the same people, even to the point of risking a breakdown in our united community in Newry last weekend. I think my own depression hangs over the province – and it hangs over many of us – and it is not surprising that in flashpoint situations it produces violence, anger, and hysteria, as well as opportunities for more subversive theories of change to briefly appear.[72]

What was most worrying for him was the upsurge in naked sectarianism:

> From the very beginning, we have understood that the only way to talk of civil rights was in terms not of them and us, Orange or Green, but for all … The point has been reached, I think, where we must consider desperately whether we are going to be defeated; whether lunatics like Bunting and Paisley in the tension raised by our agitation will sow the seeds throughout this community of religious war. It may be the case that we have exposed how meaningless community relations were; but what after exposure can we offer to produce a new community – which will never again polarize?[73]

To avoid such an outcome, Boyle argued that it was critical to modify some of the more extreme tactics and attitudes that the PD and other civil rights activists had displayed. 'If the long–term ambition is of uniting Catholic and Protestant, we must remember when considering our short-term actions.'[74]

These observations came at a time when Boyle's own political thinking was beginning to crystallize. He now identified himself as a socialist, as did Bernadette Devlin, shaped by a sense that 'the most effective solutions to the problems we discussed always turned out to be the solutions offered by the left'.[75] Yet Boyle did not formally affiliate himself with any socialist organization or theory. Instead, he defined his approach as 'left and reform-ist'.[76] And this put him more and more at odds with Michael Farrell, who was talking in increasingly explicit terms about revolution. So was Eamonn McCann, who described the conditions Boyle found so bleak as 'pre-revo-lutionary', and told the same interviewer: 'The transformation necessary to implement these reforms is revolution.'[77]

Mixed into Farrell's thinking was another element that Boyle found troubling: a militancy that became profoundly anti-unionist, displaying 'good old-fashioned nationalism. A feeling that Ireland has been occupied, Ireland has been wrongly divided.'[78] Boyle confessed that he had never felt that way, and his loathing for hard-line unionism was combined with a deep scepticism about traditional Irish nationalism. 'I could never be a Unionist, but more than anti-unionism, an anti-partitionist. For me, that was an issue which wasn't on the agenda, and efforts to insert it into it was ultimately damaging to civil rights movement. Ultimately it was what it fell apart on.'[79]

Boyle was not alone in being slow to recognize the depth of sectarian hatred and the dangers that civil rights agitation would intensify it. His comrades in the PD were, by and large, young, innocent and ignorant of Northern Ireland's troubled history. Years later, Boyle acknowledged that the majority of PD activists saw the events at Burntollet as a means of maintaining pressure on the government, to challenge arbitrary power, and confront the Unionist regime. The young activists had no memories of earlier periods of sectarian tension and violence. 'I certainly didn't know, or have a feeling for the depths of antagonism that existed in the sense of territory that existed in Northern Ireland,'[80] Boyle acknowledged decades later. 'Each generation can't be told,' he ruefully observed.[81] As Boyle and his youthful comrades were about to discover – painfully – they would have to learn the hard truths about Northern Ireland for themselves.

[5]

A Three-sided Civil War

JUST AS BOYLE began to realize that Northern Ireland was standing on a precipice, Terence O'Neill called a surprise election for the province's legislature, scheduled for 24 February 1969. He was gambling on winning support from the middle ground in both communities and thus strengthening his hand against the hardliners in his own party. Within People's Democracy, the move triggered a debate about whether to field candidates or to boycott what many members felt was a sham election.

There were two types of elections in Northern Ireland. One was for local councils, the other for the territory's parliament at Stormont. In local elections, only the designated 'occupier' of a house and their spouse could vote, and limited companies could appoint up to six electors. So some adults had no vote, and others, especially certain Protestants, had several.[1] It was this policy, buttressed by local electoral districts and wards blatantly gerrymandered to ensure Protestant control, that was the target of perhaps the most potent slogan of the civil rights movement: 'one man, one vote'. (In the late 1960s, when the issue of women's rights was emerging, few activists in

Northern Ireland seemed troubled by the sexism of the slogan, which was always intended to mean 'one adult, one vote'.)

For elections to Stormont, and for the North's twelve members of the British Parliament at Westminster, however, there was full adult suffrage. Despite widespread scepticism about the process, most of the leading figures in the PD, including Boyle, supported the idea of participating. He laid out his reasons in ten pages of notes, which he used for a presentation at a PD meeting. While acknowledging the unlikelihood of a PD representative being elected, fielding candidates, he argued, would provide an important opportunity to bring the organization's civil rights agenda to a wider audience. 'This election is an extension of our plan to inform the public. We involve people in the general level – we have guaranteed publicity for those we cannot reach – through the media.' By modifying their tactics and participating in the election, the PD had an opportunity to 'present policies and candidates with policies'.[2]

It was a view Bernadette Devlin strongly backed. 'It was our golden opportunity,' she wrote. 'We didn't want to get into Parliament, but here was the chance we'd been waiting for to explain our policies to the people. The police were bound by law to protect a parliamentary candidate; we could send an election manifesto into every home in eight constituencies with the Post Office paying for our propaganda.'[3]

Depressed and worried about the rise of sectarianism, and opposed to the traditional republican approach of focusing on partition, Kevin Boyle identified another crucially important point. 'This is the first election which is not about the border. It's about the internal power struggle in the Unionist Party.' This, he wrote, gave the PD the opportunity to raise what he viewed to be 'the real issues – jobs, homes, liberty. We have it in our power and ONLY US to lay down the beginnings of normal democracy – to use this bogus event for the highly responsible and necessary end of pressing demands and putting the real issues to THE PEOPLE.'[4]

The PD decided to run candidates for eight seats at Stormont, in the process trying to challenge traditional sectarian voting patterns. As Devlin explained, 'in Northern Ireland ... and if there was a sufficient majority of either Protestants or Catholics in a constituency, the seat was never contested ... We took on both parties in a non-sectarian platform for radical policies.'[5]

Boyle organized the press conference to announce that the PD would stand, and introduced the candidates. He was also deeply involved in drafting the PD's manifesto, which sought to link the battle for social justice with broader calls for reform. It contained both the standard civil rights demands, as well as calls for a much more active state intervention in the economy along socialist lines. Still, in Boyle's view, 'this was not a revolutionary manifesto'.[6]

Boyle was also involved in an attempt by his brother Louis to secure the nomination to be a Unionist candidate in Newry. The logic, in Louis' mind, was clear: O'Neill 'was trying to reach out to moderate opinion, including Catholics, for support'.[7] What better way to seek that support than to nominate one of the only Catholic Unionists in Northern Ireland? 'I consulted Kevin and he encouraged me to go ahead and indicated that while the resources of the PD were not available to me, there could be considerable sympathy and maybe passive support for me standing as a candidate.'[8] Indeed, Kevin managed to convince the PD not to field a candidate in Newry 'in order to give Louis a clear run'.[9]

Louis wrote directly to Terence O'Neill seeking his endorsement. But from the prime minister, and the Ulster Unionist headquarters, he got only silence. A few days later, the Ulster Unionist Party selected a Protestant businessman to run in Newry. Louis was furious. Prepared to expose himself to personal risk by standing as a Catholic Unionist, his party had rejected him. Kevin shared his brother's 'sense of disappointment and anger'.[10] At Kevin's suggestion, they decided to leak the story to the *Irish News*, which, the following day, featured the headline 'Wooing of Moderates Fails Its First Real Test ... Mr Louis Boyle to tell PM of his dismay'.[11] Kevin told the *Irish News* reporter that, while he disagreed with Louis' politics, 'he had always admired his courage and sincerity, especially his refusal to allow his religion to determine his political allegiances'.[12] It was clear to Kevin that the Ulster Unionist Party 'was so bigoted it just couldn't cope with the fact that here was somebody who was a well-known Catholic prepared to stand pro-O'Neill'.[13] Within a matter of weeks, Louis determined that there was no future for him in the party, and resigned. Kevin helped him draft his resignation statement. As Ed Moloney, a friend of both brothers, noted, 'Louis' story was important, because it sent a bigger and wider message to the Catholic community – that if someone like Louis, who was a decent spud, and wanted to accept the union, and wanted to be part of the Unionist Party, could not be accepted, then no one could be accepted.'

It became increasingly clear that O'Neill's juggling act was not working. 'Here was a man saying that the future was contingent on Catholic support for him,' Kevin Boyle noted, 'but he could not field a single Catholic candidate, and he was endorsing all kinds of people [who were] clearly anti-Catholic.'[14]

When the results of the election came in, they were a disaster for O'Neill and his hope of consolidating a moderate centre. Anti-O'Neill Protestant hardliners did surprisingly well. O'Neill himself came within 1414 votes of losing his own seat at Stormont to Ian Paisley, and in a matter of months, he would be forced from office.

On the other side, PD candidates exceeded expectations. As *The Irish Times* noted, while 'none was returned to Parliament, all, except one in Belfast who lost his deposit, polled heavily … The significance of the People's Democracy vote is that the movement itself regarded its intervention in the election as propagandist and an effort not to allow Civil Rights demands to get lost in the general confusion.'[15] In Devlin's view, 'the PD gained an electoral mandate that was not gained by that element again until Sinn Féin were brought into the electoral process many, many years later.' She and Farrell both believed that the upsurge of support triggered by the attack at Burntollet was critical, and undercut the argument that the march had served only to make things worse. It was, in her words, 'a significant vote for a bunch of reprobate students who [in staging the Belfast to Derry march], according to the historical analysis, against the popular will had done a reckless and unpopular deed.'

Indeed, the stature of the PD had grown in the previous weeks to the point that, just days before the election, Boyle and Farrell were voted onto the executive of the Northern Ireland Civil Rights Association. Farrell recalled: 'We were brought in to sort of create greater unity in the movement, and maybe jazz up the rather sleepy leadership of NICRA. People didn't really know who they were. NICRA really never had any great status.' Ann Hope, a NICRA activist, later wrote that within the organization, 'there was unease at our apparent lack of activity. Some felt we were losing the initiative,' and that there was 'strong support' for adding Farrell and Boyle.[16] However, tensions soon emerged with the more cautious leaders of NICRA. Indeed, the organization's official history describes the move to recruit the two men as an effort 'to nullify the PD influence by co-opting' them.[17]

If that was the intention, it quickly became clear that the tactic had backfired. In early March, Farrell and Boyle proposed that the People's Democracy and NICRA jointly stage a march from the centre of Belfast to the parliament at Stormont. There was heated debate, with opponents warning that the route of such a march would go through predominantly Protestant East Belfast and this would almost certainly spark trouble. The upshot was that four members of the NICRA executive who were opposed to the march resigned. After a 'long, acrimonious and confused debate' at an emergency general meeting later in the month, it was finally agreed that the march should not take place.[18]

But the differences between those demanding immediate reform – reflecting the impatience growing in the Catholic community, which the People's Democracy was both articulating and encouraging, and those advocating a more cautious approach, were now out in the open. Nonetheless, the pressure from Boyle and Farrell was having an effect. As Bernadette Devlin wrote, the Civil Rights Association, 'which had been a not very effective pressure group, suddenly found itself a sort of spokesman for a popular movement consisting of very disparate elements indeed'.[19]

Meanwhile, a by-election had been called for 17 April to fill the seat of an Ulster Unionist member of the Westminster Parliament for Mid-Ulster who had died in December. Divisions on the Catholic side meant that at least two contenders would run, likely splitting the Catholic vote in what was a majority Catholic area, thus ensuring a Unionist victory. Devlin, who had performed well as a PD candidate in the local elections in February, came under pressure to run as a unity candidate. She had no interest in doing so. 'I didn't want to stand for election to Westminster,' she wrote later. 'I didn't know anything about Parliament … I didn't respect the system, and even if I had, that wasn't the sort of politician I wanted to be.'[20] Nonetheless, under pressure, she agreed, and, with just two weeks before the vote, plunged into the campaign.

Devlin had emerged as one of the most passionate and effective speakers produced by the civil rights movement. She campaigned energetically across the province, sometimes to cheers, sometimes 'through hails of broken bottles and stones',[21] pushing a non-sectarian platform of sweeping reform. 'That was a campaign that was crazy – absolutely crazy,' she recalled. 'But there was a coherent logic to it in the midst of the craziness. We were the PD, radicals, we were civil righters. We were not Green; we were not Orange. We spoke everywhere.' Boyle understood her appeal. 'She was from the area and she knew the constituency … She has this ability to speak almost in a poetic fashion, and then she's also very, very human, she appeals to people, not as an abstract leader. And she's very direct, she's very warm, and I think people are just charmed.'[22]

Boyle played an active role in her campaign, joining her at rallies, his analytical manner of address a sharp contrast to her own impassioned style. 'I was effectively an orator or a ranter,' she acknowledged. 'Kevin was a much better indoor than outdoor speaker. [He spoke] with all the rationale and logic and calmness of indoor speakers … People listened to him.' Boyle felt that Devlin was torn about her political stance. 'I think she was half-impressed with my indirect approach to politics,'[23] he remembered. But she was also impressed with the 'more strident approach' of more radical figures like Farrell and McCann. Years later, Devlin would say that Boyle, Farrell and McCann 'occupied three different places in the political spectrum [and] were the three most important influences on my own political development'.

Initially almost unnoticed, Devlin's campaign picked up momentum and she became something of an overnight media sensation, with reporters and camera crews tracking her every move. When the results came in on 18 April, she had swept to victory with the largest anti-Unionist majority since the seat was created in 1950. At age twenty-one, she was then the youngest woman ever elected to the Westminster Parliament.

That weekend, while 'reporters and photographers settled round the house like swarming bees, demanding idiotic phony photographs of the MP sitting on the rug surrounded by all her little cousins',[24] violence flared in Derry. In the city centre, civil rights supporters staged a spontaneous protest rally against a government ban on a march from Burntollet Bridge, site of the notorious January attack. A crowd of Paisleyites gathered and scuffles broke out. At this point, the police intervened and drove the demonstrators back into the Bogside, triggering a riot which lasted until late at night. One group of RUC men broke into a house and beat the owner, Samuel Devenny, knocking him unconscious in front of his family. Three months later he died.

As police in full riot gear moved through the area, Devlin paid a visit, encouraging local people to resist by building barricades. 'We weren't in favour of attacking the police or spreading wanton violence,' she wrote, 'but we felt the police had no business coming into the Bogside terrorizing people.'[25]

The rioting spread to Belfast for the first time since the start of the civil rights movement as Catholics there protested about the behaviour of the police in Derry. At the same time, two bombs went off near Belfast's main reservoir and electricity supply. The government immediately blamed the IRA. In fact, the illegal Protestant paramilitary Ulster Volunteer Force was responsible.

The weekend disorders led to an emergency debate on Northern Ireland in the Westminster Parliament on 22 April, the day Devlin was due to take up her seat in the House of Commons. The night before, she was at Boyle's flat in Belfast until 2 am, worrying about what she had got herself into and brainstorming what to say in her maiden speech. For all the excitement, she was less than thrilled at the idea of becoming a conventional politician. She remembered that night 'berating who it was may have got me into this, and how I was going to be got out of it. Even though I was now elected, I was saying, somehow among the three of you [Boyle, Farrell and McCann], you got me into this.'

'She went back to Cookstown,' Boyle remembered,

> had two hours' sleep, and was up for the six o'clock plane to London. Then she gave this absolutely magnificent performance in a packed House of Commons ... and she gave a speech totally off the cuff, just like that, whereas all the others have apparently great difficulty in making their maiden speeches.[26]

Devlin delivered her speech in what one reporter described as 'her biting Irish accent and forceful style'.[27] 'There can be no justice while there is a Unionist Party,' she declared, 'because while there is a Unionist Party they will by their gerrymandering control Northern Ireland.'[28] She was suitably cynical about the response of her fellow MPs. 'They all said "Hear! Hear!" and thought it was delightful stuff, which showed the House up for what it was.'[29]

The speech was a sensation, fuelling media attention and turning Devlin into an international celebrity – the poster girl for protest in Northern Ireland. A *Daily Express* headline screamed 'She's Bernadette, she's 21, she's an MP, she's swinging,' while *The Observer* described her as 'Cassandra in a Mini-Skirt'.

Boyle was bemused watching the creation of what he called her 'Joan of Arc kind of image. The things that happened. It was like a moth going to a candle. She was a media darling.'[30] But celebrity did little to blunt Devlin's outspokenness. In an interview with the *Observer*'s Mary Holland the following weekend, she worried that 'we're going to have a three-sided civil war. There will be Protestant bigots on one side, and Papist bigots on the other. And there will be a few, a very few of us in the middle asking them to stop and they'll both hate us most of all.'[31]

The day after the interview was published, Terence O'Neill, who, just a few days earlier had grudgingly accepted the principle of 'one adult, one vote', resigned as prime minister, abandoning his efforts to find a middle ground in Northern Ireland. 'When the history of this time comes to be written,' Devlin had presciently noted to Mary Holland, 'I think O'Neill will be seen as at best the fool, at worst the villain, of the piece. For the whole five years he's been in office, he's been raising Catholic expectations with his liberal chat, but he hasn't been strong enough to do anything about it.'[32] In Protestant areas of Belfast, bonfires were lit to celebrate O'Neill's departure. He was succeeded by James Chichester-Clark, a farmer and former minister of agriculture, described by one British journalist as 'wholly inarticulate' and 'regarded in political circles as a man who had never had an original idea in his life'.[33]

As spring moved into summer, low-grade street violence continued, with Boyle, who by now had been appointed NICRA's press officer, worrying about a further intensification of sectarianism and fearing that it was 'likely to explode'.[34] His concern was widely shared within the civil rights movement, amid mounting alarm that O'Neill's resignation would only embolden loyalist extremists, while intensifying Catholic frustration at the lack of further reform. The Civil Rights Association, Ann Hope wrote,

> realized if they did not return to the streets and organize demonstrations over which they would have control in an effort to relieve the frustrations of the minority, the conflict would rapidly become one not between inter-denominational forces of reform and the Unionist monolith, but rather a sectarian feud between aggrieved militant Catholics and working-class Protestants.[35]

The result was a NICRA ultimatum to the government in mid-May 1969 that if a timetable for reforms was not announced within six weeks, they would again take to the streets. With no progress by late June, a demonstration was called for the town of Strabane on 28 June. Meanwhile, the Protestant Orange order, a pillar of Unionist influence, announced plans to hold its own march through the predominantly Catholic village of Dungiven on the same day. The idea of Protestant marchers parading down Dungiven's long main street created 'great resentment' among its Catholic residents, Farrell recalled. 'Civil rights marches had not been allowed to go through the centre of any town.' For Boyle, it raised

> the whole question of discriminatory law enforcement or biased applica-
> tion of the law in relation to processions … The Orangemen could march
> through a largely nationalist area but nationalists, or Catholics organized
> under some other banner, could not demonstrate in areas which were
> known to be hostile to the civil rights movement.[36]

'Dungiven people first wanted to block the whole village,' Boyle recalled, 'stone the Orangemen, and not let them through.'[37] Boyle, accompanied by Eilis McDermott, rushed to the town. 'I was very worried about the possibility of violence. I also wanted to see what this new phenomenon of civil rights could do with Dungiven's intractable Orange/Green quarrel,' he said.[38]

Boyle met with local residents. He argued that

> a civil rights movement that had been struggling for freedom of procession
> ought to allow people [meaning the Orangemen] to march where they liked
> … but considering that this demonstration was a provocative one, some
> kind of protest could be made which would not obstruct the procession.[39]

Boyle proposed an alternative approach, which he described as civil disobedience: 'Shut down all the shops, pull down all the blinds, and put up posters asking … you can march; can others?'[40] Despite considerable resistance, Boyle's argument prevailed. He drafted a leaflet that members of the People's Democracy circulated in the small town, and also organized buses to take some local residents to a civil rights rally in nearby Strabane.

On the morning of 28 June, Kevin arrived in Dungiven. He toured the town with a loudhailer, appealing to residents to stay inside. To his horror, he discovered that a few local Catholic teenagers had painted 'Up the IRA' on the road across from a local church. 'I could sense tension. I saw the letters on the street and started wondering – what am I going to do about this?' Boyle asked one of the teenagers, 'Don't you think you should clear it away?' The youngster retorted, 'Why don't you do it?'[41]

Boyle took a can of paint, 'and I remember walking up the centre of that empty, watching town with this paintbrush … I felt that something could go wrong here. I just painted it out and that was that.'[42] But Dungiven's residents largely followed Boyle's appeal to stay indoors, and, apart from the Orangemen tearing down all the posters the PD had put up and assaulting foreign TV crews covering the event, the march went off with minimal trouble, as did the march in Strabane the same day. After weeks of mounting tension, it was at least a small success for the civil rights movement.

Now, however, the height of the Protestant marching season was approaching. For decades, during July and August, Protestant groups, including the Orange Order and, in Derry, the Apprentice Boys, had marched, often through Catholic areas, in a display of symbolic muscle-flexing, intended to show Catholics who was in charge. The first big marching day was 12 July, when the Orange Order held parades throughout Northern Ireland to mark the victory of the Protestant King William of Orange over the Catholic King James II at the Battle of the Boyne in 1690. The second great day of Protestant triumphalism was 12 August – highlighted by the annual march in Derry of the Apprentice Boys, an organization that celebrates the Protestant victory over Jacobite forces there in 1689. In the wake of disturbances on 12 July, there were calls from civil rights leaders and the Catholic community for the government to ban the Derry parade, which, even during the best of times, served only to antagonize Catholics. Yet, repeating a pattern seen in previous loyalist marches, the government could not bring itself to impose a ban. Fear of a backlash from loyalist hardliners outweighed fears that the Apprentice Boys could spark off more violence on the streets.

Indeed, despite all the incidents of the preceding months, as one British journalist observed,

> that sunny August, there was still a strange feeling of make-believe about Ulster. Riots had taken place but they had withered away again after one day, or two, or three. The destruction, by the standards of American race riots, for example, had been limited. The casualties had been unpleasant, but not yet fatal. Many people talked very seriously about the awful

dangers of the situation, of the risk of a really calamitous outbreak, yet in a way nobody believed it. Too many people were too young to remember what happens when passions are really roused, and all semblance of control is lost.[43]

On 11 August Boyle spoke with Devlin, who told him she was heading to Derry. 'I said, "Well, I'll stay in Belfast because I think it's going to be a very eventful couple of days," but I had no clear idea of what was going to happen.'[44]

On the morning of 12 August, as the Apprentice Boys prepared to march, the mood in Derry's Catholic Bogside area was highly charged. There had been intermittent clashes with the RUC for weeks, and memories of the death in mid-July of Samuel Devenny at the hands of the police were still raw. Rumours that the Bogside might come under attack from the loyalists or the police had led local residents to stockpile rocks, bricks and petrol bombs, and erect barricades. For the most part, however, the parade – 15,000 Protestant men in dark suits and bowler hats marching along the walls enclosing the old city of Derry and looking down on the Bogside – passed off peacefully, despite taunts from some of the marchers directed at the Bogsiders below. Then, early in the afternoon, as the parade passed an entrance to the Bogside, Catholic youths began to throw stones at the marchers. Young Protestants in the crowd retaliated, and a skirmish ensued.

The police, wearing riot gear, then moved towards the Bogside, an act that 'transformed the disturbance from being an incident engaging a handful of police and a few youths into a war between the residents of the Bogside and the RUC'.[45] The Catholics built more barricades and sought to repel the police with barrages of rocks and Molotov cocktails. The frustrated and embattled police responded with great quantities of tear gas – the first time it had been used in the United Kingdom – but this only 'provoked more fury from the Bogsiders'.'[46]

Bernadette Devlin was in the thick of it:

We threw up barricades of rubble, pipes and paving stones – anything we could get our hands on – to prevent the police from coming into the area and, in their own words, 'settling the Bogside once and for all' ... The police answered our stones and petrol bombs with stones of their own, and with ever-increasing supplies of tear gas.[47]

As what was now being called The Battle of the Bogside raged into a second day, Boyle and other members of the executive of the Northern Ireland Civil Rights Association held an urgent meeting in Belfast. Boyle felt it was 'almost like a civil war confrontation and we would have to do something quickly to stop it'.[48] True to his long-standing instinct of trying to play the role of peacemaker, at his suggestion the executive agreed to send a delegation to Stormont to meet the Minister of Home Affairs, Robert Porter, in the hope of negotiating a halt to the violence. Their proposal was that, in Boyle's words, 'if the police would withdraw from the Bogside, then the people would remain within the barricaded area and would not come into the city, and therefore the present police tactics were unnecessary ... We believed that the people would stay inside if the police withdrew and the firing of gas canisters stopped.'[49] The other part of the strategy was to 'put to them [the Northern Ireland officials] an ultimatum that if they didn't take the police out of the Bogside, we would cause demonstrations to be held all over the North that would force the police out of the Bogside, or at least prevent reinforcements.'[50]

Boyle was in charge of trying to arrange the meeting, but could get on the phone only a non-committal civil servant. 'I said, "Look, ring me back within an hour telling me this interview has been fixed up with your Home Affairs Minister ... If you don't ring, we'll just announce that to the press and hold our demonstrations anyway."'[51] Shortly after, the official called back to confirm the meeting. With journalists anxious for word from NICRA for the evening news, before leaving for Stormont Boyle issued a press statement he had drafted, threatening new demonstrations to take the pressure off Derry. Because of the long-standing sectarian tensions in Belfast, the statement was explicit that no civil rights protests would be organized there.

Under questioning from reporters, however, Boyle suggested that the situation was fluid and that it might, at some point, become necessary to stage something in Belfast.[52] His threat was published in several newspapers, including *The Irish Times*:

> A member of the executive, Kevin Boyle, announced that if the Minister would not agree to withdraw police from the Bogside, the only tactic left open to the association was to draw the police from Derry by holding meetings in a dozen other places in the North outside Belfast in defiance of the ban. If the situation did not improve, he said, further meetings might be called in Belfast tomorrow night.[53]

The threat to call for protests in volatile Belfast was a 'silly mistake', Boyle said some years later.[54] But the comment fuelled tensions in an already volatile situation.

In the mid-afternoon of 13 August, Boyle and the nine other members of the NICRA delegation arrived at Stormont to be told that the Minister of Home Affairs was not in fact available to see them. They were met instead by the Minister's Parliamentary Secretary, John Taylor, a hardliner. The group protested, but presented their argument to Taylor anyway. 'We put to him the suggestion or plan that if the police withdrew and gas was stopped … the people would stay inside the barricaded areas and we could ensure that they did so. We said if he was not willing to do this, we would be left with no alternative but to arrange [other] demonstrations.'[55] Taylor procrastinated. Boyle and others in his group 'formed the view that he had no intentions of telling the Minister what we had put to him'.[56] Instead, Taylor told them that Prime Minister James Chichester-Clark was going to speak on television at six o'clock that evening and they should simply wait and watch.

To most of his colleagues, Chichester-Clark's address was disappointing. However, Boyle detected one ray of hope in his appeal to people in Derry to disregard rumours of police reprisals if the Bogsiders backed off. 'I thought … he might be willing to attempt a ceasefire in the Bogside. Others were sceptical, but I talked them round to my point of view.'[57]

Calls were coming in from local civil rights groups around the province asking if they should go ahead with demonstrations planned for 8.30 pm that evening, since many people had seen the images from Derry on television and spontaneous demonstrations were already starting. Boyle's response was to urge that they hold off if possible while he and his colleagues tried to get in direct touch with the prime minister.

At that point, he was finally able to reach Bernadette Devlin on the phone in Derry, and he spelled out the proposal he had been pushing at Stormont. 'She was sceptical because she felt it was too late but was willing to try, assuming we could get in touch with the authorities.'[58] The NICRA group finally spoke directly with Chichester-Clark on the phone at 8 pm. The prime minister was, in Boyle's words, 'annoyed' that he had not been told about the NICRA delegation's visit to Stormont.[59] Chichester-Clark nonetheless said that he was open to trying to find a plan for the police to withdraw from the Bogside.

'We were shocked,' Boyle told the subsequent Scarman tribunal of inquiry, 'because it was the same plan we had proposed in the early afternoon, and were convinced that if it had been negotiated then, it could have succeeded.' Boyle even wondered whether the ideas of his NICRA group had even been conveyed to the prime minister.[60] 'That was Kevin,' Devlin would say years later. 'When you are sitting there and the towns are blowing up, he's still trying to find a way.'

After this phone call, Boyle managed to get through to Devlin again, only to be told that the RUC's attempt to withdraw had failed. As they were withdrawing, 'two officers in the second or third rank let off more CS gas and started the whole thing up again'.[61] Still, Chichester-Clark indicated that he was open to trying again. In another phone call, Devlin told Boyle that 'It's no longer in control. Nothing can be done.'[62] As he hung up, 'someone came running through the door to say there was rioting on the Falls Road in Belfast'. At this point, the NICRA leaders decided to tell local groups to go ahead and organize demonstrations, making sure 'it's a non-violent demonstration and that it's designed to block roads, to draw off the police, to involve the use of other parts of the police in the province'.[63]

The immediate spark for the Belfast violence grew out of a civil rights meeting in the courtyard of Divis Flats, an ugly high-rise block in a Catholic neighbourhood adjacent to the Falls Road. Boyle was unaware that it was taking place, but the local organizers were responding to the call to take the pressure off beleaguered Derry. Although it was peaceful and orderly, as it concluded, participants decided to march to their local police station to protest at the behaviour of the RUC in Derry. As the crowd proceeded along the Falls Road, a few windows were smashed and a small group of teenagers broke away and began to throw stones and petrol bombs at the police station. In a wildly disproportionate response, several police armoured vehicles roared out of the station. 'The crowd, forgetting in its terror all thoughts of an orderly petition ... scattered into two of the "mixed" streets running northwards up to the Protestant Shankill,'[64] fuelling fears among Protestants that they were about to be attacked.

Angry crowds from both communities faced off on streets where they had coexisted, albeit uneasily, for years. Meanwhile, other Catholic demonstrators, infuriated by the appearance of the armoured vehicles, pelted them with stones and petrol bombs. A first shot was fired, a warning from the police station. The violence that had engulfed Derry was starting to shake Belfast. 'The situation had taken over,' Boyle recalled, 'and no one was in control of it.'[65]

Late that night, the government mobilized all 10,000 members of the paramilitary B Specials. In Derry, they joined the police who were besieging the Bogside. As word spread throughout Northern Ireland's Catholic communities, the fear and anger intensified. 'I remember the fear the B Specials created in the Catholics,' Boyle recalled. 'People were genuinely scared.'[66]

If there was any chance of defusing the situation, it was now gone. 'What ruined it was the B Specials,' Devlin recalled. 'Calling up the B Specials … there was no moving back after that.' By the next day, Boyle said, 'guns were being fired, deaths were occurring, whole streets were burned … Defence associations were springing up everywhere.'[67]

In Belfast, mobs of loyalists surged into the streets linking the Shankill and the Falls, torching Catholic homes. Meanwhile, a handful of IRA men had got hold of a few old guns and, determined to protect Catholic areas, opened fire on the loyalists. For its part, the RUC responded with machine guns mounted on armoured vehicles, to deadly effect in a crowded urban area.

Eilis McDermott had grown up in Catholic West Belfast, and was by herself in Albert Street in the Lower Falls when shooting broke out. 'A woman pulled me in her door,' she later wrote:

> She had recognized me from seeing me on television. She would not let me go until she thought it was safe, and as she let me out, she said, 'Look what you've started, daughter.' I ran back to Queen's feeling bitterly angry and ashamed. I knew we had not 'started' anything and I knew she had not meant it in that way, but there was something very shaming about having been involved in some way in defenceless people being shot dead.[68]

It was a view Kevin Boyle came to share. 'In retrospect, one feels guilty,' he told an interviewer, decades later, 'because the truth is that we didn't know. I certainly didn't think that the whole phase of agitation was actually simply gradually building up to a complete polarization of the communities. We just didn't think in those terms.'[69]

Throughout 14 August, Boyle, along with other NICRA leaders, was on the phone to the British army's small base in Lisburn, outside Belfast, and to the Home Office in London, appealing for troops to be deployed to separate the communities and protect the beleaguered Catholic areas. The need was 'to bring in the army and bring them quick'.[70]

'It was a horrible, horrible atmosphere,' Louis Boyle recalled. 'The tension was just awful. No one went out. The buses had stopped. The pogroms were going on.'

'Belfast that night looked like a vision of the apocalypse,' one historian has written, with 'houses and shops ablaze, petrol bombs streaking through the sky, the sound of gunfire, sirens and screaming, everywhere men and women shouting and running.'[71] More than a half-dozen people were dead; hundreds had been injured. Northern Ireland had spun out of control. With the province on the brink of full-scale civil war, the British prime minister Harold Wilson finally called in the army.

It would be thirty more years before British troops would leave the streets of Northern Ireland.

[6]

Calm and Cheerful
Ulster Militant

THE BRITISH SOLDIERS who arrived in mid-August 1969 imposed an uneasy peace on the Catholic ghettos of Belfast and Derry. Beneath the surface, however, the sectarian passions unleashed by the violence continued to seethe. Stories were rife of the B Specials and the occasional RUC officer acting in concert with loyalist rioters in battles with Catholics, and any relationship between a large proportion of the Catholic community and the police had been destroyed.[1] For many Catholics, the presence of the army was reassuring. 'I was relieved when the British army came in,' Eilis McDermott recalled.[2] For Kevin Boyle, their presence provided the community with protection and eased the crisis, creating a 'honeymoon period' while the soldiers kept marauding loyalist mobs at bay.[3]

Nonetheless, barricades erected in Belfast and Derry at the height of the violence remained, both to protect residents from loyalist attackers and as a declaration of non-cooperation with the hated authorities at Stormont. In Belfast, a loose collection of community groups called the Central Citizens Defence Committee (CCDC) coordinated the manning of the barricades and maintained order behind them. The group operated above a pub called the Long Bar in Leeson Street in the Catholic Lower Falls. The bar was owned by Paddy Leneghan, whose eighteen-year-old daughter Mary would start at Queen's University in the autumn of 1969, study law with Kevin, and, nearly thirty years later, under her married name of Mary McAleese, be elected president of the Irish Republic. The pub was also the base for an underground radio station, known as Radio Free Belfast, set up by PD activists. Broadcasting political analysis written by Farrell, Boyle and others, community announcements and music, it operated for three weeks until the army shut it down.

With tensions still high, in October the People's Democracy officially endorsed the creation of an Irish Socialist Republic. The driving force for this explicit ideological commitment was Michael Farrell. While Boyle went along with it, he was not entirely comfortable. In handwritten comments from the meeting where the decision was taken, he noted Farrell's argument that Protestant workers 'will only be won away from Paisleyism by involving them in struggles – with their fellow Catholic workers – against redundancies, for higher wages, and for more houses'. In the margin, Kevin wrote: 'HOW?' And when Farrell declared that the 'PD should acknowledge that the only solution lies in a socialist republic', Boyle added, in an acknowledgment of the very different views held by the Protestants, that 'we also accept that the people of the North have the right to decide this in future'.[4]

Against a backdrop of Catholic alienation from the state and growing Protestant anger, Farrell's sentiments were, as Boyle noted, wildly unrealistic. Just how unrealistic became evident in mid-October, when the British government, in response to pressure for reform, announced plans to disarm the Royal Ulster Constabulary and replace the B Specials with a new, non-sectarian military unit, later called the Ulster Defence Regiment, under British army control. To hard-line Protestants, it was yet another sign that the government was being 'soft' on the Catholics, and triggered rioting on the Shankill Road – what journalist Max Hastings described as three days of 'insane fury'[5] – as Protestants clashed with police and the army. On 11 October an RUC constable was shot and killed – the first policeman to die in the Troubles, murdered, ironically, by a loyalist gunman.

Three weeks later, Boyle, McDermott and Frank Gogarty, a Belfast dentist who was the chair on NICRA, set off for New York. Their purpose was to consolidate Irish-American support for the civil rights movement. But they soon ran into trouble by endorsing a new organization, the National Association for Irish Justice. Intended as an umbrella group for sympathetic Americans, the NAIJ was seen by many conservative Irish Americans as too left-wing, an impression heightened by McDermott's language in her speech to an NAIJ conference. Packed with references to 'imperialism', 'class consciousness', and 'wooing the Protestant working class away from Paisleyism', she declared that 'for me and for my comrades in Belfast, socialism is the only thing that makes sense.'[6] McDermott's meeting on the same trip with the radical Black Panthers, where she was greeted by three leather-clad men who formally made her an 'honorary Black Panther sister', further alienated conservative Irish Americans.[7] Despite an impassioned appeal from Gogarty at the NAIJ meeting for Irish-American unity, soon after returning from the States Boyle came under sharp attack from James Heeney, head of the right-leaning American Congress for Irish Freedom, who publicly accused Boyle and his comrades of being pro-communist. Boyle retorted that Heeney was 'reactionary and bigoted'.[8]

The sharp differences were also reflected within the Northern Civil Rights Association. Three members of the group's executive, including Conn McCluskey, the driving force behind the Campaign for Social Justice in 1964, which paved the way for the civil rights movement, echoed Heeney's claim, publicly denouncing Boyle and Gogarty for antagonizing conservative Irish Americans. In February 1970, at NICRA's annual conference, Boyle and Farrell decided not to run again for the group's executive. In a statement, People's Democracy denounced the critics. With Boyle and Farrell's departure, it said, 'we hope they [PD's critics in NICRA] will finally shut up'.[9] Meanwhile, in a development which would have enormous consequences for Northern Ireland, the republican movement also split. Tensions had been growing between leftists like Cathal Goulding, who had been guiding the movement towards conventional politics with a Marxist orientation, and traditional republicans, overwhelmingly conservative and deeply Catholic, who believed the use of force was the only way to achieve a united Ireland. They were exacerbated by Goulding's call to end a hallowed IRA tradition – refusing to recognize or take seats in Dáil Éireann (the Irish parliament) in Dublin and at Stormont, bodies the republicans had long viewed as illegitimate.

The differences came to a head in the wake of the August 1969 violence, when the IRA was unable to play what the dissidents believed was its primary role of protecting Northern Ireland's Catholic population. Indeed, graffiti on the walls of Belfast's Catholic ghettos that summer declared 'IRA = I Ran Away'. The traditional republican hardliners blamed Goulding's leadership for ignoring the IRA's military side. They were joined by young men from the ghettos who had been radicalized by recent events and who saw a need for guns to defend Catholic communities from the militant loyalists and the police. Among them was Gerry Adams, who would, in the view of the security forces and many journalists and scholars of the Troubles, emerge as the future leader of the IRA. In early 1970 the dissidents broke away and established the Provisional IRA. Goulding's faction thereafter became known as the Official IRA. The organization's political wing, Sinn Féin, also split along similar lines. As winter turned into spring, the Provisionals organized and collected weapons – some acquired with funds from sympathetic politicians in the Irish Republic – and waited for the opportunity to strike.

At this point, the relationship between the British army and the Catholic population remained, if not completely friendly, at least not openly hostile. With the RUC effectively expelled from Catholic areas of Belfast and Derry, however, that accommodation began to change, as the army was forced into a policing role it was not equipped to handle.

The tensions were most evident in places like Ballymurphy, a desolate Catholic housing estate on the western edge of Belfast. It was an area of high unemployment and low incomes with few facilities and a strong sense of Irish nationalism. Among those who lived in Ballymurphy was Gerry Adams. On Easter Day 1970, the local army commander gave permission to a group of Protestant Orangemen from the nearby Protestant housing estate of New Barnsley to march along the main road overlooking Ballymurphy. As outraged nationalists threw rocks and petrol bombs at the parading loyalists, the troops responded with CS gas, choking protestors and ordinary citizens alike. Rioters fought hand-to-hand with soldiers attempting to arrest those identified as ringleaders. The violence went on for forty-eight hours. 'This was the first serious conflict, the first time there was trouble between the Catholics and the troops,' Boyle recalled.[10] For many Catholics, and not just in Ballymurphy, it was the moment when the honeymoon with the British army ended. The soldiers were seen as no better than the hated police, and large numbers of unemployed and alienated young Catholics flocked to the newly formed Provisionals.

Boyle and his People's Democracy colleagues watched the violence with alarm. For him, it was yet another sign of Northern Ireland's depressing slide into open sectarian conflict. In a letter to a friend he confessed, 'Always in the North, things go too fast. I don't think we could distribute housing leaflets in the Shankill now.' The letter noted that many Protestants were fixated on 'Popery and Dublin', while Catholics obsessed about 'England and unionism'. He wrote, 'I have never felt more like flotsam in a whirlpool whose direction and energy I cannot understand.'[11]

Within days, however, Boyle had recovered his spirits and was helping the PD set up the Ballymurphy Youth Organisation, seeking to channel the grievances of young people on the housing estate into political activity rather than violence. 'The whole point was to attempt to constructively deal with frustration,' Kevin recalled. 'What had to be done was to mobilize these kids to deal with some of the major social grievances which clearly affected them: unemployment, lack of training, lack of a hope of ever getting a good job in the area, no play facilities, nowhere to take their girlfriend except to a street corner.'[12]

He attended a series of meetings in Ballymurphy, at least one of which attracted over 200 people.[13] 'We told them they were not approaching their objectives in the best way. While at the end of the day we might agree that British troops might be regarded as enemies, the only way was to get together to fight for their own objectives in a political way.'[14] He helped to organize marches against unemployment and low wages, and to raise money to create a defence fund for youngsters facing legal problems from the riots.

To underscore the need for recreational facilities in Ballymurphy, Boyle and his PD colleagues decided to stage a protest football match on the well-tended lawn in front of Belfast's City Hall. As the Ballymurphy kids kicked the ball around on a Saturday afternoon, Boyle and other activists handed out leaflets to surprised shoppers passing by. Then the police arrived.

'They just didn't know how to handle this,' Boyle remembered, 'and they did the stupid thing – they tried to catch the kids.' But after so many skirmishes with security forces, one thing at which the youngsters excelled was eluding the police:

I remember this very clever young guy stopped with the ball under his foot. The policeman took advantage of this. 'Now look here,' the cop said. 'You can't play ball here, not allowed.' The policeman put his hand down to take the ball, and the guy let him get his hand down just that far and pushed the ball aside a wee bit with his foot. Then, of course, the policeman bent further, and the next thing he knew he was lying on the lawn. The police obviously had got to the point where they couldn't just beat these kids and [they] left.[15]

There were also efforts to use football to build bridges with the neighbouring Protestant New Barnsley housing estate, but a proposed match between youngsters from the two communities never came off. Meanwhile, Provisional IRA supporters in Ballymurphy, whom Boyle described as having 'come into power all of a sudden as the barricades came up' during the recent rioting, began to feel threatened by the young getting organized.[16] It was not long before those involved in the community group came under pressure from the IRA to back off. By his own admission, Boyle's attempt to create a non-violent, political alternative to militant republicanism in this one neighbourhood had failed.

That summer Northern Ireland's descent into violence accelerated. The previous autumn, following the clashes in Derry in August 1969, Bernadette Devlin had been charged with 'riotous behaviour' and put on trial. Despite her defence that she had helped organize the throwing of stones and petrol bombs at the invading police and militant loyalists because she and the others in the Bogside feared for their lives, she was found guilty, and sentenced to six months in jail. She remained free on appeal. But at the end of June 1970 her appeal was rejected. As she drove with Eamonn McCann and other supporters to a rally in Derry before turning herself in, police stopped her convoy of cars outside the city and bundled her off to Armagh jail. In the Bogside, which had been quiet for several weeks, rioting began within minutes, but it paled in comparison with what would happen that weekend in Belfast.

The end of June marked the start of Northern Ireland's marching season, and the authorities were again faced with the dilemma of whether to ban traditional Orange parades and risk the wrath of the loyalist community, or allow them to proceed and risk infuriating the nationalists. In the summer of 1970, the decision fell to a new British government. In June, the

Conservatives had won a British general election – an election in which Devlin, just days before she was sent to jail, held on to her parliamentary seat. The new Conservative prime minister, replacing Labour's Harold Wilson, was Edward Heath. Like his predecessor, he struggled to find the right balance as Northern Ireland's rival communities edged closer to civil war. With Orange parades scheduled for Belfast in the last weekend of June, Heath's Home Secretary, Reginald Maudling, decided to permit the marches to go ahead with an enhanced security presence. As violence flared in Derry following Devlin's arrest, however, trouble between Protestant and Catholic crowds also broke out in Belfast, and when Protestant mobs attacked the Catholic Short Strand enclave in East Belfast while the army appeared to stand by, gunmen of the Provisional IRA joined the battle. Six people were killed that weekend, while the Provisionals established themselves as the defenders of Belfast's besieged Catholic community.

The following weekend, soldiers searching a house in Belfast's Lower Falls came under attack from an angry, stone-throwing crowd. The army responded with vast quantities of tear gas, and then imposed a curfew, confining close to 20,000 people to their homes for three days. For the authorities it was a political disaster, compounded when the army brought two Unionist ministers to tour the area in armoured cars, and confirming for most Catholics that the soldiers were just another oppressive tool of Unionist rule. As Boyle noted in an interview a couple of years later, 'relations with the Catholics were destroyed for ever'.[17]

The cascading violence pushed the civil rights movement to the sidelines. Boyle, as an advocate of non-sectarian, peaceful protest, began to worry that he was becoming politically irrelevant.[18] Despite the mayhem around him, however, he also managed to continue with his teaching obligations at Queen's University. To the amazement of his students, he never let the Troubles intrude directly into the classroom. Michael O'Boyle, a Catholic from Belfast, had started studying law under Boyle in 1968. 'Although we were aware that Kevin was fully involved with the protest movement,' he recalled, 'there wasn't a sentence of that that made its way into the classroom. He was a classic university teacher in his day job,' introducing students to *Smith and Hogan's Criminal Law*, the classic 600-page textbook.

Whatever his inner doubts, and despite the turbulence of the situation and his own political activities, Boyle always presented a calm and positive face to the outside world. Indeed, in 1972, the *New York Times* would use the headline 'Calm and Cheerful Ulster Militant' in a profile of Boyle.[19]

'He seemed to be one of these people who gave the impression of not being under pressure when he must have been under unbearable pressure,' observed Joe O'Hara, a Belfast Catholic who also studied under Boyle:

> You come across these people who are quite rare, who are carrying an enormous, multi-faceted burden, and yet seem to be able to absorb it, always remaining open, friendly, kind, supportive and calm, as if your problems were the real pressure point, whereas in your private moments, you knew damn well you could never possibly be under the kind of pressure that Kevin was. As to how he did it – it must have been a Stakhanovite work ethic on the one hand, and something in him that absorbed the pressure, and that made other people, who are under insignificant pressure, feel supported.

In early 1970 Boyle had begun sharing a flat with John Fairleigh, a professor of psychology at Queen's and a former editorial writer at the *Belfast Telegraph*, Northern Ireland's leading newspaper, which had always taken a moderate political stance to the current conflict. Slightly older than Boyle, Fairleigh was a liberal Protestant with a strong interest in legal issues and had attended the same one-year law programme at Cambridge as Boyle, although the two did not meet there. Like Boyle's students, Fairleigh remembered his flatmate as 'a very gentle, charming, flexible, pleasant guy. We were very close. There couldn't have been an easier person to live with.'

Fairleigh and Boyle were joined by Tom Hadden, who had arrived in Belfast in the autumn of 1969 to teach law at Queen's. Hadden, a Protestant, had also spent a year doing the Cambridge postgraduate law course, where he had become friendly with Boyle. He was the son of a well-to-do doctor from Portadown, a town south-west of Belfast with a history of sectarian violence dating back to the nineteenth century. It was so well known for the extreme unionism of its Protestant residents that Hadden jokingly described his home town as 'a bad word for loyalism'. Like Fairleigh, Hadden considered himself to be a liberal unionist. By his own admission he was a 'slightly awkward' personality, soft-spoken and almost painfully shy. Yet beneath the surface Hadden had a keen intelligence, a sharp wit, and was a superb writer. Indeed, within months of moving in with Boyle and Fairleigh, he started a magazine called *Fortnight*, which, naturally, published every two weeks.

It became an indispensable journal of the Troubles, attracting contributors from all perspectives, including Boyle, often identifying critical trends and breaking crucial stories before the conventional media, and, under Hadden's stewardship for much of the time, lasting for forty-one years.

As he settled into his new residence, Boyle mentioned to Hadden that they had once met in a Cambridge garden where Hadden had shown him how to play croquet. 'That was a snapshot of our very different backgrounds,' Hadden later wrote, 'myself as a privileged young Cambridge graduate from a medical family in Unionist Portadown, Kevin as the son of a taxi driver in Nationalist Newry.'[20] Yet Hadden's friendship with Boyle soon evolved into an intellectual partnership the two would maintain for the rest of their lives.

The flatmates started teaching one another about their respective communities, which led to awkward and sometimes frightening episodes. One evening Boyle took Hadden to a boisterous pub on the Falls Road, in the heart of Catholic Belfast. They arrived to find a group of young Catholics sitting around a table. 'Everybody was saying I'm Seán or Seamus or whatever,' Hadden recalled. 'And it came around to my turn, and I said, "I'm Tom from Portadown." There was total silence. It was like – I wasn't supposed to be there.'

On another occasion, the two were driving back to Belfast from Hadden's family home in Portadown when they ran into a loyalist band parade. With the road blocked, Hadden, who had grown up with such parades, suggested stopping for an ice cream and watching the march pass by. But Boyle was terrified. 'Kevin was worried he would be identified and lynched,' Hadden said. 'So we both had that learning curve about the other community.'

Fuelling the alienation of Northern Ireland's Catholics – reflected in the almost daily riots, searches, arrests, shootings and bombings – was a widespread belief that the province's legal system was, as Boyle, Hadden, and another colleague, Paddy Hillyard, later documented, 'part and parcel of the Unionist power structure, and therefore unable to uphold any serious challenge to the regime'.[21]

In late 1970 Michael Farrell had written an article for the People's Democracy newspaper *Unfree Citizen*, claiming that most of Northern Ireland's judges had been leading Orangemen with a long record of anti-Catholic bias, backing up his position with quotations they had made. Farrell recalled that he 'was summoned by the police, who threatened to prosecute me for an offence called "scandalizing the courts"' – this despite the fact that the substance of his article was true. Farrell asked Boyle to accompany him to the police station for the interview. 'Kevin was quite taken aback,' he said. 'They were really scraping the barrel at that stage. It was some ancient nineteenth-century or even earlier law.' In the end, formal charges were never brought.

In April 1971 twenty-eight Catholic priests in Belfast publicly declared that they would refuse to fill out government census forms because Catholics did not have equality of citizenship. Hundreds of other people held a public burning of census forms in the Catholic New Lodge Road area. In a statement to journalists, the priests cited an incident where a man was sentenced to a year's imprisonment for shouting 'Up the IRA'; meanwhile, elsewhere on the same day, men and youths shouting 'Up the UVF' and 'To Hell with the Pope' were neither arrested, convicted nor imprisoned, despite the presence of police and soldiers who knew the law was being broken.[22]

In early 1971 Boyle began a serious study of the issue, enlisting the help of his students, including Francis Keenan, who had briefly studied to become a priest before deciding to do law at Queen's. 'People were starting to talk about the law,' Keenan recalled. 'Who were the judges? Where did they come from? What background had they? And what was it that made them give what were perceived to be the biased decisions of the day?'

One element of the study was to look at appointments to judicial office in Northern Ireland over several decades. Speaking to a journalist, Boyle said that

> it was impossible to avoid the interpretation that appointments were made to legal office as a reward for political service to the Unionist Party [and that] in riot situations non-Unionists faced the more serious charges which attracted imprisonment and Unionists less serious charges meriting fines or suspended sentences.[23]

Boyle's research was one of several projects undertaken by the Queen's law faculty in response to the growing crisis. William Twining organized a group, including Hadden and Mary Leneghan (the future Mary McAleese), to study the use of emergency legislation; they wrote a report called *Emergency Powers – a New Start*. At the same time, Hadden began working with Paddy Hillyard, a professor at the New University of Ulster in

Coleraine, to examine cases handled by the province's Magistrates' Courts. Hadden and Hillyard's research would later lead to a broader study in collaboration with Boyle, which produced an influential book called *Law and State: The Case of Northern Ireland* in 1975.

Meanwhile, as the situation deteriorated, the tribunal headed by Leslie Scarman, a High Court judge appointed by the British government to head an inquiry into the disorders of 1969, was nearing the end of its proceedings. Boyle had given a statement in the autumn of 1969, but in April 1971 he was called back to the Law Courts in Belfast for further testimony. One of his questioners was Desmond Boal, a lawyer acting on behalf of the Orange Order. Boal was a close political ally of Ian Paisley and had represented him in several court cases. A formidable cross-examiner, his courtroom skills were legendary. As the bemused tribunal looked on, Boal and Boyle engaged in an intense verbal duel over the latter's role in the incident in Dungiven in June 1969, where he had organized residents to close shops and businesses and remain indoors in a silent protest against a triumphalist march down the main street by Orange Order members.

Boal sought to portray Boyle as a hypocrite, an agitator and a trouble-maker intent on encouraging the locals to confront the Orange march – leading to exchanges such as the one recorded in the official transcript:

> Boal: You did not want to encourage the people or the feeling in the people [of Dungiven] that they ought to allow the right of the Orangemen to walk.
>
> Boyle: If that is as Mr Boal says it is, why did I need to go over to Dungiven?
>
> Boal: I say you did not, and I put to you, you had no business to be there.
>
> Boyle: My concern was to ensure that the Orangemen exercised their right to march.
>
> Boal: Is that the reason you were in Derry when there was trouble there? Is that the reason that you were in the Falls Road when there was trouble there? Is that the reason you have been in Northern Ireland whenever there has been trouble?
>
> The Chairman: Mr Boal, keep control please.[24]

Years later, Francis Keenan recalled that Boyle 'immensely enjoyed' the exchange.

Scarman's voluminous report finally came out in April 1972. Despite efforts by the Northern Ireland authorities and loyalists like Desmond Boal to blame the violence of 1969 on civil rights leaders like Boyle, as well as on the IRA, Scarman concluded that the disorder was the result of the 'complex political, social and economic situation in the North', rather than the result of any plot.[25]

Ironically, despite his political views, by the mid-1970s Boal would agree to defend in court not only Protestant militants but Catholic ones too, and he and Boyle – who, for his part, would also defend Protestants as well as Catholics – worked on a number of cases together.

But that was still some years off. By the late spring of 1971, tensions in Northern Ireland were at breaking point. The province's ineffectual prime minister, James Chichester-Clark, had resigned in March and was replaced by Brian Faulkner. With a business background, Faulkner – cunning, ambitious and ruthless – was widely viewed as Northern Ireland's most capable Unionist politician. A hardliner on security issues, as Minister of Home Affairs in the 1950s he had been responsible for suppressing the IRA's border campaign through the use of internment without trial, and immediately began pressing the British government for a tougher military response to the present unrest.

Meanwhile, Boyle, after an absence of several months, returned to his role as the press officer for the Civil Rights Association, while still maintaining his links with People's Democracy, although he had become much less active. The violence, and the accompanying shift in the political climate, had pushed civil rights into the background, and the composition of the NICRA leadership had changed. Some moderates had left to join the centrist Social Democratic and Labour Party (SDLP), which was seeking to position itself as the voice of constitutional nationalism in Northern Ireland, while others, radicalized by recent events, were drawn to the Provisional IRA. The result was that NICRA was now largely dominated by the 'Official' republicans – the group from whom the more militant Provisionals had broken away. The Officials still opposed the use of force and continued to emphasize left-wing politics. Other key players were members of Northern Ireland's Communist Party, many of whom were Protestants and came out of a trade union background, together with some independents who did not belong to any grouping. While NICRA continued to campaign against both sectarianism and police and army repression, it was much less the broadly based front of its early days. As Boyle himself acknowledged, 'the Civil Rights Association became irrelevant'.[26] But on 9 August 1971, that was to change.

[7]

The Last Engagement

EARLY ON the morning of Monday, 9 August 1971, British soldiers rounded up 342 men in dawn raids and interned them without trial. None were charged with any offence; the hated Special Powers Act did not require it. The authorities could simply arrest and hold them indefinitely.

For months, Brian Faulkner had been calling for internment as a way to crush the IRA, which he blamed for the current crisis, ignoring the broader alienation of the Catholic community. Edward Heath's government was reluctant to take such a drastic step, but the violence continued to intensify, with regular gun battles and an average of two bombs a day.[1] 'The people of Belfast were becoming used to the distant thump of another explosion, the plumes of smoke, the smell of cordite, the sight of bleeding, crying casualties.'[2] Meanwhile, the army and police confronted almost continuous rioting in Catholic areas. In mid-July soldiers had shot dead two Catholics during a disturbance in Derry. 'Allegations by the British that the two men had been armed or were about to throw gelignite bombs when shot infuriated the small nationalist community, which knew both men well enough to know this was untrue.'[3] The deadly cycle of army and police repression, riots, and the IRA's use of bombs and guns, was spinning out of control.

As news of internment spread, so did the fury among the Catholic population, exacerbated by the fact that almost every man arrested that morning was a Catholic. As one British journalist wrote, 'every Catholic area of the country was the scene of fighting and bitterness Ireland had not witnessed for half a century'.[4] Much of the province was in a state of open war. As columns of smoke darkened the Belfast sky, barricades manned by armed IRA men were erected in Catholic areas, and the crackle of gunfire echoed across the city as battles broke out between the Provisional IRA and British soldiers. The Official IRA, some of whose activists had also been interned even though it had not joined the Provisionals' campaign of violence, announced that it too was joining the fight. Whole streets were consumed by flames. In two days, seventeen people were shot dead.[5]

As a lawyer and university professor, Kevin Boyle was not interned, although his long-time comrade Michael Farrell was among those detained. But, like so many others, Boyle was outraged. 'I was deeply angry, physically angry after internment,' he recalled. 'And if an oddball like myself felt these emotions, you can imagine what people felt who were living in these areas where army and police were coming in marauding and raiding during the night.'[6] Boyle quickly concluded that the Stormont government's move was 'a blunder of enormous proportions. The British military picked up all the wrong people.'[7] Typically, however, despite his fury, he immediately began to think of practical steps that could be taken in response to internment that would not further accelerate the cycle of violence. 'The main question was, how could the ordinary population be mobilized into non-military resistance?'[8]

The next evening, 10 August, Boyle, on behalf of the Civil Rights Association, met representatives of the SDLP and other anti-Unionist groups in Dungannon. As the SDLP announced that it was withdrawing from any contact with government, Boyle pushed the idea of a non-violent civil disobedience campaign that would take the form of people refusing to pay their rent or rates until internment was ended. 'It was a way to show that we rejected the regime and that the regime would be resisted,' he said.[9]

For Boyle, this was crucial. 'He was pathologically opposed to violence,' recalled Nicholas Ragg, an Englishman who was then a professor of social work at Queen's University. 'He was wholeheartedly committed to peaceful solutions. The rent and rates strike was a kind of activity Kevin established as a peaceful alternative to violence.'

Boyle was given the job of devising a strategy and specific tactics to make the strike effective. Using his legal knowledge, he drafted leaflets to explain to people what to do as they withheld their rates and rent. Despite the intense anger about internment, there was widespread anxiety among ordinary people over the possible consequences of the strike. 'We taught them all they needed to know of the normal questions when you go in a hall for a meeting of people who don't want to pay their rents,' Boyle said. 'Can they throw me out of a house? Can they put me in prison? So we worked out all the answers to these questions.'[10]

Support for the strike was so strong that it became difficult for the authorities to retaliate. At its peak, an estimated 20 per cent of the entire population joined in.[11] 'It was an extraordinary situation,' Kevin later observed. 'The nationalist population had withdrawn their consent to be ruled by this government.'[12] And this was just one step in a campaign to paralyse the Northern Ireland administration. Boyle and Nicholas Ragg also got the idea of encouraging people to apply to local government authorities for emergency grants or supplementary benefits. By law, the functionaries handling such applications were required to provide a written answer to any inquiry. In meeting after meeting, Ragg or Boyle would dictate language for such an inquiry, and have those in attendance sign. 'And then at the end of the session,' Ragg said, 'we'd collect all these bits of paper, fold them up, address them, and post them, so that the supplementary benefits office the next day would receive about 500 applications for grants. The idea was to paralyse them, which it did.'

For Boyle, it was not just the purely economic impact that mattered. 'It was a battle of images,' he recalled. 'The British position and the Unionist position was that a small band of terrorists were intimidating masses of the population. Our position was saying this is not a struggle of a small minority, this is a mass rejection of this regime.'[13]

The depth of that rejection was intensified as it became clear that many internees were being tortured in custody. Most were held in Long Kesh, a bleak former Royal Air Force base nine miles south-west of Belfast. With its Nissen huts, barbed-wire fences, searchlights, armed sentries and guard towers, Long Kesh – later renamed the Maze – resembled a German World War II concentration camp. Reports soon emerged of savage mistreatment – detainees beaten, hooded, forced to stand spread-eagled against a wall for hours, kept awake for days on end. The British army had used these techniques in counter-insurgency campaigns in colonies like Malaya, Kenya, Cyprus and Aden, but the idea of such methods being applied to British citizens an hour's flight from London shocked the British public, and exacerbated the anger within Northern Ireland's Catholic communities. Boyle shared that anger, and, in the coming months would develop a legal strategy to challenge army behaviour before the European Commission of Human Rights.

At the time, however, the focus remained on more immediate forms of protest. For NICRA, largely marginalized in recent months, the rent and rate strike provided a crucial opportunity to reassert itself as the organization in the best position to coordinate a mass campaign of non-violent resistance and civil disobedience. But maintaining that position was not easy, not least because internment fuelled support for the IRA. Boyle and Ragg encountered this even at their gatherings to promote the strike. 'People came in asking how to get ammunition and where to buy machine guns and that sort of thing,' Ragg remembered. 'We had to weed that out.'

As he had often done on other occasions, Boyle tried to use the strike to bring together the various opposition groups. Travelling to the Irish Republic, he met the IRA's political leaders to urge that they endorse the strike. Boyle proposed that each opposition organization operate on its own locally, but that all of them send delegates to a central coordinating body that would be loosely affiliated with the Northern Ireland Civil Rights Association.

However, he found that both the Provisional and the Official IRA – wary of each other and of ceding any authority – were reluctant to cooperate. Moreover, the Provisionals remained focused on their military campaign. At one anti-internment meeting in the border town of Dundalk, Boyle encountered Joe Cahill, a veteran IRA gunman who in 1940 had narrowly escaped a death sentence after being convicted of involvement in a shootout with Northern Irish police. Now a senior figure in the Provisionals, Cahill had made a defiant appearance at a press conference in Belfast under the noses of the British army to show that the IRA was still in business. 'He was an action man,' Kevin said. 'He didn't bother with the politics. He was a military man.'[14] Boyle's initiative stalled. 'I over-reached myself in my ambitions as a synthesizer,' he acknowledged.[15]

Indeed, among some activists there was growing frustration at what was seen as the excessively moderate approach of NICRA, which had refrained for organizing large-scale demonstrations for fear of exacerbating already frighteningly high levels of violence. In mid-autumn a group of more radical figures, including Michael Farrell, who had just been released after six weeks in detention, joined supporters of Sinn Féin, the Provisional IRA's political wing, to set up the Northern Resistance Movement. Bernadette Devlin, who had herself become increasingly radical, was also involved. She described the Northern Resistance Movement as trying to 'carve out a ground' between a purely political struggle, and what she called the all-out 'war' of the Provisional IRA. The NRM was openly critical of what it saw as the excessively moderate Civil Rights Association and sought to undermine NICRA's control of the rent and rates strike, while some of its members openly sympathized with the political goals of the Provisionals. 'There was no doubt that some of those involved were closer to Provisional Sinn Féin than other organizations,' Boyle later acknowledged. 'They were nationalists.'[16]

The development led to sharp differences between Boyle and his one-time comrades. Boyle described the decision of People's Democracy to throw in its lot with the Northern Resistance Movement as a 'fatal event'[17] that would, within a matter of months, lead to his removal from the group's leadership. As he noted in an interview with a British journalist in early 1972, 'the more militant elements in PD were not happy working within the umbrella of the CRA. They were basically Provisionals.'[18]

While the rent and rate strike and the violence continued, anger was growing on the Protestant side too, exacerbated by the fact that internment had obviously failed in its stated goal of bringing the IRA's campaign to a halt. Indeed, hard-line loyalists increasingly believed that they might have to take matters into their own hands. In late autumn, around the time the Northern Resistance Movement was formed, loyalist vigilante groups established the Ulster Defence Association (UDA). It eventually attracted thousands of Protestant supporters, and, along with the even more extreme Ulster Volunteer Force (UVF), would be responsible for some of Northern Ireland's most gruesome sectarian attacks.

Even though he was seen as a 'moderate', with his public role both as NICRA's press spokesman and as a leading advocate of the rent and rate strike, Boyle was a highly visible figure. As tensions worsened in the autumn he became increasingly worried that he might become a target of loyalist extremists. He later told a British journalist, 'the fear was not of British bullets but of Protestant bullets'.[19] Indeed, in making his way to and from meetings around Belfast with Boyle, Ragg remembered that 'we had to go wherever we were going through the Catholic areas, through very circuitous routes, to ensure that if we broke down we would be in friendly territory'.

Although support for the rent and rate strike remained strong, after several months there was no sign that the government was considering an end to internment. Evaluating the situation, Boyle concluded that the strike by itself was too passive, not generating either sufficient media coverage or broader popular enthusiasm for non-violent resistance. 'There had been meetings, but the reality was not only the people who had been lifted in August of '71, but that people were continuing to be detained and arrested, and we regarded this as a moral outrage.'[20] By mid-October 1971 Boyle began urging NICRA to resume organizing demonstrations in the streets. In their executive meetings, he argued that one key justification for holding large-scale street protests was that 'you belied the "small band of terrorists" theory. You showed you had a whole community alienated. You could not have a military solution.'[21]

As the Civil Rights Association pondered the issue, at the beginning of December the Northern Resistance Movement announced plans for a demonstration on Christmas Day. 'We felt NICRA just wasn't doing enough,' Farrell recalled, 'so we called the Christmas Day protest.' Within the Civil Rights Association, there was concern, as Boyle observed, that with the march 'the NRM was trying to upstage us'.[22] The upshot was that in mid-December NICRA's executive met at its headquarters – 'a pair of tatty rooms above a Belfast watchmaker's shop'[23] – to discuss calling their own demonstrations.

The debate was intense. Concerns were again raised about the prospect of violence, although Boyle argued that the injustice of internment was so great that 'despite the risks of sectarian confrontation, we have to think about bringing people on to the streets to protest against this policy'.[24] Pressure to do more from the broader Catholic community was growing too. 'There was pressure not only from these organizations [like the NRM] but genuinely from the community calling on NICRA to become more active in demonstrations,' he recalled, 'especially when the news leaked out of the torture and inhuman treatment that had been going on inside these camps. That was a factor in creating more pressure.'[25]

As the discussion continued, Boyle urged that the group organize one demonstration a month. Kevin McCorry, a Belfast native and one of only two full-time paid organizers at NICRA, suggested that they start in Belfast at the beginning of January. Boyle proposed a follow-up demonstration in Northern Ireland's second city. 'I have the unfortunate record,' he acknowledged to a reporter some weeks later, 'of being the first to have suggested the Derry march.'[26] The suggestion marked a fateful moment. The march in Derry, which would be held on 30 January 1972, would lead to the deaths of fourteen people at the hands of the British army and become known as 'Bloody Sunday' – a vital turning point in the history of Northern Ireland. When Boyle made the initial proposal, however, no one anticipated such an outcome. 'The idea was to create more pressure,' he told a commission of inquiry many years later. 'There was no thought of provoking violence.'[27] The same meeting agreed that after Derry there would be a third march, to be staged in Newry.

Five days before Christmas, Kevin and other NICRA leaders held a press conference in Belfast to announce their new campaign. Although called a 'programme for peace', it was presented in the form of an ultimatum to the government. Unless the British authorities released all internees unconditionally, abolished the Special Powers Act, ended the current Unionist administration and introduced legislation to guarantee civil rights, a new series of demonstrations would begin. Reporters asked about the danger of provoking violence. Boyle responded that, despite such concerns, 'people were no longer prepared to tolerate internment'.[28]

Somewhat surprisingly, the Northern Resistance Movement's Christmas march passed off without incident, and on 2 January Boyle joined 5000 other protestors on the Falls Road in Belfast for the first of NICRA's anti-internment demonstrations. Hostile troops, some hurling insults, blocked their intended route to a nearby park. The soldiers eventually let the marchers use the footpath to pass through barricades to the other side of the park, where they reassembled to listen to speeches by civil rights leaders. Although a few youths threw stones at the troops as the gathering dispersed, there was no serious trouble.[29]

Nonetheless, soldiers and police took photos of the march leaders, including Boyle. Three weeks later, he was one of twenty-six organizers charged with violating the government's ban on marches, and ordered to appear in court in mid-February, where he faced a mandatory six-month prison sentence. Upon receiving the summons, Boyle wrote to an administrator at Queen's University. He began by explaining and justifying his action. 'Personally, I did this in protest against the continuing illegalities involved in the operation of internment, especially the use of force in interrogations. I regard my actions as being political in motivation and the decision to defy the law is a matter of conscience.'[30] He went on to say that the route and timing of the demonstration was designed to minimize the possibility of conflict, and that the march had passed off without incident.

Then, predictably, Boyle turned to practical matters; namely, how his likely conviction and jail term would affect his students. He said that, if convicted, an appeal would take up enough time for him to finish most of his teaching obligations before having to go to jail. 'Being in prison would not affect my teaching duties,' he wrote, 'except I shouldn't be available to give any advice to students.' He also expressed confidence that 'it would be possible to arrange to correct examination papers and tests while in captivity without too much bother'. As for his other academic obligations, such as study and research, he wrote, 'there are many precedents for such being successfully carried on from a prison cell, and I don't envisage too many problems in satisfying the University that such duties can and would be carried on'.[31]

Meanwhile, at a meeting of the NICRA executive on 14 January, planning for the Derry march moved ahead, with a detailed discussion of possible routes. The initial idea was to march to the Guildhall in the centre of Derry, but Boyle noted that it was likely that the army and police would prevent this, and urged that an alternative route be agreed on. The executive then decided that while the Guildhall would remain the official destination, the march would stay within the Catholic Bogside area, with a rally held at what was known as Free Derry Corner. Amid some concern that the local Civil Rights Association in the city was not as well organized as the broader group, the NICRA executive decided to appoint a four-person subcommittee to coordinate the arrangements, and asked Kevin McCorry to act as chief steward in charge of crowd control on the day. From this point on, Kevin Boyle himself was not directly involved with detailed planning for the march.

Boyle would insist afterwards that, as the last Sunday in January approached, neither he nor any of his NICRA colleagues had any premonition that the Derry march would be anything other than a 'normal' Northern Ireland protest – a parade and speeches against the backdrop of some stone-throwing by a few youths at Derry's famous 'Aggro corner', where army barricades would block an entrance to the Bogside, perhaps a modest riot, but nothing out of the ordinary for those turbulent times. 'There was no sense among the civil rights people that this might be a confrontation on a different order than any other.'[32]

Indeed, he and his colleagues were relieved that the march was going to be held in Derry, because they viewed Belfast as the place with a strong risk of sectarian confrontation. Late in the week, Boyle was asked by BBC radio in Belfast to pre-record an interview to run the following Monday, the day after the march. The final question was: 'Mr Boyle, do you think that you will feel on Monday that this march has been a success?' Boyle replied, 'If there has been a large, peaceful manifestation of public alienation against the regime, yes, certainly I will.'[33] Boyle anticipated so little out of the ordinary that he decided he wouldn't even attend the Derry protest. He spent that Sunday at home in Belfast catching up on his academic work. 'I didn't even think about the demonstration until six o'clock Sunday evening, when I turned on the news. I couldn't believe what had happened. Thirteen people had been killed. I felt as if I had a concussion.'[34]

Several hours earlier, Boyle's PD colleagues Rory McShane and Bernadette Devlin had stood on a windswept hillside in the Creggan estate overlooking the centre of Derry waiting for the march to begin. McShane remembered Devlin turning to him and saying, 'We'll be lucky to get out of here today with less than three or four dead.' McShane was shocked. Like Boyle, he was not anticipating anything more than the usual small-scale riot on the fringes of what he expected to be a peaceful demonstration.

But in the run-up to this day, the attitude of the British army had hardened. The authorities felt under acute pressure. Although the government insisted that it was defeating the IRA, soldiers and police were being attacked daily. Twenty-four British soldiers had been killed by IRA snipers in 1971, and just three days before the 30 January march, two policemen were shot and killed in Derry.[35] The security forces were on edge, and were expecting the march to turn violent. Moreover, loyalist hardliners, whose own gatherings had also been outlawed under the ban on parades and marches announced at the time of internment, were furious that civil rights supporters were defying the ban and, in their eyes, getting away with it.

It was against this backdrop that between 10–15,000 marchers set off on a sunny, cold afternoon. The atmosphere was cheerful and relaxed. A lorry bedecked with a NICRA banner and carrying several of the march leaders and speakers, including Bernadette Devlin, moved slowly at the front of the crowd, which chanted slogans and sang 'We Shall Overcome'.

As Boyle and others had predicted in the planning meetings, the army had set up a barbed-wire barricade to prevent the marchers from reaching the Guildhall in the city centre, so the vast majority turned towards Free Derry Corner, where a rally and speeches were planned. A handful of teenagers, however, began throwing stones and bottles at the soldiers manning the barricades. It was the kind of low-grade clash that happened almost every day in Derry. The soldiers initially responded with water cannon, rubber bullets, and then with vast quantities of CS gas. As the remnants of the choking, gasping crowd fell back into the Bogside, troops from the notoriously tough First Battalion Parachute Regiment were ordered into the area to arrest what the army called 'hooligans'. Moments later, the soldiers opened fire. In a matter of minutes, the Paras fired a hundred rounds. Thirteen people were killed. Thirteen more were wounded, one fatally.

Decades later, a Commission of Inquiry established by the British government concluded: 'The firing by soldiers of 1 PARA on Bloody Sunday caused the deaths of thirteen people and injury to a similar number, none of whom was posing a threat of causing death or serious injury.'[36]

Back in his flat in Belfast, Boyle was in a state of shock, 'devastated' in the words of his brother Louis, furiously smoking his pipe as stunned students and fellow activists came and went, trying to take in the news. For many, the shock swiftly gave way to intense anger, but Francis Keenan, who shared the flat with Boyle, recalled that his friend remained 'completely level-headed' as he tried to analyse the consequences. Boyle's conclusion was that the Northern Ireland government had lost all moral authority, and that London would soon be forced to stand down the parliament at Stormont and impose direct rule.

The shock waves from Bloody Sunday rippled across Ireland and Britain. In Dublin a large crowd burned the British embassy to the ground. In London a furious Bernadette Devlin called the British Home Secretary, Reginald Maudling, a 'murdering hypocrite' during a debate in Parliament and then slapped him in the face. Riots and gun battles broke out across Northern Ireland. Mobs set up new barricades in Catholic areas. The British army was forced to bring in more reinforcements. And hundreds of young Catholic men were lining up to join the Provisional IRA.

The immediate question facing Boyle and the Civil Rights Association was whether to go ahead with the planned third demonstration, scheduled for the following weekend in Newry. The Northern Ireland government urged NICRA to call off the march, warning that any violation of the parade ban would be stopped. Press reports said that the British army was planning to seal off Newry and saturate it with troops.[37] Fears grew that a repeat of Bloody Sunday was in the offing. In Boyle's words, 'it looked as if a massive confrontation was building up'. Even his colleague and mentor William Twining appealed to him to cancel the march.

But Kevin and other NICRA leaders were determined to go ahead. The key question was how to ensure that there would be no violence. 'We wanted a non-violent demonstration,' he recalled. 'We couldn't prove that we were stronger than the British army in military terms, but we wanted to show the massive rejection of the regime and the solidarity of our numbers.'[38]

On 2 February Boyle and Francis Keenan drove to Derry for the funerals of the thirteen victims. Boyle, as a member of NICRA's executive, was escorted to reserved seats in the church along with Keenan, but nearly 20,000 others stood in a driving rain and listened to the service on loudspeakers. Boyle then drove to Newry for a meeting with local activists. 'I didn't have to tell them how important it was going to be.'[39] He also contacted the Provisional IRA, both to ask that they keep a low profile during the event, and also for organizational help. 'They then volunteered the point, "Of course, there would be no military action." We said we knew that. We don't believe the British propaganda about Derry, but you could be useful nonetheless.' In fact, the IRA provided the march organizers with walkie-talkies to enable smoother communications during the protest.[40] At the same time, Boyle got in touch with British army headquarters. He stressed that, unlike Derry, march organizers were determined to ensure that there would be no confrontation at the barricades.

The following day, at a NICRA press conference in Belfast, Boyle emphasized to reporters that 'we are not searching for a confrontation with the army'. His goal, he later acknowledged, was to 'make explicit what I had communicated separately – that we would not force our way through any barricade'.[41] He was also at pains to draw a distinction between NICRA's goals and those of the IRA. 'This is a civil rights march. The purposes of our campaign do not embrace a united Ireland, nor is violence our method.'[42] To underscore this point and reduce the danger of clashes, organizers asked people from the Irish Republic, whose border was just a few miles from Newry, not to attend. The fear was that so many people would come and, 'in a little place like Newry one of the consequences would be a breakdown of control'.[43]

That weekend, Northern Ireland held its breath. Soldiers surrounded Newry and set up barricades, searching everyone entering the city. Nonetheless, on Sunday afternoon, thousands of people gathered, supervised by 500 stewards determined to maintain order. Although army helicopters swooped low, broadcasting warnings that the march was illegal and participants could be prosecuted, the march passed off peacefully, highlighted at the end by a minute's silence. 'It gave a solemnity to the occasion,' Boyle recalled. 'People were so fulfilled by the demonstration that there wasn't a single stone thrown in Newry that evening.'[44]

NICRA leaders hailed the march as a success. To Boyle, however, it was becoming increasingly clear that the kind of political activity to which he had devoted so much energy was a dead end. With the IRA's campaign and the army presence, he realized 'the streets were impossible to go on to'.[45] As Devlin observed, 'The Bloody Sunday march killed NICRA. It killed the civil rights movement. The way I saw it, and the way Kevin saw it at the time, was that the space for mass organizing on the streets was killed in Derry, and its funeral was in Newry.'

For Boyle, Newry was, as he put it, his 'last engagement.'[46] It was time to pull back from the kind of activism that had dominated his life since 1968.

[8]

Emergency Application

LESS THAN two months after Bloody Sunday, on 24 March 1972, the British government suspended the parliament at Stormont and assumed direct rule of Northern Ireland from London. More than half a century of Protestant domination and one-party rule by the Unionists came to an end. To the British, Bloody Sunday had made clear what was already becoming evident – with the Catholic community alienated from Stormont and violence out of control, Brian Faulkner and the local authorities in Belfast were simply not capable of managing the situation. With Faulkner's removal, William Whitelaw, a Conservative MP who had held a number of important positions in London, was appointed Secretary of State for Northern Ireland.

He immediately made a series of conciliatory moves to lower the political temperature. Some detainees were released, and charges were dropped against Kevin Boyle and others who were facing mandatory six-month jail terms for violating the ban on marches and parades. But the abolition of Stormont had a severe effect on the Unionists, who saw what they viewed as their chief bulwark against Catholics and the IRA disappear. For its part, the IRA was convinced that a further intensification of its campaign would force the British to withdraw from Northern Ireland. The result was a sharp increase in violence: 1972 was to prove the most lethal year in the history of the Troubles. Almost 500 people died, nearly 5000 were injured, there were almost 2000 explosions and over 10,000 shooting incidents.[1]

By now, Boyle had begun to distance himself from both the Northern Ireland Civil Rights Association and People's Democracy. Disagreement with PD's increasingly extreme politics had led to him being booted out of the organization's leadership body in February. And in that same month, he stepped down as the NICRA press spokesman, although he continued to be a member of the organization. As Bernadette Devlin observed, 'for people like Kevin, there was nowhere to stand now in terms of activism'.

Michael O'Boyle, the Belfast native who had studied law with Boyle and become a close friend, had just qualified as a barrister, and he embarked upon a path that would eventually take his career to the European Commission and Court of Human Rights. At this moment, O'Boyle believed, the dark turn in the political situation caused Kevin Boyle considerable anguish. 'It must have been a very perturbed period for someone like Kevin – an engaged intellectual. He must have felt a certain confusion or even guilt at what had been unleashed through student protests.' It was a question Boyle pondered for years. Not long before his death, he told an interviewer, 'I work on the basis that it wasn't worth a single life. This is my own moral position.'[2]

Still, as someone who tried not to let political differences undermine personal relationships, Boyle remained on cordial terms with activists in both organizations, and maintained his contacts with other opposition groups. And in a climate where he had concluded that street politics were no longer workable, his stepping back from the day-to-day activism of recent years opened the door for a new focus – an effort to use the law to try to right the wrongs that existed in Northern Ireland.

Not long after Bloody Sunday, Boyle visited Dublin to meet with Seán MacBride. MacBride was the son of a nationalist hero executed by the British after the Easter Rising in 1916, had been chief of staff of the IRA in the 1920s, and then a politician and Irish foreign minister. He was also a passionate advocate of human rights and a founder member of Amnesty International who, in 1974, would be awarded the Nobel Peace Prize. Boyle was looking for advice. With the situation in the North increasingly grim and the space for politics shrinking, Boyle asked MacBride for ideas about a possible international setting to raise the question of human rights abuses.

It is not known what MacBride said to Boyle, but a few weeks later, he sent Boyle a document written by Frank Newman, a law professor at the University of California at Berkeley and an early pioneer in teaching international human rights law, about making individual complaints to the UN Commission of Human Rights.

In the meantime, a couple of weeks after meeting Boyle, MacBride had lunch with another visitor, a 26-year-old American named Hurst Hannum. A recent Berkeley law graduate, Hannum had studied with Newman and become interested in human rights issues. During his third year of law school, Hannum had written a paper on possible international remedies for violations of human rights in Northern Ireland. In the process, he made himself something of an expert on the obscure topic of the European Convention on Human Rights. Enacted in 1953 by the original ten member states of the Council of Europe, including the United Kingdom, and inspired by the Universal Declaration of Human Rights adopted by the United Nations in 1948, the Convention was a response to the horrors that Europe had experienced during World War II. Its goal was to consolidate democracy and protect human rights and fundamental freedoms in Europe by requiring the signatory countries to adhere to a series of basic rights. These included the right to life and personal liberty, a fair trial, freedom of speech and association, and the prohibition of torture or inhuman and degrading treatment or punishment.

During his lunch with MacBride, Hannum talked of his interest in applying human rights law in Northern Ireland. Knowing no one there, and given the dangers, he had not planned to visit the North. MacBride, however, told Hannum about a 29-year-old lawyer from Belfast who had recently been asking about international remedies for human rights violations, and he urged him to meet Boyle. It was the beginning of one of the more important partnerships and friendships in Kevin Boyle's life.

In mid-March Hannum took the train from Dublin to Belfast. Shortly after arriving, he heard a loud explosion. A bomb had gone off in a Protestant neighbourhood a few minutes' walk from Queen's University. Having never seen the aftermath of a bombing, Hannum, curious, walked over to take a look, and was startled when he noticed the street sign where the blast had occurred. It read Hurst Street. 'I didn't know quite what kind of omen this was,' he recalled, 'but then I looked Kevin up. We met, and I ended up staying for two and half years, so I guess it wasn't a bad one.'

In the aftermath of the abolition of Stormont and the imposition of direct rule, the situation on the ground was getting worse. With a vicious cycle of continuing IRA violence, sectarian attacks by loyalist extremists, and increasingly tough measures adopted by the police and the British army, complaints of intimidation, beatings and mistreatment at the hand of the security forces were also rising.

'This was '72,' Hannum recalled. 'It was the worst year of the Troubles. A lot of people were getting beaten up and tortured, whether they were IRA or just suspects. Everybody was looking to do something about it.'

Around midnight on 20 April 1972, British soldiers raided a house in Belfast and arrested three men suspected of being IRA members responsible for setting off bombs in the city. The three – 29-year-old Gerard Donnelly, twenty-year-old Gerard Bradley and seventeen-year-old Edward Duffy – were taken to the Broadway military post, an army barracks in Belfast. For the next eighteen hours, they were subjected to treatment so brutal it became the foundation of a landmark case that Boyle and Hannum would bring against Britain at the European Commission of Human Rights.

During his interrogation by soldiers and members of the police special branch, Gerard Donnelly claimed that he was thrown to the floor, kicked in the ribs and battered around his genitals. 'They tore open my trousers and kicked me repeatedly; gave me karate chops, beat me with what seemed like a piece of hosepipe; penetrated my penis with something; attached an electric lead to my penis and gave me shocks; squeezed my testicles; produced a razor blade and threatened to cut off my privates.'[3]

Gerard Bradley and Edward Duffy were assaulted, kicked and had their arms twisted. Duffy's left arm was broken. Confined in a guard room as Duffy and Donnelly were being questioned in an interrogation room, Bradley repeatedly 'heard the others cry out'. Eventually all three were locked in the same room. Bradley said the other two men 'seemed to be in great pain, and [were] very weak-looking and bruised'.[4]

Ever since the introduction of internment, the Civil Rights Association, working with a community group called the Association for Legal Justice, had sought to chronicle the many instances of mistreatment and abuse reported by those who had been detained. The previous autumn, the two organizations had helped to publicize the British army's use of what were called the 'five techniques' of sensory deprivation: prolonged wall-standing in a painful position, hooding, subjecting prisoners to noise, deprivation of sleep, and removal of food and water. Developed for counter-insurgency campaigns in British colonies fighting for their independence, these methods, used on those detained during the internment operation, sparked intense controversy. In March 1972 British Prime Minister Edward Heath announced that the five techniques would no longer be allowed. However, he stated that what was euphemistically called 'interrogation in depth' would continue. Francis Keenan, Boyle's former student, was devoting much of his time to helping NICRA track cases of torture. Soon after Donnelly, Duffy and Bradley were arrested, the mother of one the men came into the NICRA offices asking for help and support.

Meanwhile, Hannum and Boyle had been brainstorming strategies to highlight the heavy-handed behaviour of the security forces. Hannum, through his research at law school, was familiar with the way the European Convention on Human Rights worked. This was something about which Boyle knew little. At most, there was a vague awareness among people in the legal field 'that there was this outside international body that was independent and impartial and had nothing to do with the UK', Michael O'Boyle recalled.

Together, Boyle and Hannum came up with the idea of bringing a case on behalf of a number of individuals against the British government to the European Commission on Human Rights. Based in the French city of Strasbourg, the Commission had been established to adjudicate violations of the Convention and to determine if complaints had enough validity to be sent to a separate European Court of Human Rights. In the early 1970s the Commission and the Court were obscure tribunals, infrequently used, even less widely known, and prone to rejecting most of the cases brought before them. Nonetheless, both men felt that it would not be hard to document army and police violations of Article 3 of the Convention, the prohibition on torture and inhumane and degrading treatment.

The challenge was that under Article 26 of the Convention, cases of abuse would be accepted only if the applicants had already exhausted so-called 'domestic remedies', meaning that all possible steps in their home country had been taken to seek redress for their grievances. The article had been included in the Convention to ensure that the tribunal would be a last resort, to be used only if national governments proved incapable of finding a resolution. There was, however, a qualification: domestic remedies had to be 'adequate and effective'.

Boyle and Hannum devised an approach to exploit this language. They would argue that so many detainees were being mistreated, it constituted a 'systematic administrative practice' by the British government of mistreating prisoners. Because the practice was so widespread, the two claimed there was no prospect of adequate and effective domestic remedies, meaning that the Commission should accept the case even if there were, on paper, still avenues for redress within Northern Ireland.

This legal argument had never been made before, according to Hannum. 'As we alleged, this widespread practice of torture and ill treatment was going on despite the laws. So our argument was that there weren't any real remedies, because the theoretical remedies were already there, and they obviously weren't working.'

'Reliance on British justice in those days had been tested and found wanting,' Michael O'Boyle observed. 'The local courts were not interested in examining cases of torture. They were interested in convicting people of firearms offences and what-have-you. It was that kind of climate that encouraged Kevin, because this was legally wrong. This was turning a blind eye to wrongdoing and [was] legally indefensible.'

To make the case that there was a systematic pattern of mistreatment, Boyle and Hannum needed to assemble a group of plaintiffs from across Northern Ireland. Working closely with the Northern Ireland Civil Rights Association and the Association for Legal Justice, they identified seven men. 'The seven were from different areas in Northern Ireland,' noted Francis Keenan, who helped Kevin and Hurst to prepare the case. 'And they were chosen on that basis, to get it as geographically widespread as possible.' Boyle and Hannum also made a conscious decision to focus on incidents that had occurred after London had imposed direct rule in March 1972. This would enable them to pin the responsibility for human rights violations directly on the British government, rather than on the discredited and now dissolved Unionist regime at Stormont.

The first three plaintiffs were Donnelly, Duffy and Bradley, whose injuries were so severe that all had been hospitalized after their interrogation – Donnelly for two weeks, Bradley for one week, and Duffy, who had two operations to repair his broken left arm, for six weeks. Two more men identified by Keenan came from Newry. They were twenty-year-old Anthony Kelly and 29-year-old Thomas Kearns. Both were arrested on 29 April 1972, allegedly while planning an ambush on British soldiers. Kelly claimed that, while in detention, he was hit on the back of a head by a rifle butt, and made to run through a line of soldiers who kicked him, banged his head against a cabinet, and forced him to sing 'God Save the Queen'.

Kearns alleged that he too was hit on the neck by a rifle butt, forced to stand spread-eagled against a wall for an extended period, and also made to sing the British national anthem. Both also claimed they were given drugs slipped into cups of tea. At their trial in Newry, they had been represented by Rory McShane, another of Boyle's recently graduated law students. Boyle contacted McShane to ask if the two would be willing to be part of the case. 'Kevin was driving it, was saying we're going to have a go at this,' McShane recalled. 'I went and spoke with them and the guys were happy to come on board and give their evidence.'

Twenty-six-year-old Francis McBride was the sixth plaintiff. Arrested in his hometown of Rasharkin, County Antrim, on 13 April by police investigating an explosion the previous day, he claimed to have been pulled by his hair, slapped in the face, hit on the neck with a rubber pipe, and threatened with being shot. The final plaintiff was John Carlin, a native of Derry. Detained in the city on 28 April, he alleged that he had been beaten, slapped on the face and thrown onto a wrecked car, where he was spun around and punched.

Hannum and Boyle spent much of May huddled in the Queen's University law library, refining their legal arguments to submit to the European Commission. 'We did an awful lot of talking,' Hannum recalled:

> I would do the first drafts of most things, and then we'd talk more. The ideas were equal. If anything, the ideas came more from Kevin than from me, except for the purely technical international side, which I sort of provided at that stage, as Kevin almost literally knew nothing about international law. He'd been entirely involved in the domestic stuff. He was fascinated by the idea that there was an international aspect to this, because he was from the North, and this was a local struggle.

It was the first major case for both men. For Hannum, who had just passed the bar exam in the United States the previous January, it was his first case of any kind. Looking back years later, he wryly acknowledged that 'neither of us really knew what we were doing'.

Closeted together day after day, the two men grew close. 'I looked up to Kevin as the one who knew what was going on and knew all the politics of everything,' Hannum recalled. 'And he looked up to me as the one who had the technical knowledge of this weird place in France that we were actually trying to get something out of.' Their friendship and shared work on human rights led Hannum to decide to stay on in Belfast, where he would live for the next two and a half years.

Hannum knew Boyle had been involved in the civil rights movement, and was impressed by the range of his contacts and his depth of knowledge. But he was astonished as he gradually discovered 'how important Kevin had been in the preceding several years, how much of a public figure he was'. Typically, Boyle didn't talk about it. 'There was simply no ego there. There was this real humility. He would never have said that he was a star. I had no idea I was working with one of the most important people in the civil rights movement.' Boyle was not someone who advertised his previous achievements. Instead, with this case offering a new avenue to push for human rights after the failure of street politics, he rolled up his sleeves and got to work.

On 27 May 1972 Boyle submitted a formal document for what was called an 'Emergency Application' on behalf of Donnelly, Duffy, Bradley, Kelly, Kearns, McBride and Carlin to the European Commission of Human Rights. The application detailed the abuse the seven men had suffered at the hands of the security forces, and sought a ruling not only that their rights under Article 3 of the European Convention had been violated, in that their treatment constituted a 'systematic administrative pattern' of brutality. It also requested a temporary injunction to halt such behaviour while the case was being investigated, and requested that the investigation of the allegations, as well as a broader inquiry into 'the system of interrogation currently employed by the security forces' in Northern Ireland, be expedited as a matter of urgency.[5] The application addressed the question of domestic remedies, arguing that 'no individual remedy can adequately deal with the system of interrogation as such', and that even if financial compensation was offered, 'one cannot be adequately compensated for the physical and massive psychological wounds which result from such systematized terror and intimidation'.[6]

In bringing this case, there was another motive. The previous autumn, the government of Ireland had brought its own case to the European Commission against the British government over the introduction of internment. The Irish case also specifically included detainees subjected to the controversial five techniques of interrogation. Among activists in Belfast, however, there was widespread cynicism about Dublin's motives, and much concern that the Irish would settle the case and Britain would get off the hook. A new case would ensure that pressure on London over the mistreatment of prisoners would continue. 'We were afraid that the inter-state case would be settled between Ireland and the UK, and that that would be the end of the whole torture issue,' Francis Keenan recalled. 'So the idea was to say to the Irish government – if you settle it, we're still here.' In fact, the Irish government did not settle. The case dragged on for years before the Commission, in 1976, ruled that the five techniques did amount to torture.

Just seven weeks after Boyle and Hannum's application was filed – a remarkably short time – came the first response. The Commission decided that it had no power to issue an injunction, but it agreed to expedite an examination of the case, although that would still likely require waiting for several more months. In the meantime, the situation in the North got steadily worse, with daily bombings and shootings, the growing strength of armed loyalist paramilitary groups, and no progress on the political front. Talks between the British government and the IRA, initiated by William Whitelaw, had led to a brief ceasefire in June, which quickly broke down. One day in July, Nicholas Ragg stopped by to visit Kevin at his apartment near Queen's University. 'I remember sitting in his flat,' Ragg recalled, 'and we counted nineteen explosions across Belfast in a half hour.' The day became known as Bloody Friday, when twenty-two IRA bombs devastated the centre of Belfast, killing nine people and injuring 130.

Against a background of unremitting violence, Boyle had decided earlier in the spring that he needed a break and he arranged for a post-doctoral fellowship in the Department of Sociology at Yale University for the 1972/73 academic year. As Boyle wrote to an American colleague, he wanted to 'leave the battlefield for at least a term'.[7] One additional reason was that his long-time romance with Eilis McDermott was on the rocks.

At the start of September Boyle left Belfast for New Haven, Connecticut. Before leaving, he received a note from Edwina Stewart, a long-time member of the executive of the Northern Ireland Civil Rights Association. She had worked and debated with Boyle for years, and was now one of those backing the case he had lodged with the European Commission of Human Rights. 'Good luck at Strasbourg,' she wrote. 'Good luck in the States. And don't go marrying a Yank!'[8]

With its leafy campus, Gothic buildings and placid atmosphere, Yale was a sharp and welcome contrast from Belfast. Boyle plunged into academic work, conducting research on the history of policing in Ireland, teaching a couple of courses, supervising an independent study project for a student interested in Irish history, and travelling around the United States lecturing on Northern Ireland. His topics included 'Ireland: Civil Rights and Law', 'The Irish Struggle' and 'Irish Problems: New Solutions'. Boyle wrote to a friend in Belfast, 'In these academic pastures, I am grazing profitably. I have been able to replenish myself after effectively four years on the streets and away from academic thought and theory.'[9] As much as he enjoyed being in the States, however, he was struck by the country's pervasive racism. During a visit to Detroit, he wrote, 'these very streets remind me of the ghettos of Belfast'.[10]

The conflict at home was never far from his mind. A letter from his sister Anne in late October highlighted the grimness of the situation. 'Things are getting worse here', she wrote. 'The courthouse in Newry was demolished last Sunday, and most of the surrounding buildings have been wrecked, I thought the whole town was gone.' Anne told him about a particularly scary episode involving their brother Louis, who had been stopped at a roadblock by the loyalist paramilitary group, the UDA, and dragged out of his car, which was then driven off. Louis, never one to be intimidated, 'went straight to the office of the battalion nearby and, after much pressure, the army intervened and got his car back. He was very lucky he didn't get shot.'[11] Indeed, as the new year began, loyalist death squads intensified a campaign of sectarian assassinations, arbitrarily targeting any Catholics they could find on the streets.

Meanwhile, Boyle and Hannum waited for word from the European Commission. They were well aware that their clients were not paragons of innocence. 'Three of them were pretty hard-core IRA guys,' Hannum noted. 'But there's no doubt in this case they were the ones who were probably beaten up most badly.' In Boyle's absence, Hannum had continued to gather evidence in Belfast. On one occasion while taking statements in the company of a British journalist and a local priest in the Catholic neighbourhood of Ardoyne, which at this point was still largely a no-go area for the troops, he was detained by the army. 'We were stopped by members of the First Parachute Regiment, a notorious bunch, as we were leaving the area, and they took us into custody,' Hannum recalled, remembering their particular interest in the statements they had been collecting:

> We were put into an armoured car and taken to a barracks, where we were kept standing in a corridor facing the wall for about two hours. Apart from a 'what the fuck do you think you're looking at' while we were standing there – I had turned my head, I suppose – we weren't mistreated.

But they were formally arrested under the Special Powers Act and told they were suspected of being members of the IRA. Once word of their detention reached higher-ranking army officials, however, Hannum and his two companions were allowed to leave, and even received an apology of sorts from a senior officer. 'We just had to check you out,' the officer told them. 'Glad that you were well treated, just like everyone else.'

During the 1972 Christmas break, Boyle flew to San Francisco, where Hannum was also visiting, and the two worked to pull together their arguments for the European Commission. In January Boyle joined tens of thousands of other demonstrators in Washington to protest about the inauguration of President Richard Nixon and the wholesale Christmas bombing of North Vietnam's capital, Hanoi, which Nixon had authorized. Boyle was, he wrote, 'curious about the phenomenon of student protest [in the US] – the movement that one has seen and heard so much about'.[12] It was a bitterly cold day as the protestors marched from the Lincoln Memorial to the Washington Monument. Boyle was struck by what seemed to him to be the 'uneasy coalition' of pro-peace and left-wing groups, including radical Puerto Ricans, which, he wrote, 'reminded me of PD'. Still, he came away heartened by the 'positive values' of the protestors despite the bleak political climate.

Although away from Belfast, Boyle had not given up hope of reviving his frayed relationship with Eilis McDermott, even paying for her to visit him in New Haven. But the romance was clearly coming to an end. Boyle confided to a journal he kept that 'I suffered considerable depressions because I was on my own and did not feel any more that Eilis loved me, as she had.'[13]

In the spring of 1973 the European Commission announced that a hearing would be held in Strasbourg from 3 to 5 April to determine whether the case was admissible. As he prepared to leave for Strasbourg, Boyle received a troubling letter from Claire Palley, the dean of the Queen's law school. Palley was a refugee from apartheid South Africa and the first female law school dean in the United Kingdom. 'I write to you now personally and as a friend,' she began. 'You should seriously consider your own personal safety in coming back to Northern Ireland. If last year you had threats against your life you took seriously, then is it not foolish in the current situation where assassinations have begun for you to come back to the Faculty? No Faculty is worth your life.'[14] Boyle put the letter aside.

At the beginning of April, Boyle, Hurst Hannum, Gerard Donnelly and Gerard Bradley flew to Strasbourg. The other five plaintiffs remained in detention. Donnelly, Bradley and Edward Duffy had all made 'admissions', while in detention, to causing multiple explosions, but claimed that their statements were made under duress, and after a court hearing the evidence against them was declared inadmissible and they were released. In early March, however, Duffy, who was supposed to accompany the others to Strasbourg, had been rearrested under the Special Powers Act.

Michael O'Boyle, who, before taking a job with the European Commission in Strasbourg, had acted as an informal advisor to Boyle and Hannum, remembered that, initially, French officials did not want to let Donnelly and Bradley – accused terrorists – into the country. 'These were people who had been lifted on suspicion of terrorism … I don't know how they managed. Eventually the French authorities let them in.'

As the hearing began, Boyle and Hannum discovered, not altogether to their surprise, that the act of bringing the case had infuriated the British. 'We were royal pains in the asses to the British, who really resented what we were doing,' Hannum recalled:

> Part of that was just the normal defensive reaction of any government. But this idea – that there was this widespread pattern of abuse throughout Northern Ireland that the British government either tolerated or encouraged or at least ignored but had knowledge of, and particularly the way the case was formulated to avoid spending years going through the domestic courts – I think this was something that they took very seriously, and that they did resent.

The British had assembled a high-powered team of half-a-dozen lawyers and several security people. 'It was the two of us against ten Brits,' Hannum said. 'They just wanted us to go away.'

During the hearing the British lawyers declared that they did not accept that the seven men had been brutalized. The British lawyers also denied that there was any 'administrative practice of ill treatment'. Instead, hoping to paint Boyle and Hannum's clients as 'bad guys', they sought to emphasize the crimes with which the plaintiffs had been charged: murder, causing explosions and the illegal possession of firearms. While acknowledging that complaints of mistreatment had been made, the British countered that these allegations were now under investigation, also noting that the government had ordered an end to the use of the controversial 'five techniques' of sensory deprivation. In addition, the British challenged Boyle and Hannum's effort to link the individual complaints of their seven clients with a broader, officially sanctioned practice of brutality, insisting that individual plaintiffs 'could only complain about a particular action that affected him, and the Commission had no power to consider whether there were other actions which might form an administrative practice'.[15]

In response, Boyle and Hannum argued that whether any of their clients had been charged or convicted of a particular crime had no bearing on the allegations of mistreatment. They defended linking the individual claims – the violations of Article 3 of the European Convention – to a broader administrative practice of brutality by arguing that it was the 'direct application to each of them of this practice' that had led to the abusive behaviour. Boyle told the eleven Commission members that the seven men

> suffered their injuries as part of a systematic, repeated, and official interrogation procedure known as interrogation in depth, whereby acts of physical beating, psychological intimidation, and sensory deprivation were either officially authorized, condoned, or tolerated at various levels in the chain of command.[16]

To protect their clients from further mistreatment, they called on the Commission to order that 'such practices in breach of the Convention be stopped'. In particular, they asked that the Commission cite the continued existence of Northern Ireland's draconian Special Powers Act, which had been used to justify internment, as a law that permitted abuses to occur.[17]

The British countered that an applicant had 'no right to be protected from something which had not yet happened'.[18] They maintained that the claims of violations of the Article 3 ban on torture or inhuman or degrading treatment were also inadmissible because each of the seven applicants had 'failed to exhaust the remedies available to him under domestic law'.[19] They noted that two policemen and a soldier had actually been prosecuted in a Belfast court because of the complaints raised by Donnelly, Duffy and Bradley, and had been acquitted. Moreover, the British lawyers said someone who was mistreated in custody also had the right to bring a legal action for compensation.[20]

Boyle and Hannum responded that no adequate and effective domestic remedy could exist where there was a continuing administrative pattern of violation of the Convention. Moreover, because 'the injuries inflicted on them [the men] in breach of that Article took place within a system of interrogation and officially tolerated torture, inhuman and degrading treatment or punishment', the two lawyers asserted that their clients 'were not bound to exhaust domestic remedies before seeking relief before the Commission'.[21] They argued that

> it was evident that the existence of a widespread pattern of torture and brutality would necessarily intimidate those who might wish to complain about the treatment they had received. The circumstances created an atmosphere where complainants must be assumed to have serious hesitation in pursuing any action against the Government.[22]

They also noted that 'as a result of the jury system in Northern Ireland, where only those who own property are entitled to sit on the jury panel, the jury was primarily, if not entirely, Loyalist or Protestant in composition [and] tended to be prejudiced against suspected terrorists and in favour of the security forces.'[23]

Since the suffering of their clients was merely one part of a larger pattern of brutality and torture directed against a political minority, Boyle and Hannum maintained that 'the Government responsible for such activities should not be allowed to continue to violate Article 3 of the Convention and at the same time argue that, as long as compensation was available, such violations could not be examined by the Commission'.[24]

After two and half days of oral hearings, the Commission issued its decision. To the shock and dismay of the British lawyers, and the astonishment of Boyle and Hannum, the case was declared admissible. A fully fledged legal inquiry of the British mistreatment of detainees in Northern Ireland would now follow. The two young lawyers were euphoric. 'Our initial win on the admissibility decision was pretty extraordinary,' Hannum recalled:

> For these two guys – this, young, politically active, charismatic Kevin Boyle, and this young American who thought he knew a lot about this stuff, and at least knew a lot about it in theory, to go up against what was a pretty hefty British team, with what was at the time a fairly unusual legal argument … it really was feeling that the underdog actually won one.

'They had overcome the biggest hurdle,' observed Michael O'Boyle, 'which related to one of the Convention requirements that you had to exhaust all your domestic remedies. They had basically won the case that … remedies for torture or alleged torture were ineffective – which was a huge step forward.'

With newspaper headlines like 'N.I. "Torture" Claims to be Investigated'[25] the admissibility decision made a significant political impact, increasing pressure on the British, while showing that an international legal avenue might offer hope of redressing deeply held grievances about the behaviour of members of the security forces.

But this initial victory was just the first step. The next stage would be a detailed investigation involving dozens of witnesses; it would last for months. And despite the surprising decision, Boyle continued to struggle with mixed feelings, including a degree of self-doubt about his own role. In a letter to a friend in Belfast, Judge Turlough O'Donnell, a week after the ruling, he wrote:

> I'm not foolish enough to imagine that to get to this point shows great untapped talents in me as a practitioner. Without the help of my colleague in handling issues of fact, I should have been lost. I am glad I did it (especially as no one else was interested) but it more or less persuaded me that whatever my diffuse talent is capable of, it probably lies in academic fields. That is not to devalue practice, quite the reverse. It's just not me.[26]

Hurst Hannum, who remained one of Boyle's closest friends, struggled to understand why Boyle felt this way:

> There was a part that was just modesty. But I think there was some self-doubt. In those very early days, he used to say 'Hurst taught me everything

I know about international law.' In the early days that was true. But that had nothing to do with his political acumen and his good lawyerly tendencies, marshalling facts and organizing things. He had very good instincts. I think he doubted his purely intellectual or theoretical talents. I am not a theoretical person either. But I think he really did grossly underestimate all these other talents he had … He was very intelligent … He may well have been filled with self-doubt, but he was incredibly successful.

In any event, following the Commission's ruling, Boyle returned to New Haven to wind up his affairs at Yale and finally found time to respond to the letter from Queen's law school dean Claire Palley. While acknowledging her concern, he said he was determined to come back to Belfast. However, recognizing the potential dangers, he asked if it would be possible for him to rent a flat from the university, which would mean not having to publicize where he lived to estate agents or others. The problem was that, having already rented university housing for two years, he was no longer technically eligible to do so, and he asked Palley if an exception could be made for him, given the circumstances. To his dismay, the university was unable to help him. With some trepidation, he returned to Belfast in the summer of 1973.

[9]

It Is Very Hard to Be Happy in Ireland Now

AFTER NEARLY a year away, Boyle returned to Belfast to find that Northern Ireland had settled into a grim routine of almost daily bombings and shootings, the most frightening new development being an upsurge in sectarian assassinations by loyalist paramilitary groups. The month of June 1973 began with two civilians being shot dead by loyalist gunmen. A few days later, six elderly Protestants died in an IRA car bomb attack, while a Catholic civilian was shot and killed by British soldiers. The month ended with the kidnapping and savage murder of a prominent Catholic politician, Paddy Wilson of the SDLP, and his female companion, a Protestant. The killers, members of the UDA, stabbed Wilson thirty times, and his girl-friend twenty times. That same day, a civilian employed by the British army was shot dead by the IRA.

The violence was taking place against a backdrop of continued polit-ical stalemate. For Boyle, it was a depressing return home, his bleak mood intensified by the end of his long romance with Eilis McDermott. The rela-tionship had been 'extremely important to him', Hurst Hannum recalled.

'It was a tough break-up.' During those unsettled months, Boyle unburdened himself in long letters to two women, one of them a former girlfriend named Judith from his days in Cambridge in 1967; the other, Eileen, was someone he had got to know at Yale. Boyle's letters do not exist, but he kept the replies from both women. 'Your last note sounded like you're pretty damned depressed,' Eileen wrote. 'How much of that is due to the war – you know, the fact that people don't leave their houses at night – as well as the pressure on you specifically to give your whole life to a cause.'[1] 'I imagine,' Judith wrote, 'that it is very hard to be happy in Ireland now.'[2]

Adrift emotionally and struggling to determine what kind of role he could play, Boyle wrote of his political uncertainty to a friend, 'I am kind of footloose at the moment.'[3] To another he wrote, 'There is much happening to me and nothing at the same time. I am in a "retreatist" mood.'[4]

It was apparent to his friends and fellow activists that the year at Yale had accentuated the transformation in his political thinking, which had begun in the wake of Bloody Sunday. Boyle's antipathy to the Provisional IRA's effort to bomb Northern Ireland into a united Ireland had intensified, and he had little patience with the radical positions of organizations like People's Democracy, by now reduced to an extreme left-wing fringe group. His old comrade Michael Farrell remained a leading figure in PD, but years later he expressed understanding of Boyle's evolving views. 'Kevin was not a Republican. He was against discrimination and wanted to build a fairer society. His philosophy would have been much more based on the law, the rule of law, and human rights ... Once he got involved in the Strasbourg case ... he could see another avenue for dealing with things.' Uneasily settling back into teaching at Queen's and navigating the daily perils of life in Belfast, Boyle and Hannum waited for the European Commission of Human Rights to move forward with the hearings that would be the next step in their case.

As the violence continued, in late 1973 the British government attempted to craft a new political compromise, convincing Brian Faulkner, who had been removed as Northern Ireland's prime minister when direct rule from London was introduced the year before, to share power in a new executive with the moderate Catholic SDLP and the small, non-sectarian Alliance Party. The agreement, finalized during negotiations in Sunningdale, England, in mid-December, also included the creation of a cross-border Council of Ireland to discuss possible cooperation between Northern Ireland and the Republic.

From the moment the new executive took office in January 1974, however, Protestant hardliners denounced it as a sell-out, the first step to the union with the Republic they so dreaded. Faulkner's own Unionist party repudiated the deal, determined at all costs to block its implementation. For its part, the IRA saw the power-sharing arrangement as a threat to its own ambitions, and stepped up its activities. Throughout the long, dark winter of 1973/74, the Provos continued to set off bombs and kill soldiers and policemen, to the growing fury of the loyalists, who intensified their own campaign of sectarian assassinations, with British troops trying to keep the warring communities apart while also conducting what amounted to counter-insurgency operations against the IRA.

One evening in the late winter of 1974, Kevin's brother Louis Boyle, now working at the Northern Ireland Community Relations Commission, went for a drink at the Botanic Inn near Queen's University in south Belfast, the area least affected by the violence. There, he bumped into some friends who introduced him to an attractive young woman named Joan Smyth, a secondary school French teacher. As someone went to the bar to fetch drinks, there was a bomb scare. Louis' friends rushed out one door; he and Joan escaped through another exit. There was no bomb, but since the group were now scattered, Louis and Joan went off for a drink elsewhere.

In the following weeks, Louis and Joan got together occasionally for drinks. One evening Louis mentioned that his brother had just bought a house on Marlborough Park, a quiet, leafy street not far from Queen's. It was Kevin's first home purchase, and, for someone with his left-wing polit-ical leanings, had produced mixed feelings. 'I have bought a house,' Kevin wrote to a friend. 'Not, I hope, the first step in the *embourgeoisement* of Boyle!'⁵ Indeed, Louis used precisely that word – *bourgeois* – to jokingly describe his brother to Joan when he invited her to a housewarming party Kevin was holding. At the party, Kevin did little more than shake hands with Joan. It was his first meeting with the woman who, two years later, would become his wife.

Joan Smyth was a Protestant. She had been born on 14 October 1948 in her grandmother's home in the small village of Jerrettspass, five miles from Newry, and had grown up in the countryside. Her father ran a large dairy farm and her mother worked as a civil servant in the nearby market town of Omagh. Joan was one of five children, with two brothers and two sisters. They were, in her words, 'a typical Northern Ireland Protestant family', but, like her parents, Joan was largely apolitical. Her father employed both Protestants and Catholics, had easy relations with neighbours regardless of religion, and when he died in 1967 many Catholics came to pay their respects. Not long before his death, Joan remembered her father saying that he would no longer visit a neighbour who had expressed strong support for the extremist views of Ian Paisley.

For Joan, youthful rebellion took the form of escaping from Northern Ireland altogether. While Kevin was at the centre of the civil rights protests in 1968 and 1969, she went to France as an au pair in the summer of 1968 after completing her first year at Trinity College Dublin. She then spent the 1969–70 academic year in Paris, becoming fluent in French and returning to France every summer. After receiving her undergraduate degree from Trinity, she completed a postgraduate teacher training programme at Queen's and was offered a good job teaching French in the town of Ballymena. However, she turned it down because she did not want to leave the livelier social scene in Belfast, and soon after took a position as a French teacher at Park Parade Secondary School in the heart of Protestant East Belfast.

A couple of weeks after the housewarming party, where Boyle had been in the company of a secretary from the law faculty – one of several casual flings he had in the wake of his break-up from Eilis McDermott – Louis Boyle called and invited Joan to dinner at Marlborough Park. The gathering was hosted by Kevin's younger sister Bernadette, who, along with her husband Paul, lived on the ground floor of Kevin's three-storey house. Paul was an electrical engineer who, like many innocent Catholics, had been interned in 1971. Newly married, the young couple could not yet afford a place of their own.

After dinner Kevin said he wanted to go to a poetry reading by John Hewitt, a Belfast native who had become known for poems exploring issues of prejudice, identity and sectarian hostility. Louis had already gone home, and Bernadette, uninterested in poetry, demurred, so Kevin asked Joan if she would like to accompany him. The event was being held at the Europa Hotel in the city centre, which at that time had the dubious distinction of being the most frequently bombed hotel in the world. Barely a half-dozen people were at the reading. As Hewitt read, Kevin asked Joan if he could borrow a pen and started taking notes. 'That was Kevin,' she recalled, 'academic to the core, always taking notes.' Leaving the Europa, Kevin said that Tom Hadden was having a birthday party the following weekend. Would she like to come?

The people at Hadden's party were a mixture of academics, lawyers and others with a keen interest in Northern Ireland's political situation. It was a mixed crowd, both Protestants and Catholics, and, for Joan, an entirely new, exciting and even rather intimidating gathering. 'I heard conversations that would make the hair of many Protestants stand on end.' As she chatted with Kevin, he never mentioned his own radical political background. Whether it was his natural self-effacing manner, embarrassment, or even guilt at how the civil rights movement had descended into violence was something she never determined. But he simply did not talk about his own role. 'Looking back,' she joked, 'if I had known who he was, I probably wouldn't have gone out with him.' They made plans to get together again the following weekend, but Kevin failed to show up. It was not until the autumn of 1974 that they would meet again.

In the meantime, Boyle and Hadden, along with Paddy Hillyard, a lecturer in social administration at the New University of Ulster, were engaged in an ambitious research project on the role of the law in the Northern Ireland conflict. They embarked on their study against a backdrop of significant changes to the territory's legal system. Although it was evident that internment was both politically and militarily self-defeating, the British government refused to abandon the policy. But in 1972 it had appointed Lord Kenneth Diplock, the most senior judge in Britain's highest court of appeals, the House of Lords, to chair a commission to explore ways of improving legal procedures to deal with the continuing violence. At Diplock's recommendation, in 1973 the widely hated Special Powers Act was replaced by the Northern Ireland (Emergency Provisions) Act. Internment was continued, but the rules governing the behaviour of the security forces, as well as procedures for detention, were modified.

Until this point, there had been no serious academic study of how Northern Ireland's legal system had operated since the start of the Troubles. Boyle, Hadden and Hillyard decided that they needed to monitor accurately what was actually happening in the security services and the courts. Hadden and Hillyard – a Dublin-educated Protestant who had moved to Northern Ireland at the outbreak of the Troubles – had already gathered some information on the working of the courts. Along with Boyle, they amassed a collection of data that documented sharp differences in the way the security forces and the courts were dealing with Republican and Loyalist defendants. 'What we were showing,' said Hillyard, 'was that a Catholic would be found with a firearm and the book would be thrown at him, while if a Protestant was found, they weren't charged with the most serious offences.' Indeed, one of the tables in their study showed that Catholics charged with possession of firearms with criminal intent received sentences averaging 6.3 years, while Protestants charged with the same offence got 4.2 years.[6] This was one of many reasons why their data also showed that 88 per cent of Catholics believed an individual in Northern Ireland could not get a fair trial, while only 27 per cent of Protestants held the same belief.[7]

It was partly because of such concerns, but more because of the problem that potential witnesses or jurors were being intimidated by paramilitaries on both sides, that Lord Diplock also recommended major changes in the way terrorist suspects should be tried. In cases of suspected paramilitary activity, Diplock called for cases to be heard by a single judge acting both as judge and jury. It was a controversial move, with critics claiming that it was switching from no trial under internment to internment with the pretence of a trial. In their research, however, Boyle, Hadden and Hillyard concluded that, in fact, the evidence showed that the Diplock system was actually working reasonably well, and that 'the suspension of jury trials was clearly successful in removing an important source of difference in the treatment of Protestant and Roman Catholic defendants'.[8]

As the three men assembled their research, there was a further dramatic deterioration of the situation. In the spring of 1974, loyalist extremists opposed to the power-sharing executive, which had taken office in January, organized a general strike. With the paramilitary UDA heavily involved, roads were blocked, cars hijacked, and bands of men carrying clubs intimidated thousands of workers into staying at home. At the same time, loyalists set off bombs in Dublin and the Irish border town of Monaghan, killing thirty-two people, the worst death toll of any single day during the Troubles. At one point Kevin was so anxious about his own safety that he briefly fled Belfast to take refuge at the home of friends across the border.

That same spring, the new British government announced the formation of yet another committee. This one, headed by Lord Gardiner, a former Lord High Chancellor, was asked to examine the 1973 Emergency Provisions Act and explore other ways of dealing with the continuing violence. In mid-summer, the Commission began holding hearings in Northern Ireland and accepting submissions from dozens of organizations and individuals. Hadden, Boyle and Hillyard decided to turn their research into a 54-page submission, which they hammered out in an isolated cottage along the Atlantic coast of County Donegal over the summer of 1974. The paper was presented to the Commission in September, and Hadden subsequently delivered oral testimony. The central argument was that internment should be ended and replaced with an improved version of the Diplock Courts. They maintained that the British army, which operated mainly in Catholic areas, was abusing the procedures for questioning and detaining people, resulting in large numbers of wholly innocent people being arrested.[9]

The writers described the army's approach as a 'military security policy' in which Catholics were the targets of a counter-insurgency campaign aimed at recording the names and other personal details of nearly every person living in nationalist areas, so that suspected IRA members could be identified and interned. Hadden recalled British journalist friends being taken on army tours of the Catholic ghettos at the time and being asked to pick any house. 'The army minders would then say we can tell you the colour of the wallpaper, we can tell you how many people are living there,' Hadden recalled. 'And then they would bang on the door and show that they knew who was supposed to be there. It was not very nice. But it was all part of the strategy that you know where everybody is.'

This approach stood in sharp contrast to what the three academics called a 'police prosecution policy' implemented in Protestant areas by the Royal Ulster Constabulary. Unlike in the Catholic ghettos, the RUC was still largely welcomed in loyalist neighbourhoods and its behaviour was marked by the use of conventional police techniques and procedures 'in which the main emphasis is on proof of specific criminal charges'.[10] The result, they said, was that the Protestants got the benefit of rule of law treatment, while Catholics faced continuing harassment and internment. This produced 'an imbalance in the number of Republican and loyalist suspects dealt with in the courts and by extra-judicial detention'[11], which served only to fuel support for the IRA.

In its final report, the Gardiner Commission accepted much of what Boyle, Hadden and Hillyard proposed. The report criticized the way current detention procedures operated, noting that the behaviour of the security forces only intensified a sense of injustice among ordinary people, especially Catholics, and called for the phasing out of internment as part of a broader reassessment of British policy.

In the autumn of 1974 the first hearings in the case of Gerard Donnelly, Thomas Kearns, Anthony Kelly, John Carlin, Edward Duffy, Gerard Bradley and Francis McBride finally got under way. Duffy and Bradley were still being held at the Maze prison, and McBride at a different jail in Northern Ireland. But the other four, now released, accompanied Boyle and Hannum to Strasbourg. The hearing lasted a week in early November, and was held before three members of the Commission. It was the first opportunity for the men Boyle and Hannum were representing to tell their stories in person. The two lawyers patiently led their clients through a grim recitation of their experiences, with Kevin, as was his style, always calm, courteous and going out of his way to show great respect for the judges. Donnelly described the police administering electric shocks to his genitals, and how he saw Bradley and Duffy 'in great pain'.[12] A doctor who had examined Donnelly at the time testified that anyone should have noticed this 'distressed condition'.[13]

Kelly, Kearns and Carlin all testified that they had been forced to stand spread-eagled with their hands against a wall for prolonged periods as security personnel kicked them or hit them with rifle butts on the legs, back and head. This occurred even though the British government had announced in March 1972 that such behaviour, one of the so-called 'five techniques' of interrogation previously used in counter-insurgency campaigns, would no longer be permitted. John Carlin recalled being kneed in the groin, repeatedly punched and slapped, threatened with a pistol and a lighted cigarette, and being forced to get down on all fours and bark like a dog.

The British government lawyers made little effort to deny these specific allegations. Rather, they stressed that the applicants had all been arrested for terrorist activities. Moreover, the lawyers argued that the claims of mistreatment, as part of 'administrative practice' of abusing detainees sanctioned by the government, could not be considered by the Commission because the applicants had failed to exhaust domestic remedies within Northern Ireland. Specifically, the British noted that Donnelly, Duffy and Bradley had initiated civil proceedings against the authorities in 1972, and the remaining four applicants began similar proceedings in 1974.

In response, Boyle and Hannum acknowledged these steps, but contended that the theoretical availability of redress was undermined by consistent harassment and obstruction by the security forces, designed to intimidate anyone thinking of filing a complaint about mistreatment. To buttress their case, Boyle and Hannum asked Rory McShane, Kevin's former student and old PD comrade, to testify. McShane was now a practising lawyer who had defended Thomas Kearns and Anthony Kelly. He testified about the legal procedures. 'My argument was that monetary compensation was available but that wasn't enough to stop the practice,' McShane recalled. John Hume from Derry, a leading figure in the SDLP and longtime civil rights activist, also flew to Strasbourg to make a similar argument. Hume testified that he shared Carlin's distrust of the police, noting the frequency with which complaints against the police or army led to reprisals. He added, 'in the history of the major complaints against the security forces in Northern Ireland by the people whom I represent, I have yet to see a case in which they have been satisfied, and I could give you a list the length of my arm if you want'.[14]

As Boyle juggled with the Donnelly case, the Gardiner submission, other research, and his normal teaching load, that same autumn he reconnected with Joan Smyth. Walking down University Street one day, Joan heard footsteps behind her and someone calling her name. It was Kevin, who apologized profusely for not having been in touch, and asked if they could meet up. From that moment, the romance began in earnest. It was in many ways the attraction of opposites, but each seemed to meet a need in the other. Boyle was cerebral, an intellectual, a workaholic – but he offered Joan entry to a world she found as stimulating as it was unfamiliar. Joan, with her fluent French, European travel, cultural taste and deep emotional sympathy, was for Kevin, in Hurst Hannum's words, 'almost exotic, because everyone Kevin knew was political'. As she recalled, 'I had lived in Paris. I spoke French. He wanted so much to have this aspect in his life.'

But there was the one fact that loomed over everything: Joan was Protestant, Kevin was Catholic. Neither was religious. Indeed, both had consciously broken with the rigid traditions in which they had grown up. 'I was trying to kick away my religion,' Joan said. 'So was Kevin.' They shared stories about how each had become disillusioned with Northern Irish society – Kevin talking about not having met a Protestant until he was seventeen, and Joan noting similar experiences from her side. 'We were both struggling, thinking, finding ourselves. We discovered quickly that we shared much in common.' But the sectarian divide shaped the entire environment in which their relationship was developing.

Joan was still teaching at the Park Parade Secondary School. It was a rough neighbourhood. In class, she spent the majority of her time simply trying to keep order rather than teaching. Many of the students were from families so poor, their only chance to wash came from once-weekly visits to nearby public baths. The fathers of many of her students were members of the paramilitary UDA. Police were often deployed just outside the school to keep the Park Parade students from fighting with the kids from a school in a nearby Catholic neighbourhood.

Joan found many of her colleagues to be as prejudiced as her students and their families. 'I never heard anything like the bigotry I heard in the staff room,' she recalled. Although she was extremely discreet about her relationship with Kevin, the news got around. Even the few friends she had among her fellow teachers talked about the 'notorious' Kevin Boyle. 'As word spread, there were some teachers who, when I passed them in the corridor, would look the other way.' The dangers were real. 'Protestant girls involved with Catholic boys could be tarred and feathered,' she noted, 'even killed.'

And for Boyle, as a prominent Catholic political figure, the romance also carried risks. 'To many people, it was very strange,' Hurst Hannum recalled:

> I can remember Kevin saying on more than one occasion that there was this feeling among die-hard Republicans – it wasn't suspicion in a political sense, but they just couldn't understand how he could end up with a Protestant. It was as simple as that. She's a Prod. How could you? I didn't know of any discrimination or dislike among Kevin's friends, but eyebrows were raised.

'It was a very dangerous time for Kevin,' Joan remembered. One night, when staying at his house at Marlborough Park, she remembered hearing the gate open and footsteps outside. Kevin went downstairs to investigate. 'The next thing I knew,' she recalled, 'the house was surrounded by police, and a big Land Rover with searchlights lit up the street.' At the time, Kevin tried to reassure her that it was nothing, just a false alarm. Year later he admitted to her that the police had found and taken away an explosive device. 'He had quite a lot of enemies,' she said. And the stress took its toll in other ways. 'I can remember Kevin having nightmares,' Joan said, 'calling out, "Don't shoot! Don't shoot!" in his sleep.'

Despite his nightmares and his frustration, Boyle continued to try to play a constructive role. In the spring of 1975 the British government, in an effort to generate political progress, organized an election to choose members of a 'constitutional convention'. The idea was that the Convention, a purely advisory body, would come up with fresh ideas for creating a local government representing both communities. But the results of the ballot gave a majority to hard-line loyalists opposed to power-sharing.

Maurice Hayes, a Boyle family friend who had previously headed the Northern Ireland Community Relations Commission and had employed Louis Boyle there, was now a civil servant assigned to work with the Convention. Kevin sent him a document about legal reform. It impressed Hayes so much that he passed it along to the Convention secretariat. Another official there circulated the document but, Hayes discovered, only after removing Boyle's name. 'The inference being,' Hayes recalled, 'that we don't want to be associated with these wild guys out in the wings.' A furious Hayes insisted that Boyle's name be put back, and that he be paid for the essay. However minor, the episode served to underscore the depth of Northern Ireland's divisions, which led to the collapse of the Convention in less than a year.

It was around the same time that Boyle decided that he had had enough. He applied for jobs at University College Cork and University College Dublin, as well as at the University of Warwick, where his early mentor, William Twining, had already moved for similar reasons. To one friend, Boyle wrote, 'the issue was not really one of promotion here but increasing depression about the North as a whole ... I would never consider abandoning [Northern Ireland] but for the general political atmosphere'.[15]

In early summer he was offered a position as a law lecturer in Cork. But four days later, Queen's, which had become aware of Boyle's frustration, finally promoted him to senior lecturer and gave him a pay raise. With some-what mixed feelings, Boyle decided to stay, noting to a friend, 'I still feel I have some contribution to make,' while acknowledging that 'it would not surprise me if at the end [of next year] I am looking for a job elsewhere again'.[16]

The following week, on 23 June 1975, the final hearing in the 'Donnelly case' got underway. It was held in Northern Ireland – the first time in many years that a European Commission hearing had taken place in the territory of an accused country. The proceedings were secret. Despite considerable press interest, few details were made public. As a reporter for *The Irish Times* noted, the government's 'Northern Ireland Office maintained its embar-rassed silence'.[17]

For the first two days, Boyle and Hannum accompanied the three commissioners, who came from Norway, Denmark and Germany, to the Maze prison, where Bradley, Duffy and McBride were all now detained. The Maze sat on a dreary, windswept plain nine miles south of Belfast. Within its corrugated iron walls and miles of barbed wire were hundreds of prisoners – the vast majority members of the IRA, but also its loyalist counterparts, the Ulster Defence Association and Ulster Volunteer Force.

The commissioners, who had diplomatic immunity, were treated respect-fully, but Boyle and Hannum had their bags searched and were frisked. Hannum was struck by the size of the prison, with republicans held in one part, and loyalists in another. As was the case for the four other applicants in Strasbourg the previous November, Bradley, Duffy and McBride recounted stories of beatings and harsh interrogations. Bradley repeated his descrip-tions of being beaten by soldiers as he lay in a corridor at the Broadway military post in Belfast after his arrest. Duffy had been the most seriously injured of all seven men, suffering a fractured left elbow at the hands of the security forces that required two operations to fix.

For his part, McBride told the Commissioners that he had responded to a question from police during his interrogation by saying 'I know nothing about it' only to be 'pulled to his feet by the hair by [a] police officer and slapped around the face, while another police officer prodded or punched him with outstretched fingers to the sides of the stomach'. As the beating continued, the police officers taunted McBride that they 'would make him remember about the explosions' in which they claimed he was involved. McBride testi-fied that he was crying while bleeding from punches to his face.[18]

With the testimony at the Maze over, the focus shifted to the government's witnesses. For security reasons, Britain insisted that the rest of the hearing be conducted at a military base in England. The British concern was understandable. Any member of the security forces identified as being complicit in the mistreatment of detainees would immediately become a target for IRA retaliation. But the British went to such extremes that they refused to allow higher-ranking members of the government or security forces to be questioned, and insisted that the faces of any police officers or soldiers who did testify not be revealed and that they be identified only by a number/letter combination – 1A, 2L, 3M and so on.

Boyle and Hannum were furious. Not knowing for sure whom they were questioning made cross-examination extremely difficult. Indeed, Hannum was so angry he wanted to boycott the proceedings. 'Were the British accusing us of planning to leak information to the IRA? I just thought they were really outrageous.'

The night before this part of the hearing began, Hannum and Boyle debated what to do, 'over a few whiskies, as we often did. And Kevin came up with what was by far the better idea.' Boyle proposed that each time the British introduced a new witness, he and Hannum would tell the commissioners that, under such unfair circumstances, they would not participate in any cross-examination. 'This, in effect, left it to the Commissioners to take over the role of cross-examiners, which they did very well.'

During the cross-examination, the witnesses' denials of any mistreatment were so sweeping that Boyle and Hannum became convinced that it was a deliberate cover-up. The refusal to acknowledge any abuse was certainly consistent with the British government's position, spelled out in a letter to the Commission after the November Strasbourg hearings, that it did 'not admit … the ill treatment as described'.[19] For instance, Major 1A, the officer in charge of the army post where Donnelly, Duffy and Bradley had been taken after their arrest, insisted that he 'received no reports that would have indicated that Mr Donnelly, Bradley and Duffy had been ill-treated'.[20] When a commissioner asked about Anthony Kelly's bloody face, witness 2L 'noticed nothing unusual about his appearance. Specifically, he did not notice a bruise below Kelly's right eye.'[21] In the case of Francis McBride, 'all the relevant police officers who had contact with McBride in police custody denied that they had assaulted him or witnessed any assault on him'.[22] At one point, the questioning descended into farce. 'One policeman was talking about one of the applicants [McBride] who had two black eyes,' Hannum recalled. 'The cop said he must have fallen into a door. Then one of the Commissioners asked how he got the other black eye. With a straight face, the cop said he must have fallen twice.'

Summing up after the hearing, Boyle and Hannum argued that 'despite the medical and other evidence of injuries to each of the seven applicants, not one of the Government witnesses admits to seeing or participating in any conduct which might explain these injuries'.[23] The account of the security forces was 'a concerted attempt to cover up the truth' and frustrate the Commission's inquiry.[24]

The next step was for each side to submit final written arguments. Here, the focus shifted again to the thorny question of domestic remedies. Later that summer Donnelly, Bradley and Duffy settled their civil suits by accepting payments of several thousand pounds each from the government. In November McBride also accepted a small payment, with no admission of liability from the authorities. The cases of the other three were still pending. The British claimed this proved that there was a system for effective redress of claims of abuse within Northern Ireland.

Boyle and Hannum, however, argued 'the vast majority of compensation awards in Northern Ireland are made not because of the machinery described by the Respondent Government, but in spite of such machinery through the extra-legal form of *ex gratia* payments to complainants. Liability is rarely, if ever, admitted by the Government.' Moreover, they noted, 'such settlements do not detract from the fear on the part of the claimants in Northern Ireland about the consequences of taking proceedings against the security forces'.[25] For the authorities, they claimed, the payments were simply the cost of doing business and continuing with a policy of mistreating suspects – in effect, paying for the right to torture. Indeed, they argued,

> the improbable evidence by Major 1A in the cases of Donnelly, Bradley, and Duffy that not a single person in Broadway military post made any report which reached him regarding the torture of the three applicants must be seen as further proof of the cover-up and toleration of ill treatment that pervades the security forces.[26]

On Monday 15 December, the European Commission threw out the case. In an 88-page ruling, it decided that not enough evidence had been presented to show that the domestic remedies available to the seven applicants were ineffective or inadequate. The ruling noted that three of the applicants had received payouts from the government, and four others had started legal proceedings against the army and police. 'The possibility of obtaining compensation in a civil action', the Commission wrote, 'constitutes in principle an adequate and effective remedy for the violations of Article 3 [of the European Convention on Human Rights – the prohibition of torture or degrading treatment or punishment] alleged by the applicants.'[27]

As a result, the Commission avoided having to deal with the details of mistreatment the seven men had suffered, other than to say

> the fact that ill treatment may be tolerated at the middle or lower levels of the chain of command, for example at the level of an officer in charge of a police station or military post, does not in the opinion of the Commission mean that the state concerned has failed to take the required steps to comply with its substantive obligations under Article 3 of the Convention.

As Hurst Hannum noted, 'they never did come to a finding on the merits'.

But the result was not entirely negative. For one thing, the Commission conceded that there had been a 'cover-up' by some police and soldiers and that vital evidence might have been deliberately suppressed by the security forces.[28] However, as Hannum observed, it was just that 'the cover-up was at the lower and middle levels of the security forces. They didn't find a cover-up at [the seat of the British government] at Westminster.'

In the following months Hannum and Boyle struggled to make sense of the Commission's decision. 'It is an extremely puzzling decision if you approach it logically,' Boyle wrote to Hannum, who had by now returned to the United States. To Boyle, it was 'an extraordinary proposition that your police can go on beating up people so long as you take reasonable steps … you just "do your best" and pay for casualties'.[29] The two men wrote a long and highly critical academic article analysing the case for the *American Journal of International Law*. Its title was 'One Step Forward and Two Steps Back'.[30]

Although the written judgment did not say so explicitly, Boyle and Hannum suspected that one key reason for the Commission's reluctance to formally condemn the British government was the result of an improvement on the ground in Northern Ireland since the case had first been brought. As Boyle wrote to a friend, the mere fact of the case led 'to a significant decline in the cases of brutality in interrogation'.[31] In a letter to Hannum, Boyle emphasized 'the point about taking into account post-1972 events in their decision. I agree with the point. I am satisfied that's what happened here.'[32]

Despite the legal setback, what became known as the 'Donnelly case' turned out to be a watershed. It was the first time the European Commission had ever acknowledged that there was a concept of an administrative practice that systematically abused human rights, and that individuals had the right to complain about it and ask Strasbourg to investigate. 'The admissibility decision essentially accepted our innovative arguments that a practice of continuing violations obviated the need to exhaust domestic remedies, thus leading to the subsequent fact-finding hearings,' Hannum noted. 'Ultimately, forty-one witnesses were heard, a remarkably high figure at the time, particularly in an individual case.'

As Michael O'Boyle observed, 'in terms of its jurisprudential impact, the notion of administrative practice has since been accepted and applied on a regular basis. There are situations that occur where even if there are theoretical remedies, the situation on the ground means they won't be applied. Donnelly was the first.' Today, as Brice Dickson, a Queen's University law professor who wrote a book on the European Convention on Human Rights and Northern Ireland, observed, the European Court would not be so quick to dismiss allegations of brutality simply because the victims had received compensation. 'The Court has recognized that if you let governments just pay off victims, that's a way of essentially avoiding condemnation by the Court,' he said:

> And the more general point about Donnelly was that it made lawyers in Northern Ireland realize you could use the European Convention in a way that would actually benefit people. Although Donnelly ultimately failed, it almost succeeded, so it kept the light alive and paved the way for other cases.

Indeed, in a matter of months Boyle had submitted a new case to Strasbourg – and this one would make history.

[10]

Civilized Standards Pay

THE SMALL college town of Amherst, Massachusetts, was a world away from the mean streets of Belfast. But in late August 1975, it was the setting for an unusual gathering. For nearly a week, many of the key figures in the Northern Ireland conflict met there for a series of presentations, workshops and informal conversations. The event was organized by a group of young, well-meaning Irish Americans from the Boston area who decided they had to do something to help end the violence in Northern Ireland. They invited dozens of people, including leading figures from the Official IRA, a break-away Republican group called the Irish Republican Socialist Party (IRSP), which had its own armed wing, the leaders of the extreme loyalist Ulster Defence Association, representatives of various political parties on both sides of the sectarian divide, and scholars, including Kevin Boyle, journalists, and clergymen. Only the Provisional IRA, whose representatives were denied visas by the US government, the loyalist UVF, and officials from the British government, who refused to attend, were absent.

The conference had many jarring moments. Men who would have likely killed one other if they met in Belfast joked, drank and debated in the bucolic hills of western Massachusetts. One afternoon the group was taken to a local fair in an exercise intended to help build personal relationships. Andy Tyrie, the burly, moustachioed chief of the UDA – a man known for having organized numerous bombings and murders – grabbed a toy rifle and jokingly pointed it at Seamus Costello, the equally ruthless head of the IRSP. Both men howled with laughter. Two years later, Costello would be shot dead on the streets of Dublin.

Boyle had few illusions that a conference like this would achieve anything. However, as a featured speaker, he used the occasion to pull together his thoughts about how the Troubles had evolved, and why – crucially, in his view – the legal system had failed to prevent the conflict from worsening, and why the abuse of repressive laws by the state was helping to fuel rather than contain the violence on both sides. His basic orientation, he said, was 'respect for the human rights of all, and that approach has dictated my involvement in active politics, practical law, and academic study of the conflict'.[1] He noted that the early goal of the civil rights campaign was 'to change the political environment through legal reforms', and that 'the creation of the proper legal channels for the redress of grievances' could have helped overcome divisions between Protestants and Catholics and spurred them to work together to battle poverty and deprivation.[2]

The lack of public confidence in Northern Ireland's legal system as a means to achieve justice, Boyle argued, had convinced the Catholic community, and, to a degree, the Protestants, that the 'law was a repressive force'.[3] The behaviour of the Northern Irish and British governments had simply reinforced this view. 'The abuses of power, from the constant complaints or torture and unjustified shootings by the security forces, to the regular screening of the young people of both communities,' he said, 'have served to feed the violence and to ensure that military power alone will not end it.'[4] Only political arrangements, which 'underpin the institutional structure of law … such that they can be endorsed and accepted by both communities, will act as a break on the violence from any side'.[5]

That prospect was nowhere in sight. Indeed, by the latter part of 1975 the IRA's short-lived ceasefire had ended, sectarian murders were increasing and political movement had come to a halt. Northern Ireland had entered, in the words of Ed Moloney, what was 'arguably the darkest period of the Troubles, nearly two years of slaughter in which the loyalists and the IRA vied with each other in an often indiscriminate sectarian killing game'.[6]

Against that grim backdrop, Boyle clung stubbornly to his belief that the law remained the best avenue for him to play a constructive role. Despite his teaching obligations, research and outside projects like the Donnelly case, he began to develop a thriving local legal practice. The cases he took were typical of that time, representing people from both communities accused of rioting, disorderly behaviour, possession of firearms and a variety of terrorist offences. In a letter to a colleague, sociologist Laurie Taylor of York University, written after defending a youngster charged with hijacking a vehicle at the age of fifteen, Boyle set out some thoughts about this legal work. As a defence lawyer, he said he got 'fairly close' to those he represented, who were generally 'young people 16–21, from both sides of the fence'.[7] Most of them, he felt, were just 'ordinary kids: they were not psychopaths ... their political thought is rarely developed ... In sum, these young people are not Che Guevaras but they are not hoodlums, the Mafia etc. as the official line goes. They are basically almost a random sample of the class, community, and age group they come from.'[8]

Many were tried before a single judge in the so-called Diplock Courts. These courts remained contentious. The judge acted both as judge and jury, and the critical evidence was often a confession from the defendant – which, given the history of abuse of prisoners by the security forces, was often legally unsound. For Boyle, the decision to participate in such proceedings, and thus acknowledge their legitimacy, was a controversial step. According to Hurst Hannum, it was a move that many in Boyle's circle viewed as 'politically suspect'. But it was yet another example of his pragmatism. Whatever crimes they were accused of, Boyle believed defendants were entitled to representation, and that was a service he could provide.

Somewhat more unusual was that, in some cases, Boyle worked with Desmond Boal. A loyalist hardliner, Boal was Ian Paisley's lawyer and had engaged in a sharp verbal duel with Boyle while questioning him during the Scarman Tribunal hearings on the roots of the 1969 violence. But Boal was recognized for his courtroom skills, and his politics did not prevent him from agreeing to represent Catholics – just as Boyle's politics did not stop him from representing Protestants. And on a personal level the two men got along well. The available documentation is limited, but Boyle's appointment diaries show that he worked with Boal on a case in early 1975 defending Francis Gallagher, a Catholic being tried before a Diplock Court on unspecified terrorist charges.

Later in the year, they worked together again, this time defending a Protestant taxi driver arrested when his taxi was found near Hightown Road, an isolated road on the outskirts of North Belfast that *The Irish Times* characterized as 'an established dumping ground for assassination victims'.[9] The defendant was charged with failing to assist the police, a crime technically called 'misprision'. At first, he insisted that he knew nothing, but later he changed his story to claim that someone had taken his vehicle – an inconsistency which made the police even more suspicious. However, Boyle and Boal argued that he couldn't be charged with misprision if he himself was a suspect, since he could hardly be expected to incriminate himself. It was a technicality, but the defendant got off.

Boyle played a key role in another controversial case, this one involving John Deery, a Catholic from Derry who had been detained and charged with two counts of the possession of firearms. Four months after Deery's arrest, and before his case came to trial, a new law was introduced that doubled the maximum sentence for such offences from five to ten years. In a climate where combating terrorism remained the government's top priority, when Deery was convicted the judge applied the new law and imposed a six-year jail term. At this point, Deery's solicitor asked Boyle to handle an appeal. Boyle argued not only that it was fundamentally unfair for someone to face a longer prison term than the law allowed at the time the offence was committed, he also maintained that it was a violation of two international conventions to which the United Kingdom subscribed: the UN International Convention on Civil and Political Rights, and the European Convention on Human Rights. In a fifteen-page ruling, Northern Ireland's Lord Chief Justice, Sir Robert Lowry, agreed with Boyle's reasoning, and cut Deery's sentence from six to three years. In addition, Lowry specifically thanked Boyle 'for his clear presentation and his thoughtful provision' of legal texts to back up his arguments.[10] Boyle was thrilled that a United Kingdom judge had referred to the European Convention in his ruling, writing to Seán MacBride that 'I believe this is the first occasion that it has been cited in this country!'[11] As a result of the decision, prisoners in more than a hundred other similar cases were allowed to appeal, and the ability of Northern Irish judges to impose harsher sentences than the law allowed at the time defendants were arrested was seriously curtailed.

Handling cases on a weekly basis prompted Boyle to think about practical ways to limit the damage from so many young people being arrested and jailed. In the same letter to Laurie Taylor, he wrote that

> how they are handled on arrest – and particularly the young – can be a factor in their overall approach to their situation … I mean – on arrest don't treat them as tough criminals – abuse them etc. They should not be thrown into prison while waiting on applications for bail: they should not be handcuffed by Tom, Dick, and Harry when brought periodically to remand courts. They should be separately dealt with at all times – and, sympathetically dealt with, they will respond, in my view – because in my opinion commitment to para-militants is not produced automatically from mixing with other 'political' prisoners, so much as determined by the attitudes to them of 'Officialdom' from the prison officer to the judge … Civilized standards pay.[12]

Despite the phasing out of internment, the treatment of prisoners – both Catholic and Protestant – remained a burning issue, and was frequently the subject of political debates and intense media coverage. Boyle's accessibility, comfort level with the press, dating back to his time as the spokesman for NICRA, and ability to explain complex legal matters in a straightforward way, made him an important resource to many journalists covering the Troubles. David McKittrick, a former Queen's student, who in 1973 joined *The Irish Times'* Belfast bureau – and later became one of the most distinguished journalists to chronicle the Troubles – regularly relied on Boyle: 'I found him a very useful guy. I would be in touch with him a fair amount because there were a lot of legal bits going on in Northern Ireland. Kevin was able to lead me through a lot of the intricacies.'

On one occasion, the Standing Advisory Committee on Human Rights, a largely toothless body set up by the British government in 1973, produced a report. McKittrick, who wrote a weekly column called 'Northern Notebook', decided to do a piece on it, and called Boyle. 'I remember asking him what to think.' Boyle, who in this case did not want to have his name used, was scathing. The column, entitled 'All That Effort – and So Little to Show for It', was largely a verbatim summary of their conversation.

Boyle also became an important resource for Peter Taylor, a young British reporter who in the mid-1970s began research for a book on the police and army abuse of detainees; he later became a prominent expert on terrorism. The book, *Beating the Terrorists,* provided a damning account of the ill treatment of suspects, most notably at the RUC's notorious Castlereagh interrogation centre in East Belfast. 'I owe Kevin an enormous amount,' Taylor recalled, 'because he was my mentor in those early years. And he opened my eyes to the way in which the British state was using the law to defeat "terrorism". As a result of talking to Kevin, my coverage of the conflict changed, and I began to question British security policy.'

Beating the Terrorists documented – with names, dates and chilling details – numerous instances in which detainees were beaten, burned with cigarettes, forced to assume painful positions for prolonged periods, were stripped and humiliated, and sometimes threatened with death. Taylor consulted regularly with Boyle as he did the research and writing. 'He helped me navigate through the legal and political jungle of emergency legislation, the European Convention on Human Rights, and the European Commission,' Taylor said.

> To have Kevin's imprimatur on the analysis and the detail of the cases was hugely … important. It gave me the confidence to write what at the time was a highly … controversial book, because it was about interrogation, it was about the abuses of interrogation, about inhuman and degrading treatment. His place in my reporting of the conflict was absolutely crucial.

Boyle's instinctive sympathy for the victims of repression extended beyond the immediate circumstances of the Troubles. One of the earliest causes in which he had been active, even before the civil rights movement, was gay rights. A chance encounter in Belfast in late 1974 would pave the way for Boyle to bring a landmark case that would decriminalize homosexuality in Northern Ireland, and lead to its legalization in other parts of the world as well.

Although the ban on homosexuality in the rest of the United Kingdom had been lifted in 1967 – a step Boyle had vocally supported – the extreme conservatism of Northern Ireland society, on both sides of the sectarian divide, prompted the British government to leave it in place in the North. Moreover, not only was gay male sex still against the law, it was punishable by life in prison. Although the law was infrequently enforced – the security forces had enough to cope with in the face of the pervasive violence – the territory's gay community lived in a climate of isolation and fear.

Nonetheless, a few activists were beginning to organize. One of them was Jeffrey Dudgeon, a 28-year-old shipping clerk who had been active in the civil rights movement. Conscious of his sexual orientation since he was fourteen, Dudgeon had in 1974 joined the Homosexual Law Reform Society, established in January of that year to press the British government to extend the 1967 law to Northern Ireland. Dudgeon was also involved in helping to found a gay counselling service called Cara/Friend – Cara being the Irish word for friend.

One afternoon, Dudgeon was walking home from work when he bumped into Boyle on College Gardens Street near the Queen's campus. The two had met when Dudgeon had briefly been a member of People's Democracy. As Boyle later told an interviewer, 'he knew I was interested in the Homosexual Law Reform Society'.[13] Indeed, after the passage of the 1967 law, Boyle had continued to publicly call for its application to Northern Ireland, even finding time in early 1969, shortly after the People's Democracy march to Derry, to co-author an article for a local magazine on the topic of 'The Case for Reform'.[14]

Dudgeon was aware that Boyle was in the midst of fighting the Donnelly case, which involved individuals petitioning the European Commission for redress of human rights abuses. As they talked, Boyle came up with another unconventional idea. 'We should take a case to Strasbourg,' he told Dudgeon, to challenge Northern Ireland's ban on homosexuality. 'Kevin said, "Look, you could win this case,"' Dudgeon remembered. '"It will only cost you a postage stamp to start it off. Why don't you do it?"'

It took almost a year before Dudgeon and his fellow gay activists decided to act on Boyle's suggestion. In late October 1975 Dudgeon wrote to Boyle to say that the Homosexual Law Reform Society, which had recently renamed itself the Northern Ireland Gay Rights Association, wanted to challenge the law in Strasbourg, and asked Kevin to handle the case. Dudgeon included with the letter a collection of documents to show that repeated efforts had already been made within Northern Ireland to redress 'this denial of human rights' – in other words, to exhaust domestic remedies – but had been 'met with a stony silence'.[15]

Boyle was delighted. The very next day he wrote back to accept the assignment, and noted that all the documents Dudgeon has sent had 'dispelled for me any few doubts that a case would be merely a debating proposal'.[16] Boyle immediately asked Francis Keenan to work with him, and consulted another former student who was also now a lawyer, Michael O'Boyle, on the best arguments to make. 'Kevin waltzed into my office,' O'Boyle recalled, 'and said:

> 'I've been approached by Dudgeon. Do you think this would pass muster under Strasbourg law?' I looked at some of the decisions and I said to him, 'Well,' you'd have to challenge it before the Northern Ireland courts.' I couldn't see that the Northern courts would do anything with it, because they'd be obliged to follow the statute. So I thought that the way was wide open for him to bring a case to Strasbourg.

Keenan was even more emphatic, noting that because Northern Ireland and the rest of the United Kingdom, unlike the Irish Republic, did not have a written constitution, 'We didn't have to go to the High Court and try to seek a declaratory order. We could go straight to Strasbourg.'

Soon after, Kevin sent Michael O'Boyle a three-page memo of what he described as 'random thoughts to help kick things off'.[17] The starting point, he wrote, would be to spell out all 'the relevant criminal offences in the law of Northern Ireland that do not apply to England'. Boyle then raised the possibility of claiming violations of at least seven of the fifty-nine articles in the European Convention on Human Rights. These ranged from Article 8, the right to privacy, to Articles 9 and 10, the right to freedom of thought, conscience, religion and expression, to Article 14, the prohibition of discrimination on the grounds of sex, race, colour, language, religion, political or other opinion, or national or social origin.[18]

One tricky question, Boyle noted, was whether Dudgeon could file a case if he himself had not been a direct victim of the law:

> Am I absolutely right in stating that it is unnecessary for Applicants to be a victim in the sense the legislation has not been used against them but nevertheless violates their rights? Clearly an individual is not a victim merely by virtue of existence in his country of legislation which appears to conflict with the Convention. He must be personally affected. Are the above restrictions in penal law of country evidence of being affected?[19]

As Boyle wrestled with these questions, the Northern Irish police provided the answer. On 21 January 1976 Dudgeon was making tea at his home on Dunluce Avenue in Belfast when the doorbell rang. Outside were six members of the Royal Ulster Constabulary. Two days earlier they had raided the home of one of Dudgeon's friends, Kevin Merrett. Merrett was involved with an eighteen-year-old man whose worried parents had called the police. Inside Merrett's home, the police discovered the list of the gay activists who had volunteered for the Cara/Friend counselling hotline, and, one by one, they started to go after them. Searching Dudgeon's flat, the RUC discovered a small amount of marijuana belonging to his house-mate, Richard Kennedy, which provided them with the excuse to describe the raid as a search for drugs, not the targeting of gays. But they also seized Dudgeon's diary, papers, and personal letters. He was arrested and taken to the RUC's Castlereagh interrogation centre, the place that journalist Peter Taylor, with Boyle's help, was about to expose as the site of repeated abuse of people detained as suspected terrorists. For four and half hours Dudgeon was questioned about his sexual behaviour and attitudes, with the police making what he described as 'humiliating remarks' about the material in his correspondence.[20] 'It did leave me feeling wretched and humbled by having my diary and letters read out to me,' Dudgeon recalled. 'However, we viewed it as par for the course in our lives to that date. There was a degree of pride and solidarity in holding out against the police and making things as difficult for them as possible.' Eventually, Dudgeon was asked to sign a statement about his 'homosexual activities' and told his file was being forwarded to the Director of Public Prosecutions with the intent of charging him with 'gross indecency between males'. 'I felt they would not win,' he said, 'but did not realize how relentless they and judicial authorities generally are to bring things to a successful conclusion once they embark on a course of action.'

Over the next five months, twenty other gay men in the North, all involved in the homosexual law reform movement, were detained and questioned. Dudgeon believed that the police viewed the activists as members of a conspiracy, 'because we weren't just arguing for law reform, we were indulging in criminal behaviour as well'. Boyle and Keenan were convinced that Dudgeon's arrest and possible prosecution significantly strengthened their case. 'He was clearly a victim within the meaning of Article 8 [of the European Convention on Human Rights], which is the right to respect for his private life and correspondence,' Keenan recalled, 'because the police had arrested him and interviewed him and prepared a case for the Department of Public Prosecution and warned him – we'll be keeping an eye on you.'

Boyle continued to craft the arguments for the case, which he and Keenan submitted to the European Commission of Human Rights in May 1976. In a series of handwritten notes, one can see the development of Boyle's thinking during this process. Boyle observed that not only was 'homosexual activity, whether in public or private, with or without consent', illegal, but that 'indeed, any demonstration of homosexual attitude [was] probably a criminal offence'.[21] In his musings, Boyle wrote that the 'source of these laws is of course Christianity – the church concept of sinful behaviour – impressed into law within British point of view … All this led in this century to debate between private and public morality – which continues to be debated.'[22] That led him to refer to the Wolfenden Commission. Set up by the British government in 1957, the Commission had recommended that homosexual behaviour between consenting adults in private should no longer be illegal. More broadly, it reframed the terms of the debate in Britain over whether and how the state should regulate public and private morality, although it would take another decade before Parliament voted to decriminalize homosexuality. Boyle noted to himself Wolfenden's conclusion that 'there was an area of private behaviour that was none of the government's business … which was reflected in the 60s in more liberal attitudes to homosexuality'.[23] Boyle also highlighted the fact that the law made homosexual behaviour between men illegal, but not between women: '[The] hypocrisy of the law [is] seen in [this] well-known fact. The fundamental principle, it seems to me, should not be based on questions of public or private, consenting or non-consenting – but equality of treatment by the law.'[24]

The application filed with the European Commission in May 1978 expanded on these themes. It started by documenting Dudgeon's suffering: 'His fear was directly caused by the existence of offences against homosexual behaviour in the criminal law. He had permanently suffered prejudice, including psychological distress, and fear of harassment, blackmail, prosecution and resultant exposure.'[25] Boyle submitted copies of letters, pamphlets and other material to show that Dudgeon had been involved with organizations seeking to reform the law in Northern Ireland. But not only had such efforts been unsuccessful, they had increased Dudgeon's risk of facing prosecution. The ban in the North, Boyle argued, 'made potentially criminal [any] advocacy of changes in homosexual laws. Explicit association in groups, clubs, or societies by homosexual persons could be indictable.

Counselling activities, befriending agencies and the like, so far as relating to homosexual persons, were of uncertain legal status.'[26]

Through what was described as the 'criminalization' of Dudgeon's status as a gay person, Boyle and Keenan argued that the right to respect for his private life guaranteed under Article 8 of the European Convention had been violated. The Convention did allow a state to limit this right, but only in the 'interests of national security', or 'for the protection of health or morals'. But, referring to the Wolfenden Commission, Boyle noted that public attitudes about homosexuality were changing. 'The evaluation of what restrictions were necessary could not be an absolute one for all time,' he noted. 'The Commission might take into account behaviour and changes in moral opinion.' To buttress their argument, Boyle and Keenan presented the Commission with a document spelling out all the recent changes in laws dealing with homosexuality in every country in Europe.[27]

The application also referred to the fact that homosexuality was treated differently in Northern Ireland from the rest of the United Kingdom, arguing that 'there was no objective and reasonable justification for the difference in treatment'. Moreover, under Northern Ireland's law, only male homosexuality was illegal. The law simply did not refer to women. 'If restriction on homosexual conduct were justifiable, there was no logical basis … for distinguishing between male and female homosexual conduct'. These differences, they contended, were violations of another article of the Convention, Article 14, which banned discrimination based on 'sex, race, colour, or religion, national or social origin, association with a national minority, property, birth or other status'.[28]

Boyle and Keenan were optimistic. 'We were extremely hopeful that it would be successful,' Keenan recalled. 'We informed Jeff that we thought it would be successful.' But such were the sensitivities that, in the initial application, it was decided not even to use Dudgeon's name. The title of the document was 'X against United Kingdom'. 'I did not want publicity,' Dudgeon remembered, 'but it became obvious that the value of the case and our ability to take advantage of the educational aspect that was so important was damaged by having no person to give it a human face.' Still, it was not until many months later that Dudgeon and Boyle felt comfortable referring to Dudgeon by name.

While Boyle waited to see what the Commission would do – a wait that, on the basis of the Donnelly case, could take months, or even years – the bloodshed in Northern Ireland continued. The day after Dudgeon's arrest in January, loyalist gunmen in Belfast had killed a Catholic in his home and a Protestant mistaken for a Catholic, while the IRA had killed two Protestant policemen and a Catholic they suspected of being a police informer. On the day that Boyle and Keenan submitted their application to Strasbourg, the IRA shot and killed an off-duty policeman. And in April 1976, the violence claimed the life of Eilis McDermott's brother Seán. Only twelve when Kevin and Eilis had helped to found People's Democracy, Seán had been shaped by the climate of violence in which he had grown to be a teenager. Like many young men living in Belfast's Catholic ghettos, he had joined the Provisional IRA, and been interned. An Irish journalist who knew him wrote, 'this boy was still in his teens, yet the fire that burned inside him was … terrifying'.[29] On a grey Monday afternoon, Seán and several other IRA men set off bombs in a hotel in the suburbs of Belfast. In the ensuing chase, police shot him dead. He was only twenty.

In late spring Kevin and Joan took a brief break from the tensions of Belfast and set out for a small seaside village in County Donegal. They were visiting Boyle's colleague Nicholas Ragg, who had worked with him on the rent and rates strike after the introduction of internment in 1971. En route, they pulled over to admire the scenery. As Joan recalled, 'Kevin began to wax lyrical, as was his wont. After talking for a while, he came to a conclusion. I remember being amazed at this complicated peroration.' Joan was also more than a little startled. Although he hadn't said so explicitly, Joan thought – but wasn't absolutely sure – that Kevin was asking her to marry him. 'It was a typical Kevin stream of consciousness. I wondered. Had that been a proposal of marriage?' The 'five-minute circumlocution', as Joan described it, was indeed that. She accepted, although they never announced a formal 'engagement'. 'It was not fashionable in the trendy 70s to do anything as traditional as that, in our circles anyway.'

Neither Kevin nor Joan wanted a traditional religious wedding. 'I had spent years breaking away,' Joan said. 'I was going down a non-religious path. I didn't want anything to do with the church.' Boyle too had moved away from the Catholicism in which he had been raised. But choosing an appropriate setting, balancing the concerns of their respective families, let alone finding someone who would conduct a ceremony for a couple from a Protestant and a Catholic background in the violent environment of Northern Ireland, was very difficult. And not only because of questions about what kind of ceremony it would be. 'When Kevin started thinking about getting married', Joan noted, 'it was a time when there would have been attempts on the lives of mixed marriages. Protestant girls [dating or married to Catholic men] had been tarred and feathered and tied to a lamp post.'

They decided to hold the wedding in London but had to struggle with the details of the ceremony, not least because the church required any Catholic marrying a non-Catholic to secure a dispensation. For advice, Boyle consulted an old friend, Herbert McCabe, a Dominican priest who lived in Oxford and worked at Blackfriars, the intellectual centre of the Dominican Order. McCabe was an unconventional figure. He was, as one newspaper put it, 'gregarious and with a fondness for drinking'[30] and was known to sing Irish nationalist songs at his local Oxford pub. A political radical who supported the 'liberation theology' that emerged in the Third World in the 1960s, McCabe was the editor of *New Blackfriars,* a magazine for Catholic intellectuals, although he had been suspended from the position for three years in the late 1960s after accusing the church bureaucracy of corruption. He suggested that Boyle contact another liberal priest, Father Alan Cheales, an Anglican who had converted to Catholicism, who was based at a parish in north London and had conducted mixed marriages.

Cheales, like McCabe, had left-wing political views, working with young people and the homeless, and supportive of Third World liberation movements. Kevin and Joan found him friendly and sympathetic, saying he would be happy to conduct the wedding in any church of Joan's choosing. For his part, Kevin decided that his father would be hurt if they simply got married in a local register office, so he agreed to a church venue. But Cheales told Kevin that in order to receive the dispensation, the church would require him to sign a form promising to 'endeavour' to bring up any children as Catholics. Kevin told Cheales he was uncomfortable with this. Cheales replied that a verbal commitment would be sufficient. Kevin's response was that this would be hypocritical. Putting the matter aside, Cheales looked at his calendar to find a suitable date. What about Thursday, 28 August?

Both Kevin and Joan wanted to keep the wedding simple, small and low-key. Joan wrote to all their siblings to tell them, but urged them not to spend any money on gifts. As the wedding day approached, they had still not received the dispensation, so Cheales told them to go to Westminster

House, the headquarters of the Catholic Church in London. As they walked into the building, with its dark wood panelling and red velvet curtains, Kevin worried that he would have no choice but to make the verbal promise. A young secretary came out, opened the letter of dispensation and said, 'I see you have not made the written promise.' Joan recalled that 'our stomachs churned'. But then the secretary continued, 'But I take it you've made the verbal promise, so please wait.' Kevin and Joan said nothing. A few minutes later, she returned, gave them a document in Latin, and said, 'Have a very happy day.' 'We went out feeling like naughty schoolchildren,' Joan recalled. 'We gave the document to Father Cheales. He didn't ask, and we said nothing.'

Kevin and Joan were married in the Ladies Chapel of St Dominic's Priory in north London. She wore a blue dress, he a brown checked suit. Only a dozen people attended, because neither Kevin's father nor Joan's mother, who was looking after her ailing father, could come. It was a low-key service. Father Cheales presided, and Dora Valayer, a French Presbyterian minister who had befriended the couple during an earlier visit to Belfast, also participated. As Kevin noted in a subsequent letter to his early Belfast mentor William Twining. 'It was exactly as I had compromised for ... It satisfied all tastes without the mass, incense, and usual undertakings ... The most instructive part of the entire affair was learning that if you are determined enough ... the apparent unbending rules of the Roman Catholic Church can be set aside.'[31]

The next day, the couple stopped for a night in Blackpool, where Kevin's parents had gone on their honeymoon. Having overcome the challenges, Boyle was thrilled. 'We are as a unit very good for each other,' he wrote to William Twining. 'I am madly in love.'[32]

[11]

Did We Really Live Through That?

ONE EVENING in late 1976, Boyle returned to his home in Belfast's leafy and relatively secure Marlborough Park after a long day in court dealing with a murder case. He was upset and distracted, wrestling with what he saw as a moral dilemma. His legal practice, by the standards of the time, was a lucrative one – a single appearance in court could generate a fee of £50 or more – but Boyle was wracked by guilt. 'He said he could never live with himself making money off the backs of young people who could have been influenced by something he said through a loudhailer during a civil rights march and taken the law into their own hands,' Joan Boyle recalled. 'He said the time was coming to make a decision. Was he going to stay as a barrister and make lots of money, or was he going to do academics, his first love? He decided the academic life was the one he wanted to pursue, but he would continue to be involved with cases at the European Commission and Court from time to time.'

It was an important turning point. As 1977 arrived, Boyle gradually began to scale back the number of cases he brought before the Northern

Irish courts. And his thoughts increasingly turned to the idea of leaving Northern Ireland.

Certainly, the political situation provided few reasons for optimism. As journalist Jack Holland wrote:

> By 1977, a pall of despair had settled on Ulster. The optimism of the civil rights days was spent. The centres of the two main cities, Belfast and Derry, were dead after dark. The Peace Line had become a wall fifteen feet high, dissecting West Belfast, a crude expression of the segregation that sectarian violence had imposed on the city. Heavily armed foot patrols of British soldiers edged their way slowly around the streets of the working-class housing estates, the constant whir of helicopters above them.[1]

As Kevin concentrated on his work, Joan started a bilingual secretarial course, held in a building across the street from the Europa Hotel in central Belfast. 'Every Friday afternoon,' she recalled, 'as I was doing the course, there would be a bomb scare. You would look out of the classroom and see a long corridor, and were not sure which way to run.'

The political front was equally depressing. Britain's new Northern Ireland secretary, Roy Mason, appointed in late 1976, had abandoned his predecessor's efforts to make political progress. His emphasis was on security, using the Diplock Courts to imprison those suspected of paramilitary activity, often on the basis of confessions obtained through harsh interrogations. At the same time, the British government decided that the 'special category' status granted to prisoners associated with paramilitary groups, a step taken in 1972 during ultimately unsuccessful attempts to negotiate a ceasefire with the IRA, should be ended.

Newly convicted prisoners, now held in cell compounds known, because of their shape, as the H-Blocks, would be treated like 'ordinary' criminals to undercut their claim to be freedom fighters rather than terrorists. In protest, republican prisoners refused to wear prison clothes, preferring to sit naked in their cells covered only by a blanket. Boyle, while unalterably opposed to the IRA's campaign of violence, believed 'it was not sufficient to say they were just ordinary criminals'. Rather, he saw young working-class men drawn into what he described as 'a kind of war' and facing legal problems that would not have existed without the Troubles.[2]

Moreover, persistent claims that suspects were being ill-treated by the security forces to obtain questionable convictions before the Diplock

Courts had become a source of growing controversy, prompting journalist Peter Taylor to put together a controversial television report in which Boyle played a key role. Taylor, whose book *Beating the Terrorists* would become the definitive account of the police abuse of detainees, produced a programme for London's ITV station called *Inhuman and Degrading Treatment*. It featured interviews with two ex-prisoners who alleged that they had been mistreated, the doctor who had examined them, and Kevin Boyle. In what Taylor recalled as 'pointed but measured criticisms', Boyle analysed the workings of the Diplock Courts and expressed concern that the Director of Public Prosecutions was unwilling to bring charges against members of the security forces accused of mistreating prisoners.[3]

The programme, as Peter Taylor wrote, 'raised a storm of protest, especially at Westminster. Politicians were outraged, not at the possibility the subjects were being ill-treated, but that a programme investigating the allegations had been made and transmitted.'[4] As the government denounced Taylor, however, Amnesty International, which had just won the 1977 Nobel Peace Prize, announced that it was sending a mission to Northern Ireland to investigate, and Amnesty's Secretary General, Martin Ennals, wrote to Boyle asking him to meet the Dutch lawyer, two Danish doctors and an Amnesty staff member who made up the delegation.

It was Boyle's first direct contact with Ennals, an Englishman who had taken charge of the organization in 1968 and would help turn it into one of the world's most powerful voices for human rights. It was also the start of a relationship with Amnesty that would lead to Boyle himself being asked in the 1980s to undertake a series of missions dealing not with Northern Ireland, but with Africa. Boyle met the delegation at his office in Belfast, sharing with them insights based both on his academic research and on his personal experiences of arguing before the Diplock Courts on behalf of defendants accused of terrorism.

When the report was published in 1978, Amnesty concluded that the 'mistreatment of suspected terrorists by the RUC has taken place with such frequency ... to warrant a public inquiry'.[5] The resulting public outcry forced a reluctant British government to appoint yet another commission, headed by Judge Harry Bennett, to investigate. Boyle was among the experts invited to make a submission. When the Bennett Report was published some months later, it acknowledged cases of mistreatment and issued a series of recommendation to prevent further abuses. After publication, as Taylor noted, 'complaints of assault during interview fell … and there was an important change in emphasis in favour of hard evidence over confessions'.[6]

Meanwhile, the slow-moving machinery of the European Commission of Human Rights continued to grind. In mid-December 1976 the Commission met to examine the admissibility of the application on behalf of Jeffrey Dudgeon that Boyle and Francis Keenan had submitted the previous May, and it decided to ask the British government for 'observations' on the case. In February 1977 British government lawyers submitted a thirteen-page document.

The British government simultaneously defended the existence of Northern Ireland's laws banning homosexuality while seeking to create the impression that the laws were so infrequently and lightly enforced that Dudgeon's complaints lacked validity, noting that 'the maximum penalties prescribed were not to be understood as likely'.[7] To reinforce this point, the British stated that London 'was considering the need for [new] legislation … in the area of homosexuality',[8] implying that the most objectionable elements of the existing laws might be reformed.

While acknowledging that the current laws 'could in principle constitute an interference with Dudgeon's private life within the meaning of Article 8'[9] of the European Convention on Human Rights – which guaranteed the right to respect for private and family life – the British argued that previous European Court decisions had left a 'margin of appreciation to the state'[10] in deciding whether homosexuality should be criminalized. In addition, the British argued that the government could choose to differentiate between the behaviour of males and females (since only homosexual activity between men was treated as a crime) 'for the protection of health and morals'. For these reasons, the British government urged the Commission to dismiss the Dudgeon case.

Two months later Boyle and Keenan submitted their own written response. While acknowledging the talk of possible changes in the law, they pointed out that 'no indication has been given of the reforms, if any, which are under consideration'.[11] They contended that the 'onus of proof' to justify restricting the private sexual life of male homosexuals was on the government, and that London's claim to be protecting the 'health and morals' of society was outdated and did not reflect 'advances in knowledge concerning the nature of homosexual activity and change in medical opinion'.[12]

Boyle and Keenan noted that 'the virtual unanimous expert medical opinion is of the view that homosexuality cannot be categorized as a disease or illness'.[13] Indeed, they pointed out that, even as the law in Northern Ireland banned homosexuality, the Northern Ireland government had given a £750 grant to the counselling service for gay people, which Dudgeon had helped to set up. 'It is inconsistent to maintain that restrictions are necessary in the criminal law on grounds of public morals while authorizing expenditure on services which encourage homosexual persons to associate with other homosexuals.'[14]

Boyle and Keenan also argued there was 'no logical basis' for distinguishing between male and female homosexual conduct, highlighting the introduction of provisions in UK law outlawing discrimination on the basis of sex.[15] Finally, they noted that the existence of a maximum penalty of life in prison for someone convicted of violating Northern Ireland's laws against homosexuality showed the 'lack of a reasonable relationship of proportion'[16] between the so-called offence and the sentence, further underscoring the inconsistencies at the heart of the government's position.

As Boyle and Keenan waited for the Commission to decide whether or not to admit the case, Ian Paisley launched what he called the 'Save Ulster from Sodomy' campaign. Promoted as a religious crusade and drawing support from Paisley's fundamentalist supporters, the campaign eventually collected 70,000 signatures backing a demand that the ban on homosexuality should remain in place. Dudgeon and his fellow gay rights activists were undeterred. Dudgeon's one-time room-mate Richard Kennedy set up a table 'bedecked by glitter and balloons' in Belfast city centre, next to one manned by Paisley supporters.[17]

For his part, Boyle was growing increasingly optimistic. In mid-1977 he wrote to David Norris, a gay Irish academic who had brought a court case in Dublin challenging the Irish Republic's own ban on homosexuality, which was as strict as that in Northern Ireland. Boyle urged Norris to consider to file his own case in Strasbourg if the proceedings in Dublin were unsuccessful, using the same arguments Boyle was making. Boyle offered to help in any way possible, noting that 'from sources at Strasbourg, I gather that the [Dudgeon] case is well regarded, which means it might get somewhere, and indeed the indication that the U.K. government has proposals to change the law in the North is to some degree influenced by the case.'[18] Indeed, the British government apparently had a similar evaluation of Dudgeon's prospects, and in the summer of 1977, hoping to avoid defeat in Strasbourg, it appealed to Dudgeon to drop the case 'because of the possibility of new legal proposals on homosexuality for Northern Ireland'.[19]

However, Dudgeon and other leading figures in the Northern Ireland Gay Rights Association decided to reject the British appeal, and Francis Keenan wrote to the Commission that

> the applicant thought that the language used by the Secretary of State [for Northern Ireland] referring to proposals for legislation on 19 July 1977 did not make clear precisely what was intended by way of government action [and] he is therefore anxious that the Commission undertakes examination of admissibility of his application as soon as possible.[20]

In late May 1977 Boyle received a letter out of the blue from Peter Glazebrook, a professor of law at Cambridge University whom he had met during his year in Cambridge. 'Dear Kevin,' it began, 'this letter is certainly impertinent.' Glazebrook went on to tell Boyle that he was helping University College Galway as it struggled to improve its law department. A decision had been made to establish a chair in law. Was Boyle interested?

Although he knew nothing about Galway, Boyle was intrigued. 'For some time, Kevin had been getting restless at Queen's, with its stuffy and conservative atmosphere,' Joan recalled. And despite his continued engagement with issues of human rights and civil liberties, he was increasingly dispirited by the gloomy situation in the North. 'The general misery of the Troubles, the constant bombs and murders on a daily basis,' Joan noted, 'would have got anybody down.' Boyle replied immediately to Glazebrook expressing interest in the position.

The Cambridge law professor responded with more details, noting that the university's newly appointed president, Colm Ó hEocha, was looking to build 'a law school which has a really fresh feel about it, free from the fustiness of existing law schools in the Republic. There is, I think, real scope and a real challenge for a young and energetic man.'[21] Glazebrook, who had been acting as an external examiner for the law departments of three other Irish universities – in Dublin, Cork, and Galway – was lobbying strongly with Ó hEocha for Boyle. 'Kevin was the ideal person for Galway,' he recalled many years later. 'He was young and vigorous, and already had an Ireland-wide reputation as a human rights campaigner.'

Soon after, Boyle was invited to Galway for an interview. Meeting Ó hEocha and others, he proposed the development of what he called a 'distinctive legal approach'[22] for the law faculty, taking into account his interest in social justice and human rights. He also suggested raising funds for a law library from Irish-American lawyers in the US, an idea that particularly appealed to Ó hEocha.[23]

What Boyle did not know was that the university's decision to recruit a chair in law was the result of deep internal turmoil. As the only major university in the west of Ireland, UCG had long been a resource-starved backwater. This was reflected in its law courses. When Boyle applied for the job, the university did not have a single full-time law professor. The handful of law students took courses from a few local lawyers who doubled as part-time professors, teaching in the evenings and on weekends. The dean of the law faculty wasn't even a lawyer, but a professor of French. Yet he was a full-time university employee, and had thus been given the law title as well.

The part-time teachers had become increasingly frustrated by the university's unwillingness to invest more resources in law. In a radical move, in the autumn of 1976, they had gone on strike. 'We had to do something about the ridiculous situation here,' recalled Leonard Silke, a local lawyer who gave tort law classes. 'There was no library. There were no Irish law books. There was a little handbook on criminal law. Nevertheless, the students we had were paying the equivalent fees of other students, but were not getting the equivalent return.'

The strike lasted into the 1977 spring term, and was settled only following the intervention of Margaret Heavey, a classics professor. 'Ma Heavey', as she was known, was a formidable figure. An elderly spinster who taught Latin and Greek, spoke mainly in Irish and used English reluctantly, she was widely respected on campus. In the winter of 1977 she invited the strikers to dinner with a small group of university officials, orchestrating a conversation that ended with promises that the university would advertise to hire full-time law professors. The decision was strongly supported by Glazebrook, who agreed that Galway's law students were 'getting a raw deal', and had been strongly urging President Ó hEocha to upgrade the law faculty.

Although a biochemist and oceanographer by training, Ó hEocha was deeply involved in the search, committed, in Glazebrook's words, 'to bringing Galway up to the standards of a proper university'. As Silke recalled:

Colm Ó hEocha was like a really good horse trainer. He could spot talent. He spotted Kevin as a young barrister and advocate. He was looking for an inspirational person, someone who would be the energy behind a new force – not just a faculty of law but a faculty of thinking about law. He recognized that what was needed was someone who could inspire young people to go out and work in the area of justice.

In Kevin Boyle, Ó hEocha had found his man.

There was just one catch. As the only university in the part of Ireland where the Irish language was still widely used, Galway had prioritized the hiring of professors who could teach in Irish, and applicants were required to pass a language test. Boyle had studied Irish in school, at one point becoming quite proficient, but it had been years since he had spoken the language, and, with his schoolboy Irish, he failed the test. So eager was Galway to hire him, however, that this was overlooked when the selection committee said no other candidate who could meet the Irish language requirement was available.

On a cold, bleak day in early January 1978, Kevin and Joan left Belfast for Galway in his battered Citroën. It was a bittersweet departure. 'We were very sorry to leave Belfast and so many friends,' Joan recalled, as well as an environment that, despite its troubles, had long been home. Moreover, many of Kevin's lawyer friends wondered what he was doing abandoning his high profile in the centre of the action for a backwater in the remote west of Ireland. But he had ambitions, and was determined to prove the sceptics wrong. 'We were up for the challenge,' said Joan. And there was another factor: Joan was now four months pregnant, and 'we were concerned about bringing up children in Belfast in the Troubles'.

Located 230 miles south-west of Belfast and 115 miles west of Dublin, Galway sits on the Corrib River, which flows into Galway Bay and the Atlantic Ocean. It had grown from a fishing village into the most important city in the west of Ireland, although in 1978 it remained a small and unspoiled place, lacking the political, economic and intellectual vibrancy of the Irish capital. As Kevin observed, the west was 'the area of Ireland to suffer most in the Famine, and from where most immigration occurred. It has also been until recently the most neglected part of the country.'[24] It was picturesque, quiet and safe, and was a place where Kevin and Joan could decompress and begin to lead relatively normal lives. 'It was only when we got out of Belfast,'

Joan recalled. 'That's when the hair stood up on the back of your neck. Did we really live through that?'

Despite Galway's overwhelmingly Catholic population, Kevin and Joan found their 'mixed' marriage was not an issue. The people they met were friendly and welcoming, and simply didn't care. When their son Mark was born five months after they arrived, Joan recalled, 'strangers came to my door with gifts. I will never forget it.' In the eastern part of the city, a short drive from the university, which Kevin described in a letter to an acquaintance as 'a most beautifully situated campus on the banks of the Corrib',[25] they bought a modest house on Wellpark Road. And, in what was for them a big investment, they also purchased a four-bedroom cottage on 1.6 acres of land in the village of Camus in Connemara, a place of rugged hills and unspoiled beaches. It was to become their favoured refuge from the pressures of daily life, especially following Mark's birth and the arrival of a second son, Stephen, two years later.

Boyle quickly plunged into building a law department and restructuring the teaching of law. 'If I try hard enough,' he wrote to a friend, 'I should be able to get a good law school off the ground in the West of Ireland.'[26] It was an immense challenge. He was the only full-time law professor. There was no law library, and resources were limited. 'He had to start from scratch,' said Jim Ward, then dean of the Galway business school who became a close friend. But Boyle had a clear vision of what he wanted to do.

In an introduction to the law school, which he drafted for prospective students, Boyle wrote 'law is not taught at UCG with the traditional purpose of preparing students for careers in legal practice as barristers and solicitors. The objective has been to broaden the scope of legal study and the range of career options which graduates who have read law may take up.'[27] A series of major innovations soon followed. One was the introduction of law as an undergraduate BA degree. This allowed students to study law in the same way as history, economics, or any other subject, without having to make the commitment to become a lawyer. In his introduction to the new undergraduate programme, Boyle wrote that the study of law could 'provide an excellent basic education for careers in a large number of fields in modern society'.[28] Writing to Seán Donlon, the Irish Ambassador to the US and an old friend, he said:

I wish to see an emphasis on mixed degrees involving law and languages, and law and the study of social and political administration. It seems to me there is evidence of over-production for the private profession and under-production of graduates who have legal training which would be of use in the public service.[29]

At the same time Boyle created a graduate programme offering an LLB (Bachelor of Law) degree, with the specific goal of attracting mature students in full-time jobs. Classes were held in the evening and on weekends. The programme offered all the courses required for someone who wanted to become a lawyer, but was designed so that 'people who wish to study law as part of their careers'[30] would also benefit. Marie McGonagle, a Northern Ireland native then living in Galway who had a day job with a book publisher and two small children, was one of those who took advantage of the weekend programme. 'His goal was not just to produce people who would become lawyers,' she recalled. 'For Kevin, law was a means to a better society.'

In addition, Galway would now offer an LLM or Master's degree in law, which was a research degree requiring the writing of a dissertation. In his introduction, Boyle encouraged research projects on 'early Irish law and institutions, criminology, public administration, constitutional law, international law, and business law'. And he also referred to his abiding passion, 'developing a special research programme in the area of Human Rights' with the goal of 'attracting students of high academic attainment for research in this field'.[31]

In his own teaching, apart from the usual technical legal subjects, Boyle specifically sought to connect with students just beginning to study law. 'He used to give inspiring lectures,' Leonard Silke recalled:

> He was introducing law to them. The students absolutely adored him. For example, he would give a lecture on bail or on the criminal and civil system. He was introducing youngsters to the whole idea of law, justice and human rights. The students could visualize right from wrong. How does a lawyer help address these problems? His approach was: how can you use the law to change people's lives?

Gerard Quinn, who was a second-year law student in 1978, felt that much of Boyle's teaching was shaped by the conflicting ideas swirling in his own mind. 'He was always coming in with problems he couldn't figure out by himself,' Quinn said. He believed Boyle's interactions with students, engaging in debates on such philosophical questions as whether it was possible to have meaningful rule of law in a sick society, and the relationship of the individual to power, were crucial to Kevin's own intellectual development. As Boyle listened to students, Quinn said, 'you really got the sense that he was having those debates in his own mind'.

Donncha O'Connell, who attended some of Boyle's lectures, and would later become dean of the Galway law faculty, observed that 'Kevin was a very good mentor. He was an enabler. That is a very good quality in a professor.' Indeed, as Mary Kelly, who did a law degree, then returned to Galway to teach in the 1980s, and became a close friend, remembered, 'if he saw you had any promise, he made opportunities for you'. Kelly was not the only student who would later become a colleague and be asked by Boyle to work on projects with him. Gerard Quinn, who in the 1980s would collaborate with Boyle on cases before the European Commission of Human Rights, and in the early 2000s on efforts to get the UN to endorse a treaty protecting the rights of the disabled, was another. 'If he found a student who was particularly enthusiastic about something he himself was interested in,' Quinn said, 'he would ask them to write a three- or four-page paper.' It was both a classroom assignment, and a tool for Boyle to help clarify his own thinking. 'As a teacher,' Quinn remembered, 'Boyle was different.'

The teaching, according to Silke, helped to further crystallize Boyle's most original idea – to create a human rights centre at the law school. It would be the first anywhere in Ireland. Boyle outlined the concept in a letter to Declan Costello, a judge at Ireland's High Court in Dublin:

> The thinking behind the notion includes my belief that there is a need for such a centre to encourage academic research and education on the subject of rights and responsibilities, both as regards Irish domestic law and the international plane … Ireland, North and South, has of course the problem of balancing rights and security considerations in the present emergency, which require continuing study.[32]

And Boyle was blunt about his other consideration. 'Such a centre would help put the faculty on the map.'[33] To his old friend Hurst Hannum he wrote, 'Why not? You must admit that however hare-brained some of the ideas – I do keep trying.'[34]

Hannum was not the only friend with whom Boyle brainstormed his unconventional ideas. He talked regularly with Michael O'Boyle, then based in Strasbourg at the Secretariat of the European Commission of Human Rights. In the university, he found a strong supporter in Michael D. Higgins, a Galway graduate who had taught sociology there since 1969. Higgins, who was also a member of Ireland's Labour Party and would, in 2011, be elected president of Ireland, was sympathetic to Boyle's views on the law. 'I do remember having these discussions that you could use law and legal measures as instruments for the achievement of significant social progress,' he recalled. 'I was very supportive of him setting up a centre. Having a significant figure with his background and engaging in contemporary and current issues was very important for Galway.'

Another key supporter was Mary Robinson, then a young lawyer and junior member of the Irish Senate, who, in 1990, would become the third Boyle friend – along with Higgins and his former student Mary McAleese – to be elected president of the country. Boyle enlisted Robinson, then already seen as a rising political star, to lobby the university's president about a Human Rights Centre. 'I certainly encouraged Kevin,' Robinson recalled. 'It was a very brave thing for him to do at a time when no such centres existed.' It was the start of a close friendship and professional collaboration that, more than two decades later, would lead to Boyle's appointment as Robinson's chief legal advisor when she served as UN High Commissioner for Human Rights.

Boyle was also strongly encouraged in this project by Seán MacBride, the Irish human rights activist who had first connected Boyle and Hannum. MacBride agreed to chair the fledging institute's advisory board, whose members included Hannum's old law professor Frank Newman and Dublin judge Declan Costello.

However, for all his ambitious plans, Boyle struggled with the university's chronic lack of resources. Soon after arriving, he was able to hire one more full-time professor, Dennis Driscoll, an Irish American from New Jersey with a background in international human rights law, and then a third member of the law faculty the following academic year. But money remained tight. 'The major problem will be funding,' he wrote to Hannum. 'I really think I need to identify one or two well-off Irish-American liberal lawyers who would be prepared to give money to such a centre.'[35]

Nonetheless, by 1980, the Irish Centre for the Study of Human Rights, with Boyle as director, assisted by his deputy Dennis Driscoll, was underway. It was the only such programme in Ireland.

[12]

David and Goliath

BY THE TIME Kevin Boyle moved to Galway, the number of cases submitted every year to the European Court of Human Rights and the European Commission – the latter the body that initially heard cases and decided which ones should be referred to the Court for adjudication – was still modest, in the low hundreds. Those cases declared admissible by the Commission were even fewer, just six in 1974 and four in 1975.[1] Indeed, of the 7313 cases submitted between 1955 and 1975, only 131 had been admitted, less than 2 per cent of the total.[2] Moreover, the cumbersome and time-consuming procedures involved discouraged many from trying to make use of these tribunals to seek a redress of their grievances.

However, both the European Court and Commission were gradually emerging from obscurity. The number of states that had ratified the European Convention on Human Rights, whose guarantees the Commission and Court were designed to protect, had nearly doubled. Slowly, the Court was beginning to be perceived as an embryonic supreme court of Europe, at least in the field of human rights, although it would take several more years before that position would be fully established.

The Donnelly case had made Kevin Boyle something of a pioneer in using Strasbourg to seek justice for those whose rights had been denied. Now, as he settled into his new job in Galway, he was waiting for a decision from the Commission about the application he had submitted in 1976 on behalf of Jeffrey Dudgeon. Although Boyle remained consistently hopeful, some of his friends and colleagues were far less confident. Among them was Michael O'Boyle, who had helped Boyle draft the initial application before leaving Belfast to join the Commission secretariat. 'I was not optimistic in the slightest because of previous cases,' he recalled. 'It would have been so easy for the Commission to reject, either because Dudgeon was not a victim and had not been formally charged with a crime, or that the state had wide latitude to regulate homosexuality as it saw fit.'

Yet on 3 March 1978 the Commission's fourteen members met in Strasbourg and declared Dudgeon's application to be admissible. In a seventeen-page report, the Commission acknowledged Boyle's contention that the ban in Northern Ireland on homosexual behaviour violated Dudgeon's right under Article 8 of the European Convention 'to respect for his private and family life'. Concluding that the case raised 'important issues concerning the interpretation and application of the Convention', the statement said Boyle's argument deserved an 'examination on its merits'.[3] After two years and numerous written submissions, this was an important step forward. 'It was a huge achievement to get it into the Commission,' Dudgeon recalled. 'Every step along the way was closer to victory.'

'What made the difference,' Michael O'Boyle observed years later, 'was that we were reaching an era where attitudes to the gay community were changing in many communities. Prohibition was no longer the norm in Europe. Since the proceedings of the Commission are a reflection of these laws, they must have found Northern Ireland's ban of homosexuality extremely strange.'

Indeed, the Commission's decision came as the British government, under pressure from Dudgeon's Northern Ireland Gay Rights Association, and well aware of developments in Strasbourg, was putting the final touches to a proposal to bring the territory's laws on homosexuality more into line with those in Britain. For the previous two years, the Northern Ireland Standing Committee on Human Rights had, at London's request, been studying the issue, and had strongly recommended reform. The idea was supported by many moderate political figures on both sides of the sectarian divide, and the Presbyterian Church had signalled a willingness to accept changes. The Catholic Church in the North, however, remained cautious, while the fundamentalist Reverend Ian Paisley and other Protestant hard-liners were adamantly opposed. For their part, Northern Ireland's twelve members of Parliament, fearful of antagonizing the province's most intran-sigent voices, had also said little in public.

Nonetheless, the proposals, announced in July 1978, generated headlines by calling for the law on homosexual behaviour in Northern Ireland to be changed from crimes punishable by life in prison into an activity that was legal between consenting males over the age of twenty-one. The proposal called for a three-month process of public consultation, yet it remained far from clear that the measure would eventually be enacted, given how intense opposition was from the most vocal critics. But it provided the context for Boyle's next step, a series of 'observations on the merits' of the case submitted to the European Commission in August.

In his submission, Boyle wrote that if the new law was passed, Dudgeon would drop his claim, under Article 14 of the European Convention, of discrimination on the basis of where he lived, since Northern Ireland's laws would now be the same as those in Britain. But Boyle wrote that Dudgeon would maintain the argument that he was the victim of discrimination on the basis of sex and sexual orientation, since restrictions, including a higher age of consent only for male homosexuals, would remain in place. The European Convention on Human Rights, he declared

> ought to require not simply more liberal laws in relation to the treatment of homosexuals, but since homosexuals are protected equally with others by the Convention, then the goal ought to be full equality. It is only when such equality exists that the unjustifiable prejudice against and fear of homosexuals will dissipate.[4]

Six months later, in March 1979, British government lawyer Audrey Glover submitted a response. The fourteen-page document began by noting that public opinion on the issue in Northern Ireland remained deeply divided, and stressed the scale and intensity of the campaign against reforming the law. Under these circumstances, she said, the government in London had not yet made up its mind about proceeding with the new legislation. Glover went on to argue that because Dudgeon had not actually been prosecuted, he could not claim that his right to privacy under Article 8 of the Convention had been violated, and that the mere existence of the ban on homosexual behaviour was not sufficient to sustain his case. Flatly declaring that 'the fact that the law on homosexuality in Northern Ireland is different than [*sic*] that in England does not amount to discrimination',[5] she argued that the government was entitled to a 'margin of appreciation' to decide on the most appropriate laws governing morality, especially in a society like Northern Ireland. And she maintained that the difference in the way the law dealt with male and female homosexuals was also reasonable, referring to a German study

> which showed that male homosexuals exhibit a tendency to proselytise other males, especially adolescents. The moral factors in Northern Ireland do not exist to anything like the same extent in relation to female homosexuality. For these reasons, the government submit that the differential treatment has an objective and reasonable justification.[6]

She concluded by dismissing Dudgeon's claim that he had been the victim of any violations of the European Convention.

The stage was now set for a dramatic showdown at a hearing in Strasbourg. It took place in July 1979, three years after Boyle's initial application. The day-long session was held in a small conference room at the Commission's headquarters in Strasbourg. Jeffrey Dudgeon remembered it as a 'sterile, airless room with very heavy furniture and dark wood walls'. Fourteen members of the Commission were seated around one end of a large oval table, while at the other end, on one side, dressed in crisply pressed pinstripe suits, was a high-powered team of British lawyers, 'the cream of the UK legal system' in Michael O'Boyle's words; as a junior Commission lawyer, he was observing the proceedings. On the other side sat Dudgeon, 'small and slight', as one spectator recalled, plus Keenan and Boyle, the latter wearing a faded sports jacket with patches on the elbows.

Among those observing the proceedings was Françoise Hampson, a young law professor who had just started teaching at the University of Dundee and was spending a few months as a Commission *stagiaire*, a form of glorified intern. A decade later, she and Boyle would become colleagues and close friends at the University of Essex, and in the 1990s they would return to Strasbourg as partners to argue dozens of controversial human rights cases. Now, however, observing from the interpreter's booth, what struck Hampson was the contrast between the two sides. 'You're looking at David and Goliath,' she recalled. 'It was the visual impact of just a couple of people against the state.'

The hearing got underway against the backdrop of a dramatic development. Just four days earlier the British government had announced that it was abandoning proposals to lift Northern Ireland's ban on homosexuality. The decision undercut London's claim that the lack of prosecutions and the possibility of reform made Dudgeon's application effectively irrelevant, and served to reinforce the power of Boyle's argument. 'By definition, the law interferes with his private life,' Boyle told the Commission, 'as it criminalizes behaviour he might indulge in. The degree of interference is a denial which makes consent or non-consent immaterial, and it is a denial that extends to acts or behaviour in private places.'[7] Boyle went on to note that 'this total prohibition is enforced by the most serious sanctions known to law, a sanction otherwise reserved for such acts as murder and rape'.[8]

Turning to the question of whether such a ban might ever be justified on the grounds of public morality, Boyle said it would require evidence both that the 'overwhelming majority' of citizens opposed removal of the laws, and proof that such a move 'would actually injure or damage seriously the moral standards, the moral sense, of that community'.[9] Using the government's own language from an earlier written submission, Boyle pointed out that the views of the majority of people in Northern Ireland were 'not known concerning the question of homosexual law reform'.[10] Moreover, he emphasized that even among some religious leaders who disapproved of homosexuality, 'there is a clear area of divorce between the moral and the criminal'.[11] Furthermore, he drew attention to a report from Northern Ireland's Standing Commission on Human Rights, which cited the province's assistant chief constable as acknowledging that in Britain, 'no particular problem had been encountered as the result of the passing of the 1967 Act' legalizing homosexuality between consenting males over twenty-one.[12]

'Calm, collected, very lawyerly, but with a good Irish turn of phrase,' as Michael O'Boyle remembered, Boyle also mocked the government's argument that the lack of prosecutions for homosexual offences in Northern Ireland undermined the strength of Dudgeon's case:

If the government takes the line that the total prohibition is necessary to protect the morality of Northern Irish society, it is surely contradictory and damaging to the morality of Northern Irish society not to prosecute, because if the law is not enforced, it cannot have any deterrent effect, and if it cannot have any deterrent effect, it cannot, as it were, protect the morality of society.[13]

Turning to the issue of the different legal standing of male and female homosexuals, Boyle ridiculed the British contention, articulated in Audrey Glover's written submission, that 'the moral factors present in Northern Ireland do not exist to anything like the same extent in relation to female homosexuality'. What did the government actually mean, he asked? Where were the studies of lesbianism in the North to back up this claim? 'No evidence has been produced.'[14] 'The truth,' he concluded, 'is that the laws that exist are irrational, anomalous, sexist, and incompatible with the Convention.'[15]

The lead British lawyer was Nicolas Bratza, the Oxford-educated son of a mother whose family had produced lawyers in Britain for three generations and a Serbian violinist father who settled in London after World War I. Bratza later became a vocal human rights advocate, as well as a close friend of Boyle, and in 2011 was elected president of the European Court of Human Rights.

In this case, however, he was defending a law that Boyle was arguing represented a flagrant violation of human rights. Bratza began by analysing the meaning of the word 'interference', as used in Article 8 of the European Convention in relation to the laws banning homosexuality. He insisted that it was necessary to 'examine not merely what the legislation provides in abstract terms, but the extent to which and the manner in which the authorities exercise their power to prevent the proscribed acts or punish those who have indulged in them.'[16] He repeated what had become a central feature of the government's position; namely that Dudgeon, despite his arrest in 1976, had never been prosecuted. More broadly, he stressed that since the state had not in recent years charged any males over twenty-one with violating the law, 'no interference ... with the right to respect for private life has been shown to exist'.[17]

At this point, one of the commissioners, German lawyer Jochen Frowein, a professor of international law, interrupted Bratza to challenge the logic of his argument. Was Bratza not neglecting a central reason for having a law

– to ensure that citizens knew what they were free and not free to do – by emphasizing only how the law was being applied, rather than what it deemed illegal?[18] Bratza replied by arguing that the 'unique situation' of Northern Ireland meant that 'the purpose of protecting the moral fabric of society may be achieved by maintaining a law such as the laws of 1885 on the statute books without in fact necessarily using the powers to prosecute in any given case.'[19]

Commission member James Fawcett, a British barrister and professor of international law, was unconvinced: 'If you concede that the existence of the statue has a purpose to protect the moral fabric of the country', he asked, 'if that is its purpose, how can it be said that it does not affect or influence private life? It seems to me very difficult to argue that a law is necessary if it is conceded that in a good deal of certain areas it is not used.'[20] On the defensive, Bratza answered by saying 'I accept that what appears on the statue book does have an effect on private life in the sense that it affects the way people think and it may indirectly, or even directly, have an effect on the way they behave. That I accept. I do not, however, accept that that would necessarily give rise to an interference with the right to respect to private life for the purpose of Article 8(1) of the Convention.'[21]

Bratza continued his argument by denying that legal restrictions on male homosexuals were 'founded on irrational prejudices against one sexual minority', pointing out that 'until very recently' laws against homosexual behaviour had been on the books in many European countries.[22] He also returned to the theme that every government deserved a 'margin of appreciation in determining the context of the social and moral requirements of their society', and that it was not the rule of the European Convention to impose 'uniform moral standards' on all the member states.[23] James Fawcett interjected again: 'But is that not exactly what the fourth paragraph of the preamble of the Convention is saying? Surely this is the purpose of the Convention, and it cannot be said that the Convention, if it is used to achieve this purpose, is somehow defeating what is a kind of national sovereignty.'[24]

Dodging the question, Bratza turned to the issue of public opinion in Northern Ireland. He noted that opinion in the North had always been much more conservative than in the rest of the United Kingdom, which, in his view, both explained and justified the difference in laws. He also asserted that many in Northern Ireland believed the legalization of homosexuality in Britain in 1967 had 'led to a decline in moral and social standards which has had a strong and damaging impact'.[25] Justifying the law's different treatment of male and female homosexuals, he repeated the claim made previously by Audrey Glover that male homosexuals tended to proselytize, while females did not. Moreover, he said that in other European countries, even if the difference was not written in law, prosecutions for homosexual activity were almost exclusively directed at men. For all these reasons, he called on the Commission to dismiss the application.

Boyle then took the floor again, and immediately attacked Bratza's argument that, although Dudgeon may have been affected by the law, that did not mean his right to privacy had been interfered with. To the hushed room, Boyle read out the full text of Article 8 of the European Convention on Human Rights. 'Everyone has the right to respect for his private and family life, his home, and his correspondence. There shall be no interference by a public authority with the exercise of this right.'[26] Boyle paused, and, for emphasis, repeated, 'no interference with the exercise of this right'. He went on to stress that 'prosecution is only one aspect of interference. The law which justifies that prosecution is in itself, because of the provisions, interference. If one takes the view that there must be prosecution before there is interference, then one is in the position of arguing that it is only those who are caught, as it were,' who faced interference with their private lives.[27] In any case, Boyle reminded the commissioners, even if Dudgeon had not been not formally charged, Dudgeon had been arrested, questioned and threatened by the police because of his homosexuality.

Boyle contended that the apparent policy of non-prosecution, which Bratza had cited, might well in itself violate British law:

> It is a principle common to all the democratic states in western Europe that the Government of the day cannot dispense with the enforcement of the law. If, for example, the chief of police was to give an instruction that no burglaries in a certain town were to be prosecuted, that was clearly unlawful and would be challenged.[28]

As for the 'margin of appreciation', he argued, 'the notion that a total prohibition of all homosexual life for persons in Northern Ireland ... goes far beyond any previous illustration of the application of the margin of appreciation doctrine'.[29] With the British government's decision not to proceed with legislative reform, he said, one is condemning a minority of anything between seventy and a hundred thousand persons who are homosexual to the prospects of no change and the prospects of no rights, and that is the circumstance under the Convention which the applicant would submit and invite the Commission to hold is unacceptable and intolerable.[30]

As the hearing came to an end, Michael O'Boyle, who had watched the proceedings with other members of the Commission secretariat, turned to his colleagues. 'We all thought that Kevin had done a brilliant job,' he recalled. 'I was proud of his performance.' Keenan remembered feeling 'extremely hopeful that the case would now be successful'. Jeffrey Dudgeon was equally upbeat. 'Kevin argued a very clear case,' he recalled. 'I felt it was just a question of when.'

The answer came nine months later. On 13 March 1980, the Commission, by a vote of nine to one, declared 'that the legal prohibition of private consensual homosexual acts involving persons aged over twenty-one years of age breaches the applicant's right to respect for private life under Art. 8 of the Convention'.[31] In a 43-page report, the Commission gave a powerful endorsement to the case that Boyle had presented.

The report said that Dudgeon could legitimately claim to be a victim of the law, even though he had not been prosecuted, noting that 'in the circumstances the Commission sees no reason to doubt the general truth of his allegations concerning the fear and distress he has suffered'.[32] It concluded that the United Kingdom government had not proved any need to maintain such a draconian law to protect public morality: 'The available evidence does not suggest that to allow private acts between consenting adults would have any very significant impact.'[33] There was 'no pressing social need' in Northern Ireland that required maintaining the ban. Yet the Commission dismissed Boyle and Keenan's argument that, owing to the difference in treatment between homosexuals in Northern Ireland and Britain, Dudgeon had been the victim of discrimination under Article 14 of the Convention. Having found a violation of a specific article of the Convention – in this case the right to privacy protected by Article 8 – the Commission said it was 'unnecessary to examine whether the restriction in question also had a discriminatory character'.[34]

Nonetheless, it was a major triumph, especially since the Commission referred the case to the European Court of Human Rights for final adjudication. In those days very few cases made it to the Court. Even though there would be a hearing and other proceedings, having got this far, the outcome appeared to be a foregone conclusion. Dudgeon, Boyle and Keenan seemed on the cusp of a historic victory.

During the course of the case, periodic differences over how to approach the case had emerged between Boyle and Keenan on the one hand, and Dudgeon and the activists of the Northern Ireland Gay Rights Association on the other. NIGRA itself was split between those holding moderate views and some with more extreme positions. 'There was a rather radical band of people who wanted more,' Dudgeon recalled. 'Could we go further? Could we get a bit more out of it? And that was where I was coming under pressure – let's try for more.' Some of the NIGRA activists had been frustrated that Boyle had not given even more emphasis to Dudgeon's claims of discrimination under Article 14, the claim the Commission had eventually rejected. 'We were being political,' Dudgeon said, 'and Kevin was being legal. As a lawyer, he was perfectly right. He thought he could win, he did his best to win, and he won on Article 8.' Still, the resentment, and the desire to use the case as a broader platform for the gay rights agenda, remained. And when the case was referred to the European Court of Human Rights, the radicals made their move.

In early July 1980 Boyle and Keenan both received formal typed letters on NIGRA stationery signed by Jeffrey Dudgeon. With the case going to the Court, the letter stated that the NIGRA executive had decided 'to deal directly with the Commission and thus no longer work through lawyers'.[35] Boyle and Keenan were, in effect, fired. The reason appeared to be explicitly political. 'In this way, we can offer to the Commission advice and consultants on both the broader issue of gay reform – aside from the law itself – the new sociology on, of, and by gay people, as well as the specifically localised aspects of politics, the police, religion, etc., where we are the obvious and accepted experts.'[36]

Boyle and Keenan were stunned. 'Kevin was devastated,' Joan Boyle recalled. 'He was very, very hurt. He was near tears.' To Francis Keenan, 'it was unpardonable'. Ironically, NIGRA's decision was based on a misunderstanding of how proceedings worked before the European Court. When a case was referred there by the Commission, the Commission in effect became the representative of the applicants before the Court, although in practice, the Commission allowed the applicants' lawyers to appear as well. Dudgeon and his fellow NIGRA activists, however, appeared to believe that they could act on their own behalf at Court proceedings, and thus no longer needed legal representation. They wanted the limelight for themselves. As the months passed, however, Dudgeon discovered that the Commission was not responding to his letters, and it was made clear that he would need to have his own lawyer to remain directly involved. Having burned their bridges with Boyle and Keenan, this led to NIGRA hiring Lord Tony Gifford, a left-wing London lawyer known for supporting radical causes, to represent them.

It was nine months before Boyle could bring himself to write to Dudgeon, finally prompted to do so by news of Gifford's hiring. 'I am personally deeply hurt,' he wrote, 'when, after five years' involvement in a case that one has suggested oneself, to find that at the very last stage, another barrister is being briefed.'[37] Boyle's bitterness was palpable:

> Following your letter of 1 July 1980, I was naive enough to imagine that our relationship and your personal regard for my involvement in this matter would have at least led to a personal letter explaining why the decision had been taken to remove Francis and myself from the case. If the reasons included your view that the case was too narrowly argued, I wish to say that in my professional judgement it was the proper way to proceed, and I still hold to that view.[38]

Boyle told Dudgeon that NIGRA's notion that it no longer needed legal representation was hollow, and he predicted that Lord Gifford would make the same kind of arguments before the Court that Boyle had done before the Commission.

And that is in effect what happened. On 22 October 1981 the European Court of Human Rights issued a historic judgment. Acknowledging that its decision was based on the report of the Commission, shaped primarily by the arguments Boyle and Keenan had made, the Court declared that 'the very existence of this legislation continuously and directly affects his private life'[39] in violation of Article 8 of the European Convention. As Boyle had emphasized to the Commission, the Court noted the dramatic change in public attitudes and legal opinion in Europe regarding homosexuality:

> There is now a better understanding, and, in consequence, an increased tolerance, of homosexual behaviour ... it is now no longer considered to be

necessary or appropriate to treat homosexual practices of the kind now in question as in themselves a matter to which sanctions of the criminal law should be applied; the Court cannot overlook the marked changes which have occurred in this regard in the domestic law of the member states.[40]

The Dudgeon case was a milestone and had a sweeping impact. The law in Northern Ireland was soon changed. The case became the basis for the eventual legalization of homosexuality in the Irish Republic, after David Norris, to whom Boyle had written about Dudgeon in 1977, won his own case in Strasbourg in 1988 using essentially the same arguments. The Dudgeon judgment led as well to the decriminalization of homosexuality in Cyprus, and was a factor in the decision by several former Soviet bloc nations to repeal their anti-sodomy laws when it joined the Council of Europe in the 1990s.[41] And, in a landmark 2003 decision by the US Supreme Court, which struck down an anti-sodomy law in Texas, Dudgeon was cited by Justice Kennedy, who wrote the majority opinion. It was the first time a decision of the European Court had ever been cited by the highest American court.

Decades later Dudgeon acknowledged that 'Kevin was totally instrumental in it happening, which is why I always felt guilty he was denied the pleasure of being a winner. The guilt thing was very strong in me, and in a lot of others.'

The two men never spoke again.

[13]

It Was a Long Shot

EVEN AS he fought the Dudgeon case, Boyle was drawn into what would become arguably the most controversial issue in Northern Ireland during the late 1970s and early '80s – the battle over the treatment of IRA prisoners, which would lead to the hunger strikes of 1980 and 1981 that would become a turning point in the tortured history of the Troubles.

The British government's decision in 1976 to phase out 'special category' status for paramilitary prisoners and treat them like ordinary criminals had generated strong resistance from inside the H-Blocks at the Maze prison. Rejecting the government's characterization, jailed IRA men refused to wear prison uniforms – choosing instead to remain naked except for a blanket – or to engage in prison work. It was the start of what became known as the 'blanket protest'. By 1978 some 300 men were involved, and the dissent mutated into the 'dirty protest', with IRA prisoners refusing to clean out their cells and smearing the walls with their excrement. In response, the prison authorities took away almost all the 'privileges' to which detainees were normally entitled. They were not permitted to exercise or associate with other prisoners, were deprived of reading or writing materials, denied access to radio, TV, the library and the canteen, banned from receiving food parcels and allowed only one letter and one visit per month.

It was a bitter test of wills, waged out of public view in cold and filthy cells between prisoners who saw themselves as fighters for Irish freedom, and a government determined not to give in to what it saw as a bunch of terrorists – a sentiment reinforced as the IRA began to systematically target prison officers for assassination, killing eight by the end of 1978. However, as word of the appalling conditions spread, especially after Ireland's Cardinal Tomás Ó Fiaich visited the Maze and expressed shock and revulsion at what he saw there, public support in Northern Ireland's Catholic community for the prisoners, and, by extension, for the Provisionals, began to increase, heightened by London's refusal to compromise.

In Belfast, Francis Keenan, who, although no friend of the IRA, had represented some republican prisoners and regularly visited the Maze, watched developments with growing alarm. 'I saw on the ground that every week, more and more people were supporting the Provos,' he recalled. 'The H-Block protests were only aiding and abetting the Provisionals' campaign.' Unless something was done, Keenan worried, that trend would accelerate. 'I knew we had to make an intervention – to do something in a non-violent manner.' In a series of conversations with Boyle, Keenan proposed bringing a case on behalf of the prisoners to Strasbourg, in the hope that the European Commission might lay out guidelines for handling prison protests that both sides could accept. 'The ultimate prize was that we could settle the case and effectively solve the issue before the Provos became the winners,' said Keenan.

Boyle, who had a long record of supporting non-violent methods to tackle injustice in the North while simultaneously trying to undermine public sympathy for the IRA, was enthusiastic. He asked Keenan to go to the Maze and start collecting statements from prisoners, while Boyle began to work out how to craft the arguments to be presented in Strasbourg. In a letter to Hurst Hannum, Boyle wrote,

> we are doing a fairly major job, Francis and I, in raising a whole series of questions about the administration of the prison ... Neither of us are [sic] especially interested in special category status or its restoration, but simply in the argument that there are minimum standards, within which the state must respond to prisoners who are protesting.[1]

Over the course of nearly thirty visits to the Maze during the spring and early summer of 1978, Keenan identified four prisoners for the case, and took down hundreds of pages of testimony. Kieran Nugent had been convicted of car hijacking in 1976, and was the first man to protest by refusing to wear a prison uniform; Thomas McFeeley was sentenced in 1977 to twenty-six years for assault with a firearm and robbery; John Hunter was jailed for five years in 1977 on explosives charges; and William Campbell was serving a twelve-year sentence for possession of firearms. As participants in the protest, all had faced a variety of sanctions and punishments at the hands of the prison authorities.

Boyle and Keenan filed a lengthy application with the European Commission of Human Rights in late August 1978. They spelled out conditions in the Maze in graphic detail, and made an unconventional legal argument – that the authorities were withholding as 'privileges' things that were, in fact, fundamental rights. They asserted that the policies of the prison contradicted minimum standards for prison discipline and punishment laid down by the Council of Europe in 1973, and were in violation of the European Convention on Human Rights. Indeed, the application accused the government of violating nine articles of the Convention. These included Article 3, which banned 'degrading and inhuman treatment or punishment', with the applicants claiming 'that the official response to their actions has been excessive and wholly disproportionate to their refusal to wear prison uniforms'.[2]

Boyle and Keenan's submission specifically cited the imposition of what was called the 'No. 1 diet' – three days in which the protesting prisoner was given only soup, bread and black tea – and the use of 'Rule 24', which allowed the authorities to put prisoners into solitary confinement for no stated reason.[3] The document also claimed that there had been violations of Article 8 – the right to privacy – because the prisoners, owing to their refusal to wear prison uniforms to go to the normal toilet facilities, were required to use the chamber pots in their cell in full view of other inmates and prison guards.

More broadly, the applicants claimed that the right to freedom of conscience and belief under Article 9 had been violated because the authorities were requiring them to wear a prison uniform and work, 'despite their deeply held beliefs'.[4] They also alleged violations of Article 10 – the right to freedom of expression – because they were being limited to receiving and sending one letter a month, asserting as well that these limitations violated their right to correspondence guaranteed under Article 8. Violations of five other articles were also claimed, including Article 13, the right to an effective domestic remedy for their grievances.

Boyle and Keenan were well aware that they were unlikely to prevail on all their arguments, that the case was a long shot, and was extremely politically sensitive. 'It is going to be messy and drawn out,'5 Boyle wrote to Hannum. The key question, Keenan told an Irish radio reporter, was how far the authorities should go. 'How do you punish dissident prisoners? Do you use corporal punishment? If that fails, do you use the rack and thumbscrews? There must be some minimum code for prisoners who disobey.'6

If Strasbourg could force the British government to spell out in clear legal terms its responses to the complaints, the two men calculated, perhaps the basis of a compromise might emerge. The authorities, however, were not happy when the case was filed, and even less so when it crossed a major procedural hurdle in October 1978, as the Commission asked the British government for a written response to the application. An official in the Northern Ireland Office wrote a memo saying that if the government lost the case, the prisoners 'would become prisoners of war – or political prisoners. Obviously, therefore, the granting of any of these claims is out of the question. But should the regime be modified without in any way making a concession on these claims?'7 Indeed, while both sides waited for the Commission to decide its next step, the government was already changing at least some of the most objectionable procedures. That same month, the prison authorities quietly abandoned the use of the 'No. 1 diet'.

From his sources in Strasbourg, Boyle learned that the Commission was debating whether to admit the case, but had deferred a decision because of internal divisions over what was described to him as 'one of the most difficult cases they have to consider'.8 He wrote to Hannum that

the political overtones, not surprisingly, are very obvious. Should they admit it, the reasoning goes, it will be 'victory' in the propaganda war for the Provos. We point out that if they reject it, equally it will be 'victory' for the government ... my hope had been that the Commission could have acted as an intermediary, and induce some movement in a situation that remains intractable ... but we shall see.9

With Dudgeon still awaiting a final resolution at Strasbourg, Boyle was now juggling two controversial cases before the European Commission, along with his regular teaching duties in Galway, his efforts to get the Human Rights Centre up and running, and his continuing scholarly research. The central focus of his own research was the study, undertaken with Tom Hadden and Paddy Hillyard, of 'the legal control of political violence' in Northern Ireland, which would lead to the publication of *Ten Years On*, a follow-up to their important 1975 study, *Law and State*.

The new study contained numerous practical suggestions to the government, the British army, the police and the courts for more effective and humane policies to deal with the Troubles. A section on prisons spelled out the underlying thinking behind Boyle's approach to the Thomas McFeeley case: 'There are strong pragmatic grounds for seeking to avoid the kind of adverse publicity and propaganda which has resulted from the attempt to force those who see themselves as different from ordinary criminals to accept the status of ordinary criminals.'[10] Boyle and his colleagues argued that there was 'no criminological evidence to support the now traditional view that prisoners benefit from being required to submit to strict prison discipline and to work'.[11] Instead, they urged that 'those who refuse to wear prison clothes or to work should be permitted to do so'[12] and that the government should adopt such a policy for all prisoners, 'showing that the state is prepared to respect deeply held convictions without in any way restricting its right to punish and to detain in custody those who commit serious criminal offences'.[13]

By the spring of 1980 the protest in the H-Blocks had been going on for four years, while beyond the prison walls the violence continued unabated. The previous summer had been particularly bloody. The worst moment came in August 1979, when the IRA assassinated Queen Elizabeth's uncle, Lord Mountbatten, his fourteen-year-old grandson and two others who were on holiday with them in the Irish Republic. On the same day, eighteen British soldiers were killed in a single attack in Warrenpoint, County Down, the seaside town close to the border where Boyle used to go swimming every summer as a child. It was the single most successful attack the IRA would stage during the Troubles.

To their immense relief, Kevin, Joan and their two boys, now safely ensconced in Galway, no longer had to suffer the daily stress of living in

Belfast. But Boyle remained deeply engaged with Northern Irish issues, and not simply through his legal caseload and academic work. In a practice that was to become something of a trademark, Boyle, a consummate networker, was sending a steady flow of letters to influential figures on both sides of the border, offering analysis, advice and practical suggestions. He maintained a regular correspondence with Robert Lowry, the chief justice of Northern Ireland, with other judges and lawyers in Belfast and Dublin, and with leading journalists and political figures. In the wake of the Warrenpoint and Mountbatten killings, for example, he wrote to a senior official at Ireland's Department of Foreign Affairs, urging that Dublin and London set up a joint judicial inquiry into security on the border. 'I would envisage the Commission's writ as including scrutiny of the legal and technical features of cooperative law enforcement on the border,'[14] he wrote. Always pragmatic, he noted that such a Commission would reassure public opinion on both sides, and reduce the danger of rumours and misrepresentation. There is no evidence to suggest the Irish government ever acted on Boyle's proposal, while Britain's new prime minister, Margaret Thatcher, who had taken office in May 1979, was deeply shaken by the attacks and committed to an uncompromising battle with the IRA.

Thatcher's attitude was reflected in the government's continuing refusal to give in to the demands for political status by the prisoners on the 'dirty protest'. In May 1980 Boyle and Keenan's hope that their case in Strasbourg might provide an opening to resolve the situation was dashed. The European Commission rejected the application made on behalf of Thomas McFeeley and the three other republican prisoners. The Commission concluded that there was no 'right to a special status for political prisoners'[15] under Article 9 of the European Convention (the right to freedom of conscience and belief) and dismissed almost all the other arguments in the application, in particular the contention that the prisoners had been 'forced' to go naked or remain in their cells under appalling conditions.

These circumstances, it said, were 'self-imposed'[16] and not the responsibility of the British government. 'If they had to slop out naked or covered only in a blanket or towel', the statement said, 'it was because of their persistent refusal to wear prison clothes.'[17] On two elements of Boyle and Keenan's case, however, the Commission chose to 'adjourn', or defer making a decision, on admissibility. These were the claims of violations to the prisoners' right to correspondence guaranteed under Article 8 of the Convention, because of limitations on the number of letters they could send and receive, and to their right under Article 13 to effective domestic remedies for their complaints.

At the same time, the Commission was critical of what it described as 'the inflexible approach of the state authorities which has been concerned more to punish offenders against prison discipline than explore ways of resolving such a serious deadlock'.[18] It explicitly urged the government to allow the prisoners not to wear prison clothing while exercising, and while consulting outside medical specialists.[19] As Queen's University law professor Brice Dickson observed in his book on Northern Ireland and the European Convention, 'this was a very rare example of a European Convention organ "daring" to give direct advice to a State as to how best to resolve a difficult domestic issue and its utterance is an indication of how seriously the Commission considered the stalemate in the prison to be'.[20] Indeed, in the immediate aftermath of the Commission's decision, the government did institute some modest changes to the prison regime.[21] But it was not enough to satisfy the protesting prisoners. Within a matter of months they decided to resort to the ultimate step – a hunger strike to force the authorities to give in to their demands.

As a weapon of last resort, the hunger strike had a hallowed place in the history of Irish Republicanism, dating back to the struggle against the British in the early decades of the twentieth century. On 27 October 1980 seven prisoners at the Maze, including Thomas McFeeley, began refusing food, vowing to starve themselves to death unless the British government agreed to grant them the right to wear their own clothes, to refrain from prison work, to communicate freely with other prisoners, to receive one letter, parcel and visit per week, and have lost remission time restored. Watching from Strasbourg, Michael O'Boyle, now on the secretariat of the European Commission, observed: 'We all knew with our knowledge of Irish history that a hunger strike is really bad news in terms of fanning the flames of extremism and recruiting young people into the IRA.'

But the strike lasted only fifty-three days. As one striker approached death, it came to a confusing end. The protestors were convinced that the government was prepared to make concessions – even as the British were indicating otherwise. Francis Keenan, who had been visiting Thomas McFeeley every week, gave the news to Michael O'Boyle in a 2 am phone call, saying that McFeeley had been persuaded to give up the protest. But the prisoners came to feel that they had been duped, setting the stage for a second hunger strike, with far deadlier and more politically consequential results.

As the prisoners made plans, the continuing violence moved closer to Boyle. Ronnie Bunting had been a student at Queen's, a member of People's Democracy, and had participated in the march from Belfast to Derry in January 1969. Later on, however, he helped establish a breakaway republican paramilitary group. In the autumn of 1980 he was murdered by loyalist gunmen in front of his wife at his home in Belfast.

Then, in January 1981, Bernadette Devlin McAliskey and her husband Michael were both shot by three masked members of the loyalist Ulster Defence Association who burst into their home as they were preparing their children for school. Although badly wounded, both miraculously survived. As his old PD comrade Michael Farrell, then a teacher at Belfast's College of Technology, wrote to Boyle, 'things are distinctly grim here at the moment'. Regarding the first hunger strike, Farrell said that what the protestors saw as a 'British trick/concession has only aggravated the situation and greatly embittered the prisoners. There is a lot of tension.'[22] Indeed, Farrell was informed by the police that after Devlin, he was next on the loyalist hit list. Farrell hurriedly left Belfast and moved to Dublin.

It was against this backdrop that a second hunger strike began on 1 March 1980. Unlike the previous one, this time the protestors planned to go in stages, with a new prisoner joining the strike every fifteen days to create sustained pressure on the government. The first man to refuse food was Bobby Sands, the 27-year-old commander of the IRA prisoners at the Maze. Just days after Sands began his hunger strike, a Nationalist member of the Westminster Parliament from the rural Fermanagh–South Tyrone constituency died suddenly of a heart attack. The leaders of the IRA's political wing, Sinn Féin, pushed for Sands to be nominated as a candidate for the seat, both as a propaganda move and also in the hope that his election would increase the pressure on Margaret Thatcher to compromise.

On 9 April, the fortieth day of his hunger strike. Bobby Sands was elected to the British House of Commons. Meanwhile, in Dublin, the government of Charles Haughey was growing increasingly anxious, not only about the welfare of the protestors, but about the growing political clout of

Sinn Féin and its impact on the politics of the Irish Republic. Desperate to find a solution, Haughey appealed to the European Commission on Human Rights to get involved, but the Commission said it could do so only if one of the hunger strikers or their representative filed a case in Strasbourg. On 23 April, after meeting Haughey, Sands' sister Marcella agreed to do so, appealing to the Commission to send a delegation to Northern Ireland to meet her dying brother. Michael O'Boyle convinced the president of the Commission, James Fawcett, 'that this was the right thing to do if we could bring the hunger strike to an end, because it spelt disaster for political developments in Northern Ireland'. The ostensible reason for the Commission's visit was to confirm Sands' intention to proceed with the case, but the possibility now existed that the Commission might find a way to play a mediating role to end the crisis.

Two days later, two members of the Commission, a Dane, Carl Äage Nørgaard, and Torkel Opsahl, a Norwegian, visited the Maze prison. They were accompanied by Michael O'Boyle and the secretary of the Commission, Hans Kruger. But Sands abruptly told his lawyer Pat Finucane that he was not prepared to go ahead with the case, and said he would meet the commissioners only if Gerry Adams and other leaders of Provisional Sinn Féin attended as well. 'The IRA were trying to transform the visit into a full-blown negotiation about "special category" status,' O'Boyle recalled.

The commissioners made clear they were not in a position to act as mediators, especially in the absence of a case. The initiative collapsed. On 5 May, Bobby Sands died. His death triggered widespread rioting in Northern Ireland, and tens of thousands of people attended his funeral. As spring turned to summer, more hunger strikers died, but Margaret Thatcher was unyielding. Political status for the prisoners was out of the question. 'Mr Sands was a convicted criminal,' she declared after his death. 'He chose to take his own life. It was a choice his organization did not allow to many of its victims.'[23]

Kevin Boyle watched the hunger crisis with growing dismay. 'He was very upset,' Joan Boyle recalled. Sympathetic to the predicament of the prisoners, and disgusted by what he and many others saw as Thatcher's intransigence, Boyle was deeply concerned that her behaviour was going to drive more people into the arms of the Provisionals.

Almost lost amid the worsening crisis was the fact that in mid-May, less than a month after the collapse of the Sands case, the European Commission had reconvened and decided that the two remaining elements of the original McFeeley application – the complaints of violations of Articles 8 and 13 of the European Convention – were admissible. The Commission informed the British government that it was welcome to submit whatever proposals it wished as part of a process known as a 'friendly settlement', in which the Commission would offer its services to both sides in the hope the two parties could resolve the issue. The Commission also proposed what were in effect 'proximity talks', inviting the government to send representatives for an informal meeting, while asking Boyle and Keenan to travel to Strasbourg as well. 'A move for a friendly settlement would be a form of pressure on both sides,' Keenan recalled. 'It would especially put pressure on the British government to be more reasonable.'

Thatcher remained adamant that she was not interested in using the Commission as a channel to negotiate with the IRA, and had no new proposals to offer,[24] but she did agree to respond to the Commission's invitation to send representatives to Strasbourg. She wasn't alone, however, in her scepticism. Although Keenan remains uncertain about the precise date, he recalled being summoned with Boyle to a meeting with the Provisionals' leader, Gerry Adams, under somewhat melodramatic circumstances. The two men had been driving to the Maze prison to see Thomas McFeeley when a car raced up and signalled for them to pull over. The driver was Pat Finucane, the lawyer who had represented Bobby Sands and was now advising the Provisional Sinn Féin leadership. 'He told us we were not to go to the Maze,' Keenan said, 'and that Mr Adams wanted to see us.' Sitting in their car by the side of the road, Keenan and Boyle discussed what they should do. Keenan felt strongly they should ignore Adams. 'If we gave in at that stage,' he remembered telling Boyle, 'we were effectively saying to our clients that we were not acting totally on your behalf. We are acting on your behalf only insofar as Adams permits us to do so.'

'Look, Adams is in control of the situation,' Boyle responded, 'and you have to talk to him. We have to go in and make our point here.'

Keenan eventually reluctantly agreed, and the two men turned around and drove to Sinn Féin's heavily fortified headquarters on the Falls Road in Belfast. Adams, accompanied by an aide, was civil but dismissive. According to Keenan, 'he said we were more or less giving false hopes to the prisoners' that the Commission could actually do anything. 'The clear impression given by Adams was that we were very good boys but that we were out of our depth and totally naive.' The meeting was inconclusive, and the two men came away with the impression that Adams wasn't seriously interested in a settlement.[25] As they left, Boyle turned to Keenan and said, 'You're right. We should just ignore Adams.' For Boyle, it was an unsettling experience to meet with someone who, in his view, had 'endorsed killing. I didn't find it easy to talk to him,' he told an interviewer years later.[26]

With no end in sight to the hunger strike and a mounting death toll both in prison and on the streets, Boyle and Keenan travelled to Strasbourg to explore whether the McFeeley case offered any hope of breaking the deadlock. On 3 June Michael O'Boyle and Hans Kruger of the Commission secretariat held separate talks with Boyle and Keenan on the one hand, and a group of British officials and legal experts on the other. In deference to British sensitivities, the Commission officials made clear that these were not negotiations on a friendly settlement, but rather exploratory discussions – talks about talks – on the possibility of the Commission's involvement.

The British position, however, remained unyielding. They were not prepared to negotiate with the IRA, and viewed proposals the applicants had submitted for improving prison conditions, relayed by Boyle and Keenan, as a smokescreen for the prisoners' real demand, to be recognized as political prisoners. For his part, Boyle maintained that the prisoners were not fixated on the term 'political status', but on the need for changes in their treatment. He also said the prisoners wanted the Commission to be involved in the implementation of any agreement that was reached. In response, the British representatives said London was continuing to review improving conditions for all prisoners, irrespective of the hunger strikes. One idea that was raised was for a 'cooling-off period' to ease the pressure on both sides. Boyle and Keenan responded that they did not believe the prisoners would accept such a move in the absence of a broader agreement. The day ended with no accord.

Soon after an election in the Irish Republic led to a change of government, with Garret FitzGerald, widely seen as a more moderate and less polarizing figure that the abrasive Haughey, becoming taoiseach in early July. Like his predecessor, FitzGerald was anxious to find a way to end the hunger strike before the Provisionals reaped even more political benefits. Soon after the new taoiseach took office, Boyle and Keenan arranged a private meeting to brief him on the McFeeley case. With the two elements of the original application still under consideration, they told FitzGerald that it might yet be possible for the Commission to play a constructive role. As efforts by numerous other parties – the International Committee of the Red Cross, a Catholic lay organization called the Irish Commission for Justice and Peace, a representative of the Vatican, leading Irish-American political figures, and a secret negotiating channel between the British and the IRA – came to nothing over the course of the summer, the two men, with FitzGerald's support, tried to keep this one alive. Indeed, so eager was the taoiseach for progress with the Commission that at one point he kept a government plane on standby at Shannon airport, a short drive from Galway and Boyle's summer cottage in Connemara, in case Boyle and Keenan had to fly to Strasbourg at short notice.

'The H-Block affair and its ever-increasing seriousness has preoccupied us here,' Boyle wrote to an American friend in late July. 'The telephone traffic and the preoccupations of this last two weeks seems [sic] anomalous in the atmosphere of Connemara. You will understand I cannot say much to you now except that we still have hopes our "vehicle" may ultimately deliver a solution.'[27] In the meantime, in Strasbourg, Michael O'Boyle was working what was dubbed a 'blueprint' – a new set of specifics that could be discussed if the 'friendly settlement' mechanism were activated. As O'Boyle recalled, the blueprint was 'a document setting out how the remaining McFeeley complaints could be used as a springboard for settling the wider issues at the root of the claim for "special category" status – the requirement to wear prison garb and work and, and the right to correspond with the outside world. It could have provided an elegant way of climbing down without losing face.'

In late August Boyle wrote to FitzGerald:

> The position remains that the Commission has prepared a 'Blueprint' document for resolution of the crisis which it would send to the UK and ourselves as McFeeley's representatives, if the parties were interested. We are, but the UK has indicated it is not. While not being privy to the contents of the Blueprint, I am convinced from discussions with Strasbourg it could be the vehicle for final resolution, particularly on the enforcement side. At the same time, it would be sensitive to the need to resolve the dispute within the principles laid down by the UK government.[28]

In early September a second meeting was finally arranged. Boyle and Keenan returned to Strasbourg, along with a team of British officials and legal advisors. But, as Michael O'Boyle recalled, at the last minute the British had been given instructions 'not to engage with the Commission or Kevin or Francis'. Boyle and Keenan were told the British officials were actually in a nearby room at Commission headquarters, but it fell to O'Boyle to break the news to the two men that 'the process was aborted and no meeting would take place. They were very upset; I suppose because of what the future had in store.' The reason for the abrupt turnaround was Margaret Thatcher, who had had an eleventh-hour change of heart and, in O'Boyle's words, 'pulled the plug'. It was hardly a surprise. Thatcher had been wary of being drawn into such a process for months. 'She obviously wanted to make it absolutely clear that the time for ambiguity was over and that there would be no discussions in whatever form,' O'Boyle noted. As Boyle told a reporter: 'What is wrong is the British Prime Minister is simply not prepared to move the little distance necessary to settle it.'[29] To O'Boyle, a Belfast native, 'an important historical opportunity was missed to stop the hunger strikes in their tracks. It was a great pity.'

By now, though, the hunger strike was running out of steam. One after another, the families of the protestors intervened by asking the authorities to revive the strikers as they slipped into unconsciousness. In October, the hunger strike was called off. On the face of it, it appeared Mrs Thatcher had won. In fact, however, the entire episode produced a wave of new recruits to the IRA, and set the stage for Provisional Sinn Féin to emerge as a formidable political force in both halves on Ireland. It was precisely the outcome that Boyle, Keenan and O'Boyle had feared, predicted, and, with their ultimately unsuccessful efforts in Strasbourg, tried to prevent.

'I always realized it was a long shot,' O'Boyle acknowledged years later, 'but it was one worth trying.'

[14]

Professor Aer Lingus

AS THE CHAOTIC, bloody, and frustrating year of 1981 drew to a close, Boyle wrote a long letter to Sir Robert Lowry, the chief justice of Northern Ireland, who had become a good friend. In it, he tried to spell out the complicated political and moral balancing act with which he was struggling as he assessed his role in the Troubles:

> I will confess it is not easy to maintain the position I have tried to hold to over the years, which is a civil libertarian focus that broadly doesn't take sides between republican and unionist perspectives. I say broadly because the position we (Tom Hadden, Paddy Hillyard and myself) have adopted is that Northern Ireland, whatever its problems, is a legitimate entity, and that the Provisional violence is illegitimate because of that fact. In other words, it is not the practical argument against violence ('how can you shift the one million Protestants') on which we base our position, but the moral argument based on the right of the Northern Ireland majority community to insist on deciding upon and maintaining its national identity. Having said that, I must tell you that as a Roman Catholic married to a Presbyterian, my personal position is that all discussion on Northern Ireland should begin on the premise that each community has a very good case to make for its position. Where you go from there is of course the problem.[1]

Despite the lack of space for conventional politics and the fact that he no longer lived in Northern Ireland, Boyle remained deeply engaged in efforts to bridge the province's political and sectarian divide. In early 1982 he flew to Boston to participate in a symposium with academics, politicians, community workers and journalists, as well as some American experts. The conference, organized by a group of Irish Americans, was held at the John F. Kennedy Center. It featured John Hume, Boyle's old friend from civil rights days, now the leader of the moderate and largely Catholic SDLP, Harold McCusker, a prominent Unionist politician, and Edgar Graham, a young Queen's University law lecturer who had studied law when Boyle was still teaching there in the 1970s and was considered to be a rising star in the Unionist Party.

Despite their political differences, Boyle and Graham were exploring the possibility of working together on some law-related projects, and they shared the stage for a panel on 'Law and Justice'. Here, Boyle argued that the law would be a crucial instrument in any settlement since it was the way to guarantee the rights of all citizens of Northern Ireland, but he warned that abuse of the legal system, in the way people were detained, interrogated and tried, was contributing to the ongoing crisis.

One of those attending the symposium was Orlando Delogu, a professor at the University of Maine law school. Delogu, a founder of the Maine Civil Liberties Union and an expert on environmental law, had become friendly with Boyle when the two men initiated a partnership between their respective law schools the previous year. For Delogu, new to the complexities of Northern Ireland, the formal presentations at the symposium were much less interesting than the informal conversations afterwards.

'The real meetings began in a hotel room around 8.30 pm and went on until 2 am,' he recalled. 'These people were all at loggerheads in Northern Ireland, and now they were on a first-name basis and talking to each other until the wee hours, with the talk getting more robust as the bottles of Bushmills whiskey were drained.' Delogu was struck by Boyle's description of the process. 'Kevin called it bridge-building,' he said, adding, 'Kevin said to me "They've got to get to know one another. They are decent people, but they are just so trapped in their backgrounds. They have to understand there must be a settlement because it can't go on like this."'

Underscoring the consequences of the continuing deadlock, just days before the Boston symposium, Kevin's friend Sir Robert Lowry narrowly escaped an IRA assassination attempt in Belfast. And the year after the symposium, Boyle's fellow panellist Edgar Graham would be murdered by two Provisional IRA gunmen on the Queen's University campus. The killing of a close academic colleague shook Boyle profoundly. 'He was horrified, deeply shocked, and sad,' Joan Boyle recalled.

The Troubles could suck someone in, becoming an all-consuming preoccupation, and Boyle maintained an intense and deeply personal involvement. Yet he had a seemingly inexhaustible supply of energy, and Northern Ireland remained just one of a number of his steadily expanding commitments. Indeed, his students nicknamed him 'Professor Aer Lingus' because he always seemed to be heading to nearby Shannon airport to fly to conferences and meetings. The juggling, however, was more difficult than Boyle generally let on. In a letter to Delogu, he confided, 'life is too busy, Orlando. It is only when I have time to write to you that I remind myself that life can be fun too. But I still am hopeful that it will not be too long to go when I can get some of this load off myself.'[2]

The demands on his time, however, only increased, with the building of the university's law school and human rights centre a top priority, under-pinned by his vision of training students to use law as a way of making a better world. In the autumn of 1981 Boyle spelled out the vision in a talk to the Irish Society at Cambridge University. One of those present was Conor Gearty, a law student from Ireland. Gearty remembered Boyle as 'impossibly glamorous – sort of like George Clooney, with a beautiful voice and this very strong perspective rooted with great intelligence in human rights'. Boyle's presentation, as Gearty wrote years later,

> dazzled, enthused and intellectually intimidated all those present. Here seemed to be a new way to do law: get on top of all the stuff, the cases, the statutory provisions, the complex scholarship – all the ramparts with which law protects itself from external scrutiny – and then deploy them not to mystify and stifle the people but rather to empower and therefore to enrich them.[3]

For Gearty, it was the inspiration to pursue what would become his own distinguished career in human rights law.

The foundation of Boyle's approach was teaching. Given his tiny faculty and limited resources, Boyle initiated an exchange programme with the

University of Maine's School of Law. Orlando Delogu – warm, ebullient, always dressed in blue jeans and red braces and with an impressive handlebar moustache – spent a term in Galway, cementing what would become a lifelong friendship. As the head of the law programme and a prominent public figure, Boyle often found himself in a lonely place, unable to share his concerns with those working for him or with whom he was politically involved. 'You make decisions and take the blame if things don't work out,' Joan Boyle recalled. 'With Orlando in the early days, Kevin could talk openly about his hopes and disappointments. He could voice frustrations where he could not be as open with the few colleagues he himself had appointed.'

Other colleagues from Maine followed Delogu, with members of Galway's law faculty making return visits, while a student exchange programme got underway as well. Boyle also managed to lure law professors from the University of Georgia, the University of Detroit and the University of South Carolina on visiting lectureships, in addition to bringing back such old colleagues as Hurst Hannum for shorter teaching stints. Hannum was asked to conduct a three-week seminar on humanitarian law, as well as the question of criminal process and human rights. The courses were popular, and the student number grew steadily. The fledgling Irish Centre for the Study of Human Rights was beginning to make a mark. An inaugural conference – on using the European Convention on Human Rights – was held in early 1982. Boyle brought in a series of speakers and slowly began to assemble a law library, acquiring material from the United Nations, the Council of Europe, the International Court of Justice and elsewhere. It was a small collection – lists of pleadings, the texts of judgments and reports – but it was a start. The Centre was also awarded a contract by the Council of Europe for a planned Human Rights Documentation Centre to help keep the Council abreast of human rights issues in Ireland. Its major significance, Boyle wrote to a friend, 'is recognition for the Galway effort, and a modest sum of money we can put towards the library'.[4] Boyle himself was increasingly emerging as one of Ireland's most visible public intellectuals, appearing regularly in the media, sought-after as a speaker and gradually beginning to put his department and the Institute on the map. For all the pressure, life in Galway was good. Joan and Kevin would later look back on that period as the 'magical years'. They found the university community to be stimulating and diverse, with a lively mix of nationalities – Irish, British, American,

Finnish, South African – while the locals were exceptionally warm and welcoming. They became part of a group of people, mostly in their thirties, all fairly new to the university and raising young families. Kevin was sociable, constantly inviting people home for dinner. Boyle's colleague Leonard Silke remembered that 'they would use their house to invite people who would be interesting. It was very great fun, stimulating and uplifting. Kevin and Joan were extraordinarily good hosts.' Boyle's ambitions for the law department and human rights centre, however, were frustrated by one major obstacle – a chronic lack of resources. Located in Ireland's hinterland, the university remained a backwater, acutely short of almost everything. For example, he was able to pay Hannum only $1000. To another American colleague he was wooing, Boyle apologetically wrote, 'We offer very modest remuneration', although he noted that a visiting scholar would have a 'chance to be abroad for a period and get to know another legal system'.⁵ In handwritten notes, Boyle vented his frustration. Although he had given the university a plan when he took the job in 1978, he wrote, 'there has been a virtual total failure to follow through on the resources to implement it. The faculty is a victim of its own success. There is a high demand … students higher … students demanding more. The staff cannot cope.'⁶

With little tradition of philanthropy in Ireland, Boyle remained convinced that the best chance of finding significant financial support was the Irish diaspora in the United States. He believed that Galway – the embarkation point for tens of thousands of Irish emigrants over the decades – had particularly close links, and thus a particularly strong claim, on the loyalty of Irish Americans. Looking for help and advice, he reached out to Bert Lockwood, the director of the University of Cincinnati's Urban Morgan Institute for Human Rights. Established in 1979, with Lockwood as the initial director, the Institute was the first programme devoted exclusively to international human rights at an American law school. Lockwood was a long-time human rights activist who had worked with rights lawyers in South Africa in the 1970s, and would eventually serve on the board of Amnesty International. He saw Boyle as a fellow pioneer in the emerging field of human rights education, as well as 'a model for anyone who has an aspiration to be an activist lawyer', and was happy to assist him in making connections in the United States. Boyle made a number of trips for meetings Lockwood arranged with prominent Irish-American lawyers in and

around Cincinnati and Chicago. He came away with some modest dona-
tions, enough to keep the Human Rights Centre afloat, but was frustrated
to discover, as Lockwood observed, that many Irish Americans 'are Irish on
St Patrick's Day but that was about as deep as it went. Kevin was very disappointed that it did not yield the money he had in his dreams.' Indeed, Boyle
discovered that the only cause some Irish Americans were interested in
funding was the armed campaign of the Provisional IRA, which he wanted
nothing to do with.

But operating on a shoestring did not blunt Boyle's prodigious energy or
willingness to involve himself in multiple causes. As he established himself
in Galway, word of his presence spread, and he was soon swamped with
requests for assistance from local people who had heard of his reputation
as an advocate for the underdog. One appeal for help came from a street
trader in Galway who was having trouble with his licence. A student in one
of his classes raised the issue of the mistreatment of Ireland's Travellers, a
traditionally itinerant group who had lived on the margins of Irish society
for centuries, and who were present in substantial numbers around Galway.
This – combined with pressure from Joan, who was growing frustrated with
his frequent absences, to find a cause closer to home – led Boyle to embark
on an ambitious project to draft a charter of rights for the Travellers.

To move ahead with the charter, Boyle adopted what would become a
regular feature on numerous projects: he asked his students to get involved.
'That was typical of Kevin,' said his former student Gerard Quinn. 'He'd
find someone with a particular interest and say "let's do something on that".'
Along with the student who originally raised the idea, Boyle invited Mary
Kelly to work with him on the Travellers project. 'If he saw you had any
promise,' she recalled, 'he just made opportunities.' Kelly remembered that
Boyle 'was worried about the Travellers. Communities didn't want Travellers
living in their neighbourhood. Often they would be forced to live by the
side of the road with no proper facilities.'

The challenge was to devise guidelines that would protect the Travellers'
distinct culture and way of life so they wouldn't be forced to integrate
simply to receive the basic social services to which all Irish citizens were
entitled, and to give them a new status in law. Boyle presented the charter at
a conference of the National Council for Travelling People held in Galway.
'Irish attitudes have come close to denying that Travellers have any inherent

rights,' he told the gathering. 'It is necessary to draw attention to the fact that Travellers are human persons who are entitled to human rights.'[7] Eventually, many of the specific ideas in the charter, which Boyle described as a combination of rights recognized in the Irish constitution and in such documents as the Universal Declaration of Human Rights, became a central feature of a broader effort to improve the lot of the Travellers.

Boyle's belief in the value of an international legal framework to protect human rights, reflected in his academic and legal work, was deep. Years later, he wrote about the 'civilizational advances' represented by the 'extraordinary appeal of the belief in universal rights and freedoms to be enjoyed by all without distinction'.[8] Building on the Universal Declaration, by the mid-1970s scores of countries had signed the International Covenant on Civil and Political Rights (ICCPR). Along with the International Covenant on Economic, Social and Cultural Rights, which also took effect in 1976, the ICCPR was intended to give legal force to the Universal Declaration. The ICCPR obligated countries to protect such basic rights as the right to life, freedom of speech, religion and privacy, freedom from arbitrary detention and torture, and the right to a fair trial. Yet by the early 1980s it was evident that many nations were not in full compliance. Among human rights activists, there was growing concern about governments limiting implementation or 'derogating' from the treaty – that is suspending certain civil and political rights – in response to a crisis. Although the ICCPR allowed a government to derogate in the event of an emergency, all too often that was simply a pretext for cracking down on political opposition or consolidating power. Kevin Boyle's experience of internment in Northern Ireland was just one example.

In the hope of curbing such abuses, Bert Lockwood's Urban Morgan Institute for Human Rights, along with two other NGOs, convened a meeting of leading international law experts in Siracusa, Sicily in April 1984. Boyle was one of the thirty-one lawyers and scholars asked to attend. The goal was to create legal guidelines for governments deviating from their ICCPR commitments. As Lockwood recalled, the idea was 'to ensure that rights would be preserved and that it was only under very limited circumstances that you could infringe on these rights'. Lockwood and Boyle played active roles in the drafting of what became known as the Siracusa Principles, an authoritative legal interpretation of when and to what extent a state could limit rights affirmed by the ICCPR. The closely argued 76-paragraph document emphasized that such curbs were justified only when 'absolutely necessary', and should be accompanied by minimal limitations on rights. The Principles were adopted by the UN's Economic and Social Committee in 1985. In subsequent years, they became – and remain – a key point of reference in legal and political debates over such contentious issues as how to deal with terrorism or introducing quarantines to combat epidemics. For Boyle, though, this was just one of many projects. Gerard Quinn, who studied under him and had won a postgraduate fellowship at Harvard, delayed his departure for a year to work with Boyle on one dealing with mental health in Northern Ireland, and another with language rights. The latter case was prompted by a query from the local authorities in a predominantly Catholic county in the North who were frustrated that they were not being allowed to put up road signs in both English and Irish. Although only a small minority of Northern Catholics spoke the language, this was seen as an important symbol of Irish identity, and, for that very reason, was opposed by many Protestants and had long been banned. To assist them, Quinn and Boyle prepared a paper surveying the status of language rights across Europe. The issue was never resolved, however, and, ironically, nearly forty years later, the status of the Irish language remains one of the most divisive questions hampering full implementation of the Good Friday Agreement intended to bring the Troubles to an end.In the early 1980s, however, the Irish language was a peripheral issue in Northern Ireland, far less important than the many controversies surrounding the continuing violence and the behaviour of the security forces. For Boyle, and many others, the period after the end of the IRA hunger strikes was particularly grim, as the popularity of the IRA and its political wing, Sinn Féin grew, while street disturbances, terrorist attacks and sectarian murders took a continuing toll. A number of deaths, mainly of Catholic civilians, were caused by the police and the British army using plastic bullets. Four inches long, one and a half inches in diameter, and weighing five ounces, the plastic bullet had been designed as a less lethal tool for riot control than so-called live bullets, and had been in use for nearly a decade in the North. They were often the weapon of first resort for security forces in breaking up demonstrations or disturbances. Fired from close range, however, they were deadly. As the horrifying cases piled up – people killed, blinded, suffering skull fractures, permanent brain

damage, ruptured kidneys, or severe haemorrhages – the anger and alienation of the Catholic community, which felt itself to be a particular target,
grew, exacerbated by the unwillingness of the authorities to deal with the
issue. In Belfast, two activist priests, Fr Raymond Murray and Fr Denis Faul,
organized a campaign to ban plastic bullets, and asked Kevin for help. Boyle
was moved by the plight of victims like fifteen-year-old Derry schoolboy
Paul Whitters, who died after being hit in the head by a plastic bullet fired
by a policeman, and twelve-year-old Alec McLaughlin, who lost an eye.[9]
'I don't exaggerate,' he wrote to Hurst Hannum,

> when I say the issue of plastic bullets and their misuse is an even worse
> scandal than interrogation was in the early 1970s. It isn't even the deaths
> and injuries, but the complete lack of response by the authorities. Déjà vu
> might be your feeling when you hear of no prosecutions, inadequate inves-
> tigations, and so on. The general political situation is now so bad and there
> is so much war-weariness that no one wants to know, basically.[10]

The two activist priests organized an 'international tribunal' in Belfast,
with participants from Britain and the US joining concerned local citizens
to mobilize popular opinion to press for a ban on plastic bullets. Boyle
submitted an eight-page paper in which he argued that the policies of the
British army and Royal Ulster Constabulary governing the use of plastic
bullets raised serious legal questions. The paper began by taking issue with
the government's use of the antiseptic-sounding term 'baton rounds' to
describe the bullets. This, he noted, was deliberately being done to portray
the plastic bullet as 'defensive in nature and restrained in its capacity to
cause injury'.[11] In contrast, the much more accurate term 'bullet' suggested
'an object potentially lethal in its intent and notoriously liable to cause
injury to innocent and uninvolved people'.[12] Categorizing the plastic bullet
as a lethal weapon, he wrote, 'has a bearing on the legal position'.[13] Boyle
argued that soldiers and police 'and those who command them' could not
be in any doubt about the capability of plastic bullets 'to kill, maim, and
disfigure', raising the question of whether in legal terms, employing 'such
force was reasonable – was it justified in the circumstances? If the force
used was excessive, then a crime has been committed.'[14] He noted that in
almost all the situations where plastic bullets were usually fired in Northern
Ireland – soldiers or police facing crowds of youths throwing rocks, bottles

or petrol bombs – the threat to the security forces was not sufficient to justify using such a potentially lethal weapon. He cited numerous examples of a 'very clearly unlawful use of these weapons in non-riot situations',[15] and was sharply critical of military and police commanders for failing to implement strict rules of engagement to prevent such behaviour.

Following the tribunal, Boyle enlisted Hannum and students from the Galway Human Rights Centre to work on a submission about the issue for the UN's Subcommittee on Human Rights in Geneva. He had no illusions that this step, or the appeal from the Belfast gathering, would solve the problem, but he was convinced that, as he wrote to Hannum, 'raising the issue of plastic bullets internationally'[16] would create additional pressure on the authorities to curb such abuses. As a long-time analyst of what he and his collaborators Tom Hadden and Paddy Hillyard called the 'legal control of political violence' in Northern Ireland, Boyle was keenly interested in the behaviour and policies of the army and police. The misuse of plastic bullets was, in his view, just one example of how the laws governing the use of force by the security forces were either inadequate, unclear, loosely enforced, or ignored. This was not only leading to unnecessary deaths and injuries, but, he believed, was adding to the major obstacles in the face of any solution to the continuing violence. Fuelling the controversy was a series of bloody incidents in which the security forces had killed a number of people under questionable circumstances, sparking accusations that the authorities were following a 'shoot to kill' policy towards suspected terrorists to avoid the headache of securing sufficient evidence to win a case in court. Despite his numerous other commitments, Boyle took a new case, challenging the army's rules on the use of lethal force, at the European Commission of Human Rights in Strasbourg.

The incident in question was not new. A decade earlier, on 26 October 1971, at a time of intense Catholic fury in the wake of internment, 26-year-old Thomas McLaughlin and two other Catholic men set out to rob a bank in Newry, Boyle's home town. Across the street, four British soldiers were waiting on the roof of a two-storey building, deployed after the army received intelligence about the impending robbery. According to the army, the soldiers called on the men to halt, and when they didn't, they opened fire. The three men were killed. For years, McLaughlin's widow, Olive Farrell, sought compensation, but a jury rejected her civil action against the British

Ministry of Defence in 1977. A retrial was ordered after an appeal, but this decision was reversed by Britain's House of Lords in November 1979. Following that setback, Farrell's lawyer wrote to Boyle asking if Farrell had any grounds to bring a case before the European Commission of Human Rights. Boyle was convinced that she had a strong case.In making his argument to the Commission, Boyle argued that the standards for the use of lethal force in UK domestic law did not conform to Article Two of the European Convention on Human Rights. Under UK law, lethal force was justifiable if it 'was reasonable under the circumstances'. Article Two, which enshrined for all citizens a basic right to life, said it was only legitimate to kill if 'absolutely necessary'. Boyle contended that this was a standard 'qualitatively more exacting than the standard of reasonable force',[17] and, in this case, had clearly not been met. Specifically, he noted that the soldiers who killed Farrell's husband and the two other men were in no personal danger from the three victims. No warning shots had been fired. The three men were hit while running away, and the soldiers had shot to kill. Moreover, he stressed that UK law was frustratingly vague, did not specify criteria governing the use of deadly force, and that British courts 'have resisted the specification of any such criteria, preferring to deal with each case on its facts'.[18] In Northern Ireland, he said, the absence of such criteria meant that soldiers were given 'a flexibility far removed from the strict requirements and justifications of Article Two of the Convention'.[19] To a lawyer friend, he wrote,

> my bottom line would be that if the concepts are to be in practice coterminous, the UK law must spell out rules and criteria specifically distinguishing lethal from non-lethal force, and in effect codify the relevant principles that there is no doubt as to such common principles as last resort and proportionality.[20]

In response, the British chose not to argue the substance of the incident as much as to fight on procedural grounds, claiming that Farrell had not fully exhausted the available domestic remedies and so her application should be dismissed. But the European Commission was not impressed, and at the end of 1982 declared the case admissible. For Boyle, it was another significant legal victory. 'This could have quite radical implications for the rules governing the use of firepower in the UK, where it is intended to kill,'

Kevin told a reporter from *The Irish Times*.[21] 'Congratulations on Farrell,' Hurst Hannum wrote. 'It could well be one of the most significant cases the Commission has dealt with in a while.'[22]

By the autumn of 1983, Boyle was getting clear signals from contacts in Strasbourg that the Commission was ready to send the case to the European Court of Human Rights, where the odds of eventual victory were high. The development prompted a major shift in the position of the UK government. Eager to avoid a high-profile legal defeat, and the attendant pressure to change the army's rules of engagement, they indicated a willingness to settle the case by offering Olive Farrell the compensation British courts had previously denied her. For Boyle, this prospect posed a dilemma: on the one hand, he was thrilled his client might finally receive what she had been demanding; on the other, a settlement meant foregoing a judgment on the broader issues, which would thus be left unresolved. Boyle wrote to Farrell's original lawyer, Richard Ferguson, stressing the need to ask for a substantial pay-out, while acknowledging that if it was offered, 'we would have to abandon'[23] hope for a court ruling that her husband's rights had been violated. He concluded, however, that 'ultimately, the client must come first, provided, however, that there is some substantive sum of money involved'.[24] The upshot was a meeting in London, convened under the auspices of the Commission, where the British government agreed to give Farrell a payment of £37,500 and to issue a statement saying that the death of her husband was 'an unfortunate mistake'.[25] The British also agreed to cover a portion of the legal costs of the Strasbourg proceedings. 'The fees will not make us rich,' Boyle wrote to Farrell's lawyer, 'but they will buy a very good meal in what is the eating capital of Europe.'[26]

[15]

On This, We Can Do Business

BY EARLY 1983, Boyle was becoming convinced that focusing so heavily on the behaviour of the police and army alone was not making enough of a difference. This was despite his involvement in so many cases dealing with abuses committed by the security forces – abuses that, he believed, fuelled support for the IRA. Violence was continuing, and in the wake of the 1981 hunger strikes, support for the Provisionals, especially their political wing, Sinn Féin, was growing. For Provisional leaders like Gerry Adams, who had seen large numbers of Northern Catholics elect Bobby Sands to the Westminster parliament at the height of the second hunger strike, the incentive to engage in electoral politics as a complement to the IRA's military campaign was strong. As Adams' colleague Danny Morrison famously told a Sinn Féin conference: 'Will anyone here object if, with a ballot paper in this hand and an Armalite [rifle] in this hand, we take power in Ireland?'[1] Indeed, in the 1983 British general election in which Margaret Thatcher won a second term, Sinn Féin received 100,000 votes in Northern Ireland, and Adams himself was elected as the member for West Belfast.

In keeping with Sinn Féin's abstentionist tradition, he refused to take his seat in Westminster.

For Boyle, as his long-time collaborator Tom Hadden acknowledged, it was clear that 'neither research nor legal action had hindered the Provisionals' advance'. It was time for fresh thinking.

Boyle's view was shared by Garret FitzGerald, with whom the lawyer had developed a warm relationship. The two men, along with John Hume and others, had the same concern: that the growth in support among Northern Catholics for the 'physical force nationalism' of the IRA and Sinn Féin was at the expense of the 'constitutional nationalism' of Hume's moderate SDLP. FitzGerald was also concerned that Sinn Féin might make political inroads in the Republic. He later wrote, 'There was now a danger of a major destabilisation of the situation following the gain in support for Sinn Féin and the IRA.'[2] In the spring of 1983, building on a concept initially developed by Hume, FitzGerald convened the New Ireland Forum. The goal was to bring together the leading parties and individuals associated with constitutional, non-violent Irish nationalism, North and South, to explore new ideas for breaking the impasse.

The politics of the Irish Republic were fractured. The mere fact that the main political parties, Fine Gael and Fianna Fáil, were participating was a significant development. The hard-line nationalist leader of Fianna Fáil, Charles Haughey, was FitzGerald's bitter adversary. The two parties were descended from the factions that had fought the Irish civil war in 1922–23. Fine Gael emerged from those who supported the treaty with Britain that led to the partition of Ireland; Fianna Fáil was formed by those who rejected the move. The two were joined in the Forum by Ireland's Labour Party and the SDLP. Because of its support for the IRA's campaign of violence, Sinn Féin was excluded. In a conciliatory gesture, the Ulster Unionist Party was invited but refused to participate, although two younger, more liberal Unionists gave presentations in an individual capacity. FitzGerald appointed Colm Ó hEocha, the president of University College Galway, as chair of a process that became in effect a think tank for all shades of constitutional nationalist opinion. Ó hEocha was assisted by a staff seconded from the Irish civil service.

Over the course of the next eighteen months, the Forum held eleven public meetings, twenty-eight private ones and countless informal discussions, with debate stimulated by over 300 written submissions. Boyle was encouraged by the process. It was, he said in a subsequent talk,

> the first time the Irish political parties and leadership have come together to attempt to agree a definition of the problem and find a solution, to give the outlines of what they would see as a New Ireland. It is generating much hope in Ireland that it will be at last an initiative that can break the political stalemate and the cycle of violence.[3]

In mid-June 1983 Boyle and Tom Hadden decided to make their own submission. Both men quickly realized that for all the talk of fresh thinking, the final Forum report was likely to focus on traditional nationalist goals, although framed in a more conciliatory manner and with an acknowledgment of the need for Protestants in the North to give their consent. This focus became explicit in late autumn, when Deputy Prime Minister Dick Spring wrote to Boyle to ask if, in addition to his own submission, he would be willing to draft separate papers on the legal implications of three possible scenarios: a unitary state, a federal/confederal model and an Ireland sharing with Britain joint authority over Northern Ireland.[4] Boyle agreed to do so once he and Hadden had finished their own submission.

The two men drafted their own paper in a manner similar to their earlier collaborations – brainstorming together, Hadden writing up the ideas, Boyle responding, and Hadden then rewriting. They consulted with others, including Mary Robinson, an increasingly influential figure in the Labour Party, who broadly shared their outlook. 'I met both of them together, and each of them separately,' she recalled. 'I knew they were trying to push for a broader perspective and how there should be a better understanding of the North in the South. We had lots of conversations.'

Using their practical experience, academic training and the deep insights from the roots each had on the opposite sides of Ulster's sectarian divide, Boyle and Hadden came up with an analysis that differed sharply from the conventional wisdom. 'It was fairly clear what the main options of the Forum were,' Hadden recalled. 'They just seemed to want to say [about Northern Ireland]: you're an illegitimate state. You belong to us, whether you like it or not.' In contrast, Boyle and Hadden wrote, 'it is necessary for those who accept the consent principle to reject the traditional thesis which grants no legitimacy to the position taken by the Northern Ireland majority.'[5] In their 27-page paper, the two men identified what they viewed as the central contradiction in any effort to convince Northern Protestants to agree to a new, all-Ireland political structure. 'The drawback is that there is no evidence whatsoever that Northern Protestants will give their consent to any such plan, and that any effort to coerce them into doing so would destroy the idea of unity by consent.'[6]

In view of what they called this 'unpleasant fact', Boyle and Hadden argued instead for an alternative – to see the Forum not as a blueprint but as 'a process of constitutional and legislative change, which could help to produce peace and stability without threatening the constitutional position of Northern Ireland as part of the United Kingdom.' Specifically, they proposed that Britain and the Irish Republic both 'recognise the respective rights of the majority to determine the constitutional status of Northern Ireland and the minority to express their Irish identity in ways which do not conflict with that status'.[7] If the right of Northern Catholics to express their Irish identity was legitimized, Boyle and Hadden wrote, then the government of the Republic should respond by granting 'full and explicit recognition of the constitutional status of Northern Ireland as part of the United Kingdom'.[8] This would include changing Articles 2 and 3 of the Irish constitution, which formally laid claim to Northern Ireland as part of the Irish Republic. The two men also called for new legal protections for minority rights in both Northern Ireland and the Republic, and urged that in both Ireland and the UK the sweeping protections of the European Convention on Human Rights be incorporated into domestic law.

Having participated in numerous commissions dealing with Northern Ireland over the years, Boyle and Hadden were experienced operators. Even before submitting their final paper, they made sure their ideas were widely shared by quietly distributing drafts to senior Irish civil servants, as well as officials at the British government's Northern Ireland Office in Belfast. One of those civil servants seconded to work on the Forum in Dublin was Walter Kirwan, a key aide to Garret FitzGerald. He found Boyle to be

> a real charmer, and a prolific generator of ideas. The Irish government thought if you dealt with the British and went over the heads of the North you could bring about a result tending towards a united Ireland. I would attribute a lot of significance to Boyle and Hadden in getting it through our skulls that this wasn't going to be possible.

Convincing even the most moderate of Irish nationalists of the need for dramatic gestures to placate Northern Protestants in return for their acknowledgment of the Irish identity of Northern Catholics was a slow and difficult process. After submitting the joint paper with Hadden, Boyle spent several weeks writing up separate analyses of the legal issues in each of the three scenarios Dick Spring had proposed. Even though he did not himself believe in any of these options, Boyle had accepted the assignment in part to maintain his role as a player in the continuing political crisis. He worked furiously at his office in Galway, puffing on his pipe.

His assistant Geraldine Smyth, in a letter to Orlando Delogu, wrote that 'the pen has been to the paper for the past six weeks constantly. All one sees is smoke signals coming out of the office!'[9] Boyle also used the opportunity to draft an unsolicited paper on an issue about which he felt particularly strongly: the need to amend the Irish constitution. He and Hadden had mentioned this in their own submission to the Forum, but now Boyle made the case, in stronger and much more detailed legal terms, of how 'offensive' Articles 2 and 3 were to the unionists because they reflected 'clearly a unitary state model as Ireland's ultimate goal'.[10] To underscore how important this was, Boyle entitled his paper 'Document No. 2'. To anyone with a knowledge of Irish history, the term resonated. In 1921 Éamon de Valera, the first president of the Irish Republic, had written a sharp critique of the treaty that Irish negotiators had agreed with Britain to secure the country's independence, and offered his own alternative version. It became known as 'Document No. 2', and had become a byword for dissenting opinions. 'Kevin was playing with Wally Kirwan,' Tom Hadden observed, adding that submitting the paper was like 'throwing a [fire] cracker into the Forum'.

Boyle understood that his paper would be controversial, and had deliberately sought to provoke debate on the issue. What he did not know was that Kirwan, concerned about maintaining at least a facade of inter-party unity in relation to the Forum's report, decided to suppress the document. In a handwritten note on the top of Boyle's paper, he wrote, 'I decided it should not be passed to party leaders as likely to promote disagreement.'[11] Years later, Kirwan recalled that 'the issue was very sensitive'. Opening a debate about modifying the constitution, he feared, would mean the chances for an agreed report 'would go out the window'.

The Forum report was published on 2 May 1984. Scores of Irish journalists and nearly a hundred from Britain attended the launch in Dublin. As Boyle had been advised, the report offered three scenarios – a unitary state, a federal/confederal structure and joint authority – although in all cases supporting the principle of consent and the need to assuage Protestant anxieties. In Ireland's complex political situation, however, in order to placate Charles Haughey, the document described the unitary state as the 'ideal framework', which it 'would like to see established'.[12] Predictably, the Unionists in the North rejected the report.

The British reaction was more cautious, with Mrs Thatcher indicating a willingness to hold discussions with Dublin – thus achieving one of FitzGerald's key goals, which was to provide 'a basis for a new approach with the British government'.[13] Indeed, for all its drawbacks, the report marked the start of a significant shift in Irish nationalist thinking, moving away from the long-held article of faith that the South should simply absorb the North, and recognizing the need to come to terms with a suspicious Unionist population who defined themselves as Protestant and British. Significantly, after detailing the three scenarios, in a section entitled 'Realities and Requirements', the report declared that 'the Parties in the Forum also remain open to discuss other views which may contribute to political development'.[14] It was a crucially important phrase. To Tom Hadden, it was an acknowledgment that at least some elements of the analysis he and Kevin had submitted had been accepted. Years later, Walter Kirwan conceded that Boyle and Hadden 'exercised a significant influence' in the process, and that many of their ideas 'foreshadowed later developments in actual British-Irish agreements'.[15]

In June 1984, in a conscious effort to shape the official response to the Forum report and increase the chances of practical progress, Boyle and Hadden recast their own Forum submission. As usual, they found themselves in agreement on most issues. Hadden recalled, 'there wasn't very much we argued about'. Boyle, however, repeatedly stressed the need to be as careful and balanced as possible. 'One of his jobs,' Hadden acknowledged, 'was to stop me saying things that would get up people's noses, which I sometimes do. He would spot something that I had written that would get up the noses of nationalists, and he would say "you can't say that".' For his part, Boyle greatly admired Hadden's insights. 'The man's a genius,' he would often exclaim to Joan. The new paper had the somewhat clumsy title of 'How to Read the New Ireland Forum Report: Searching Between the Lines for a Realistic Framework for Action.' They began quietly circulating copies to senior government officials in Dublin, Belfast and London, and also arranged for the paper to be published that autumn in the British journal *Political Quarterly*.

Despite Boyle's admonitions, in their critique of the Forum report he and Hadden did not mince words. 'The report's prescriptions are totally unrealistic,' they wrote, 'and can only be pursued, if at all, in ways that are inconsistent with the principles it asserts.'[16] They challenged the nationalist mythology that British 'occupation' of Northern Ireland was the source of the problem, asserting that 'the underlying reasons for partition were that the vast majority of the inhabitants in the North and the South of Ireland had incompatible loyalties and commitments, and very large numbers in each part had shown their willingness to fight for those commitments'.[17] They also criticized the Irish Republic for missing 'no opportunity to assert the Catholic, Gaelic, and non-British ethos of the state, and in so doing to confirm the fears and prejudices of Northern Protestants and to deter them from contemplating any form of unity or even mutual respect'.[18]

Asserting that 'traditional Irish republicanism and the least attractive aspects of Ulster unionism' were 'mutually self-supporting', they called on the Republic to show 'its willingness to embrace the pluralist values and attitudes on which so much emphasis is placed in the Forum report'.[19] Amplifying the argument in their Forum submission, they again called for the Republic to recognize the legitimacy of Northern Ireland 'as presently constituted', and urged that any immediate action 'be directed toward a fuller recognition of the identity, rights and interests of the nationalist minority in the North, rather than the unionist minority in Ireland as a whole'.[20]

The two men then put forward what they called 'an alternative framework for action', which, they argued, should be underpinned by a binding international agreement between London and Dublin. 'What we were saying,' Hadden recalled, 'was that the two governments have got to get together and sort themselves out. You have got to sort out your joint acceptance of the current constitutional position. It is not helpful to have one saying Northern Ireland is illegitimate.'

At the core of their argument was a guiding principle that recognized the 'long-standing interdependence of the peoples and states of Britain and Ireland', while abandoning 'traditional and outdated concepts of national independence and exclusive state sovereignty'.[21] Boyle and Hadden particularly emphasized the need to give 'legal effect' to the validity of both traditions in Northern Ireland. They called for steps to end linguistic and cultural discrimination against nationalists, such as repealing laws banning the display of the Irish flag and the naming of streets in Irish. They also advocated Southern input into security issues in Northern Ireland, joint training for the Irish police and the RUC and consular representation of the Republic in the North. In return, they urged the Republic to give up its legal claim to Northern Ireland, and offered specific proposals on power-sharing and minority participation in government and measures to protect basic rights, including the passage of a Bill of Rights for the North.

Throughout the autumn of 1984 the two men made numerous public appearances. They spoke to a large gathering at University College Dublin. In Belfast, they met with members of the Northern Ireland assembly, and Boyle gave a speech to the central council of the SDLP in the town of Dungannon, where the first civil rights march had been held in August 1968. To the SDLP, Boyle was blunt: once the unionists and the British recognized the legitimacy of nationalist identity in the North, there were only two choices for Northern Ireland, 'either the road to Lebanon, with the Republican and loyalist paramilitaries turning Northern Ireland into warring enclaves, or the accommodation of these identities within the State on conditions of equality of treatment and respect'.[22] The response from the SDLP was sceptical, with the party's deputy leader, Seamus Mallon, raising doubts and warning that any moves to remove Articles 2 and 3 from the Irish constitution would be 'very actively opposed'.[23]

Amid the controversy, however, Boyle and Hadden were gaining a critically important ally: Britain's prime minister Margaret Thatcher. As early as March 1984, the Secretary of State for Northern Ireland, James Prior, had sent a copy of Boyle and Hadden's Forum submission to Thatcher's private secretary for foreign and defence affairs, John Coles, with a note saying he thought that the prime minister 'might wish to see this document, whose analysis of the problems in Northern Ireland and the proposals for action are of interest'.[24] Prior had underlined sections of the accompanying document to which he particularly wanted to draw Thatcher's attention. These included the key points in what Boyle and Hadden had described as a 'framework for action', most notably

> the <u>acceptance</u> and <u>recognition</u> <u>by all parties</u> of the <u>differing identities and loyalties</u> of the two communities within Northern Ireland; the extension of this <u>acceptance</u> and <u>recognition</u> in the context of relationships between the United Kingdom and the Republic; the protection of <u>majority</u> and <u>minority</u> rights on a political level <u>within Northern Ireland</u>; and the protection of <u>communal and cultural rights</u> through law for both communities within Northern Ireland and the Republic.[25]

While the fact that Thatcher had been given a copy of Boyle and Hadden's work remained private, media coverage at the time contains enough oblique references to indicate that the government in London, as well as that of Garret FitzGerald, was taking a serious look at their ideas. 'People were clearly talking about what we had written,' Tom Hadden recalled. *The Irish Times* on 24 September, for example, reported that the 'How to Read the New Ireland Forum' paper was 'known to have received careful study by both the Irish and British governments'.[26]

That November, Ed Moloney, the newspaper's well-connected and highly respected Belfast correspondent, devoted an entire column to analysing the impact of Boyle and Hadden's activities. Clearly reflecting what he had been told by British officials, Moloney wrote that 'their ideas have been warmly greeted in British government circles,'[27] although he reported that the two academics' high profile had generated conspiracy theories in the North, with intense speculation that they were being used, as Hadden recalled years later, 'as a front for the two governments'.[28] Indeed, to underscore the growing influence of Boyle and Hadden, Moloney's article was accompanied by a cartoon drawn by Rowel Friers, a native of County Down who became known for his satirical political cartoons during the Troubles. It showed two pinstriped government officials walking by a huddle of anonymous-looking men; one bureaucrat says to the other, 'They must be producing a new Boyle-Hadden document.'[29] Later that year Boyle's ideas were given further weight when he was approached by an editor from Penguin Books. According to Hadden, the publisher 'said it had been directed to us by British officials in London' eager to see a book version of their 'How to Read the New

Ireland Forum' paper. Boyle and Hadden agreed to meet with Penguin staff in London on 19 November 1984.

As it turned out, the night before their Penguin meeting, Garret Fitz-Gerald had travelled to Chequers, the British prime minister's country residence, for a summit with Thatcher. The meeting took place amid unprecedented secrecy and security. A month earlier, Thatcher had narrowly escaped an assassination attempt when the IRA detonated a bomb in her hotel in Brighton; she had been attending the Conservative Party's annual conference. Five people died. Thatcher was shaken but unhurt.

For Thatcher, the attack underscored the need to intensify the battle against the IRA's terrorism. To FitzGerald and others, including Boyle and Hadden, it demonstrated the urgent need to move towards a political settlement that would undercut support in Northern Ireland's nation-alist population for the Provisionals' campaign of violence. The Chequers meeting was FitzGerald's first opportunity to discuss Northern Ireland in detail with Thatcher since the release of the New Ireland Forum report. He recognized that all three models proposed by the Forum were unlikely to be workable in the near future, despite his own preference for the idea of joint authority. In the run-up to the meeting, he had therefore gone out of his way to focus attention on the 'realities and requirements' listed in the report, in particular the offer to 'discuss any other proposal that may contribute to political development'.

Thatcher and FitzGerald met privately that grey and foggy Sunday night, and then twice with key aides on the morning of 19 November. The only official record of the private meeting is a five-paragraph summary that Thatcher subsequently gave her team. In it, she said that FitzGerald had offered to put Articles 2 and 3 of the Irish constitution to a refer-endum, in the hope of changing the claim to the North – something Boyle had forcefully advocated – 'provided that something was done at the same time to restore nationalist confidence in the North. The question was what and how.'[30] Thatcher pressed FitzGerald on why he thought the minority in the North remained alienated, given the steps that had been taken to end discrimination. FitzGerald responded that many national-ists still felt excluded from the decisions that affected their lives. In his memoir he wrote that he told Thatcher, 'I was prepared to do my part by asking the people of the Republic to amend their constitution if she would agree to changes in Northern Ireland that would end the alienation of the minority.'[31]

The meetings the next day, with other senior officials in attendance, were wide-ranging – what FitzGerald described as 'a long discursive argument ranging over a whole series of problems'[32] and what Thatcher called the 'fullest, frankest, the most realistic bilateral meeting I have ever had with the taoiseach'.[33] Media reports at the time, and many subsequent accounts of the summit, have stressed the points of disagreement. This narrative has taken on added weight because of comments made by Thatcher at her post-summit press conference. When asked her view of the three models proposed by the New Ireland Forum, she responded, with her customary brusqueness, that 'a unified Ireland was one solution. That is out. A second solution was confederation of the two states. That is out. A third solution was joint authority. That is out.'[34]

The comments caused offence across all sectors of opinion in Ireland, and gravely embarrassed Garret FitzGerald. But lost amid the controversy of what was incorrectly interpreted as a blanket dismissal of new ways of thinking about the problem was the fact that, in the joint communique issued after the summit, the two leaders explicitly stated their interest in a settlement in which 'the identities of both the majority and minority communities should be recognised and respected, and reflected in the structures and processes of Northern Ireland in ways acceptable to both communities'.[35]

Such language echoed the arguments Boyle and Hadden had been making for months, as, indeed, did Thatcher's dismissal of the Forum's three models. 'I suspect that Maggie Thatcher got her "out, out, out" on the basis of what we had said about each of the options', Hadden observed. 'We said none of these options were actually terribly realistic, except in slightly more diplomatic language.' All this lends weight to an anecdote that Kevin shared only with his wife and Tom Hadden: that FitzGerald privately told him after the summit that, at one point, Thatcher had taken a copy of 'How to Read the New Ireland Forum' and, in Hadden's recollection, 'plonked it down on the table saying something like "On this, we can do business."'[36]

Boyle asked both Joan and Hadden not to mention the episode. In Joan's recollection, 'he said not to talk about it to anyone because it could put Tom's and his life at risk from the IRA'. Hadden, however, thinks a more likely reason was simply a concern not to betray something the taoiseach had shared in confidence.

One piece of evidence that corroborates Boyle's account can be found in a note he sent to the publicity department at Penguin Books. In September 1985 Penguin had published Boyle and Hadden's paper as a book entitled *Ireland: A Positive Proposal*. Writing on 24 July with a suggestion that the publisher send an advance copy to FitzGerald, Boyle added, 'While you must not use this for publicity I am quite friendly with Garret FitzGerald, and Mrs Thatcher has essentially bought our analysis some nine months ago [almost exactly at the time of the Thatcher-FitzGerald summit] although I am not free to explain that any further, except to assure you it is the case.'[37]

Despite the bruised feelings over Thatcher's 'out, out, out' comments, FitzGerald, perhaps in part because of his awareness of Thatcher's interest in Boyle and Hadden's ideas, kept his cool, while Thatcher was willing to allow her ministers and senior civil servants to explore possible ways forward with their Irish counterparts. After months of intense negotiations, on 15 November 1985 the two leaders signed the Anglo-Irish Agreement at Hillsborough Castle in Northern Ireland. Its central concept was the idea that Boyle and Hadden, along with John Hume and others, had long sought to establish as the guiding principle of any solution: the formal recognition of the right of Northern Ireland's majority unionists to remain in the United Kingdom as long as they wished, while acknowledging the right of Northern nationalists to express their Irish identity.

The key feature of the Agreement was to give the Irish government a direct, although purely advisory, role as the guarantor of the rights of the nationalist minority through an 'intergovernmental conference' in Belfast, to be staffed by Irish and British civil servants. The conference was designed to allow the Irish government to put forward proposals on such sensitive matters as policing, security and counterterrorism, as well as preventing discrimination, protecting 'the cultural heritage of both traditions', and the possibility of introducing a Bill of Rights.[38]

The Agreement was a watershed moment, foreshadowing some of the key elements of the 1998 Belfast Agreement. Boyle and Hadden had argued that the critical first requirement to resolve the conflict would be 'a decision by the British and Irish states to realign their relationship over a territory that was once in dispute between them so as to emphasise current realities rather than historic enmities'.[39] Indeed, in their book, *Ireland: A Positive Proposal*, they included their own version of what such a treaty might look like. The Hillsborough Agreement was such a step, fundamentally changing Anglo-Irish relations in a positive way.

In the short term, however, the accord simply fuelled the prevailing tension. The unionists were furious at what they saw as a weakening of Northern Ireland's links to the UK, and they held a series of huge rallies under the slogan 'Ulster Says No.' Loyalist violence increased sharply. For its part, the republican movement also felt threatened, both by the Agreement's obvious intention to strengthen Sinn Féin's main rival for the nationalist vote, the SDLP, and also because the notion that the North's position in the UK was a reflection of majority popular will undercut the long-standing republican argument that everything was the fault of the British 'colonial occupation' of Northern Ireland. It would take thirteen more years, and hundreds of further deaths, before most of the ideas Boyle, Hadden and others had been advocating were enshrined the 1998 Belfast Agreement, designed to bring the Troubles to an end.

Neither FitzGerald nor Thatcher ever referred to the episode Boyle shared with his wife and closest collaborator. And Boyle and Hadden, for reasons of temperament and tactics, were uninterested in claiming any kind of credit for the Anglo-Irish Agreement and the subsequent peace process. As Hadden sardonically noted decades later, 'there are so many people with their fingers on the Anglo-Irish Agreement and the Good Friday Agreement. They don't want people like me and Kevin interfering with their kudos.' But senior Irish civil servant Walter Kirwan was convinced that key elements in the peace process were in part directly influenced by the work of the two academics. Among these were 'the stress on the validity of both the nationalist and unionist identities, the need for new structures to accommodate together two sets of legitimate rights, and [the need] for effective guarantees of individual human rights and of the communal and cultural rights of both nationalists and unionists'.[40] This was a view shared by Mary Robinson, who as a senator, member of the Forum, and later, president of Ireland, became an influential figure in the search for peace and reconciliation. 'That they [Boyle and Hadden] were very influential in the thinking behind these deals,' she stated, 'is not in doubt.'

[16]

The Horrors Going on Here Are Appalling

BY THE EARLY 1980S, South Africa was dissolving into terrifying turmoil. After a decade of increasingly brutal repression, the white minority government of President P.W. Botha, facing intense international and domestic pressure, announced what it billed as a series of reforms, but continued to exclude blacks from any share in government and left the apartheid system of racial separation intact. The ensuing backlash led to the creation of a united front of opposition groups: churches, civic associations, trade unions and student bodies, who organized demonstrations, strikes and boycotts. At the same time, a groundswell of anger from the impoverished black townships fuelled repeated outbreaks of violence. Riots, flaming tyres and cars, armoured police and army vehicles rolling through these townships and almost daily funerals became a common sight.

At its London headquarters, the staff of Amnesty International watched these developments amid a growing debate about what to do. Traditionally, Amnesty had focused on arrests, imprisonment and the mistreatment of individual detainees rather than broader political issues. But the crisis in

South Africa prompted them to rethink. Malcolm Smart had studied South African history and had undertaken academic field work there before joining Amnesty in 1974. A decade later, he was in charge of the organization's research on Africa. 'Within Amnesty, there had been an internal debate for some time about how to respond to apartheid,' he recalled. Now, a consensus emerged, as Smart noted, 'to oppose all the laws and practices of apartheid, since they were essentially destructive of almost everybody's rights'. The door was open, as Smart had long advocated, for Amnesty to mount a campaign against the foundation of the apartheid regime – the pass laws – a campaign in which Kevin Boyle would play a central role.

Regulations to control the movement of blacks had existed in some form in South Africa since the arrival of the earliest, mostly Dutch, settlers from Europe in the eighteenth century. By the middle of the twentieth century, the pass laws had become the mechanism by which the white minority government controlled where black South Africans could live, work and travel. Officially, they had only permanent residence rights in the so-called African 'homelands' created by the government – usually remote and desolate areas that comprised barely 13 per cent of the country's land mass. Under apartheid, the remaining 87 per cent was reserved for whites or other non-black minorities such as Indians. Blacks were technically allowed entry on only a temporary basis to service the white-dominated economy, except for a relatively small minority who had 'permanent urban rights'. Every black over the age of sixteen was required to carry a personal identity document, called a reference book, which included a photo, personal details and fingerprints. The legal requirement to carry a pass was only for blacks. Without the appropriate permission stamped into the document, which had to be carried at all times and shown on demand to any police officer or other white official, blacks were deemed to be illegal trespassers in their own country, and subject to immediate arrest, fines or imprisonment.

Protests against the pass laws were a central feature of the anti-apartheid struggle, with numerous demonstrations, strikes and campaigns of civil disobedience. In 1960 a march to a local police station where protestors burned their passes triggered an infamous massacre in a township called Sharpeville, near Johannesburg, in which police killed sixty-nine unarmed demonstrators and wounded 180 others.

'It was the most dominant feature of black life,' Malcolm Smart said:

And now, we at Amnesty could attack the pass laws. So I was thinking – who can I get to do this, because this is a big, big job. I immediately thought of Kevin. I wanted somebody who would have empathy for the people affected by it, who would understand the rights issues, who would have energy, drive, stamina, determination, commitment. He had it. He was a perfect choice.

It would not be Boyle's first Africa project for Amnesty. In 1980 and 1981 he had observed a series of trials of anti-government dissidents in Gambia, producing what Nigel Rodley, then Amnesty's chief lawyer, described as 'simply the best trial observation report I had ever read – a superb analytical piece'.

In a long memo, Smart outlined the specific goals for Boyle's South Africa mission. The focus, he wrote, should be on the 'pass law prisoners' – those who ran afoul of the system and ended up in jail. In 1983, for example, more than 200,000 people had been prosecuted.[1] In 1986 one scholar would estimate that over the decades, more than seventeen million South African blacks had at one point or another been arrested for violating the laws governing their movement.[2] Amnesty International was particularly interested in learning how the legal structure underpinning the pass laws – and thus the system of apartheid – actually worked. Smart urged Boyle to attend as many pass law trials as he could and talk to as many of the people involved both in administering and fighting the system. The continuing turmoil, Smart believed, was generating enough pressure to raise the possibility the government might be forced to change at least some of its behaviour. 'The political situation was deteriorating,' Smart recalled. 'There were changes happening in South Africa. There was movement. It looked like there was something to push.' With the growing internal and external pressure, Amnesty's plan was to make the report Boyle would prepare the centrepiece of a worldwide campaign to abolish the pass laws.

On 3 April 1984 Boyle arrived in Johannesburg. It was the first of two visits he would make over the next thirteen months. Both were searing experiences, leaving him shaken and horrified by what he witnessed, but inspired by the people he met in the resistance movement and convinced that his long absences from Joan and his sons, whom he missed desperately, were worth it.

Kevin Boyle, aged twelve, as altar boy. In his youth, Boyle wrestled with growing doubts about his strict Catholic upbringing. © Joan Boyle

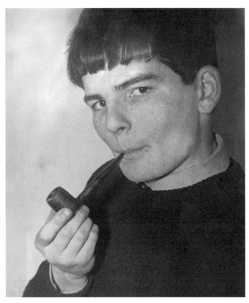

Boyle as a student at Queen's University, early 1960s. © Joan Boyle

Kevin at Louis Boyle's graduation from Queen's University, spring 1968.
Louis was one of the few Catholics to join the Unionist Party in the hope of
promoting reform from within the system. Despite their political differences,
the two brothers remained close. © Louis Boyle

Kevin and Joan Boyle's wedding, London, 28 August 1976. © Joan Boyle

Maggie O'Boyle, Kevin, Joan and brother Eugene at Boyle's cottage in Connemara, July 1978. Maggie was a doctor and wife of Boyle's close friend and legal colleague Michael O'Boyle. © Michael O'Boyle

Bernadette Devlin and Kevin Boyle at the first civil rights march in Belfast, 9 October 1968. The march, held in response to the RUC assaulting civil rights protesters in Derry four days earlier, led to the formation of People's Democracy. © The Trustees of the Buzz Logan Photographic Archive/ Linen Hall Library

Police confront Boyle and other Peoples Democracy protestors during the Long March, January 1969 © Associated Press

Boyle and Bernadette Devlin at an anti-internment rally, March 1972. Boyle was convinced that the space for street politics had disappeared after Bloody Sunday, so this was one of the final protest marches in which he participated. © Victor Patterson

Boyle and his close friend Tom Hadden at Hadden's family home in Derrybroughas outside strongly loyalist Portadown, 1994. © Joan Boyle

Tom Hadden, Joan and Kevin, with their children, 1983. Joan is holding Mark and Stephen. Rachel Hadden is on Tom's lap and Ellen Hadden sits on Kevin's knee. © Chris Hadden

Boyle with William Shawcross, the distinguished author and chairman of Article 19, spring 1989. © Joan Boyle

Boyle with writers Kazuo Ishiguro, Harold Pinter and Arnold Wesker, along with Article 19 colleague Frances D'Souza, at a news conference to publicize the letter Boyle drafted, in support of Salman Rushdie, 19 July 1989.
© Peter Orme, *The Daily Telegraph*

Boyle in Diyarbakır, Turkey, 1992. His lecture to local human rights lawyers there was the catalyst for bringing scores of cases on behalf of Turkey's beleaguered Kurdish minority to the European Court of Human Rights. © Joan Boyle

Boyle with some of the Kurdish civilians he represented in Strasbourg, 1993. His clients faced arrest, imprisonment and torture at the hands of the Turkish government. © Joan Boyle

Boyle arguing one of his many Kurdish cases at the European Court of Human Rights, mid-1990s. © European Court of Human Rights

Boyle with Françoise Hampson at the European
Court of Human Rights, May 1996. © Joan Boyle

Boyle with Hurst Hannum, Françoise Hampson and
others in Strasbourg, autumn 1999, discussing the Banković
case against the NATO bombing of the Serbian television
headquarters in Belgrade. © Joan Boyle

Boyle at the Palais des Nations in Geneva, headquarters of the UN High Commission for Human Rights, 2002. © Joan Boyle

Boyle with Tom Hadden, Hadden's wife Chris and daughter Rachel, 2002.
© Tom Hadden

Kevin and Joan with Michael and Maggie O'Boyle, winter 2002.
© Michael O'Boyle

*Kevin and Joan with Mary Robinson, her husband Nick, and Maggie O'Boyle with
daughters Lisa (left) and Eleanor (right), winter 2002.* © Michael O'Boyle

*Boyle with Francis Keenan, his long-time friend
and collaborator, 2005.* © Joan Boyle

*Boyle with his University of Essex colleague Nigel Rodley, 2009. Rodley was
Amnesty International's top lawyer for many years and later became the
UN's Special Rapporteur on Torture.* © Joan Boyle

Kevin and Joan, Norway, 2003. © Joan Boyle

Boyle with current and former students at celebrations marking the twenty-fifth anniversary of the establishment of the Essex Human Rights Centre, 2007.
© Myles Fisher

Kevin Boyle, 2008. © Myles Fisher

Kevin with Mark (left) and Stephen (right) on their first family visit to Belfast in March 2010, a month before Boyle became ill. © Joan Boyle

He was immediately swept up in the world of the non-violent opposition to apartheid. His first meetings, within hours of getting off the plane, were with members of the Black Sash, an organization of mainly white women, which helped Africans in trouble with the pass laws. The name came from early demonstrations in which the women wore black sashes as a symbol of protest and the Black Sash had emerged as a catalyst for white resistance to apartheid. Even though its members took advantage of their privileged status as whites to push the limits, they faced surveillance, harassment and occasional arrest. Joyce Harris, the vice president and one of the most prominent Black Sash figures, who joined Boyle for dinner, had once received a malicious phone call in which an unnamed voice said: 'This is the police. Your husband has just been killed in a road accident.'[3] The members of the Black Sash were widely considered to be the most well-informed experts on the pass laws, and their network of advice centres, staffed by volunteers, was a crucial resource for black victims of the system. Black Sash members took Boyle to several of these centres during his stay, giving him an opportunity to speak at length with those who came for assistance.

The next morning Boyle met Geoff Budlender. A student activist in the 1970s, Budlender had been friends with Steve Biko, the leader of South Africa's enormously influential Black Consciousness Movement, who had been killed in police custody in 1977, and, apart from Nelson Mandela, was considered to be the most towering figure in the history of the anti-apartheid struggle. In 1979 Budlender and two other liberal white lawyers had formed the Legal Resources Centre, inspired in part by organizations like the American Civil Liberties Union. The LRC was South Africa's first public interest law firm, designed, in Budlender's words, 'to make systematic attacks through the law on apartheid'. Like the Black Sash, the LRC faced regular harassment. As Budlender recalled, 'meetings were bugged, security police infiltrated the staff, people had stones thrown at their homes and the tyres of their cars slashed'.[4]

Budlender and his colleagues worked closely with the Black Sash, as well as with another public interest law organization, the Centre for Applied Legal Studies. CALS had been founded by John Dugard, a law professor at the University of Witwatersrand in Johannesburg, and a long-time critic of the apartheid system. Modest and unassuming, the soft-spoken Dugard had turned CALS into the leading centre for research on South African security legislation and policy, as well as part of a broader effort to under-mine the laws used to prop up apartheid. Curiously, despite the repressive nature of the state, South Africa's whites, perhaps because of their European Calvinist roots, had an exaggerated respect for the law, and consistently sought to justify their system in legal terms. 'South Africa was one of those bizarre countries in which there was a pretence of respect for the rule of law,' recalled Gilbert Marcus, who, in 1984, as a young lawyer, had just joined CALS and helped to show Boyle around. 'Of course, the reality was very different, but as long as South Africa pretended to respect the rule of law and the rule of the courts, it gave opponents of the regime, and particularly lawyers, a small opening to challenge the state.'

Boyle was also introduced to activists at the South African Council of Churches, the South Africa Institute of Race Relations, and to Max and Audrey Coleman. The couple had founded the Detainees' Parents Support Committee (DPSC) after their son Keith was arrested for his anti-apartheid activities. The Committee swiftly grew into a national organi-zation of relatives of the detained of all races fighting to get their loved ones out of prison. 'Because of the steadily increasing repression, we grew and grew,' recalled Audrey Coleman. 'We were handling people who were bearing the brunt of the actions of the security forces.'

All these organizations were part of a growing movement against apartheid. 'There was a camaraderie around a shared desire to unseat the apartheid government,' Coleman said, 'so we drew on each other as neces-sary.' They all helped Boyle to assemble a picture of a system as arbitrary and all-encompassing as it was cruel. In visits to several cities, he watched it in action. 'Arrests result from regular screening on the streets, and surprise raids on hostels, townships, or factories, where documents are demanded and checked,' he wrote.[5] Boyle observed

> police vans patrolling on a continuous basis and plain clothes officers dressed often in casual wear mingling with the crowds on the streets, suddenly stop-ping an African at random and demanding 'pass'. If it is not produced – or is incorrect (in the eyes of the officer) – the person is arrested and bundled into a police wagon. Thereafter, the patrol recommences its surveillance.[6]

Black Sash activists told him that police trawling operations focused on train and bus stations, where many Africans were arrested as soon as they arrived there, even if they had a pass allowing them to visit an urban area. 'The horror of that system,' Geoff Budlender remembered,

> was section ten of the Urban Areas Act. This said no black person could remain in what was called a 'prescribed area', which was an urban area, for more than seventy-two hours unless she or he had a form of qualification. The number of Africans in the cities by the time Kevin came was at least double the number of people who were legally entitled to be there. Probably more. So huge numbers of people were committing crimes every day. Their offence was being caught, rather than what they had done, because it was a routine thing which everybody did if you wanted to survive. The cities were where the jobs and the housing were.

Even with a valid pass, however, the mere presence of many black people was enough for the white police to detain them. This was just one example of the capriciousness of the system. Boyle spoke to one black man who had been arrested for failing to produce his pass on demand. The man had a pass, but his employer had taken it to register him so he could work. 'I was asked for my reference book by a plain-clothes policeman,' the man told Boyle. 'I told him it was with my employer in the building just a few yards away. But he said that's no good, you have to come with me. I pleaded – let me collect it and I will show I have one. But he just put me in the police truck. He didn't give me a chance to collect it.'[7] The man was found guilty.

The initial treatment of those arrested for violating the pass laws was usually a frightening one. Most of the victims Boyle interviewed 'complained of the behaviour of the charging officers. Insults, name-calling, slapping in the face for failing to speak up or move fast enough, being told they smelled. [These] were indignities commonly inflicted on those arrested under the pass laws.'[8]

After a night or a weekend in a cell, detainees were tried at either Commissioners' or Magistrates' courts. 'They were very disturbing places to be, according to Geoff Budlender, who had defended many victims. 'They were a place where people were processed rather than a place in which trials took place.'

As Boyle later wrote, 'the dress of those who appear in court following arrests the previous day – workers, women in shop coats, men in overalls, teenagers, people smartly dressed for the evening, others in the shabby clothes of the poor and jobless – offered eloquent testimony to the sweep of arrests through the black community'.[9]

Boyle watched court proceedings in several cities. Although his phone calls were almost certainly tapped and police informers likely attended some of his meetings, Boyle encountered no significant objections to his presence as an observer. 'The appearance of outsiders always caused a stir,' recalled John Dugard, who took Boyle to watch a court in Johannesburg:

> We would have been asked what we were doing, to which I always replied that courts were open to the public, so we had come to observe. Neither prosecutor nor commissioner were happy with our presence. This was clear. They would secretly converse after discovering that we were staying. Then they would proceed. The accused would be brought in to court. At first, the commissioners proceeded slowly because they were conscious of being observed. But then they got into their stride, and convictions were hurriedly made.

'It was one of the strange features of the system that, by and large, it was relatively open to view,' Budlender noted. 'For many years, they didn't really give a damn about what the outside world was saying. They were satisfied with their own righteousness. It was a strange thing. It was a brutal society that was surprisingly open to scrutiny.'

In court after court, Boyle watched the same grim scene unfold: the defendants lining up in corridors that led from the cells, shuffling into the dock as their names were called, with most cases decided in two or three minutes. The presiding officers were often in their twenties, young white men Boyle scathingly described as 'junior civil servants drawn from clerical and administrative grades with limited general educational attainment and no legal knowledge'.[10]

The specific details of any individual case appeared not to matter, partly because, as Boyle observed, prosecutors simply did not seem to care. 'It was clear in all trials observed that the prosecutor was not personally acquainted with the facts in any case he presented, or in a position to prove any feature of any case if called upon. On no occasion where trials were observed did the prosecutor call a witness.'[11] For their part, almost all those charged pleaded guilty, either because they had in fact broken the rules, or because they knew that a not guilty plea would lead to them being remanded in custody to await further proceedings, which could mean an even longer time in jail. 'The rational thing to do was to plead guilty,' observed Budlender, 'and get on with serving your sentence or pay the fine, whatever it was going to be, because there was no mileage in pleading not guilty. All you would do is spend weeks or months in jail waiting for your trial to happen.'

Occasionally, defendants tried to explain their circumstances. 'You would hear stories which were heart-rending,' Budlender recalled. 'Sometimes people would plead with the magistrates, and try and explain what they were doing there. But it cut no ice at all.' In one case Boyle witnessed, a woman who had been found guilty told the presiding official that she had simply forgotten her pass when bringing children of a relative into the city. The commissioner stated, 'You have to have permission to come to Johannesburg,' and imposed a sentence of thirty rand or thirty days in jail. A male defendant explained that he was just acting as a messenger between a husband living in a hostel for black workers and his wife. The commissioner told him he had no permission to be there and sentenced him to a fine of forty rand or eighty days in prison.[12] Boyle found that 'the default term of imprisonment fixed should the fine not be paid normally was an equivalent number of days' imprisonment to the number of rands imposed, and occasionally even double the fine'.[13] Many of the victims were too poor to pay the fine. In a number of cases, Boyle was so upset he paid the fines of women found guilty so they could avoid prison.

Given the acute poverty of most South African blacks, paying even the most modest fines was often impossible. The result was the vast majority of defendants went to jail. Those who had been through the experience told Boyle of appalling conditions. 'A thin foam mattress and a coarse blanket is normally issued to each prisoner,' he wrote. 'The blankets issued to black prisoners were often lice-ridden. Each cell is equipped with a toilet that is not closed off and often fails to flush. Women prisoners in particular complained of the smells and the lack of air in the cells. A cold tap and a basin is also contained in each cell but no soap or towel is provided.'[14]

Cases were usually disposed of so quickly, Boyle wrote in his report,

> that frequently, relatives, friends or employers who crowded into the court to deliver a reference book or other documentation had to make frantic efforts to present these before the defendant was remanded or fined and returned

to custody. In one case … a young woman entered the dock in Court B, and the prosecutor said 'No reference book, R.I.C.' [remand in custody]. The young woman was led from the dock, gesticulating wildly at the prosecutor that her relatives were trying to get to the front of the court. He finally turned to see someone struggling through the packed court to hand in her reference book. She was brought back to the dock and discharged.[15]

Despite the work of people like Geoff Budlender and John Dugard, there were so many people arrested that very few defendants had legal representation. During his 1984 visit Boyle saw only one case where a defendant had a lawyer, and none where an appeal was lodged. The chief presiding officer of a Johannesburg court smugly told Boyle, 'The safeguards are such that there is nothing to appeal about.'[16]

Some of those convicted were given the option of what was euphemistically called 'parole', but was in fact a thinly disguised form of forced labour. Boyle was told of Africans 'sold' outside court houses, following conviction, to local wheat and maize farmers, and of raids on black settlements deliberately timed to coincide with the harvest, when the need for what amounted to virtual slave labour was greater. Boyle heard accounts of workers on 'parole' locked in guarded compounds, whipped and beaten with sticks, and forced to work twelve hours a day or longer in the fields.[17]

As he systematically observed and collected information, Boyle, to most of the South Africans who were assisting him, remained the consummate professional, seeking to understand the workings of the system, asking questions, debating the best analytical format for his mission. 'He didn't wear his emotions on his sleeve,' Geoff Budlender remembered. 'He kept what he was feeling pretty much to himself. If, as I expect, he was experiencing pain, he didn't display it very publicly.'

But Boyle was deeply shaken by what he had seen. 'Kevin was disgusted,' John Dugard recalled. 'So was anyone with any sensitivity. The whole procedure made a mockery of justice.'

'The horrors going on here are appalling,' Boyle wrote to Joan. 'Children shot, children in prison. Meanwhile, in the Holiday Inn, the whites enjoy their holidays. Never will we come to this country.'[18] When a liberal South African academic said that there would be an open invitation for him to come and teach at the University of Cape Town, Boyle told Joan that he had replied, 'When the people who are the majority run the place, I would be delighted to show my family the fabulous sites he had shown me.'[19] Boyle found the separations from his family difficult, but in letters home he emphasized the importance of what he was trying to do. 'I miss you all terribly and ask you again to accept that this separation is for a reason we can all be proud of.'[20]

As Boyle left South Africa in mid-April 1984, a government-appointed commission, headed by Supreme Court judge Gustav Hoexter, issued a strongly worded report, condemning the pass law system as 'unnecessary, humiliating, and repugnant' and calling for its abolition.[21] In the following months, the government, trying to project a reformist image, introduced some changes to the system, leading Amnesty to ask Boyle to return in May 1985 to assess whether any progress was being made.

Kevin again connected with a wide range of anti-apartheid activists, among them Geoff Budlender, Max and Audrey Coleman, and the women of the Black Sash, including one of their most controversial figures, Molly Blackburn. A mother of seven, Blackburn had been arrested several times under South Africa's security laws. She was one of a very few number of whites to attend the mass funerals frequently held for blacks killed by the police and army: on one such occasion, a huge black crowd rose and greeted her with clenched-fist salutes as she arrived.

In all these meetings, as Kevin wrote to Joan,

> The core of the conversation is about whether the 'reforms' being intro-
> duced here are really reforms or are a subtle manoeuvre to appease world
> opinion now so conscious about South Africa. What is clearly confirmed is
> that my subject – Influx Control and the Pass Laws – are at the core of the
> issues ... so at least I am doing something important, to justify this terrible
> length of time I am away.[22]

His negative feelings about South Africa remained intense. 'It would be more bearable if I could honestly say I am enjoying myself, that I like the place,' he wrote in another letter. 'I don't. Its only compensation are the people ... I have met in the line of my work, or in the hotels, waiters, maids etc.'[23]

By the end of his trip, Boyle was not impressed with the government's so-called changes. 'Following personal observation,' he wrote,

> the conclusion must be drawn that the improvements achieved or that
> are possible of achievement are modest ... It remains a system where the

prosecutor is unable to provide any evidence independent of what can be extracted from an unrepresented, often poorly educated and confused defendant.[24]

In Boyle's mind, the changes were little more than tinkering with apartheid in order to preserve it.

Another indication that this was true came with the acceleration of the government's effort to uproot blacks from lands where they had long resided and force them to move to barren and desolate 'homelands'. 'It was a particularly brutal part of the apartheid process,' said Budlender, 'the forced removals of literally millions of people from the land which they owned or which they had lived for a long time.'

To better understand this situation, Budlender brought Kevin to the remote village of Mathopestad. The Bakubung people had legally purchased the land where Mathopestad now stood in 1912. Subsequently, however, the government declared it an area designated only for whites, but with Budlender's help the 1500 residents were resisting. To delay a decision, they engaged in long negotiations with the authorities, ostensibly over the logistics of a move, but never having any attention to agree. And they looked for any opportunity to publicize their plight internationally.

Budlender introduced Boyle to Chief John Mathope, a stocky man with a cane who favoured formal trilby hats. Earlier in the year, Mathope had hosted US Senator Edward Kennedy, and had just written to American Secretary of State George Shultz, appealing for the US to pressure the South African authorities. Mathope was adamant that the people would not move.

For Boyle, after so many grim encounters, a day in the village, with its spirit of defiance, was a refreshing change. To Joan he wrote, 'it was the best day of all'[25] during his trip. After he left South Africa and began writing his final report for Amnesty, however, President Botha's government imposed a nationwide state of emergency. In the face of intensifying opposition, including increasing numbers of whites joining the anti-apartheid movement, the police and army were given sweeping powers to break up demonstrations and riots and detain protestors and activists. Even harsher curbs on internal movement were implemented, along with draconian restrictions on the media. Tens of thousands were arrested, but the crackdown sparked greater violence. The country was on the edge of civil war, with townships turned into battlegrounds, while international pressure on the regime intensified.

In late 1985 Boyle submitted his report to Amnesty International. Nearly a hundred pages long, it carefully documented in measured tones the injustice of the pass laws. Boyle highlighted how subjecting black South Africans to arbitrary arrest and imprisonment violated numerous international human rights standards and conventions and, often, South Africa's own laws too. The victims of the pass laws, he wrote, 'have been frequently, perhaps routinely subject to cruel, inhuman and degrading treatment or punishment, some of it bordering on enforced slavery'.[26]

'It was an excellent report,' Malcolm Smart said:

First-rate stuff. We needed something to be readable, to be accessible to people, to understand the issue, to go into detail, and be accurate. We didn't pay for his time. He voluntarily gave us that. Two big trips, plus hours and hours of research and writing. But when he saw the reality, it gave him a drive and commitment to the topic. Kevin knew this was an appalling system. He wanted to get the report right. And he did.

To publicize the report, Amnesty planned a major event in Washington DC. 'The US had become the big mover on South Africa', said Smart, 'so we said – let's launch it in the States.' Boyle flew to Washington, and also stopped in Canada. In both places he made numerous media appearances and briefed journalists, lawyers, lawmakers and anti-apartheid activists. On 28 January 1986 he participated in a press conference in Washington attended by several members of the US Congress, at which the report was formally presented. Unfortunately, that same day, the US space shuttle *Challenger* exploded, knocking everything else off the news. A week later, however, Amnesty arranged a second media event, where a statement signed by fifty members of Congress was released, calling on President Botha to repeal the pass laws. The mayor of Los Angeles joined the growing campaign, as did activists all around the country. Within months, Congress overruled a veto by President Reagan and passed a law imposing sweeping new sanctions on South Africa. The move, which led many large multinational companies to withdraw from South Africa, was a major blow to the South African regime.

Just days after the release of Boyle's report, President Botha announced plans to amend the pass laws. In April he declared that the government would stop enforcing them, and that anyone in jail on pass law charges would be freed. In July the pass laws were formally repealed, the 'reference books' were abolished and restrictions on the movement of blacks to the urban areas were lifted. The most hated legal foundation of apartheid was gone. 'The sudden repeal of the pass laws in 1986 took everyone by surprise,' Geoff Budlender remembered. 'When I saw the draft law, I almost fell over. It was extraordinary.'

The combination of internal resistance – which the state of emergency had failed to quell – and growing international pressure, especially the US sanctions, had forced Botha's government, in Budlender's words, 'to show that it was in a reform mode'. Those with whom Boyle worked in South Africa are in no doubt that the Amnesty report played a significant role in the government's decision. 'I am sure it had an impact,' said Malcolm Smart. 'Boyle's mere presence as an international observer … under the auspices of Amnesty International,' added Gilbert Marcus of the Centre for Applied Legal Studies, 'was a form of putting pressure on the state.' In the years after apartheid, Marcus said, those on whose behalf Amnesty worked would repeatedly emphasize the importance of the campaign in which Boyle played such a major role. In John Dugard's view, Boyle's report 'was part of an accumulation of factors that led to the abolition of the [pass law] system'.

Repeal, however, did not end apartheid. Indeed, it was evident that President Botha was still scheming to keep blacks disenfranchised and maintain white political power. But the state had been fatally undermined. It would take several more years of external and internal pressure, and the shedding of much blood, but the end was inevitable. In 1994, Nelson Mandela, free after twenty-seven years in prison, was elected the first president of post-apartheid South Africa. Meanwhile, in Mathopestad, the stubborn resistance of the Bakubung people, which had so moved Boyle and which continued until the collapse of apartheid, paid off. They remained on their land.

[17]

Prisoners

ON 17 JULY 1984, two months after Boyle returned from his first visit to South Africa, a 32-year old prisoner walked out of Portlaoise jail in the Irish midlands. His name was Nicky Kelly. His case was one of the most notorious miscarriages of justice in modern Irish history. And Boyle had played a crucial role in securing his freedom.

Eight years earlier, on 31 May 1978, an armed gang had robbed the Dublin-to-Cork mail train near the town of Sallins, County Kildare, and made off with £200,000. Following the robbery, Kelly and two other men, all members of the Irish Republican Socialist Party, were arrested, charged and tried before a Special Criminal Court. The court, composed of three judges but no jury, was used primarily to handle terrorism-related crimes.

During their trial Kelly and his co-defendants repeatedly declared their innocence, and claimed they had signed confessions – which became the sole evidence for the prosecution – only after hours of relentless, often violent police interrogation. Kelly told the court that gardaí deprived him of food and sleep, hit him with a chair, kicked him in the groin, banged his head into lockers and pushed his face into a toilet, while denying access to a lawyer or doctor.[1] The police acknowledged the medical evidence of injuries, but, implausibly, alleged that they had been self-inflicted. When the confessions were nonetheless allowed in evidence, Kelly, certain he would be convicted of a crime he did not commit, decided to leave Ireland. In December 1978, three days before sentencing, while out on bail, he fled to the United States. In his absence, all three men were convicted. Kelly and one other defendant were sentenced to twelve years in jail. The third got nine years.

Five months after the verdict, the Provisional IRA, to which Kelly did not belong, issued a statement claiming responsibility for the robbery. In May 1980 Kelly's co-defendants had their convictions overturned on appeal, with the appeal court saying that it was not convinced that their confessions were voluntary. In New York, Kelly, confident that his conviction would also be reversed, decided to return home and clear his name. Instead, when he arrived at Dublin airport, he was arrested, handcuffed and taken directly to Portlaoise jail. In October 1980, even though his case was basically the same as his freed co-defendants, the Irish Supreme Court rejected his appeal. He faced the prospect of twelve years behind bars.

His plight sparked a major public outcry. The Irish Council for Civil Liberties, prominent political and cultural figures and even Amnesty International called for his release. There were rallies, petitions and a song recorded by one of Ireland's most popular singers, Christy Moore. The campaign was bolstered by allegations of the existence within the Garda Síochána of a 'heavy gang' who regularly used violence in interrogations on terrorist cases while officials looked the other way. Yet despite calls for a pardon, the Minister for Justice, Michael Noonan, continued to insist that the government could not overrule the courts. Sitting in his cell, Kelly despaired, and on 1 May 1983, began a hunger strike. 'I have no option but to take this extreme action to gain my rightful freedom,' he wrote.[2] The hunger strike, less than two years after ten IRA men had starved themselves to death in the North, further fuelled popular anger. Confronted by protest demonstrations outside his home, taoiseach Garret FitzGerald publicly backed his justice minister. Privately, however, he appears to have been deeply troubled, not only about the injustice Kelly had suffered, but also by the near-certain domestic political crisis if he were to die, as well as the problems the case would create for Dublin's credibility to comment on controversial judicial decisions in Northern Ireland.

Late one night in May 1983, Boyle received a phone call from FitzGerald. According to Gerard Quinn, who had done a law degree at Galway and had deferred a fellowship to Harvard for a year to work as Boyle's research assistant, FitzGerald and Attorney General Peter Sutherland wanted Kevin to file a case on Kelly's behalf as a matter of urgency before the European Commission of Human Rights. Boyle, who had been appalled at Kelly's treatment, readily agreed. 'The hunger strike was an incredible embarrassment to the government,' Quinn recalled. 'The government was in a fix. Kelly was in a fix. And Kevin was reached out to as a way of trying to create some neutral space whereby Kelly could get off the hunger strike and the government could get off the hook.'

Boyle, in collaboration with Mary Robinson (by now a prominent lawyer and an influential political figure), spent the next three weeks putting together a petition to be sent to Strasbourg outlining how Kelly's treatment was a violation of the European Convention of Human Rights. In keeping with his practice of giving his current and former students significant responsibilities, Boyle invited Quinn to conduct much of the research, which involved reading the transcripts of the original trial and all the Irish Court of Appeal decisions and trying to determine the relevant benchmarks under the European Convention. Quinn also helped in the initial drafting of the petition and subsequent documents.

On 7 June 1983, the thirty-eighth day of Kelly's hunger strike, the appeal was sent to Strasbourg:

> The applicant claims that his right to a fair trial under Article 6 of the Convention was breached, in that he was forced to confess guilt under psychological and physical abuse over a protracted period of interrogation, that his conviction solely on the basis of admissions made after such treatment, without access to legal advice or medical attention, raises not only issues of fair trial, but constitutes a violation of Article 3 as inhuman and degrading treatment. He further submits that it is inhuman treatment under Article 3 to require him to continue to serve a sentence of twelve years penal servitude for a crime he did not commit, following a trial where false evidence forced from him was the sole basis of his conviction.[3]

The petition appealed for 'urgent and immediate intervention by the Commission to save his life.' By this point, Kelly's physical condition was rapidly deteriorating. He had lost over forty pounds, his cheekbones were protruding, his complexion had gone grey, and he was suffering from continual stomach and chest pain. Doctors gave him a week to ten days to live.

The biggest immediate obstacle was that Commission procedures required that any case, to be deemed admissible, had be submitted within six months of the relevant final decision in local courts. That deadline had just passed, but Boyle and Robinson explained that the delay was caused by what they described as Kelly's fragile mental state. In a sign of how eager FitzGerald was to find a way out of the crisis, his government, the ostensible target of the petition, made clear that it had no objection to the case being heard in Strasbourg, despite the expiration of the deadline.

That night, shortly after the application had been sent to Strasbourg, Kelly agreed to end his hunger strike. The filing to the Commission was not made public at the time, and Kelly's supporters, as well as government officials, insisted there was no deal or private understanding. But after thirty-eight days, Kelly had stepped back from the brink. In a letter, Boyle expressed relief that the hunger strike was over, but told Kelly he had achieved the objective of generating 'very widespread concern about your circumstances and a general belief that you ought not to be where you are'. Explaining the next steps in the Commission process, Boyle stressed that Kelly now had an avenue to justice.[4]

Within six weeks – lightning speed for Strasbourg – the Commission responded that it was prepared to examine the question of admissibility. It asked the Irish government if Kelly had received a fair trial

> as required by Article 6 of the Convention in light of: (1) his claim that his conviction is based solely on admission statements that were voluntary? (2) the finding of the Court of Criminal Appeal that the statements of his co-accused obtained under similar conditions were inadmissible? (3) Does the conviction and sentence of the applicant solely on the basis of statements obtained against his will constitute inhuman and degrading punishment contrary to Article 3 of the Convention.[5]

The Commission sought a response to these questions by the end of October.

The nature and tone of the questions were a warning shot to the Irish government – a sign that if it was accepted despite being submitted after the six-month deadline, Kelly's case would get a serious and sympathetic hearing. Dublin replied to the questions from Strasbourg with a 35-page document. Much of it simply recounted the details of the arrest and trial of Kelly and his co-defendants. The document dismissed the question of whether the statements from Kelly that led to his conviction were voluntary by noting 'the fact that they were voluntary was found by the court of trial and affirmed on two appeals to the highest court in the state'.[6] And it was equally dismissive of questions about how the cases of Kelly and his co-defendants, which appeared so similar, could lead to their freedom and his imprisonment. The Court of Appeal, the Irish statement said, 'found that the circumstances in the applicant's case were sufficiently different from those obtaining in the other two to justify a different decision'.[7]

After receiving a copy of the Irish government's document, Boyle, Robinson and Quinn put together their response. In a 4 January 1984 letter to Kelly, Boyle wrote:

> I have just finished a very detailed study and draft of our Observations in preparation of a submission to the Commission of Human Rights. All of us have been working quite intensely on all aspects of this case. We are of course still left with the problem of the 'six-month rule', but subject to that I think we all believe and I think it is fair to tell you that we have a very strong case indeed. I personally have no doubt but that you have been a victim of the most reprehensible miscarriage of justice.

Boyle ended the letter by saying, 'Keep your spirits up and take comfort from the fact that quite a considerable amount of work is being committed on your behalf – which is no more than you deserve, given the injustice done to you.'[8] Boyle also visited Kelly at least once in prison, although the date remains unclear.

In February Boyle and Robinson sent the European Commission an 86-page rebuttal of the Irish government's position. Their document detailed all Kelly's complaints, and also raised some novel legal arguments: challenging the integrity of the Special Criminal Court where Kelly had been tried, as well as aspects of Ireland's Offences Against the State Act. The Special Courts were not a permanent feature of the Irish legal system. Under the Act, they could be brought into being if the authorities believed the established courts were incapable of dealing with a perceived threat. Faced with the activities of the IRA and a spill-over of violence from the North, the government had set up such a court in 1972. Boyle and Robinson argued that the Special Criminal Court was not in fact independent, since it had been instituted by government decision, and the judges who presided – without a jury – were also appointed by the government. This, they argued, represented a violation of Kelly's right under Article 6 of the European Convention of Human Rights to a fair trial 'by an independent and impartial tribunal'.

The document also singled out Article 52 of the Offences Against the State Act. This required anyone arrested under the Act 'to give a full account of their movements and actions during any specific period if demanded'. Refusal to cooperate could result in six months in jail. The article effectively eliminated the right of the accused to remain silent. With Kelly's interrogators alone having the power to decide if his answers were acceptable, Boyle and Robinson argued that the sole purpose of a relentless interrogation over more than sixty hours 'was to have him admit against his will to involvement in an offence he did not commit'.[9]

The document also included a series of tables, created on an early computer with Quinn's help, which challenged the contention that the circumstances of Kelly's case were significantly different from the two other defendants who had been freed on appeal. The charts compared the number of hours of detention, of formal interrogation, and of the deprivation of sleep, and contained a bar graph that clearly demonstrated how similar the cases were. 'It was the first time such technology had been used in a brief submitted to the Commission,' Quinn recalled. 'Kevin loved it.'

In Strasbourg, officials at the European Commission were impressed with the submitted materials. 'They were extremely well researched and compelling,' recalled Boyle's former student Michel O'Boyle:

> They demonstrated quite clearly that Kelly's case had been treated in a different way from those of the co-accused. The brief provided a rather extensive point by point comparison with the other cases to demonstrate that there existed no specific features to distinguish the Kelly case from the others and not quash his conviction. In reality he was being punished for going to ground [in the United States].

Yet when the Commission issued its decision on 17 May 1984, the application was deemed inadmissible. Boyle's concern about the six-month rule proved justified because the Commission's statement focused narrowly on the fact that the original petition was submitted later than six months after the final Irish court decision, and was not therefore eligible for consideration.

Boyle and Robinson did not, however, give up. Two weeks later, they submitted a confidential memorandum to the Irish government. In it, they reviewed the arguments they had made to Strasbourg, writing that we consider that if the case had not failed due to the six months' rule, these arguments or some of them would have been seriously examined by the European Commission of Human Rights. We are strongly of the view as practitioners experienced in that jurisdiction that at least some of points summarized below would have been accepted.[10]

They reiterated their view that Kelly did not get a fair trial, that his interrogation under Section 52 was contrary to the European Convention and that 'any conviction from the Special Criminal Court could now be raised at Strasbourg'.[11]

The memo ended with a forceful appeal for the government to pardon Kelly:

We believe that these legal considerations and arguments which have emerged from confidential and intense research necessitated by the Strasbourg case should be considered by the government. We think that taken together they supply a sufficient and we think compelling basis for executive intervention. The European Convention on Human Rights is not part of domestic law and cannot be considered as law in our courts. However, conformity with it is an obligation in international law ... We submit that this is the constitutional basis for government action on the Kelly case and that no issue of interfering or transgressing on the judicial power arises.[12]

On 17 July 1984, exactly two months after Strasbourg had rejected Kelly's application, Minister for Justice Michael Noonan announced that Kelly was being released on 'humanitarian grounds'. After four years and two weeks in prison, Kelly was a free man. Two days later, Boyle joined Kelly at a press conference. Outlining the details of the case he and Robinson had made to the European Commission, Kevin said the Irish government would have found it very difficult to defend its stance in Strasbourg.[13] And he stressed that the continued use of Article 52 probably would lead to more cases before the Court. On this point, he was right. It would take twenty-four more years, but in 2000 the European Court of Human Rights, in a case brought by Kevin's old comrade from the civil rights movement, Michael Farrell, ruled that Section 52 'destroyed the very essence of [the] privilege against self-incrimination and [the] right to remain silent'.[14] To Michael O'Boyle, the Kelly case stood out 'as an example of the utility of sometimes bringing ECHR proceedings in exceptional cases, even though the chances of success are slim'.

In 1992 Mary Robinson, now Ireland's president, issued Kelly a formal pardon. Not long after Nicky Kelly walked free, Boyle received a letter from another prisoner, but one with a very different story. Billy Hutchinson, aged twenty-nine, was a leading figure in the extreme loyalist paramilitary group, the Ulster Volunteer Force. He had been convicted of involvement in two sectarian murders of Catholics in Belfast in 1974, and was ten years into a life sentence. 'Dear Mr Boyle,' the letter began. 'I am a loyalist prisoner. I am serving a life sentence. The reason for writing is to find out if you would be interested in our case as life prisoners without a release scheme. We would be grateful if you could guide us in some direction that could get our case heard.'[15]

Hutchinson was the 'officer commander' for all UVF prisoners in the Maze prison, a role he had taken over from Gusty Spence, a UVF leader whose murder of Catholic barman Peter Ward in 1966 had helped fuel the tensions that led to the Troubles. During his time in prison, however, Spence had concluded that traditional loyalist violence was futile and that a political solution was the only way to end the conflict. Influenced by the evolution in Spence's thinking, Hutchinson too was moving in this direction – a transformation that would in the 1990s make him a key figure in ending UVF terrorism as the peace process gathered momentum. In 1984, though, Hutchinson was involved in a simpler, but in some respects just as daunting a task: working with a group of life prisoners to persuade the Northern Irish authorities to offer at least the hope of a parole or release scheme for inmates whose views, Hutchinson contended, had modified behind bars.

In his letter Hutchinson went out of his way to make sure that Boyle knew of his loyalist background, and stressed that he was not speaking for Republican prisoners. For his part, Boyle would undoubtedly have heard of Hutchinson, and Boyle's reputation had clearly penetrated the walls of the Maze. Indeed, some of Hutchinson's fellow loyalist inmates initially objected to Hutchinson contacting him because of Boyle's history as a leading figure in the civil rights movement. To Hutchinson, that did not matter.

'The reason why we wrote to him,' Hutchinson recalled,

> was we thought he was the one best placed. He was the one who seemed to be getting all the accolades – not just here but for his work abroad. It made more sense for us to talk to him on the basis that he was the human

rights lawyer with the best profile, and the one with the understanding of international law and human rights.

To the sceptics, Hutchinson said his response was 'hold on a minute. This guy is a professional, and what we have to assume is that he behaves in a professional way. He doesn't work on some sort of sectarian knee-jerk thing about who people are. And that means he comes without any preconceived notion about an individual or a group.'

Hutchinson's judgment was correct. Boyle quickly replied with a positive note offering to help and expressing optimism that 'there are some possibilities'.[16] A month later Boyle received a three-page memo from Hutchinson outlining the plight of the loyalist life-sentence prisoners. Although it would take another decade before the UVF declared a ceasefire, the document provided revealing insights into how the thinking of one-time-extremists like Hutchinson was changing. It claimed that many young Protestants who got involved in violence had been 'led astray by the bellicose rhetoric of demagogic leaders'.[17] This was a clear reference to Ian Paisley, who had acquired a reputation for making fiery speeches and then managing to disappear when the violence inevitably followed. It said that Hutchinson and his fellow loyalist lifers were now 'liberating themselves from the prejudices, fears, and illusions which became instilled in their minds from the advent of the Troubles ... Peaceful co-existence achieves more than violent confrontation.'[18] The document expressed remorse, noting that life prisoners 'are also human beings and recognize the suffering which resulted from their actions'.[19] It stressed the fact that the prisoners were using their time behind bars to learn new skills, take classes and forge a commitment to reintegrate into society and lead productive, non-violent lives. And yet, it concluded, the prisoners felt 'forgotten' by the outside world, except for their long-suffering families, because the authorities would not give them any idea when they might be considered for parole. It was on this question that Hutchinson had written to Boyle for advice.

In his response, Boyle, likely sensing the importance of the political evolution the document articulated, was predictably both practical and encouraging. He praised the memo, and said that if the Northern Ireland Office remained unresponsive, Hutchinson should consider making it public. He also suggested that in communicating with the authorities, Hutchinson should emphasize that lifers who were released understood they could be sent back to prison if they again became involved in illegal activities. This, Boyle said, would be a 'useful argument' that might help blunt official reluctance to consider a parole scheme, as would evidence from prisoners' families of possible employment opportunities that might be available after their release. Finally, he offered to encourage a non-sectarian group in Belfast called the Committee on the Administration of Justice in Northern Ireland, which was respected by the Northern Ireland Office and had good contacts in the bureaucracy, to work on the plight of those serving life sentences. 'Keep up your spirits,' the letter ended. 'I look forward to meeting with you.'[20]

During 1985 public pressure in Northern Ireland from both communities for changes in procedures for life prisoners was growing. As promised, Boyle lent his voice to the lobbying. 'The stuff we were doing with Kevin was great,' Hutchinson recalled. 'Some of the things he had been working on were the things that came to fruition.' Later that year the Northern Ireland Office issued a memo outlining a new policy. It stressed that life sentences were reviewed by prison officers every year, and at ten years the case would come before a Life Sentence Review Board, composed of civil servants, probation officers and a psychiatrist. While both republican and loyalist prisoners complained about the lack of openness in the process, it was a start, and by the end of the decade, it led to the release of a number of life sentence prisoners, including Billy Hutchinson. He was freed in 1990 and became an important figure as loyalist extremists became involved in the peace process. Years later, he remained grateful for Boyle's help. 'He wasn't in it for people because of the colour of the skin or their religion. He was in it for people who he felt were on the other end of an injustice that shouldn't have happened.'

As Boyle was providing advice to Hutchinson and other convicted loyalist murderers, he received an appeal for help in the case of one of the most notorious of Northern Ireland's republican killers. Dominic McGlinchey was the head of the Irish National Liberation Army, an extreme republican paramilitary group that had broken away from the Provisional IRA. Nicknamed 'Mad Dog' by the press, McGlinchey was known for his indiscriminate ruthlessness, and was linked to numerous murders and some of the most gruesome bombings of the Troubles. In 1984 he was arrested in the Irish Republic after a gun battle with police and became the first member of a nationalist paramilitary organization to be extradited from the state to the North, where he faced trial in Belfast on yet another murder case.

In August 1985 Boyle received a handwritten note from his old comrade from civil rights days, Bernadette Devlin McAliskey. He and Bernadette had lost touch in recent years when she had drifted into extreme left-wing politics and barely survived an attempted assassination by loyalist gunmen in 1981. Yet the note contained an echo of their previous closeness. 'Ever the champion of unpopular causes,' she began, 'I should like to think that I should write to you with a little more hope and less cynicism than to the rest.'[21]

Devlin enclosed a letter from McGlinchey's wife Mary, herself suspected of involvement in several killings, asking if Boyle would be willing to act as an independent observer at her husband's trial in Belfast. Her letter contained a list of alleged irregularities in her husband's case, and she pleaded 'if not for the sake of Dominic McGlinchey, than for the sake of justice in Ireland, come and see yourself'.[22] For her part, Devlin ended her note by writing, 'maybe I am the only person left who believes that even those with whom we profoundly disagree, those who themselves disregard the law, are entitled to fair and equitable treatment. I hope not.'[23]

In his response, Boyle said he could not attend McGlinchey's trial because he was not going to be in Ireland at the time. Always trying to be helpful, he suggested that McAliskey and Mary McGlinchey ask Amnesty International to send an observer. The rest of his note contained a quick update on his own activities. He mentioned the joint report he and Tom Hadden had written after the New Ireland Forum, noting to Bernadette that it was something 'with which you will disagree fundamentally'. But, Boyle added, 'you in particular and possibly you only will notice that it is at least consistent with the position I have maintained since 1968'. And he ended wistfully: 'Do you recall our naive views that we would have it all put right in a couple of months?'[24]

There is no record of a reply from Devlin. Apart from one brief encounter in Dublin years later, the two had no further contact. As for McGlinchey, he was acquitted in the case Boyle was asked to observe and he returned to his violent ways. In 1994 he was murdered in the Irish border town of Dundalk by some of his former associates.

The reason Boyle was not available for the McGlinchey trial was that for much of 1985 he was watching and working on Irish issues – and developments elsewhere – from the other side of the world. At the invitation of a fellow law professor and Northern Ireland native, W.G. 'Kit' Carson, he had been invited to spend a sabbatical year at La Trobe University in Melbourne. Carson, a Protestant who had come to despise the community in which he was raised, had left Northern Ireland in 1959 and never returned. By 1985 he held the chair in law at La Trobe, and had come up with the idea of holding a series of seminars on human rights issues that would be open to the public and broadcast on national radio.

'The concept of these seminars was different,' he recalled. 'We wanted to bridge the gap between the academy and the public. And the link was to be the ABC – the Australian Broadcasting Corporation.' Boyle's background and experience, Carson believed, made him an ideal participant in the project, which covered such topics as 'Human Rights and Crime', 'Australia: The Case for a Bill of Rights' and two subjects on which Kevin was an acknowledged expert: Northern Ireland, and, in the wake of his second mission for Amnesty International, South Africa. Carson and Boyle organized each event, inviting prominent figures from Australia and beyond, with Carson chairing and Boyle playing an important role as a speaker.

'The seminars were an enormous success,' Carson said. 'They were broadcast nationally, but even more significant was the fact that by popular request, they were repeated no less than twice (and possibly three times) on Radio Australia, which broadcasts to all over south-east Asia.'

Kevin and Joan enjoyed their seven months in Australia immensely – 'we fell in love with the place' Joan recalled – and for Boyle, the sabbatical became an important turning point. By 1985 he had been in Galway for seven years. He had built up the law department and put the university on the map with the creation of the Irish Centre for Human Rights. However, he was becoming increasingly frustrated by the lack of resources in what remained an academic backwater. Even with the support of university president Colm Ó hEocha, Boyle had been disappointed at not being able to raise more funds in the United States, where a human rights centre in Galway held much less appeal for Irish Americans than donating money to the 'cause' of fighting the British in the North. 'He felt he had done as much as he could in Galway given the financial constraints,' Joan said. 'He was getting restless.' For Boyle, his time in Australia, coupled with his second visit to South Africa, had broadened his horizons and whetted his appetite to play a bigger international role. As he later wrote to a Galway colleague, 'I found myself caught between the needs of my own career and the demands of the under-resourced faculty which would have caused me to go into reverse.'[25]

After returning to Galway in the autumn of 1985, Kevin's feeling of being trapped only intensified. To a friend in Dublin, he wrote:

> I still believe that what Ireland needs very much is an authoritative, independent centre for the study of human rights, both within Ireland and abroad, from an Irish perspective. That was my dream to create in Ireland, based in Galway. I won't say I have given up on it, but there is as you know an extraordinary tendency for inward-looking behaviour in our dear country. What strikes one from outside is the absence of a world view.[26]

His doubts and uncertainties were further heightened by the unexpected death, following a short illness, of his father in Newry. A month after getting back, Boyle wrote to Kit Carson. He described the time in Melbourne as 'one of the most exciting and fulfilling periods of our lives'. He then confessed, 'Joan and I have not settled in. The events of the last month [his father's death] have not helped, but we have more or less taken the decision that we should move.' What he had created at Galway, he acknowledged, 'cannot grow much more because it will not get the resources to do so. Anyway, it is time for a change.' Before leaving Australia, Boyle and Carson had discussed the possibility of a position for Kevin at La Trobe, and the idea of creating a human rights centre there. With this letter, Kevin formally expressed interest in a position at the university should one become available.[27]

A few months later, in early 1986, Joan was at home in Galway one morning when the phone rang. It was Martin Ennals, the former head of Amnesty International, looking for Kevin. When Joan said he was at the university, Ennals replied that he had an interesting job possibility for him, and then asked, 'how would you like to come live in London?' Despite Kevin's continuing frustration with Galway, Joan was less than enthusiastic. 'I said I would absolutely hate to come live in London,' she recalled, 'because we couldn't afford a decent house or decent schools for the boys [then eight and six] and it was an awful time to be Irish in England because of all the bombings and IRA activity.'

Ennals, taken aback, told Joan he still wanted to talk to Kevin. The job he was offering would change Boyle's life.

[18]

Document Censorship, Defeat the Censors and Help the Censored

ZWELAKHE SISULU had just sat down for dinner with his wife and children when six armed men wearing masks burst into his home in the black South African township of Soweto and dragged him away. 'I was taken to a vacant lot outside Soweto,' he later recalled. 'I believed I had come here to die.'[1] Sisulu, the son of the prominent anti-apartheid activist Walter Sisulu who was then being held in prison with Nelson Mandela, was the founder and editor of *New Nation*, a newspaper widely viewed as the 'authentic voice of black opposition'[2] to the South African government. For Zwelakhe, it was the start of a terrifying two-year ordeal in solitary confinement.

Sisulu's detention became the subject of the first campaign Kevin Boyle would wage as the founding director of Article 19, a new London-based organization created to oppose censorship and promote freedom of expression across the globe. Shortly before his arrest, Sisulu had been invited to join Article 19's International Board, which was chaired by the British writer and journalist William Shawcross and was composed of distinguished journalists, academics and lawyers from around the world. As Boyle arrived for his first full day on the job at the NGO's modest London office on 16 December 1986, he got word of Sisulu's plight. It was, Boyle wrote, 'something of a baptism by fire'.[3]

When former Amnesty International chief Martin Ennals had sought to contact Kevin the previous spring, it was to tell him about plans to establish Article 19 and sound him out about running what was envisioned as an 'Amnesty International for the word',[4] an organization that would campaign 'to document censorship, defeat the censors and help the censored'[5] in the same way that Amnesty International was doing for prisoners of conscience. The name came from Article 19 of the Universal Declaration of Human Rights, which declared that 'everyone has the right to freedom of opinion and expression'.

The organization was the brainchild of American entrepreneur and philanthropist J. Roderick MacArthur, son of the multi-millionaire John D. MacArthur, who had established the MacArthur Foundation. But Rod, as he was known, became estranged from his father, went his own way, and, after a successful business career, set up his own foundation. With a particular emphasis on human rights, the J. Roderick MacArthur Foundation became known as 'the little MacArthur Foundation' to distinguish it from his father's much larger one. Rod MacArthur died in 1984, but his three children were determined to turn his dream of a free speech equivalent to Amnesty International into reality by subsidizing the creation of a new organization with a $500,000 grant. Like Amnesty, they wanted it to be based in London, and they turned for advice to Aryeh Neier. A towering figure in the world of human rights, Neier was a New York lawyer who had been head of the American Civil Liberties Union and co-founder of Human Rights Watch. Neier in turn contacted Martin Ennals, who recommended that Boyle be considered for the job of Article 19's first director.

From his earliest days at Queen's University, freedom of expression was a cause in which Boyle passionately believed. His first published work was a 1962 article in the Queen's student newspaper about the banning of a controversial play staged by the drama troupe to which he belonged. This was followed by an article in a student magazine analysing the rigid censorship in the Irish Republic. Defending the right to speak out and demonstrate had been a central feature of his activities in the early days of the civil rights movement, and many of the legal cases in which he was subsequently involved also concerned the right of people to express unpopular views, engage in unconventional behaviour, or be safe from official retaliation for speaking or acting against authority. Boyle believed, as he would later write, that 'freedom of expression is an individual right of the human personality ... It underpins the right to participate in public life and the right to be heard by those in authority.'[6] He was fond of quoting a phrase in one of the earliest resolutions passed by a just-formed United Nations in 1946: 'Freedom of expression is the touchstone of all freedoms to which the UN is consecrated.'[7]

Indeed, even before Martin Ennals approached him, and, despite his numerous other commitments, Boyle had been working on an ambitious project for the National Newspapers of Ireland (NNI) called 'Press Freedom and Libel'. Representing all Ireland's major newspapers, the NNI was deeply concerned about the way the country's rigid libel laws were being used to stifle the media. 'The law on libel – or published defamation – in Ireland was exceedingly restrictive,' recalled Conor Brady, then the editor of *The Irish Times*:

> The presumption of guilt rested upon the newspaper or broadcaster. An apology was an acknowledgment of fault and swept away any defence. Actions against newspapers in the courts by public officials and politicians were common and were almost always successful. Awards for damages were costly and represented a significant drain on resources in media organizations where profit margins were traditionally modest. More insidiously, the punitive libel regime often acted as a brake on vigorous journalism.

Vincent Browne, one of Ireland's most distinguished journalists, was then the editor of the *Sunday Tribune*. In early 1986, at his suggestion, the NNI asked Boyle to examine the issue. 'The idea,' Browne recalled, 'was to try to persuade our parliament to change the libel law in a way that would resemble the libel regime in the US.' In the historic 1964 case of *New York Times Co. v. Sullivan*, the US Supreme Court had ruled that public figures had to prove that false statements were made with 'actual malice' and with 'reckless disregard for whether it was false or not'. The ruling set a much higher bar for libel than did Irish law. 'The goal was to get Boyle to construct the legal arguments for a change in the policy,' Browne said.

Enlisting his one-time student and now Galway law faculty colleague Marie McGonagle, Boyle threw himself into the project with characteristic enthusiasm, conducting interviews and travelling frequently to Dublin to study court records of libel cases. 'When we interviewed editors, journalists, politicians and lawyers,' McGonagle said, 'they would say for every hundred cases the media would only win five. In all the rest, the media would settle and pay out, or go before a jury, which usually did not side with the media.' By December 1986 Boyle and McGonagle had completed the draft of a report analysing Irish case law, comparing it with other international models and proposing a series of reforms. When the NNI finally published its report in 1988, however, the initial response was lukewarm. 'Politicians weren't interested,' Marie McGonagle noted, 'because they saw defamation as a weapon to obtain media coverage or to use themselves.' Indeed, she recalled the former editor of *The Irish Times*, Douglas Gageby, jokingly telling her, 'Marie, I hope you live long enough to see defamation reform.' But it was a crucial first step in a long, complex and contentious process, and it would lead, more than two decades later, to the passage of new and less restrictive legislation. As Conor Brady noted, 'the Boyle-McGonagle report was to prove the foundation upon which Irish libel and contempt laws were gradually relaxed'.

Even with this significant role on the national stage in Ireland, in the wake of his work related to the Troubles, Boyle, still frustrated by the constraints of a backwater like Galway, leapt at the opportunity when the Article 19 job came up. As part of the application process, he was asked to write a letter outlining his skills and achievements. It offers a revealing glimpse of how he saw himself at this critical turning point. For all that he had accomplished, and despite his eagerness to get the Article 19 job, Boyle remained modest and self-effacing, a trait that was evident in the letter. 'I have had to date a reasonably successful academic career,'[8] he wrote, making brief references to building up the Galway law faculty and helping to establish an association of Irish law scholars. About his early political activism in Northern Ireland he was notably reticent. 'It's enough to say about that phase that my main contribution was on the level of ideas and presentation.' The letter further developed this theme by stressing Boyle's academic research on policing and the use of emergency powers, and his role as a consultant to the New Ireland Forum.[9]

Indeed, with the passage of time, Boyle would talk less and less about what he did during the initial period of the civil rights movement. Few of his colleagues – then or later – were aware of how extensive and pivotal his role had been, and at home he rarely mentioned it to his sons. 'It was avoided,' Stephen would say years later. In his view, his parents 'wanted to spare me and Mark from having to contend with all that stuff they had to deal with'. Mark agreed. 'We didn't have to think about this stuff. It didn't have to shape your life.' Kit Carson saw a darker reason:

> Part of the explanation for his reticence in the matter is he carried a certain amount of guilt about what kind of a tiger he [had] unleashed. He most sincerely wanted all the things he believed and all the actions he took, but he had not wanted the horrible side of it to happen the way it did. I am not sure that he ever reconciled within himself the fact that that had happened.

Whatever the case, Boyle would increasingly keep memories of those turbulent early years to himself.

Kevin Boyle was much more forthcoming in his letter about the establishment of the human rights centre in Galway, his cases before the European Commission of Human Rights and his Amnesty International missions in Africa. Always an energetic networker, he also stressed his 'good relationships with many people in the international human rights community around the world'.[10] And he ended his job pitch on a simple note: 'I would like the job because I want a new challenge and I want to achieve more for human rights victims.'[11] In a letter to a friend, he was characteristically self-deprecating. The job, he wrote, 'has the merit of being an unusual solution to the academic male menopause, and also may do some good'.[12]

Boyle flew to London to meet the Article 19 board of directors. 'I didn't know Boyle,' said Aryeh Neier, 'but I knew of him. We interviewed him and were favourably impressed.' William Shawcross recalled, 'he was the most charming personality. He was outstanding, excellent, and we recruited him.'

First, however, Kevin had to convince Joan. 'Kevin found it such an exciting and totally different challenge he wanted to accept immediately,' Joan recalled. 'It was me who did not want to uproot myself and the children so soon again [after Australia] and there was a fair battle of wills over the move to England. We had a few rows about it. But Kevin won the day.' As Stephen Boyle noted, 'we were all sort of invested in Dad's career and success. It was an unspoken thing that we would not make it any harder than it was. We knew what he was doing was important.'

Kevin Boyle took the helm of Article 19 at what he later described as 'an extraordinary moment – although few realized it at the time'.[13] With the benefit of hindsight, it was clear that huge changes were brewing: the fall of the Berlin Wall, the collapse of apartheid in South Africa and of communism in the Soviet Union and a dramatic expansion of democratic freedoms around the world. Yet at the time none of this was immediately evident. As Boyle told an interviewer for National Public Radio in the United States, 'censorship is a global norm. Despite the technical capacities we have – in radio or television and print and fax and Xerox, it is not a censorship-free world. In fact, it's a world which has a gag right round the centre of it.'[14]

Boyle listed a series of examples. 'In South Africa, it is a criminal offence to write a story about what you know or have witnessed about an incident involving in the security forces. Our board member, Zwelakhe Sisulu, has been jailed. In Romania, your typewriter has to be registered in an effort to try to control the unofficial circulation of information.'[15] And he expressed concern about what was happening in the West:

> In the United States one of the major concerns is the creeping reach of national security considerations over the traditional respect for freedom of expression. In Britain, the BBC has recently been prevented from carrying interviews with a number of banned organizations, like Sinn Féin. For the first time the BBC is being told by the government whom they may interview and whom they may not.[16]

Pledging to campaign for 'journalists who are under detention, arrest, or under threat, writers whose books have been banned, and media that are threatened by a particular new law or new bill', Boyle was ready to put Article 19 – as an ideal and an organization – on the map.

'It was a huge challenge,' Joan Boyle recalled, 'and very different from academia. Kevin soon realized he would have to smarten up, and some new suits and silk ties were purchased because this was London and not the rural west of Ireland.' When the news of this sartorial upgrade got back to Galway, it caused much amusement among Kevin's old friends.

Boyle's first day on the job was consumed with the plight of Zwelakhe Sisulu. He was in touch with Amnesty International, which immediately issued an urgent appeal. Boyle released his own statement to the press, and also contacted Index on Censorship. Established in 1972 with the support of such prominent writers as Boyle's university idol Samuel Beckett and the British poet Stephen Spender, Index focused on publishing the work of writers and intellectuals who faced persecution in the Soviet Union, eastern Europe and elsewhere. Roderick MacArthur and his children had initially hoped Index would support the creation of a campaign arm to go along with its publishing activities. When that did not materialize, they turned their energy and resources into the establishment of Article 19. For Boyle and his NGO, it was the start of a complicated relationship, which would include a difficult and ultimately unsuccessful attempt to merge the two organizations. In the case of Sisulu, however, Index readily agreed to issue a briefing paper based on material that Boyle supplied.

Boyle's vision for Article 19 involved three aspects: building a data base to document censorship; conducting research on conditions in specific countries; and campaigning for those who were being silenced. One of the first people he hired was Matthew Piette, a recent Cambridge English literature graduate. Piette had become intrigued with freedom of expression issues after seeing someone on a bus wearing a T-shirt with a photograph of a gagged Samuel Beckett and the caption 'If Samuel Beckett had been born in Czechoslovakia, we'd still be waiting for Godot'. The T-shirt had been produced, with Beckett's support, by Index on Censorship, and when Piette started to volunteer at the Index office in London, he was urged to apply for a paying job at Article 19. Piette vividly remembered his interview with Boyle. 'Kevin had this vision,' he said. 'He started talking about his ambition to have Article 19 host the work of banned writers worldwide on a very, very early form of the Internet. This was the precursor of the World Wide Web. Kevin was way ahead of his time.'

Years later, Boyle would note that 'the new Article 19, focused as it was on information, seemed an ideal candidate to embrace'[17] the emerging technological revolution. To guide the creation of a computerized information bank for collecting, processing, analysing and transmitting information on censorship, Article 19 hired Friederike Knabe, who had worked on technology issues at Amnesty International. Piette, with no experience, was soon helping Knabe to process the volume of information being collected. Within a year, budget and technological problems forced Boyle to scale back his vision of a comprehensive data base, but, as he wrote, 'the discipline of systematic gathering and inputting of information in-house, including crucially on media laws'[18] played an important role as Article 19 began to produce detailed reports on the working of censorship around the world.

One of its targets was the Human Rights Committee, a body in Geneva set up by the countries that had ratified the UN's International Covenant on Civil and Political Rights. Under the Covenant, signatory nations were required to submit regular reports to the Committee, which held public proceedings. Within months, Article 19 had drafted and submitted what it called 'Commentaries', spelling out human rights failings in numerous countries, including, in 1987 alone, Senegal, Poland, Tunisia, Romania, Zaire and the People's Republic of the Congo. It was the first time that an NGO had inserted itself into these deliberations, and was as well a way for Article 19 to gain visibility at the level of the UN. As Boyle subsequently noted, 'the Commentaries encouraged both the Committee and governments to give attention to freedom of expression and media issues which hitherto had been largely ignored'.[19] At the same time, Boyle and his colleagues sought to make copies of the Commentaries available to activists in the countries themselves.

Beginning in the summer of 1987, Article 19 started to publish a regular quarterly bulletin. The first one contained a front-page statement from Boyle introducing the new organization and calling for the formation of 'an alliance of people throughout the world committed to information freedom as a human right'.[20] In the subsequent pages was a new appeal for the freedom of Zwelakhe Sisulu, as well reports on censorship in Paraguay, where dictator Alfredo Stroessner had just declared a state of siege, and in Ireland, looking at the role of Catholic church in underpinning the government's Censorship of Publications Board.

There was also a call, in the wake of the catastrophic accident in April 1986 at the Chernobyl nuclear power plant in the Soviet Union, for greater transparency from governments and the International Atomic Energy Organization in discussing nuclear safety. This last appeal was one in a series of Article 19 initiatives designed to make the case that freedom of information and its denial had repercussions beyond mere curbs on journalists or writers. Subsequent reports would examine the link between human rights and the availability of information on reproductive health, and one report, *Starving in Silence*, explored the connection between famine and censorship. As Boyle would later write, 'Chernobyl and the spread of AIDS throughout the world have contributed to the realization that full freedom of informa-tion is not a luxury but may literally be a matter of life and death.'[21]

To boost the organization's profile, Boyle travelled constantly, attending conferences, meeting journalists and scholars and giving interviews. In 1988 he appeared on American TV morning news shows and ABC's *Nightline* with Ted Koppel, while expanding his already formidable network of contacts. At a dinner in New York, for example, he was joined by such luminaries as *Harper's* magazine editor Lewis Lapham, *The Nation* editor Victor Navasky, Walter Isaacson of *Time*, Sydney Schanberg, who had won acclaim for his coverage of the fall of Cambodia to the Khmer Rouge in *The New York Times*, US diplomat Richard Holbrooke and Aryeh Neier. Neier was impressed with how Boyle was boosting Article 19's profile. 'I think the organization fairly quickly established itself as a serious place for the protection of freedom of speech.'

Boyle needed to draw on all his connections for the next ambitious project – the *Article 19 World Report, 1988*. That year was the fortieth anni-versary of the Universal Declaration of Human Rights, a document Boyle revered, and to mark the occasion he oversaw the publication of a 340-page report that explored the nature of censorship in fifty countries around the world. 'The idea,' recalled Lance Lindblom, who was president of the J. Roderick MacArthur Foundation, 'was to have a report like the State Department has an annual report, or Amnesty International had an annual report. Only this one would be on freedom of expression.' Matthew Piette remembered that Boyle 'had had this amazing network of people, and he contacted writers in every country. We had this huge fax machine and we'd be faxing back and forth. And he would give me incredible guidance.'

It was not an easy process. 'It was an absolute nightmare,' said William Shawcross, who wrote the preface. 'It was terribly difficult to do, and took forever and caused a lot of agony and a lot of puffing of Kevin's pipe to get it right.' At one point, as work on the report progressed, there was a break in at the Article 19 office, which Matthew Piette and others suspected may have been the work of South African security agents.

The fifty country reports, written by eyewitnesses, independent experts and human rights organizations, were not simply a record of repression, but, as Boyle put it, an effort 'to detail the legal standing of rights to expression and information, the structure of the media and limitations on them, and how censorship, if it is practised, functions and is justified'.[22] The reports dealt with numerous issues in the news: the emergence of *glasnost* in the Soviet Union, continuing censorship in South Africa, the silencing of dissident voices in China, the Irish government's ban on interviews with members of the IRA's political wing, Sinn Féin, states of emergencies in Central and South America and the concentration of media ownership in Britain and the United States.

Boyle convinced the British publisher Longman and Times Books, the publishing arm of *The New York Times*, to bring out British and American versions of the report. Copies were sent to every government that was a member of the UN, and Boyle embarked on a whirlwind media tour to promote the study. Publication of the report was a significant turning point. 'He was absolute stickler for accuracy, and for getting the tone right, and he displayed his enormous knowledge and his commitment and his essential intellectual honesty in his attention to detail, and I think everyone respected that,' said Frances D'Souza, an Oxford-educated scientist who had worked on development issues in Africa and would, in 1989, succeed Boyle as director of Article 19. 'The study was very important,' recalled William Shawcross. 'It set an internationally recognized standard.' And it put Article 19 on the map.

By now Boyle had assembled a small but dedicated staff, what Matthew Piette described as a 'ragtag team': young, passionate, devoted to the cause and especially devoted to Kevin. 'He had an incredible enthusiasm that just permeated the building,' Piette recalled. 'He had a very strong sense of mission, but he also had a twinkling sense of humour. It was a lot of fun.' As Frances D'Souza remembered, 'in building an organization that was growing, he had these wild and wonderful ideas, and he got these wild and wonderful people to do it. The staff loved him. You couldn't help but be fond of him. He was a straightforward, honest, passionate, bright, and funny guy.'

The work at Article 19, as Boyle wrote to a friend, was 'immensely stimulating', but stimulating 'at a cost'.[23] Kevin and Joan had chosen to live in Colchester, both because of its affordability compared to London and its proximity to the University of Essex, where he was a board member of the university's human rights centre, which had been explicitly modelled on the one he had created in Galway. But it meant that Boyle had a daily round-trip commute of 120 miles to the office at 90 Borough High Street, Southwark, in London. For their part, the transition from Galway had not been easy. Both Mark and Stephen had left close friends in Ireland, and Joan initially struggled to make friends in the more formal and reserved social climate of south-eastern England. Kevin also had mixed feelings, writing to an old Galway friend that 'I suppose I would prefer to be in the west of Ireland.'[24] Still, by 1988, the family situation had settled down. 'The children are very well-adjusted and like their local school,' Boyle wrote in another letter. 'Joan is doing a few days teaching [of French], something it is unlikely she would have found at home [in Ireland].'[25]

The pressure-cooker at Article 19, compounded by the burdens of dealing with budgets, administration and a demanding board of directors, reinforced Boyle's desire, once he felt the organization was on a firm footing, to return to the academic world. In mid-1988 the University of Essex offered him a job as professor of law and director of the human rights centre, to begin in the autumn of 1989. Despite some mixed feelings, he set a departure date from Article 19 of June 1989. In the intervening months, however, he would be caught up in a global confrontation over freedom of expression where his position would put his life at risk.

Kevin, Joan, and the boys celebrated Christmas 1988 with the prospect that the Essex job would offer a welcome respite from the brutal pace of the previous two years. The mood was further lightened by the news just before the holidays that Zwelakhe Sisulu, for whose release Kevin had campaigned since starting at Article 19, had finally been freed after two years of harsh solitary confinement. The two men would finally meet in January, at a human rights conference Boyle attended at the University of Stellenbosch, near Cape Town. Years later, Sisulu said that 'it was this campaign, I believe, that ultimately led to my release from jail sentence'.[26]

For a workaholic like Boyle, the period between Christmas and New Year was, in Joan's words, 'the only time he really relaxed'. Kevin had a long-standing ritual on Christmas Day. Drink in hand, he would call friends all over the world. In the evening, with yet another drink, he loved to watch movies on TV. But he also religiously followed the news, and during those otherwise quiet days, one story stood out for him. In September, Viking Press had published a new novel, *The Satanic Verses*, by the Indian-born British writer Salman Rushdie, who had won the distinguished Booker Prize for a previous work, *Midnight's Children*. The new book was a tale of two Muslim immigrants to the UK struggling to reconcile their Islamic roots with the temptations and contradictions of the West. Rushdie, whose Muslim family moved from Bombay to Britain when he was a child, later described the book as 'an attempt to create a work out of his own experience of migration and metamorphosis'.[27]

But some Muslims, driven by rumours rather than experience of reading the novel, took offence at the book's alleged portrayal of the prophet Muhammad. During the autumn it had been banned in India, denounced in Saudi Arabia and made the target of growing anger among conservative elements in Britain's own Muslim community, who considered it blasphemous. In December 7000 Muslims gathered for a ritual burning of the book in the English town of Bolton. With the TV on one evening during the holidays, Kevin turned to Joan. 'He said, "watch this space",' she recalled. 'He envisaged trouble ahead.' In January a second copy of the novel was burned by angry British Muslims in Bradford. A month later several thousand people stormed the US Information Centre in Islamabad, Pakistan, chanting 'Hang Salman Rushdie' and burning effigies of the writer. Several demonstrators were killed by police. In Iran, the country's leader, Ayatollah Khomeini, unaware of the book's existence, saw reports of the violence in Pakistan on Iranian television, was told by his son that Rushdie's novel was the cause, and immediately dictated a *fatwa* – a religious edict. It declared that 'the author of the book entitled *The Satanic Verses* – which has been compiled, printed, and published in opposition to Islam – and all those involved in its publication … are sentenced to death'.[28] Iran then offered a multimillion dollar reward to anyone who killed Rushdie, and said any Muslim who died in the effort would be considered a 'martyr' with a direct ticket to paradise.

It was an unprecedented threat. As Rushdie's friend the writer Christopher Hitchens, observed: 'The theocratic head of a foreign state offered a large sum of money, in his own name, *in public*, to suborn the murder of a writer of fiction who was not himself Iranian.'[29] In a personal account of his ordeal, Rushdie later wrote that Ayatollah Khomeini 'was a head of state ordering the murder of a citizen of another state, over whom he had no jurisdiction; and he had assassins at his service, who had been used before against "enemies" of the Iranian revolution, including those who lived outside Iran'.[30] As Khomeini's *fatwa* was enthusiastically endorsed by a host of Islamic fundamentalist organizations with a long involvement in terrorism, including Hezbollah in Lebanon, British authorities rushed the writer into hiding, under heavy guard, from which he would not emerge for nearly a decade

In retrospect, the Rushdie affair would come to be seen as the opening salvo in what became an enduring theme of the years that followed: the clash between Islamic extremism and western liberal democracy. In its passions and bloodshed it was a foretaste of the mistrust, tension and conflict that would characterize so much of the West's subsequent dealings with the Islamic world. It created a climate of heightened pressure and violence, targeting both liberal thinkers in Islamic nations and critics of extremist Islam in the West. Rushdie's Japanese and Italian translators were killed; his Norwegian publisher was shot three times but survived. Liberal imams in Brussels were murdered. Bombs went off in bookstores in central London. Meanwhile, the episode exacerbated tension and misunderstanding between the large numbers of immigrants from Islamic countries and the western societies in which they now lived.

Although the European Community and other western governments denounced the move, the criticism was softened by broader consider-ations, such as the plight of western hostages in Lebanon and concern about losing access to the valuable Iranian market. Meanwhile, the *fatwa* instantly created a climate of unprecedented fear among writers, publishers, booksellers and academics. Six days after the Ayatollah's declaration, Boyle organized an emergency meeting at the headquarters of the National Union of Journalists in London. In addition to members of Article 19, those in attendance included representatives from the NUJ, Index on Censorship, the international writers' organization PEN, the Writers' Guild of Great Britain and the Publishers' Association. Denouncing the *fatwa* as 'armed censorship',[31] they decided to form the International Committee for the Defence of Salman Rushdie and his Publishers, with Boyle as the chair. For Boyle, who deeply believed that freedom of expression was a universal value, which underpinned all the other freedoms he had spent his life defending, the *fatwa* was a threat that had to be resisted, whatever the personal risks. 'There are times in all our lives when you would wish it was otherwise,' he wrote later, 'but you take up the challenge.'[32]

A few days later, Boyle, the chair of Article 19's board William Shawcross, influential British playwright Harold Pinter (who in 2005 would win the Nobel Prize for Literature), Pinter's wife, the historian Lady Antonia Fraser, and a few others gathered in an ornate meeting room at the House of Commons. They decided to draft a letter in support of Rushdie and to seek the signatures of as many writers and intellectuals as possible before publishing it in newspapers and magazines around the world. 'It was crucial that the writing community, the literary world, should rally to Rushdie's defence,' recalled Aryeh Neier. 'Had that not happened, the impact of the *fatwa* and the physical attacks on people who were associated with Rushdie's book would have had a far more devastating impact on freedom of expression.'

Boyle took the lead in drafting the document. With the help of Shawcross, Pinter and others, they reached out to as many Nobel Prize winners as they could. Matthew Piette handled much of the communication and logistics. 'It was letters and fax back then,' he recalled. 'Kevin was directing everything. And all these wonderful Nobel Prize winners immediately signed it with no questions asked.' Within ten days they had a thousand signatures. There were five winners of the Nobel Prize for Literature, including Boyle's hero Samuel Beckett. Seven others who signed would subsequently be awarded the prize, among them Kazuo Ishiguro, Doris Lessing, Mario Vargas Llosa and Boyle's old friend from Belfast, the poet Seamus Heaney. Other notables included Graham Greene, Norman Mailer, Elie Wiesel, V.S. Pritchett and John Hersey. Significantly, a half-dozen exiled Iranian writers signed, as did authors from Egypt, Tunisia, Jordan, Pakistan and the United Arab Emirates, as well as from the Soviet Union and eastern Europe. It was a striking rebuff to the argument that freedom of expression was a purely western notion.

Although the letter itself was barely a hundred words, Boyle spent hours refining it. 'I remember the pains he took,' said Matthew Piette. 'He was aware it was the first big Islam versus the West controversy.' The document was very much a reflection of Boyle's values and sensitivities. 'On 14 February,' it began,

> the Ayatollah Khomeini called on all Muslims to seek out and execute Salman Rushdie, the author of *The Satanic Verses*, and those involved in its publication worldwide. We, the undersigned, insofar as we defend the right to freedom of opinion and expression as embodied in the Universal Declaration of Human Rights, declare that we are also involved in the publication.[33]

The next sentence acknowledged the strength of feeling against Rushdie. 'We appreciate the distress the book has aroused, and deeply regret the loss of life associated with the ensuing conflict.'[34] To Matthew Piette, this was typical of Boyle. 'Kevin was very strong on issues of religious freedom because of the Troubles. He wanted to accommodate the fact that there were intensely held beliefs on the other side. I think that was signature Kevin.' The letter contained two appeals. One was to 'world opinion to support the right of all people to express their ideas and beliefs and to discuss them with their critics on the basis of mutual tolerance, free from censorship, intimidation, and violence.'[35] The other appeal was to world leaders to 'continue to repudiate the threats made against Salman Rushdie and those involved in the book's publication world-wide'.[36]

On 2 March the letter was published in sixty-two newspapers and magazines around the world, with Boyle having used his extensive list of journalistic contacts to ensure the widest possible dissemination. A press conference was held in London to publicize the document. Boyle told reporters that its publication was 'an unprecedented event [that] gave an opportunity for writers all across the world to speak in one voice for freedom of the imagination and in defence of Salman Rushdie'.[37] Privately, he was thrilled. 'It was one of the world's greatest coordinated protests,' he wrote years later, '1000 signatures. Think of the challenge of agreeing a statement and responding.'[38] The letter made Article 19 a voice for Rushdie, who remained in hiding, and Boyle became the public face of the campaign – and thus a potential target. 'That took a hell of a lot of courage,' Boyle's old friend Bert Lockwood observed. 'He was quite visible.' As Matthew Piette recalled, 'we were at risk, because we were effectively representing Rushdie. We did receive threats. Although it didn't happen, there was talk of having a policeman stationed outside the Article 19 office, because it was quite dangerous.' Yet Boyle never let on, to his colleagues or his family, that he was worried. 'Kevin would have handled that,' Piette said. 'He was very good at protecting us from anxiety.' Joan Boyle had a similar recollection. 'Kevin was so swept along by the excitement and the effort of creating the initiative that I am not sure he ever felt in danger. I do not recall being particularly frightened.'

The campaign for Rushdie consumed Boyle's remaining months at Article 19. It included a meeting with Britain's Foreign Secretary, Sir Geoffrey Howe, to press for stronger British government backing for Rushdie and for pressure on Iran, numerous letters, including to the United Nations Security Council and to the head of UNESCO, regular meetings with journalists and plans to collect more signatories of the letter. Boyle also took the initiative for Article 19 to conduct a study on Britain's own blasphemy law, which, although a throwback to the Middle Ages, remained on the books. Indeed, in the early 1960s, it had been used to ban Boyle's college drama troupe from performing a controversial play about Jesus. In late May 1989 the organization published a report entitled *The Crime of Blasphemy – Why It Should Be Abolished*. It his preface, Boyle wrote that 'tolerance, understanding, acceptance and respect for the diversity of faiths and beliefs in modern Britain or elsewhere in the world cannot be secured by the threat of criminal procedure and punishment. Freedom of religion and freedom of expression may need to find a new accommodation. This can only be achieved through dialogue.'[39] He ended by urging citizens to write to their MPs and appeal for the abolition of the blasphemy laws.

In July Boyle organized a press conference held at the Institute of Contemporary Arts on the Mall in central London with Harold Pinter, Kazuo Ishiguro, the playwright Arnold Wesker and Frances D'Souza. During the previous four months, Article 19 had continued to collect signatures for the letter. Boyle showed reporters what was now a book-length document, signed by over 12,000 writers and intellectuals from sixty-seven countries. Despite the show of support, the news conference was a tense occasion. 'People were very jittery,' recalled Frances D'Souza. 'Harold Pinter was very jittery about being photographed by the press because he might be targeted.' Boyle read a message from Rushdie in which the writer, making one of his first public comments since going into hiding, acknowledged the number of letters of support he had received from Muslims, and tried to strike a positive note, saying, 'the process of mutual understanding with Islam will continue, leading to reconciliation'.[40] It was a hope Boyle strongly shared.

Throughout this process, Boyle had no direct contact with Rushdie, communicating instead through intermediaries. The two men would not meet until January 1993, when Rushdie made a heavily guarded appearance at a conference on freedom of expression that Boyle had organized in Dublin. Years later Rushdie expressed regret at not getting to know Kevin well, but remained 'deeply appreciative'[41] of the efforts Boyle and Article 19 had made on his behalf.

It would take almost a decade before post-Khomeini Iran backtracked on the threat sufficiently for Rushdie to resume the semblance of a normal life. But the religious and political fault lines exposed by his case became more acute, and the challenge of responding to terrorism and authoritarian governments in a way that preserved fundamental values like the right to freedom of expression became more complex. Even though the press conference was Boyle's last official event both at Article 19 and as chair of the Rushdie Support Committee – he now handed both roles over to Frances D'Souza as he prepared to resume his academic career in Essex – they were issues that would remain central to his work for the rest of his life.

[19]

If Human Rights Was a Religion, Essex Was the Main Seminary

EVEN WHILE handing over the reins of Article 19 and the campaign for Salman Rushdie to his successor, Frances D'Souza, Boyle, in yet another display of his talent for multi-tasking, was simultaneously writing up a June 1989 mission to Somalia for Amnesty International,[1] where he challenged dictator Mohamed Siad Barre to release political prisoners while also beginning his new job as professor of law and head of the Human Rights Centre at the University of Essex. But the transition back to the academic world was a difficult one. He was no longer in the centre of the action and he found the slower pace and cumbersome university bureaucracy frustrating. In a letter to Lance Lindblom, president of the J. Roderick MacArthur Foundation, he admitted that 'the whole business of the departure from the directorship was emotionally quite tough and disorienting' and that it was taking him some time to recover 'what is my normally upbeat outlook'.[2]

Yet he quickly began to make his mark. Boyle's vision for Essex was an ambitious one – to take a modest programme narrowly focused on law and transform it into a multi-disciplinary powerhouse that would combine human rights with other academic subjects and provide both the intellectual and practical foundation for a new generation of human rights activists. His purpose was to pursue what he described as 'the fundamental goal – the achievement of universal protection of the standards proclaimed in the Universal Declaration [of Human Rights]'.[3] To Boyle, the Declaration represented a 'moral vision … [that] introduced not only the radical idea of the equal worth of all human beings, but the equally radical idea that all human persons, all peoples and the states which represent them, had responsibility to act to promote and secure their universal and effective recognition and observance'.[4] It was the guiding light for everything Boyle did.

Since its establishment in 1982, and inspired by the human rights centre Boyle had created at Galway, what was then called the Centre for International Human Rights Law had offered an LLM degree – a master's in law with a focus on international human rights law. Boyle changed the named to the Essex Human Rights Centre and reached out to colleagues in other departments to add a new degree: the MA in the Theory and Practice of Human Rights. His idea was to enable students to learn about human rights not simply from the perspective of law but also from philosophy, political science, sociology, economics and other disciplines. His approach was unconventional. Indeed, at the time, as colleagues later wrote, 'the blinkered law faculties at Oxbridge and London did not realize the subject's importance'.[5] Even at Essex, Boyle had to employ all his charm and intellect to win over the rest of the faculty and the university administration. 'He wasn't self-consciously out to charm the birds off the academic tree,' recalled Andrew Phillips, who was then the chancellor of the university. 'But his personality, his intellect, his empathy, and his manner' carried enough weight for him to prevail. As Boyle later wrote, 'the argument that won out at Essex was that human rights is not a discipline as such, but a subject area which should be studied through the knowledge and methodologies of existing disciplines'.[6]

To turn his vision into reality, Boyle assembled an influential team that became critical to the Centre's success. Françoise Hampson had first encountered Boyle when, as an intern at the European Commission of Human Rights, she had observed him argue the Jeffrey Dudgeon gay rights case in 1978. Hired by Essex in 1983, her main academic focus was constitutional law, but by the late 1980s she had already begun to acquire a reputation as the world's leading expert on the law of armed conflict. Hampson was thin, intense, and a chain-smoker. She spoke in a rapid-fire delivery, as if her mouth could not keep up with all the ideas in her head. She was thrilled at Boyle's appointment, since, in addition to his fresh vision for the Centre, it was clear he would be supportive of, and likely personally involved in, human rights work outside the university. Hampson, who, in addition to her university commitments, had occasionally brought her own cases to the European Commission of Human Rights in Strasbourg, recalled the disapproving reaction of some traditionally minded colleagues. 'They looked at me as if I picked my nose in public. So you can imagine the sigh of relief when Kevin arrived.'

The two quickly bonded. 'With Kevin there wasn't a distinction between a social occasion and a work occasion,' she recalled. 'I don't mean he was working all the time. It just meant he couldn't turn his brain off. So we'd end up talking about things.' Indeed, their passionate but good-humoured conversations and debates became something of a campus legend. 'Françoise and Kevin were like siblings,' observed Clara Sandoval-Villalba, a student from Colombia who took classes with both and, after receiving her degree, eventually became a member of the Essex faculty. 'They would argue constantly, but they loved each other.' Boyle affectionately called Hampson 'darling' or 'sweetheart' or sometimes 'herself', and they developed a tradition of spending the New Year together, usually continuing their high-spirited arguments, which became a source of self-deprecating amusement. Joan Boyle recalled Françoise emerging from a campus talk by a guest speaker and saying to Boyle's administrative assistant, Anne Slowgrove, 'Guess what? Kevin and I have finally agreed on something. The speaker was awful!'

In 1990 Boyle convinced Nigel Rodley to leave his position as Amnesty International's chief lawyer and come to Essex. Rodley was a big catch. In the world of human rights he was a towering figure, in many ways more prominent than Boyle. A child of Jewish refugees who fled Germany in 1938 and whose father was killed while fighting for the British army in World War II, Rodley was deeply influenced in his youth by the post-war Nuremberg trials, where Hitler's henchmen were brought to account for their crimes. The first lawyer hired by Amnesty, during his seventeen years at the organization, Rodley had helped to develop the legal tools to bring tyrants and torturers to justice, including playing a central role in the drafting of the UN Convention on Torture, an international agreement adopted by the General Assembly in 1984, aimed at creating a set of rules to curb brutal or inhuman punishment. It was eventually signed by more than 160 nations. As a result, in 1993 Rodley was named the UN's Special Rapporteur on torture, a position he held for eight years even as he continued with his teaching at Essex.

In personality, Boyle and Rodley were strikingly different. Kevin was gregarious and outgoing, with his legendary Irish charm. Rodley was reserved, cerebral, almost austere. But they developed a strong professional and intellectual partnership and a warm personal relationship. 'Entirely different personalities,' Rodley acknowledged, 'but we were sufficiently unalike in terms of personal style to be really quite harmonious. We worked together all the time. We didn't have much in the way of rough edges.'

Together, Boyle, Hampson and Rodley formed the core of a programme they would soon turn into the most influential centre for human rights education in the world. 'They were a very effective trio,' observed Andrew Phillips. 'It was because of their contrasting personalities and backgrounds.' As Hampson noted, 'in the eyes of the University of Essex, they had a constitutional lawyer, me, a criminal lawyer, Kevin, and an international lawyer, Nigel'.

Along with Geoff Gilbert, a young Englishman who had joined the faculty at the same time as Kevin, after completing a doctorate on extradition law at the University of Virginia, they made their own expertise the backbone of the courses they offered. 'We were at the heart of the international human rights programme here,' Rodley said. 'That was our main collaboration internally – dividing the teaching.' Rodley taught the fundamentals of international law, especially in relation to human rights, and questions relating to the prohibition of torture. Hampson did her speciality, the law of armed conflict, as well as case law of the European Court and constitutional law, while Boyle was particularly interested in freedom of expression, association and combating discrimination. Gilbert focused on refugee law – in which he would eventually become one of the world's leading specialists – and minority rights.

There was, of course, much overlap and constant adjustment as the programme developed, but one constant was Boyle's insistence that students be given a practical sense of how they could apply what they were learning. This was reflected in the kind of exam questions Boyle would give his master's degree students. In one class, for example, he outlined a situation facing a fictional African country he called Alatia, which was facing an alarming spread of HIV/AIDS. Although Alatia had ratified all the main international human rights treaties, Boyle laid out a scenario where the government had declared a state of emergency to rule by decree. Under these decrees, all passports were cancelled, foreign travel was banned, everyone was required to be tested for the HIV virus and those infected faced compulsory quarantine. The exam question Boyle then posed was twofold:

> You are the human rights legal advisor of a national development NGO asked to prepare a human rights response to the government's actions. (1) In terms of the international standards to which the State is committed, what issues of violation or possible conflict with those standards would you highlight in your advice, and (2) what complaints under any applicable international human rights procedures would you suggest might be made about the Government's actions, and by whom?[7]

'Kevin had so many ways of making the material relevant,' noted Geoff Gilbert:

> That was the starting point. He would say – let's immerse ourselves in the really interesting stuff that is happening now. He would talk about how things that they were seeing in the news were related to what they were studying. They realized they were getting stuff they wouldn't be getting from anyone else. And Nigel was the same. Nigel had all this information that only he could give. He had been there, done it.

While Rodley was immensely respected, he could be severe and even intimidating to some students. Kevin was, in contrast, as Joan described him, 'a teddy bear', and his students adored him. He became deeply involved not only in their education but in their personal lives. 'He cared so much about them,' said Clara Sandoval-Villalba, 'and cared so much about the progress of human rights through them. At student dinners, he would talk to everyone, and would stay until the last person left.' As Nigel Rodley noted, 'he treated them with affection and respect. They really did love him.'

Students would come to Boyle for guidance about their personal problems, and every Christmas he would go out of his way to invite to his house foreign students who had not been able to get home for the holidays. 'There were waifs and strays, people a long way from home,' his son Mark recalled. 'There were Japanese, Ugandans, Russians, Bangladeshis,' added Joan. 'Just piles of students.'

Under Boyle's leadership, in the early and mid-1990s, the number of students rose dramatically, not simply because of the programme's growing reputation, but because of a series of major developments that changed the global political landscape. The collapse of communism in eastern Europe in 1989 had been followed by the fall of the Soviet Union two years later. Suddenly, nations that had suffered under decades of dictatorship were groping uncertainly towards a freer future, and struggling with the challenge of building democratic institutions. 'You had the new states who had previously been in the Soviet empire ratifying every human rights treaty in sight,' noted Françoise Hampson. 'Some states that had during the cold war thought all this human rights stuff was just political blah-blah-blah now saw that the European states who were preaching at them had themselves agreed to be subject to the jurisdiction of the European Court of Human Rights.'

At the same time, the role of the UN Security Council in sanctioning the US-led Gulf War to expel Saddam Hussein's Iraqi army from Kuwait in 1991 suggested that a new, rules-based international system might be emerging. 'You got the international community pulling together,' said Hampson:

> You got the Security Council doing the right thing. You got a coalition assembled. You got them booting out the Iraqis from Kuwait. Never had 'law-ness' seemed to do so well. It was the high-water mark for international law. In 1991, it looked like there really was the possibility of a world order emerging based on the rule of law.

It was in what Boyle described as this 'more benign and optimistic context',[8] where 'the post-Cold War environment reopened the possibility of more effective efforts to advance human rights through cooperation between states',[9] that the Essex human rights programme saw a sharp jump in enrolment. 'The relationships between democracy and rights as well as the relationship of both to development became central to policy-makers and to academic thinking,' he wrote. 'The expansion of the UN into preventive diplomacy, election monitoring, policing, peace-keeping and peace-making, as well as human rights presences in the field, created a professional demand for human rights field personnel.'[10] The potential of the new climate was further highlighted by the creation in 1993 of a new institution, the UN High Commissioner for Human Rights.

From the handful of students when Boyle arrived in Essex, the number doubled in the two years following the collapse of the Soviet Union, and then continued to increase. By 1994, including those doing the traditional LLM degree and those enrolled in the new master's programme Boyle had created, the Human Rights Centre was home to nearly seventy students from dozens of countries. Many of those who went through the Essex programme, then and later, found their attitudes and future careers profoundly influenced by Boyle's approach to human rights. 'Kevin was this visionary person, and the way he talked about human rights problems and what needed to be done appealed to a lot of students,' said Aisling Reidy, a young Irish woman who started at Essex in 1993. 'It was very easy for us to buy into the vision of rights that Kevin conveyed, both on a personal level and when he was teaching.'

After working subsequent to her graduation with Boyle and Hampson on a series of cases in Strasbourg on behalf of Turkish Kurds facing government-sanctioned repression, Reidy became the director of the Irish Council for Civil Liberties and then the Senior Legal Advisor at Human Rights Watch in New York. Other graduates included Montserrat Solana, a Costa Rican who went to work as a prosecutor at the International Criminal Court and was later named her country's ombudsperson; Canadian Colleen Duggan, who got a job working for the UN High Commissioner for Human Rights; Magdalena Sepúlveda Carmona, a Chilean who subsequently held a major position with the Inter-American Court of Human Rights; and Eugenio Aragon, who became Brazil's Minister of Justice. Indeed, over the years, the number of graduates of Boyle's programme who emerged in key positions in the world of human rights became so numerous that they were referred to as the 'Essex mafia'.

Among them was Borislav Petranov. A native of Sofia, Bulgaria, he heard about Essex while working as an election monitor for an NGO called the Bulgarian Association for Fair Elections, which had been set up after the fall of the communist regime. 'People said if you want to do human rights law, there is no better place in the world,' he recalled. 'Forget about Oxford, Columbia, or Harvard. Essex had Kevin. It had Nigel. It was *the* place.'

After posting his application, Petranov received a phone call out of the blue from Boyle, who then quickly arranged for a scholarship. The opening day of the autumn 1991 term at Essex, however, came just one day after the first free elections scheduled in Bulgaria since the communist regime was toppled. 'It was the first Bulgarian election the communist party was not going to win,' Petranov remembered. 'I told Kevin I absolutely had to be there.' The next morning, however, Petranov and his wife flew to London. They finally reached Colchester by bus at 10 pm, where they discovered Boyle waiting for them at the bus station. He drove them to the modest accommodation he had arranged, and in the subsequent weeks, Petranov said, 'Kevin and Joan surrounded us with 90 per cent love and 10 per cent curiosity.'

The two men bonded over a shared taste for wine – Petranov's family had run wineries in pre-communist Bulgaria – and their shared passion for human rights. After getting his master's degree, Petranov was admitted to Oxford to do a doctorate. 'Kevin told me – don't do something boring. Find something that would both push the field and would be really interesting for you. Why don't you do freedom of conscience and religion? And that's what I did.' Petranov also began working with Inter-Rights, a London-based NGO that helped lawyers in newly democratic countries who wanted to work on human rights issues. Boyle advised him on how to bring cases to Strasbourg, and Petranov enlisted Kevin to help in a series of training programmes being held for lawyers in Moscow, Kiev, and other places in eastern Europe.

His work with Petranov was part of Boyle's broader involvement, both personally and through the Human Rights Centre, in efforts to promote democracy, civil society and human rights following the collapse of communism. With Emile Kirchner – a German who had settled in England, taught in the Essex government department and was a specialist on European integration – Boyle participated in numerous conferences and meetings with lawyers, academics and officials working in local and regional governments, projects often funded by the EU. 'Constitutions had to be designed for these countries,' Kirchner recalled. 'There were legal and economic aspects. Kevin was always a central figure, trying to act as a bridge to Central and Eastern

Europe ... Kevin argued that we need to consolidate or nationalism might come back, or Russia might become aggressive.'

One such conference, organized by the Council of Europe, was held in Moscow in July 1994. The topic was 'political, legal, cultural, social, and economic aspects of the media in a democratic society'. The event was designed for senior government officials involved in drafting media legislation for the new Russian Federation, as well as journalists, members of parliament, lawyers and judges. Boyle was specifically asked to speak on constitutional and legislative guarantees for media freedom. Following the gathering, the British government's Office of Development Assistance asked the Human Rights Centre to draft a proposal for a series of 'democracy seminars' to be held in Russia.

As part of his effort to promote democracy in a promising but uncertain international climate, Boyle joined forces with David Beetham, a widely respected political scientist at the University of Leeds, to produce a book commissioned by UNESCO called *Introducing Democracy: 80 Questions and Answers*. 'This was not an academic book,' Beetham said. 'It was a civically designed book for newly developing democracies to give them some answers to key questions about what democracy is.' The project originated through Boyle's huge network of contacts, which included people at UNESCO. 'He was such a brilliant networker that people turned to him for anything slightly innovative that they wanted to get done,' Beetham noted. The book, which came out in 1995, contained six sections: basic concepts and principles, free and fair elections, open and accountable government, individual rights and their defence, democratic and civil society, and the future of democracy. In brainstorming what to say, Boyle asked his MA students what questions they would most like answered. He and Beetham then pooled their ideas, with Beetham writing the bulk of the text, although Boyle did the section on individual rights. *Introducing Democracy* was a big success. It was translated into thirty languages and, in 2005, the two men prepared a second edition.

The UNESCO book was Boyle's second collaboration with Beetham. The first, which began in 1991 and was much more ambitious, was *Auditing Democracy in Britain* – an attempt to assess the health of democracy and human rights in Britain. The Democratic Audit was funded by the Rowntree Trust, and Boyle secured a large grant to base it at the Human Rights Centre in Essex. 'Concern for the quality of democratic life in Britain is already a major national theme,' Boyle said at the time. 'The publication of a major audit of trends, positive and negative, from Essex can have real impact on public affairs.'[11] David Beetham had sent Rowntree his own proposal from the University of Leeds, but as soon as Essex secured the funding, Boyle invited Beetham, who had devised a unique template to make the assessment, to join forces. 'I think it was the contacts and reputation that Kevin had that sold it to Rowntree,' Beetham observed. 'And they liked having it housed in a human rights centre.'

The idea of the audit grew out of the collapse of communism and the end of the Cold War. 'Here was the UK after 1991 telling all these countries how they should construct their democracies,' Beetham said, 'when it itself had a political system that, from a democratic point of view, was deeply flawed.' It was, he acknowledged, a hugely ambitious project. 'The idea was to assess how democratic the UK was against a set of criteria, many of which did not exist then and had to be created.' With the help of Stuart Weir, the former editor of the *New Statesman*, Beetham devised thirty questions to measure the quality of democracy, underpinned by two fundamental principles. One was popular control: how far did the people exercise control over political decision-makers and the processes of decision-making? The second was political equality: how far did political equality exist in the exercise of popular control?

With Boyle acting as intellectual sounding board and the Human Rights Centre providing the operational base, over the next decade, in addition to numerous reports, pamphlets and papers, the Democratic Audit produced two major books. The first, *The Three Pillars of Liberty: Political Rights and Freedom in the United Kingdom*, with a foreword by Kevin Boyle, explored the state of human rights in Britain and found the country failing to adhere to key international standards. The second, *Political Power and Democratic Control in Britain,* looked at the way formal institutions operated, such as the executive, parliament, the civil service and the electoral system.[12] Within Britain, the studies served as a catalyst for discussions among policy-makers and scholars about the need for change. Internationally, the Audit had an even greater impact. Increasingly recognized as a respected resource on the problems of democracy, in the following years it provided consulting, training and resources to countries such as Bangladesh, Kenya, Namibia, New Zealand, Peru and Canada.

As if this was not enough even for someone with Boyle's prodigious energy, he secured funding from the Pew Foundation in the US for an ambitious study of freedom of religion around the world. Having seen at first hand in Northern Ireland the result of religious intolerance, this was an issue in which he was particularly interested. Modelled on the surveys of press freedom he had pioneered at Article 19, *Freedom of Religion and Belief: A World Report*, published in 1997 after several years of research, analysed 'how international standards on freedom of religion and belief are understood and reflected in the laws and practices of over fifty states and territories'.[13]

Boyle recruited his former student Borislav Petranov, then just completing a PhD on religious freedom, to help with the project, which assembled detailed information on the relationship of religion to the state, policies towards religious minorities or non-believers, as well as documenting numerous cases of intolerance, from the mistreatment of the Ba'hai in Shiite Iran to the plight of Christian Copts in Egypt. 'There were multiple elements of logic for doing the report,' Petranov recalled:

> One was that case law was not developed. So the thought was that if you compiled a record of laws and common themes in rules regarding religion around the world, then you could ask an international tribunal to rule on what should be the law – for example, that conscientious objection to military service should not be criminalized. So part of the logic [of the project] was to create a body of knowledge from which you could distil what the proper rules about freedom of religion and belief should really be.

Deciding on the fifty-eight countries, assembling a team of writers and editing each contribution was a monumental undertaking. Juliet Sheen, an Australian human rights activist with strong writing and editing skills whom Boyle had met at a conference in Geneva, agreed to join the effort. 'Kevin couldn't do this on his own,' she said. 'He had too many other irons in the fire.' Beginning, in her words, as a 'glorified research assistant', Sheen became so central to the project that Boyle asked that her name be added as co-editor when the book was published. It was yet another example of how Boyle the visionary would recruit able partners to implement many of the practical details for the projects he conceived. For Sheen, Boyle's concept was that the book would 'produce a snapshot of what it was like to live as a particular believer in the different nations of the world'. She and Boyle drafted a set of benchmarks for each writer to observe, and after he did an initial scrutiny, she would go over them in detail before sending them to outside experts for comment.

By any standards, as Françoise Hampson noted, *Freedom of Religion and Belief: A World Report* 'was an important book'. But in the words of Geoff Gilbert, 'it didn't get the attention it deserved'. Years later, Hampson would say 'I was gobsmacked – and still am – that more attention wasn't paid to it, especially given how central the issue has become.' Still, Petranov remains convinced it played an important role in helping to create a sounder international legal framework for religious issues, as well as strengthening the role of the UN's Special Rapporteur on freedom of religion and belief, a role created a decade before.

Working on the book reinforced Boyle's belief in the importance of the subject. In notes for a 1998 talk, he wrote that

> the phenomenon where different religions and non-religious ideologues within different countries define opposing beliefs as inferior, false, or heretical is at the core of all violations of freedom of thought, conscience, religion, and belief. It represents a direct contradiction of the most fundamental of the human rights, namely that of non-discrimination.[14]

The multiple projects on which Boyle worked, along with his teaching and professional activities and those of his colleagues, served to further burnish the already widely respected reputation of the Human Rights Centre. Indeed, as Conor Gearty, a human rights scholar at the London School of Economics, noted: 'If human rights was a religion, Essex was the main seminary, and Kevin had a lot to do with that.'

[2 0]

Can You Shoot the Messenger for the Nasty Message?

FROM ITS MODEST origins in the late 1950s, the European Court of Human Rights had, by the mid-1990s, established itself as, in effect, a kind of Supreme Court of Europe on matters relating to human rights. Its jurisdiction was now acknowledged by all forty-seven members of the Council of Europe, and covered hundreds of millions of people from Iceland to Azerbaijan. On 20 April 1994 Kevin Boyle stood before nineteen judges from nineteen different nations, all of them wearing long judicial robes and frilly white collars. Twenty-two years after bringing his first case to Strasbourg, he was finally getting an opportunity to act as an advocate in front of the highest body responsible for upholding the European Convention on Human Rights. For Boyle, whose passionate belief in the importance of international law and international guarantees of human rights underpinned everything he did, it was an exhilarating moment.

In this case, Boyle's client was Jens Olaf Jersild, a correspondent for Danmarks Radio (DR), the Danish version of the BBC, who, as Boyle told the judges, 'has ended up with a criminal record as a result of his work as a professional journalist'.[1] The hearing, which Boyle later described to colleagues as 'quite an experience',[2] was the dramatic climax to a landmark free speech case nine years in the making. In July 1985 Jersild, then a young reporter, had broadcast a television story for DR about a worrying new phenomenon in Danish society: the emergence of extreme right-wing skin-head gangs engaged in racist violence against immigrants. It was one of the first journalistic reports about a trend that, in subsequent years, would become a burning issue across Europe. Jersild's six-minute piece featured interviews with three members of a gang called the Green Jackets, who boasted of their racist views.

To Jersild, and to many Danish TV viewers, the report was a shocking revelation. 'Since the German occupation of Germany, we had never had violent racism,' Jersild recalled. 'Now, you had people saying on television that we took a bucket of white paint and we poured it onto the bed of a child so that the child would be the right colour. Not since the Nazis had this happened.'

Following the broadcast, the three skinheads were prosecuted under a Danish law that banned the public dissemination of racist views. To his surprise, however, Jersild and his producer, Lasse Jensen, were charged under the same law for 'aiding and abetting'[3] the spread of racism through their report. Convicted, their appeals, first to the High Court of Eastern Denmark and then to the Supreme Court, were rejected.

One evening soon thereafter, Jersild was drinking in a local bar when he encountered Lene Johannessen, a Danish law student who happened to be working for Article 19. Indeed, she had written a brief summary of the Jersild case for the organization's *1988 World Report on Censorship*. The two quickly became romantically involved. 'I told her my story,' Jersild remembered, 'and she immediately said, "Maybe there is a chance. We should talk to Kevin."' In London, Jersild met Boyle. Never one to walk away from a battle over press freedom, Kevin, despite his many other commitments, agreed to take the case. In a note to himself, he wrote, 'If I understand what the case is about, it seems to me the question is: can you shoot the messenger for the nasty message?'[4]

In Copenhagen, Jersild convinced the Danish Union of Journalists to pay for Johannessen to collect and translate key documents. On 25 July 1989 Boyle filed an application on Jersild's behalf with the European Commission on Human Rights. 'The case raises important questions concerning the right to free expression and the permissible restrictions of that right,' he wrote. 'The main question is whether a state can restrict the exercise of free expression where a member of the public wishes to report what another has said, without in any way adopting the views expressed by that other.'[5] Citing multiple previous decisions by the European Court of Human Rights, Boyle argued that the conviction of Jersild and his producer clearly violated Article 10 of the European Convention, which stated that everyone was entitled to freedom of expression.

In October 1991 the Commission formally asked the Danish government to respond to Boyle's original application. The government submitted a document in December, and in February 1992 Boyle provided his own response. The duelling documents provided a foretaste of the legal battle that would play out over the next two years.

In its written submission, the government asserted that Jersild was responsible for spreading racist views, and that 'the right to protection against racial discrimination took precedence over the right to free expression'.[6] Underpinning its argument, the government cited the UN's 1965 International Convention on the Elimination of All Forms of Racial Discrimination. Signed by dozens of countries, including Denmark, the Convention called for the criminalization of 'all dissemination of ideas based on racial separation or hatred'.[7] Denmark, the government said, was simply enforcing the UN's anti-racism mandate. Boyle, in his rebuttal, wrote that 'to impose liability on him [Jersild] for the racist remarks of those he interviewed is incompatible with Article 10 and with a proper appreciation of the role of the media in a democratic society'.[8] In early September 1992, the Commission met to view Jersild's programme. Soon after, it declared the case admissible. The battle lines were drawn.

Seven months later, Boyle, Jersild and Tyge Trier arrived in Strasbourg for a Commission hearing. Although twenty years younger, Trier, who was helping Boyle understand the complexities of the Danish legal system, hit it off with Kevin, partly because of their shared commitment to human rights, but also because Trier was teaching law at Copenhagen University and co-authoring a book aimed at popularizing the idea of human rights law in Denmark.

Jersild had spent the previous few months covering the war in Bosnia. Arriving in Strasbourg for the hearing, he was more interested in talking about the war than about his case. But, ever the contrarian, he had seized on a particularly controversial issue: claims that the Serbs, widely portrayed in the media as the villains, were responsible for the mass rapes of Bosnian women. While acknowledging the possibility, over coffee with Boyle and Trier, Jersild said he would remain sceptical until journalists could produce concrete evidence to back the claim of rape being used as a weapon. Puffing on his pipe, Kevin said, 'that's why we need independent reporters like you, and why we have to protect them'. Jersild replied that lawyers like Kevin were just as necessary, to which Boyle self-deprecatingly replied, 'Oh no, Olaf. We're just the plumbers.'

To Jersild, the comment provided a revealing insight to how Boyle viewed his work.

'It's a great expression,' Jersild recalled,

> because he said 'people much cleverer than us made this system – all the tubes and pipes. And then when the tubes and pipes are not working or leaking, the plumbers come in.' And Kevin was the plumber to fix that one tube or passageway. That was how he described it to me. He had a very down-to-earth idea about his job.

Tyge Trier agreed with the characterization. 'That hits it on the nail how he saw himself in this very practical way. I suppose I was the junior plumber there.'

Underscoring the importance of the case, the Danish authorities had assembled an impressive team: three officials from the Foreign Ministry and three from the Ministry of Justice, including the government's chief legal advisor. Not for the first time in Strasbourg, Boyle entered a legal battlefield looking outnumbered and outgunned. When the proceedings began, the president of the Commission asked him to speak first. Boyle immediately spelled out what was at stake. 'Was it necessary in a democratic society ... to convict and punish a *bona fide* journalist because of the criminal statements made by those he interviewed?'[9]

Directly addressing the Danish government's contention that prosecuting Jersild was necessary because Denmark had signed the International

Convention against racism, Boyle noted that when the Convention was being drafted in the mid-1960s, a number of member nations, including Denmark, were concerned that the call to outlaw all dissemination of racist ideas was too sweeping. This, he stressed, 'could give rise to difficulties in balancing such a broad prohibition with other rights, such as freedom of opinion and the press'.[10] The solution was that a proviso had been attached to the UN document before its passage in 1965 that any 'prohibition of expression of racism would be "done with due regard for the principles embodied in the Universal Declaration of Human Rights such as freedom of expression"'.[11] The prosecution of Jersild, Boyle argued, 'was precisely the kind of injustice'[12] that the clause had been inserted to prevent.

After explaining that the needs of a television report required broadcasting the actual words of those interviewed, however offensive, Boyle concluded by saying that

> in bringing to public attention the reality of the criminal activities of this group, the applicant was doing no more than following his profession as a journalist ... He was acting as a watchdog by alerting citizens to a new reality in Danish society ... He was not intent on disseminating racism but in countering it through exposure.[13]

Two different Danish government lawyers followed Boyle. Implying that the Commission would be overstepping its bounds by challenging the Danish judgment, they stressed that the case had been 'thoroughly dealt with by the Danish courts'[14] and that Jersild's conviction had been necessary 'to protect the rights of others as defined in the 1965 [Anti-Racism] Convention'.[15] They also offered a detailed critique of the way Jersild had reported and structured his piece, noting that he had taken five or six hours to do the shoot, which suggested deliberation on his part, and stressing that Jersild had served beer to the youths, which, they implied, had a sinister connotation. They also accused him of not questioning 'the use of defamatory remarks directed against black people and other ethnic groups',[16] complained that 'there was no debate in the programme' and argued that 'a solid counter-view should have been expressed'.[17] After several Commissioners asked questions of both sides, Boyle was given the last word. He emphasized that the broadcast had prompted the local authorities to act to counter the malign influence of the Green Jackets. 'It did have a positive impact,' he concluded, 'and that was its purpose.'[18]

Three months later the Commission handed Boyle, Trier and Jersild a major legal victory. In a 21-page opinion, it concluded that Jersild's right to freedom of expression under Article 10 of the European Convention of Human Rights had been violated:

> The Commission finds it established that his [Jersild's] intentions were not to disseminate racist ideology but rather to counter it through exposure … In such circumstances, it is of great importance that the media are not discouraged, for fear of criminal or other sanctions, from imparting opinions on issues of public concern.[19]

The next step would be a hearing before the European Court of Human Rights, where a positive decision would compel the Danish government to reverse Jersild's conviction.

The hearing took place on 24 April 1994. Boyle began his remarks to the judges by stressing that, even though Jersild had been able to broadcast his report in Denmark, 'the messenger was also punished'.[20] Summarizing the facts of the case, he stressed the serious nature of Jersild's journalism, his lack of sensationalism and the importance of alerting Danish television viewers to the threat posed by racist extremists. Boyle argued that because the UN's 1965 Anti-Racism Declaration contained a reference to the Universal Declaration of Human Rights, 'there was no conflict between the two treaties', and urged the Court to uphold Jersild's 'right as a journalist to seek and impart information'.[21] 'This was a clear case,' he emphasized, '… of reporting by a free media in a free society.'[22]

As in the Commission hearing, Trier was impressed with Boyle's courtroom style. 'It was kind of effortless,' he recalled:

> It was almost musical. It was elegant. He was extremely intelligent. He had this understanding where he could read the person in the room with him. Some academics or lawyers use over-complicated language, but real excellence is when you can be very precise and convincing. He was a brilliant counsel in those sessions.

Five months later Boyle was on a brief visit to Dublin when he received a call from Trier. The Court had ruled in Jersild's favour. 'Taken as a whole,' the Court decision said, 'the feature could not have objectively appeared to have as its purpose the propagation of racist views and ideas.'[23] Moreover, the ruling established two key legal principles: 'The punishment of a journalist for assisting in the dissemination of statements made by another person in an interview would severely hamper the contribution of the press to discussion on matters of public interest.'[24] Of even greater significance, the Court declared that 'it is not for this Court, nor [sic] for the National Courts for that matter, to substitute their own views for those of the press as to what techniques should be adopted by journalists'.[25]

It was a sweeping endorsement of the arguments Boyle and Trier had made. Boyle was elated. 'The case defends the right of the journalist to independently determine how to handle material, what images to use, and what to portray on TV,' he told an Irish reporter.[26] As Trier noted,

> that was the core of the case. It is for the journalist and the editor to decide how you present journalism. It's not the role of the judge to sit and say you should have included a little more of this or a little less of that. That is why the judgment still stands today. It is still being used in academia and the teaching of journalists all over the world. It is referenced all the time by the Court in other cases. It has kind of become a Kevin Boyle classic.

At almost exactly the same time as he submitted his initial application for Jersild, Boyle was playing a critical role in bringing another landmark case to Strasbourg: this one involving free speech issues in Ireland.

Almost from the start of the Troubles in Northern Ireland, the Irish government had used Section 31 of the country's Broadcasting Authority Act – which gave it the authority to ban from the airwaves anyone who might 'tend to undermine the authority of the state' – to prevent members or leaders of the IRA's political wing, Sinn Féin, from appearing on the state broadcaster RTÉ. The ban was a source of immense frustration and anger for Irish journalists, among them Betty Purcell, an RTÉ reporter and radio and television producer. 'Section 31 was hugely burdensome,' she recalled. 'It created an atmosphere in RTÉ of self-censorship.'

For years, Purcell and her colleagues had been forced to ignore or misreport stories to avoid violating the Section 31 ban. This meant not only not being able to broadcast interviews with key figures, such as Sinn Féin's leader Gerry Adams, but also confronting absurd situations such as being unable to talk to the only witness to a local fire simply because he happened to be a member of Sinn Féin. 'It was ludicrous,' Purcell said. Compounding the frustration was the fact that Sinn Féin itself remained a legal political party in the Irish Republic. Its members could run for office, but they couldn't appear on Irish radio or TV. Over the years, journalists had been reprimanded, demoted and even fired for violating the ban. 'We were banging our heads against a brick wall,' Purcell recalled.

One afternoon while Boyle was still at Article 19, he was visiting Dublin and had tea with Purcell at the National Gallery of Ireland. He told her it was worth bringing a case to Strasbourg. 'He reassured us – you can do it. It's just a matter of getting evidence, and you can do that because you're a journalist. And he said don't worry about the money and the big lawyers and the senior counsel and all that. I will do all that end.' With Boyle's help, Purcell enlisted Kevin's old friend Mary Robinson and solicitor Anne Neary to take the case. Boyle was too busy to act as the lead lawyer. But behind the scenes he remained a key advisor, along with his former student Marie McGonagle, now a professor at Galway, who had become one of Ireland's leading experts on media law, and who, at his request, provided the important historical background on Section 31. 'He was very helpful,' Purcell said, 'because he was steeped in the human rights and freedom of press perspective.'

Less than a month after Boyle had filed the Jersild case in the summer of 1989, Purcell's legal team submitted an application to Strasbourg challenging Section 31. They claimed that it violated key provisions of the European Convention on Human Rights, notably Article 10, which guaranteed freedom of expression, as well as Article 14, which banned discrimination on the ground of political or other opinion, as well as race, sex, colour or language. The use of Section 31, the application asserted, had left RTÉ's journalists 'unable to cover news stories adequately ... In particular, the result has been to deprive the public of proper analysis and information about developments in Northern Ireland'.[27]

Moreover, the application noted that because Sinn Féin – a legal political party – was banned from the airwaves, the journalists 'are forced to carry out discrimination on the basis of political opinion'[28] and 'risked dismissal from their employment if they refuse or fail to carry out Section 31'.[29] While acknowledging that the government had legitimate security concerns, the document said the Irish authorities had not demonstrated any pressing need for using such a blunt legal instrument, and, indeed, that banning reporters from challenging members of Sinn Féin in interviews was 'counter-productive'.[30]

As usual, the machinery of the Commission moved slowly, but in April 1991 a hearing was held in Strasbourg. Acting as an advisor, Boyle joined the rest of Purcell's legal team, except for Mary Robinson, who, in 1990, had been elected president of Ireland – the first woman to hold the position – and could no longer work on the case. Her place was taken by Frank Clarke, a distinguished lawyer who would later become Chief Justice of the Irish Supreme Court. The hearing took a full morning, with Clarke arguing Purcell's case by citing numerous examples of journalists being blocked from covering important news, while government lawyers claimed that Section 31 was necessary to protect national security. To buttress its case, the government submitted detailed documentation of the IRA's many terrorist attacks. However, on the very same day, to the surprise of many observers, the Commission declared the application inadmissible. The ruling said that the government's security concerns were legitimate, and noted that 'the decision not to declare Sinn Féin an unlawful organization does not imply an obligation on the government to grant Sinn Féin unimpeded access to the broadcast media'.[31]

While accepting the government's argument, the Commission nonetheless acknowledged key points made by Purcell's legal team, in particular the fact that Section 31 'produces serious effects on the applicants' work as journalists'.[32] After the ruling, Boyle told Purcell not be discouraged. 'Look,' she recalled him saying, 'the momentum is for human rights. You have placed this on the human rights agenda, and you have made the government answer. This is a lost battle, not a lost war.'

Indeed, in the wake of the decision, pressure on the government to rescind the ban increased. An editorial in *The Irish Times* in December 1993, for example, declared that Section 31 was 'a blunt instrument which has deprived the public of an essential element in understanding the conflict in Northern Ireland'.[33] The campaign even received support from the US, where the American chapter of the writers' organization PEN issued an open letter calling for the ban to be ended.[34] And earlier, in July, the United Nations Human Rights Committee in Geneva declared that Section 31 violated the International Covenant on Civil and Political Rights.[35]

The same year, a new government took office in Dublin, and Boyle's old friend and former Galway colleague Michael D. Higgins was appointed

Minister for Arts, Culture and the Gaeltacht, with responsibility for broadcasting. Higgins had long been sceptical of Article 31, and had discussed the issue with Boyle on many occasions. In January 1994 he announced that the government would let the ban lapse. 'It was a freedom of expression issue,' he recalled. 'You shouldn't be using broadcasting to achieve a security purpose.' In an approving editorial, *The Irish Times* wrote that the ban had 'served in equal measure to frustrate broadcasters, embarrass the government, and provide Sinn Féin with a sense of grievance bordering on martyrdom'. It was time, the paper said, to 'let in the light'.[36]

While helping Purcell and her lawyers to prepare their case, Boyle, with his seemingly inexhaustible appetite for work, had taken on yet another controversial freedom of press case – this one a battle over a whistle-blower's attempt to 'let in the light'. While it would be decided by the European Court in Strasbourg, the original battleground was the Norwegian city of Tromsø, 350 kilometres north of the Arctic Circle and for decades the centre of seal-hunting in Norway. Inextricably linked with Norway's traditional seafaring culture and its sense of national identity, as well as a mainstay of Tromsø's economy, by the 1980s hunting seals had become the focus of controversy. Environmental and animal rights groups, such as Greenpeace and the Humane Society, had been waging increasingly successful campaigns to ban or restrict the practice, highlighting the allegedly cruel ways in which the seals were killed.

It was against this backdrop that Odd F. Lindberg, a former freelance journalist who had written sympathetically about the seal-hunting industry, secured an appointment from the Norwegian Ministry of Fisheries to serve as an inspector on the seal-hunting boat *Harmoni* in the spring of 1988. On his return from a month at sea, he gave an interview to the local newspaper, *Bladet Tromsø*, in which he claimed that the unnecessarily cruel way he saw seals being slaughtered violated the revised government regulations. Lindberg also asserted that he had been threatened by some of the sealers who did not want him to speak out. He subsequently submitted an exhaustive report to the ministry in which he provided further details and named several of the men on board the ship. Normally such reports were made public. In this case, however, the ministry decided not to release it. Lindberg, fearing the ministry would permanently suppress the report, leaked a copy to *Bladet Tromsø*. Although omitting the names of the crew members, the newspaper published the entire report, with the headline 'Shock Report: Seal Skinned Alive'.[37] The coverage sparked widespread controversy, as well as generating international media interest from CNN and the BBC.

In March 1991 the crew of the *Harmoni* initiated defamation proceedings against the newspaper and its editor, Pal Stensas. In March 1992 the Nord-Troms District Court declared that the paper's coverage, including publication of the leaked report, was 'not intended to promote a serious debate on matters of public interest' but was of a 'sensational nature'.[38] Because *Bladet Tromsø* had 'failed to prove the truthfulness'[39] of Lindberg's report, the court said, publishing the document had defamed the *Harmoni*'s crew. The paper was ordered to pay each of the seal hunters damages of 10,000 Norwegian kroner (US$1613), while Pal Stensas was ordered to pay 1000 kroner (US$161). Steingrim Wolland, the young lawyer who had represented *Bladet Tromsø* and Stensas, appealed to the Norwegian Supreme Court, but the lower court's judgment was upheld.

Wolland, who had previously worked for the Norwegian Editors' Association on issues of media ethics and defamation law, then reached out to Kevin. The two men, who had met at an event in London when Boyle was still at Article 19, were friends. Wolland had long advocated relaxing what he and many others viewed as Norway's excessively rigid regulations governing defamation, and had written about the issue for Article 19. Their bond had been strengthened by Wolland's involvement in the campaign to support Salman Rushdie in Norway, where the publisher of the Norwegian translation of *The Satanic Verses* had been shot and badly wounded.

Wolland believed the best chance of overturning the guilty verdict and reforming Norway's defamation laws was to go to Strasbourg. Boyle immediately agreed to take the case, even though there was no fee and his clients struggled to find the funds even to cover his costs. For Wolland, this was more than just another case. Although any criticism of the seal-hunting industry touched a raw nerve in Norway, he had expected to win in the local courts, and was stung by the fact that the seal hunters' complaint had been upheld.

As in the Jersild and Purcell cases, in crafting his arguments Boyle's central theme was that Article 10 of the European Convention – the right to freedom of expression – had been violated. The Norwegian court judgment, he wrote in the initial application, 'amounts to an unjustified interference with the freedom of a newspaper to play its role in a democratic society and that in a democratic society the question of presentation of a newspaper story is primarily one for the newspaper editor'.[40] The Commission quickly declared the case admissible. After considering written submissions from both sides, but without holding a hearing, it ruled on 9 July 1998 that there had indeed been a violation of Article 10, twice citing the precedent set in the Jersild case on the need to protect the role of the press as a 'public watchdog'.[41] Boyle was heading for yet another showdown at the European Court of Human Rights.

The hearing was set for 27 January 1999. This time, the Court asked Norwegian government lawyer Frode Elgesem to go first. Directly challenging the reasoning of the European Commission, Elgesem claimed 'the Jersild formula cannot apply in defamation cases' like the *Bladet Tromsø* one, where specific individuals had been singled out.[42] He argued that the seal hunters were 'ordinary workers',[43] not public figures, and had been 'exposed to contempt'[44] as well as to 'unfounded attacks on their honour and reputation'[45] by a newspaper that had 'violated journalistic ethics'.[46] Elgesem maintained that Lindberg's controversial report was 'highly defamatory'.[47] Although an official document, he said it was 'not reliable'[48] and the paper had failed in its obligation to determine the truth of the accusations before publishing them.

Boyle responded by cutting to the heart of the matter. The question, he told the judges, was:

> When can it be justified to sanction or interfere with a newspaper when it reproduces an official report? The government claims that a newspaper may not reproduce such an official report unless it is independently able to prove every statement of fact in that report. Such reasoning is not consistent with the European Court's consistent jurisprudence as to the pre-eminent role of the media in a free society. If *Bladet Tromsø* is not entitled to rely on the official character of an official report and is in fact required to independently establish the factual basis of any report it draws from, that principle would be enormously damaging to press freedom in Europe.[49]

He also dismissed the government's claim that the seal hunters were just ordinary people whose reputation and privacy had been damaged. 'This is not just a case of a powerful media outlet ruthlessly invading the privacy or trespassing on the reputation of ordinary private persons,' he maintained. 'It is rather a story of a small local newspaper acting as newspapers should, and local fishermen caught up in a controversy of national and international importance at the time.'[50] Like Tyge Trier, Wolland marvelled at Boyle's courtroom performance. 'While others just rushed through their presentations,' Wolland remembered, Kevin 'was very good at modulating his voice to catch the attention of his listeners and emphasize certain points. He didn't use big gestures, but he was very good.'

Four months later, in May 1999, the Court ruled in favour of Boyle, Wolland and *Bladet Tromsø*. Citing the precedent of the Jersild case, the ruling stressed the importance of journalists in a democratic society being able to report on matters of public interest, no matter how contentious. In this instance, it concluded that the Norwegian courts were in violation of Article 10. It ordered that the defamation convictions of the paper and its then editor be thrown out, that they be paid damages, and that Boyle and Wolland's costs and expenses be reimbursed. Concluding that *Bladet Tromsø* had 'acted in good faith',[51] the Court used the ruling to lay out what would become a key legal principle: 'The press should normally be entitled, when contributing to public debate on matters of legitimate concern, to rely on the contents of official reports without having to undertake independent research. Otherwise, the vital public-watchdog role of the press may be undermined.'[52]

The case was a legal milestone. It would be regularly cited in subsequent court decisions on press freedom, and became an essential protection in the daily work of journalists. In Norway, meanwhile, the Supreme Court ordered a revision to local defamation laws to reflect the fact that, as Wolland put it, 'the public's right to know outweighs the right of a citizen to protect their reputation'.

Yet again, Kevin Boyle had played a pivotal role in the establishment of historic principles of international law protecting freedom of the press.

[21]

Eziyet

THE CITY OF Diyarbakır in Kurdistan lies some 630 miles south-east of Istanbul. Overlooking the Tigris river, it is one of the oldest continually inhabited cities in the world. Long the unofficial capital of Turkey's Kurdish minority, which comprises between 15 and 20 per cent of the country's population, Diyarbakır had been at the heart of a bloody conflict between Kurdish separatists and the Turkish security forces since the mid-1980s.

Kurdish grievances were deep-rooted. For decades, successive Turkish governments had banned the use of the Kurdish language, dress, folk customs and even names in an effort to force the Kurds to assimilate. In 1984 the Kurdistan Workers' Party, known as the PKK, launched an armed uprising aimed at establishing an independent Kurdish state. In the decade that followed nearly 40,000 people were killed, thousands of villages were destroyed, and ordinary Kurds, often caught in the middle, faced arbitrary arrest, imprisonment, torture and death at the hands of the security forces.

In the summer of 1992 Kevin Boyle arrived in Diyarbakır. He had been invited to give a talk to local lawyers and human rights activists. His audience in a packed Diyarbakır cinema heard him argue that recourse to the human rights machinery in Strasbourg was now a viable option for the long-suffering Kurds. The reason, he said, was that the Turkish government, seeking to join the European Union, had finally agreed to grant individuals the right to petition the European Commission of Human Rights and to accept the jurisdiction of the European Court. It was thirty years after the UK government had granted its citizens the same rights, but it was a significant step for Turkey. In the following years, it would lead Boyle and his colleagues to bring – and win – scores of cases in Strasbourg. The cases exposed the appalling practices of Turkey's counter-insurgency campaign, put pressure on the Turkish government to modify its behaviour, and made a major contribution to the use of international law to redress human rights violations during times of civil unrest. It was, as Boyle later wrote, 'one of the most far-reaching initiatives to render state action in violation of human rights accountable internationally'.[1]

Boyle's visit had been arranged with the help of one of his students. Kerim Yildiz was himself a Kurdish refugee who was doing a human rights degree at the University of Essex and, with Kevin's encouragement, had set up the Kurdish Human Rights Project (KHRP) in 1992. Based in London and working closely with activists and lawyers in Turkey, its goal was to highlight the grievances of the Kurds in Turkey, Iran and Iraq and support their efforts to seek redress. To the activists in Diyarbakır, most of whom had only the vaguest notion of how Strasbourg worked, Boyle's talk was a revelation, inspiring them to begin collecting information about possible cases to bring.

There was no shortage of possibilities. For instance, in November 1992, not long after Boyle's talk, Turkish soldiers on an anti-PKK operation entered the village of Kelekçi, set fire to nine houses, and ordered Mayor Hüseyin Akdivar to tell all the residents to leave the village. Homeless and destitute, Kelekçi's inhabitants made their way to Diyarbakır, where many were forced to live on the streets. Soldiers soon burned the rest of the village to the ground. It was one of thousands of villages destroyed in what amounted to a government scorched-earth policy to deny territory to the PKK. That same day, in the neighbouring village of Kurşunlu, soldiers on a counter-insurgency operation killed three shepherds, Mehmut Akkum, Mehmut Akan and Dervis Karakoç. Akkum and Akan were taking their animals to graze in the surrounding hills while Karakoç was travelling with his wife and mother on a road in the area where the operation was occurring.

One of the victims was shot at point blank range while the body of another was mutilated.

Later in the month, police in a nearby town burst into the home of Zeki Aksoy, a truck repairman and part-time journalist. Acting on a false tip that Aksoy was a member of the PKK, they dragged him to a prison where he was subjected to nearly three weeks of torture, including being hung by his arms and suffering electric shocks to his genitals while being denied medical treatment. Partly paralysed, Aksoy was eventually released with no charges brought. Also in November, a tank fired at the home of Ramazan Cagirga in the predominantly Kurdish town of Cizre, killing seven of his family members, including his parents, brothers and sisters. These incidents, all in the same month, were just the tip of the iceberg. Indeed, as Boyle wrote in a letter to his old friend Mary Robinson, now president of Ireland, 'the repression and violence on both sides in South-east Turkey is on such a horrendous scale compared with Northern Ireland that it is difficult to credit how little attention it gets compared to our own problems'.[2]

In a judicial system controlled by the Turkish authorities, almost none of those harmed found there was a way to seek redress inside Turkey. The result, recalled Boyle's Essex colleague Françoise Hampson,

> was that victims would go to the Diyarbakır Human Rights Association, many of whose members had attended Kevin's lecture, for help. They'd be interviewed, and if it appeared nothing could be done for them [in Turkey], then the people in the HRA would say 'do you want to go to Europe?'

It is likely that none of the potential applicants had ever heard of the European Commission or Court, but by the spring of 1993 the young lawyers in Diyarbakır had gathered material on dozens of incidents. Some of the lawyers, who were willing to bring cases before Turkish courts, were themselves detained. Their younger and even less experienced colleagues then began sending the information to the KHRP in London.

When Boyle and Hampson were in London in early May, Kerim Yildiz handed them a large folder of material. They skimmed the documents on the train back to Colchester. The details were chilling, and the number of potential cases made clear the nature and scale of the problem. 'The situation in eastern Turkey was a human rights crisis,' Hampson said. 'There was a complete mess going on there.' Boyle and Hampson organized the cases into different categories based on the legal issues involved and agreed that each would take the lead on cases most closely related to their experience or expertise. 'Kevin was dealing with village destruction and freedom of expression,' Hampson recalled. 'I was dealing with indiscriminate and targeted killings, torture and disappearances. These were a type of very widespread violations that Strasbourg had never dealt with before.' The idea, as Boyle later wrote, was to 'prosecute strategically a series of individual cases and through them to establish state responsibility for gross and systematic human rights violations'.[3]

With the European Commission's rule that an application must be filed within six months of a final decision by local courts, Boyle and Hampson picked three of the most time-sensitive cases to start with and, working through a May bank holiday weekend, drafted submissions on behalf of Hüseyin Akdivar and his fellow villagers, torture victim Zeki Aksoy, and the family members of Akkum, Akan and Karakoç. In the following months, as more and more material from the Diyarbakır lawyers arrived, they submitted on average two or three new cases every week. As Hampson noted, 'we were saying "you want torture cases? We can give you one a week. You want unlawful killing? We'll give you one a week."'

Boyle and Hampson asserted that their clients had been victims of a host of violations of the European Convention of Human Rights. For Akdivar and his fellow villagers, it was Article 8, the right to home and family life. They also argued that the house burnings and forced evictions were so serious that they amounted to a violation of Article 3, the right not to be subjected to torture and cruel and inhuman punishment. In addition, they claimed there had been violations of Article 13, the right to an effective domestic remedy, Article 14, the right to be free from discrimination, and Article 18, which imposed limits on the power of governments to curtail other rights in the Convention. In the Aksoy case, they asserted a violation of Article 3, as well as Article 5, the right to liberty and lawful arrest, Article 6, the right to a fair trial, and of Article 13. And for Akkum, Akan and Karakoç they claimed violations of Article 2, the right to life, as well as Articles 3, 6, 13, 14 and 18.

It was far from certain that, on purely legal grounds, Strasbourg would accept the flood of applications. For one thing, Boyle and Hampson had to convince the Commission that, in light of the government-imposed state of emergency in south-eastern Turkey, and the biased attitude of local prosecutors, who assumed all wrongful conduct must be the work of the PKK, whatever 'domestic remedies' the applicants might have used to seek redress were either ineffective, unavailable, or would lead to retaliation from the state. Only then was the Commission likely to make an exception to its rule that such remedies must be exhausted before a case would be considered. 'Strasbourg has always taken this very seriously,' Hampson noted. 'You've got to show that the remedies weren't working. It was a real challenge to us.'

In Strasbourg, however, there was a growing recognition that something terrible was happening in what was still part of Europe. The applications offered an opportunity to look into what appeared to be a major human rights crisis. 'The Commission immediately felt there had been injustice done and it had to be investigated,' recalled Hans Kruger, who was the then secretary of the Commission secretariat. 'We picked up the cases very quickly to try to find out what had happened.' Added Michael O'Boyle, 'everyone knew that there were serious problems of torture, killings and disappearances in Turkey. Consequently, it did not take much for these cases to get off the ground.'

Indeed, within weeks, in an important procedural move, the Commission informed the Turkish government that the three cases had been lodged, and requested written observations on their admissibility and merits. While required to respond, the Turkish authorities were furious. As government lawyers in Ankara drafted documents denying the allegations, Turkish security forces launched a major effort to intimidate the applicants. Hüseyin Akdivar and others were called to a local police station and given pre-drafted statements to sign blaming the PKK, not the army, for burning their village. They were also forced to sign statements denying that they had asked the Human Rights Association in Diyarbakır for help, instead claiming – falsely – that it was the Association who had pressed them to apply.[4]

But that paled in comparison to the fate of Zeki Aksoy. Constantly tailed by security agents, he received numerous anonymous death threats and was regularly visited by police, who kept asking him why he had gone ahead with his application. In April 1994 he was abducted by two plain-clothes policemen and shot dead. When his father Serif decided to continue the case anyway, he too was detained, and warned by the police, 'If you don't drop the case, we will kill you.' Serif fled his village to Diyarbakır and informed the KHRP in London to proceed.[5]

On 18 October 1994 the European Commission of Human Rights held a hearing for the three initial cases. As they prepared for the session, Boyle and Hampson were assisted by Tony Fisher, a Colchester lawyer who had sought Kevin's help for his own Strasbourg case, representing a British woman whose efforts to seek redress for a childhood incident of sexual abuse had been rebuffed by the British courts. By coincidence, the hearing for Fisher's case was set for 17 October, and he flew to Strasbourg with Boyle and Hampson. Also participating was Boyle's former student Aisling Reidy, a Dublin native who had recently received a master's degree from Essex and was working as an intern at the KHRP. In the years after passing the Irish bar exam, Reidy herself would argue multiple Kurdish cases in Strasbourg.

The Commission allotted each party thirty minutes to make its case. This was followed by questions from the Commissioners, and then each side was given ten minutes to sum up. Boyle spoke for Akdivar and his fellow villagers. Building on an argument that he and Hurst Hannum had been the first to develop in the Donnelly case in the 1970s, he contended that the brutal behaviour of the Turkish security forces was an 'administrative practice' authorized by the state, which explained why there were no valid domestic remedies available to the applicants. 'The way in which the remedies the Turkish authorities had said were available had proven to be totally ineffective was a key point,' Fisher recalled. 'They couldn't produce a single case where somebody had successfully gone to the administrative courts of southeast Turkey to recover damages for the loss of their livelihood and property.'

In Hans Kruger's recollection,

> the Turkish government defended itself by saying that these villagers were terrorists – that people like Aksoy and Akdivar had willingly supported the terrorists of the PKK and therefore had to be punished. And Kevin and Françoise Hampson replied that the villagers had been victims of very aggressive action on the part of the Turkish military.

Boyle and Hampson's arguments resonated. The day after the hearing, the Commission declared the Aksoy and Akdivar cases admissible, much to the consternation of the Turkish authorities. A decision on the third case was delayed, but in 1996 it too was declared admissible. However, with such diametrically opposed accounts of the first two incidents, the Commission decided it had no choice but to send a fact-finding mission to Turkey to determine for itself what had actually happened. This was a highly unusual decision. Not since Boyle's Donnelly case in the mid-1970s had Strasbourg concluded that such a step was necessary.

The hearing was set for Diyarbakır in mid-March 1995. In the months before, the Turkish authorities continued to intimidate the applicants, potential witnesses and their local lawyers, prompting Boyle and Hampson to lodge four separate protests with the Commission.[6] 'What we had been hearing at the time from the human rights activists on the ground,' Aisling Reidy recalled,

> was that in the weeks preceding the arrival of the Commission, the military had been going round to applicants and witnesses saying the Commission was coming. They'll want to speak with you, so you have to tell them that everything is OK – and basically threatening them, and that, as a result, people were going to be very scared to testify.

Arriving in Diyarbakır, they found a heavy military presence on the streets, and it soon became obvious they were under intense surveillance. 'We assumed our hotels were bugged,' Hampson recalled. 'We were definitely being watched,' added Aisling Reidy. 'We used to joke about avoiding umbrella tips [which had been used by Russian agents to poison exiled dissidents in Britain] and things like that.' Indeed, Boyle was extremely cautious even crossing the street. 'We were very careful about suddenly being caught in a "traffic accident",' Reidy recalled.

The hearing was held in a large room in an old building that had previously been a water factory. Boyle and Hampson had given the Commission a list of witnesses, including government officials whom they wanted to question. Given the level of intimidation, the lawyers were not sure who would show up, or what any of the victims would actually say. The grim atmosphere was underscored when one of the requested witnesses, Diyarbakır lawyer Mahmut Sarkar, was brought into the room in handcuffs.

Sarkar, who had attended Boyle's 1992 talk and helped collect information for many of the initial cases, had been jailed for having published a report on human rights in the region. Nicolas Bratza, who had argued against Boyle in the Dudgeon gay rights case fifteen years earlier, had just joined the European Commission, and was one of the three delegates on the fact-finding mission. 'The Swede who chaired our delegation, Hans Denelius, said that this was unacceptable, that he [Sakar] had to be released,' Bratza recalled. 'The Turks said there were security problems in doing so. And we said, "Well, we're not prepared to go ahead with him being in handcuffs." And so the handcuffs were removed.'

Despite the menacing atmosphere, Sarkar testified that he had interviewed villagers who told him the security forces had burned their homes, and that the authorities had threatened people for pursuing their claims.[7] Several villagers also appeared and, despite the threats, recounted how the military had burned their village. Under questioning from Boyle, they insisted that they were not PKK sympathizers but simply ordinary civilians. One witness told of previously being forced by a local police commandant to sign a prepared statement blaming the burning on 'terrorists', but at the hearing he repudiated the statement.[8] The same witness told of how he and Hüseyin Akdivar had also been forced to record videos exonerating the military, and then to sign notarized statements confirming what they had said. The witness told Boyle 'he was so frightened he didn't know what he had signed'.[9]

The key government witness was Bekir Selçuk, the chief State Security Court prosecutor, ostensibly in charge of investigating the incident. Stocky, with greying hair, a white moustache and fleshy jowls, he looked to Aisling Reidy like 'a bit of a ruffian, a self-important thuggish villain'. Under several hours of questioning by Boyle, Selçuk maintained that he 'could not contemplate that soldiers would burn down citizens' homes, [and] that the explanation had to be sought elsewhere, either in PKK responsibility, or in a conspiracy to discredit the state involving lawyers and organizations in Turkey and outside'[10] – the last comment a direct jab at Boyle and Hampson. 'Selçuk was attacking Kevin,' noted Hans Kruger. 'He was saying Kevin was supporting terrorists, that these cases should never have been brought, and that we [the Commission] should never have gone there.'

Boyle, however, in his deliberate, soft-spoken manner, continued his questions. 'Kevin kept asking – why had Selçuk not been told certain things? Did he not have a responsibility to investigate? Why didn't he do certain things?' recalled Reidy. 'Kevin was trying to demonstrate that Selçuk was lying,' said Hampson, 'and Selçuk was getting rattled.' Suddenly the Turkish official shouted: 'I have never been treated like this in my entire life!'

Boyle calmly took a breath, looked at the Commission members, who remained silent, and said, 'That's a pity, because I intend to carry on. My next question is …' and the interrogation continued. Selçuk's testimony was a crucial moment. As Boyle wrote in a follow-up document to the Commission, the 'attitude extensively demonstrated by his evidence effectively deprived victims of state crimes from undertaking proceedings to vindicate their rights. The hopelessness of seeking compensation or other relief for wrongdoing by the state emerged vividly.'[11]

With the Akdivar hearing done, attention turned to the case of Zeki Aksoy, where Hampson handled most of the questioning. Since Aksoy had been killed eleven months earlier because of his Strasbourg application, Hampson and Boyle were not certain that their witnesses would show up. 'Nobody knew how difficult the situation was going to be,' Hampson recalled. 'Yes, the government had a legal obligation to cooperate with the fact-finding mission, but what was it going to be like on the ground?'

In any case, eleven witnesses did appear and Hampson questioned them. She had a different style than Boyle. 'It was not abrasive,' said Aisling Reidy, 'but she was never soft-spoken. She was very direct … intense, sometimes like a steam train. She and Kevin were different, but both were very effective.' The witnesses included four Turkish doctors who confirmed key details of the tortures Aksoy had suffered. One said that Aksoy had described being strung up with his hands tied behind his back, resulting in partial paralysis.[12]

Despite Hampson's aggressive challenges, a policeman assigned to the prison where Aksoy had been held maintained that his 'interrogation took place in a calm, comfortable atmosphere with no pressure'. He said Aksoy's allegation of ill treatment showed that he was a 'contributor' to 'terrorist activities' whose goal was to 'humiliate Turkey before Europe'.[13] A local prosecutor testified that 'if the applicant had complained to him of ill treatment in custody, he would have investigated it. Since there was no investigation,' he argued, 'no such complaint was made.'[14] And Bekir Selçuk, who claimed not to be an eyewitness, argued that because of the ongoing 'crimes against the state' in south-east Turkey, 'human rights should be seen in a different context in such areas'.[15] The cynicism of the government witnesses was breathtaking. 'We started to call it the Ministry of Scenarios,' said Reidy. 'Every time there was a human rights complaint, they would go to the Ministry of Scenarios and say, OK, we need a scenario which explains what happened here. And they'd come back with this kind of made-up account of how things went down.'

Hampson, Boyle, Reidy and the Commission delegation left Diyarbakır and travelled, at the Turkish government's request, to Cizre, a small town near the border with Syria and Iraq. It was in Cizre that seven members of Ramazan Cagirga's family had been killed when a shell demolished their home. The Turkish government arranged for the group to stay at Cizre's only hotel, which allowed the authorities to monitor meetings Boyle and his colleagues had with the people they had lined up to testify. It was yet another attempt at intimidation. 'We weren't sure anyone was going to turn up for the hearing,' Reidy remembered. The next morning, however, shortly before the proceedings were due to start, there was a commotion outside the hall.

Dozens of villagers, led by the local *mukhtar* or mayor, were clamouring to testify – not about the Cagirga case, but about the injustices they had suffered. 'They were saying "you have to hear us",' said Reidy. 'They had heard that the European Commission was in town and they thought they could all come and testify.' Eventually, Commission Secretary Hans Kruger emerged to explain that, on this day, only those who had already made a complaint could testify, but that they were all entitled to submit their own applications. It was another sign that the officially inspired campaign of intimidation was not working.

Nonetheless, the witnesses in the Cagirga case were frightened. The first person who arrived to testify told Boyle, Hampson and Reidy, 'We are very scared that something will happen to us when you leave. What can you do for us?' In response, Kruger told the witnesses – and made clear the authorities understood as well – that if anything happened, the Commission would hold the Turkish government responsible. 'We said we were doing our job,' Kruger noted, 'and we would continue to do it.' During the hearing, government officials, subjected to Hampson's withering questioning, produced multiple, often contradictory, explanations for the incident. For her part, Hampson was able to convincingly show that the only kind of weapon capable of causing such extensive damage and so many deaths was a tank shell, and, as she observed, 'it was blindingly obvious the PKK did not have tanks'.

Yet again the lawyers had put the Turkish authorities on the defensive. As a report by Human Rights Watch subsequently noted, these hearings alone were a landmark event for Turkey. The spectacle of high-ranking state officials and soldiers being thoroughly examined by an official commission and called to account for violations against common people was unprecedented. This enterprising move on the part of the Commission came as a powerful shock to institutions unaccustomed to having their acts carefully examined.[16]

With the fact-finding mission over, Kruger and the three delegates returned to Strasbourg to begin deliberations with their colleagues. To reinforce the case for Akdivar, Boyle submitted a ten-page 'memorial'. The hearings and documentary evidence, he wrote, had 'established the truth' about the ordeal of the displaced villagers, while Turkish officials were determined

> to avoid the full truth of and accountability for their continuing policy of the deliberate arbitrary displacement of the Kurdish population of large parts of South-East Turkey, as a counter insurgency stratagem, from being known widely in Turkey and by the international community. The Convention has rarely if ever had to face such deliberate attempts to corrupt justice.[17]

Meanwhile, Boyle and Hampson continued to submit new applications to buttress their argument that the use of lethal force, torture, enforced disappearances and the widespread destruction of villages in south-eastern Turkey were part of a pattern of sustained human rights violations sanctioned by the Turkish government. Just a few weeks later, Kruger contacted Boyle to say that in the Cagirga case, the Commission was proposing a 'friendly settlement', in which the Turkish government would make a one-time compensation payment to Ramazan Cagirga.

Hampson was dubious, preferring to hold out for a formal legal ruling on the merits of the case. But Boyle argued that a fight with Strasbourg now might jeopardize their other cases. Moreover, the Commission was insistent. 'Rather than a ruling,' Kruger said, 'these people had suffered a great deal, and this person was willing to accept a settlement – if he was paid.' In negotiating the terms, Hampson demanded that, in addition to the money, a statement should say that both parties maintained their pre-existing positions – the Turks that the military was not at fault, but Cagirga would repeat his claim that the army was indeed responsible. Turkish officials, however, wanted to include only their version. Hampson said it should include both or no reference at all. In the end, the document mentioned that, 'on humanitarian grounds' Cagirga would receive a payment of 150,000 French francs. It was the first judgment on a Kurdish case from Strasbourg. However frustrating, Boyle and Hampson's client had received a measure of justice.

Soon after, the Commission referred the Akdivar and Aksoy cases to the European Court of Human Rights. In 1996 the Court ruled in favour of Boyle and Hampson in both cases. The Akdivar judgment concluded that the security forces had indeed burned down the applicants' homes. 'There can be no doubt,' the Court wrote,

> that the deliberate burning of the applicants' homes and their contents constitutes at the same time a serious interference with the right to respect for their family lives and homes and with the peaceful enjoyment of their possession … [with] no justification for these interferences having been proffered by the respondent Government.[18]

Moreover, the judgment criticized Turkey for failing to conduct a proper investigation, hold accountable any of the soldiers or police involved, or offer any compensation to the victims. It also noted that the applicants had already faced 'illicit and unacceptable pressure to withdraw their application' and that their lawyers faced a real risk of retaliation if they initiated further legal proceedings against those responsible. Under the circumstances, the Court said the domestic remedies in Turkey were clearly not sufficient.

'The Akdivar judgment was really, really important for the Kurdish cases,' Hampson noted. By creating conditions in which scores of applications could effectively bypass Turkey's internal legal system and be considered by Strasbourg, the ruling opened the floodgates. By the end of the decade, the Commission and Court would consider hundreds of Kurdish cases. And it would turn out to be equally important for broader international human rights law as well. 'It made it clear that this was not a formal thing,' Hampson said. 'You're looking at how remedies work in practice. The mere fact that a remedy formally exists does not mean that it has to be exhausted if it would be … a waste of time.' According to Michael O'Boyle,

> to this day the Akdivar judgment remains a first order authority on the issue of non-exhaustion of domestic remedies, which is so important in the Strasbourg system. It is a definitive statement of the law on issues such as burden of proof of remedies, the adequacy and effectiveness of remedies and the 'special circumstances' rule.

The Aksoy judgment soon followed – and it too was groundbreaking. The Court confirmed that Zeki Aksoy had indeed been tortured, and that the government had offered no alternative explanation for his injuries. 'In Strasbourg terms,' Hampson observed, 'it was a landmark.' It was the first Strasbourg judgment to confirm state-sanctioned torture in Europe, and it set out what would become an important principle in international law. 'The Court considers that where the individual is taken into custody in good health but is found to be injured on release, it is incumbent on the state to provide a plausible explanation.'[19] As Tony Fisher noted, the importance of Aksoy was that 'the exact duties of the state towards those who are in their custody were more comprehensively identified, and that's been pleaded in thousands of cases since.'

But the Court did not endorse Boyle and Hannum's notion that the abuses constituted an 'administrative practice'. Rather, as was true in the Donnelly case in the 1970s, it appeared content to focus on individual cases. Boyle and his colleagues were disappointed, writing in a journal article that 'focusing solely on the particular facts of a given case may provide substantial redress to an individual, but it will fail to address the underlying situation which is generating continued violations of the Convention'.[20] While some legal scholars have argued that the reason for this was concern in Strasbourg that such a sweeping judgment would have so antagonized Turkey that it would cease cooperating with the Commission and Court altogether,[21] Michael O'Boyle saw another explanation. 'Had the Commission determined that there existed an administrative practice,' he noted,

> it would have been deluged with even more cases that it would not be in a position to examine, and its default position was that efforts to seek a national remedy must be made wherever possible – accepting that in many cases there may be special circumstances absolving the applicants from exhausting [domestic remedies]. In retrospect this may have been short-sighted, given the volume of cases coming from the region and the knowledge that torture and killing was [sic] widespread in the east of Turkey.

Nonetheless, Boyle and his colleagues persevered. Trips to Strasbourg for hearings and to Turkey for fact-finding missions became a regular feature of his life during the mid- and late 1990s. Even for someone with Boyle's experience, however, it took considerable emotional fortitude to plunge into one agonizing episode of cruelty and suffering after another. Kevin 'always spoke of the dignity of the Kurdish peasants who were affected by the terrible crimes of that time', Joan Boyle recalled. 'He was very affected by meeting them.' In the words of Tony Fisher, 'some of the fact-finding cases were indeed very haunting, and I am sure that the evidence of some of the witnesses has stayed with us for ever.' At one point, Joan said, 'Kevin talked non-stop about a murder scene where the victim had left bloody fingerprints on a door. The boys and I had to stop him recounting that scene each time we sat down to dinner.' Back in Colchester, Joan said, 'there were many occasions when Kevin, Françoise, Aisling and Tony would be together, and they would open many a bottle of wine and talk and talk about their experiences. A very close bond was formed. They called themselves "The Survivors".'

One particularly harrowing case involved Sukran Aydin, a seventeen-year-old Kurdish girl detained by police. In prison, she was stripped, put in a tyre, rolled around, hosed with cold water and then raped by a man in military uniform. Afterwards, she was beaten, warned never to talk about what had happened, and dumped on a hillside near her village. Hearing of her ordeal, local human rights activists informed the KHRP in London, and Hampson and Boyle brought a case to Strasbourg. When the Turkish government did not respond to requests for observations from the Commission, the case was declared admissible. In July 1995 three Commission delegates flew to Turkey for a fact-finding hearing, in which Hampson, Boyle and Reidy participated. Although Sukran's father was present, she was nowhere to be found. With the Turkish authorities claiming the whole incident had been fabricated, the Commission asked for a letter from Sukran confirming her desire to continue. A young Turkish human rights activist travelled hundreds of miles over nearly two weeks before locating the illiterate Sukran in a filthy camp for migrant workers, where she pressed her thumbprint on a document saying that she wanted to pursue the case.[22]

That autumn, with no luggage and no coat, a frightened and crying Sukran arrived in Strasbourg for what Reidy described as a 'very emotional, traumatic hearing'. Françoise Hampson handled the questioning. 'It wasn't like a normal cross-examination,' said Nicolas Bratza. 'Aydin was very nervous. Françoise managed to bring out the story of how she had been treated.' So deep was Sukran's trauma that she could not bring herself to use the word 'rape', referring instead to the 'dirty things' that had happened to her.[23]

There were huge legal issues at stake. Would the European Court rule, for the first time, that rape was a form of torture? Along with the ethnic cleansing in Bosnia, and the genocide in Rwanda, enshrining this conclusion in international human rights law would have enormous implications. Françoise Hampson, assisted by Reidy, had taken the lead on the case, consulting with Boyle. But she and Reidy found Boyle to be notably sensitive in talking about the matter. 'Kevin found the facts so distressing that he didn't want to look at them', Hampson recalled. 'It was so upsetting that he was uneasy even talking about the purely legal side of how you plead the case.' To Reidy, it was clear that Kevin was 'visibly uncomfortable dealing with the issue of sexual violence. He definitely was glad that Françoise was taking the lead. He didn't like to discuss the details too much.'

But the distress was worth it. In 1997 the Court recognized that the act of rape, in and of itself, could amount to torture, adding that

> rape of a detainee by an official of the State must be considered to be an especially grave and abhorrent form of ill treatment given the ease with which the offender can exploit the vulnerability and weakened resistance of his victim. Furthermore, rape leaves deep psychological scars on the victim which do not respond to the passage of time as quickly as other forms of physical and mental violence.[24]

It was a landmark ruling, reflecting the growing public consciousness about the prevalence of rape in conflict zones and underscoring the need to develop legal mechanisms to bring to justice perpetrators of sexual violence. And it laid the groundwork for the international tribunals, which investigated war crimes in Rwanda and the former Yugoslavia to condemn rape as a tool of war and prosecute those who engaged in it. For Sukran Aydin, however, the pain never went away. Before the rape, her family had already arranged a marriage for her, which, despite the deep conservatism of Kurdish society, went ahead despite the 'shame' of what had happened to her. After marrying, she had a baby daughter and named her Eziyet. In English, the word means 'torture'.[25]

Despite all the horrors emerging from Turkey, Boyle carried on. He, Hampson and their colleagues continued to bring cases on behalf of the

Kurds throughout the 1990s, with regular victories in Strasbourg in a host of categories: the destruction of villages, torture, enforced disappearances and extrajudicial killings. The Turkish authorities responded grudgingly to their repeated legal defeats, but eventually the pressure became so strong, the government began to introduce some significant reforms. 'It helped to bring an end to the worst exactions such as torture in the police stations,' said Michael O'Boyle. 'Turkey wanted to get into the EU and the EU was following the Strasbourg judgments very closely and undoubtedly made it clear they had to bring about considerable improvement in their human rights record. These cases laid the basis for this strategy.'

As Nicolas Bratza observed, 'There undoubtedly were improvements brought about by the adverse findings of the Commission and the Court.' These included enhanced training for the security forces, judges and prosecutors, modifications to the criminal justice system, and a greater willingness to pay compensation. Moreover, the state of emergency in south-east Turkey was eased, and detainees were granted new rights. These included the right to see a lawyer of their own choosing and to be examined by a doctor without the police or military present.[26] There was still resistance from within the bureaucracy and the security forces, and continuing questions about how well-equipped the Strasbourg system was to deal with extensive state-sponsored violations of human rights – but compared to when Boyle made his first visit to Diyarbakır in 1992, the progress was significant.

For their work in 1998, the fiftieth anniversary of the Universal Declaration of Human Rights, the British Law Society and Liberty, previously known as Britain's National Council of Civil Liberties, named Kevin Boyle and Françoise Hampson lawyers of the year.

[22]

The Choice

IN 1992 Northern Ireland appeared to be heading back to the darkest days of the early 1970s. With political progress blocked owing to intransigence on all sides, loyalist and republican death squads stalked the streets. In the first six weeks of the year, thirty-one people, most of them civilians, were killed in a series of bombings and shootings. Later that spring, the IRA set off two bombs in the city of London, causing more financial damage than all the bombs that had gone off in Northern Ireland since the start of the Troubles. By the end of the year, nearly a hundred people had been killed, and the province was enveloped in despair. As Boyle and his long-time collaborator Tom Hadden wrote, 'there is a real risk of the situation deteriorating as quickly and disastrously as it did in the former Yugoslavia'.[1]

Boyle had remained deeply engaged in Irish issues, despite his numerous other activities. He was a regular participant in meetings of the British-Irish Association, an organization that for years had brought together politicians, senior government officials, journalists, academics, business and religious leaders, community workers, and former paramilitaries for private discussions on Northern Ireland-related issues. While cynics dismissed the Association, with its gatherings at stately country homes or the ornate halls of Oxford and Cambridge, as 'toffs against terrorism', in fact it played a crucial role in sustaining dialogue during some of the worst years of the Troubles, providing a safe setting to explore new ideas.

Boyle eventually served on the organization's executive committee. 'The British-Irish Association was an important thing for the exchange of views, and people who normally would not have rubbed shoulders with cabinet ministers and particularly senior officials got the opportunity to do so,' recalled Maurice Hayes, an old Boyle family friend and a senior Northern Ireland civil servant in the 1990s. 'That was the sort of setting where Kevin would shine, because the people there could suddenly could find a guy talking in objective terms which they could understand and making things reasonable and possible.' To Hayes, such efforts were part of what he called Boyle's ongoing 'missionary work' to promote a settlement.

Boyle also continued to speak and write about the Troubles. In November 1992 he was featured in a documentary on Northern Ireland produced by BBC radio along with several of the most prominent political figures in the conflict. They included Britain's newly appointed Northern Ireland Secretary Sir Patrick Mayhew, former Irish taoiseach Garret FitzGerald, John Hume, head of the SDLP, Ulster Unionist Party leader James Molyneaux, and Martin McGuinness, the one-time IRA commander who was now number two in the IRA's political wing Sinn Féin. Most of the participants stuck to their predictable positions, but the BBC host gave Boyle the last word.

Kevin used the opportunity to outline a new approach that would transcend the unionist–nationalist antagonism that had defined Northern Irish politics for so long. 'I see solutions based on states and identity within states and territory as being, in effect, anachronistic in the context of these islands,' he said:

> We need to move away from the ideas like the nation-state, the independent state, national sovereignty, to a different view, where we try to think instead of institutions which will adequately reflect the interdependence. For me, the best way to think about the solution for the future is to change ideas, is to change our discourse, our language.[2]

It was, in the words of journalist Andy Pollak, who had edited Hadden's journal *Fortnight* for several years in the early 1980s, the kind of courageous forward thinking 'that didn't go down well in a sectarian little province like Northern Ireland where politics was all about identity'.

Indeed, as the tit-for-tat sectarian killings and IRA bombings continued, public frustration at Northern Ireland's politicians and paramilitaries grew. It led, in mid-1992, to the creation of 'Initiative '92', an effort spearheaded by the then editor of *Fortnight*, Robin Wilson, and a Queen's University law professor, Simon Lee, to establish a forum where ordinary people could have their voices heard. The organizers asked Torkel Opsahl, a distinguished Norwegian human rights lawyer and an old friend of Boyle's, to chair a commission that would seek submissions from across Northern Ireland. Andy Pollak was asked to coordinate the effort. 'The idea was for an independent commission of inquiry,' he wrote, 'to which the people of Northern Ireland ... would be invited to submit ideas on possible ways forward.'³

With its slogan 'No One Asked You ... Until Now', the initiative drew an overwhelming response. As Opsahl, a soft-spoken man who had been both an Amnesty International observer at trials of Soviet dissidents in the 1960s and a long-time member of the European Commission of Human Rights, travelled across Northern Ireland with his six fellow commissioners, three thousand people took part in making written and oral submissions. It was a reflection of the desperate public desire for fresh thinking after so many years of bloodshed.

Among the contributors were Boyle and Hadden, who submitted a major paper and spoke at a public hearing in February 1993. As in their earlier joint projects, the two men brainstormed, with Hadden writing an initial draft and Boyle offering comments and feedback. The goal this time was to come up with new ideas for breaking the deadlock. Boyle wrote to Hadden in a letter that

> our collaboration is directed at transcending the sealed containers of traditional positions towards a more open-ended accommodation of the identities and loyalties, and certainly an accommodation which is sceptical of solutions which are predicated on outmoded nationalisms. We have enough evidence of where that has led from Ireland's past and from the Balkans' present.⁴

Instead, Boyle proposed emphasizing 'what can be shared, what is common between these islands and their peoples'.⁵

Two central themes shaped the Boyle-Hadden submission. First, with both Ireland and the United Kingdom now in the European Union, they called for

> recognition of a European dimension to any future settlement that may help in resolving some issues which may cause greater difficulty within an existing British and Irish framework, notably the protection of human rights, the monitoring of security activities, and minority protection.[6]

Second – and related – was the importance of strong legal protection for human rights through the adoption of a Bill of Rights for Northern Ireland, based on the European Convention on Human Rights. These and other steps, they stressed, should be incorporated into a new British-Irish agreement for the 1990s that built on the vision of the Anglo-Irish Agreement signed seven years before. A new accord, they wrote, should include 'mutual recognition', meaning the Republic accepting the legitimacy of Northern Ireland's existing status

> by agreement on identical wording on the status of Northern Ireland in both UK and Irish law. Any such statement might include both the right of a majority within Northern Ireland to opt for adhesion either to the UK or the Irish Republic, and an appropriate statement of aspiration for members of both communities.[7]

The arguments of Boyle and Hadden featured prominently in the voluminous report issued by the Opsahl Commission in June 1993. The report endorsed their call for the enactment of a Bill of Rights for Northern Ireland incorporating the European Convention, as well as reform of policing and the criminal justice system. In addition, it proposed the legal recognition of nationalism in Northern Ireland to create 'parity of esteem' between the two communities and, on that basis, it urged the establishment of a local government in which power would be equally shared. Most controversially, it argued that the British government should open informal channels of communication with Sinn Féin to test whether that party was committed to the constitutional process.

The report was criticized in many quarters, especially by some political parties who resented the intrusion of the general public on their 'turf', but it was widely read and discussed, and became an indispensable resource for those seeking to keep a nascent peace process alive. As Tom Hadden noted, 'it set the scene for the possibility of a deal because so many people, both from the community people and some of the political parties, had come to Opsahl and said "let's get on with this". It did have influence.' Indeed, by reflecting the growing desire of ordinary people on both sides for an end to the conflict and offering fresh proposals for debate and discussion, it was, in the words of Garret FitzGerald, 'a welcome antidote to the politics of despair'.[8]

While debate continued over how to break the deadlock, Boyle and Hadden were already thinking about the complex details that would have to go into any peace agreement. Even as they drafted their submission to the Opsahl Commission, Boyle had also approached the Standing Advisory Committee on Human Rights (SACHR), which advised the Northern Irish authorities on human rights issues, with a proposal to brief the province's political parties on the mechanics of any future Bill of Rights. In a letter to SACHR, Boyle outlined his idea. With the lack of political progress, he wrote

> it is essential to keep a sense of engagement on the part of the local elected politicians. One of the only areas on which there has been a consensus is on the need for more formal protections of human rights. Whatever the shape of the political arrangements that may ultimately be agreed, all parties have accepted that there will need to be a bill of rights. However, there is a good deal of uncertainty around what that entails in terms of substance of rights and procedures.[9]

At a time when the parties were barely talking to one another, Boyle stressed that 'the seminar proposal is not intended to be a political forum or to be a vehicle for political talks. It is exclusively concerned with substantive technical issues.'[10]

SACHR embraced the idea, and in late February 1993 Boyle and Hadden presided over the first of two sessions. They were held in a modest hotel outside the town of Kells in County Antrim under conditions of strict secrecy, including a pledge not to reveal the meetings to the press. Those attending included representatives of the Official Unionist Party, Ian Paisley's more hard-line Democratic Unionist Party, John Hume's SDLP and the small non-sectarian Alliance Party. Among the participants were David Trimble, soon to become the leader of the Official Unionists, and, in 1998, a signatory to the Good Friday peace agreement, as well Ian Paisley's son, Ian Junior, whose views were just as extreme as those of his father. There is no record of whether or not Boyle felt any sense of irony briefing the son of one of his chief political adversaries from civil rights days on the need for a Bill of Rights. In any case, Boyle and Hadden presented several papers they had drafted. Other academics and human rights experts spoke as well, covering a host of specifics, examples and international precedents that would need to be examined. Yet the participants soon concluded, as Hadden noted, 'that none of this could be done unless and until there was a political agreement. So a Bill of Rights would have to be part of a political agreement. It couldn't be done separately. And Kevin and I agreed with that.' Still, the meetings were one more piece in a foundation for protecting the rights of all Northern Ireland's citizens, which Boyle and Hadden were slowly starting to create.

Sinn Féin was not invited to Kells, since none of the unionists would meet with representatives of the IRA's political wing. But Boyle and Hadden established their own channel of communication. 'It was just to keep Sinn Féin informed as to what we are doing,' Hadden recalled. The exchanges were frustrating, however. At one meeting, Hadden told Sinn Féin official Tom Hartley 'we're doing all this work on human rights. What is Sinn Féin's position?' Hartley, a former Sinn Féin press officer described by Ed Moloney in his history of the IRA as 'a driving force behind the bid to politicize the Provisionals',[11] gave Hadden a blunt reply. 'Look,' Hartley said, 'realistically this is a bit difficult for us, because we are engaged in an armed struggle.'

Indeed, in the autumn of 1993, the violence reached a new peak. In October the IRA bombed a fish and chip shop in the Shankill Road in the mistaken belief that key figures in the UDA were meeting there. Ten people – the bomber and nine Protestants, including women and children – were killed. Loyalist gunmen then went on a rampage. In just one week, twenty-three people died. But the carnage spurred efforts to find a political way forward, including a controversial dialogue between John Hume and Gerry Adams – an effort to find common ground between the constitutional and physical force wings of Irish nationalism. At the same time, the British government was engaged in secret contacts, revealed only years later, directly with the Provisionals, while the Irish and British governments were also holding intensive negotiations.

The result, in December 1993, was the Downing Street Declaration, signed by British Prime Minister John Major and his Irish counterpart, Albert Reynolds. Its central feature was an affirmation of the principle of consent – that the desire of Northern Ireland's Protestant majority to remain part of the UK had to be respected – something that Boyle and Hadden had advocated for years. Both governments pledged to 'foster agreement and reconciliation, leading to a new political framework founded on consent and encompassing arrangements within Northern Ireland, for the whole island, and between these islands.'[12]

Moreover, Britain acknowledged that 'it is for the people of the island of Ireland alone, by agreement between the two parts respectively, to exercise their right of self-determination on the basis of consent, freely and concurrently given, North and South, to bring about a united Ireland, if that is their wish.'[13] The statement also noted the importance of the UK and Ireland being partners in the European Union, while the Irish side, acknowledging that elements of the Irish constitution were resented by Northern Unionists, pledged constitutional reform in the event of a final settlement.[14] To Walter Kirwan, a senior Irish civil servant then working in the Department of the Taoiseach and previously a major figure involved in the diplomacy concerning the Anglo-Irish agreement, it was a document 'which, on constitutional status issues, had moved closer to the Boyle-Hadden position'.[15]

By making an explicit reference to a united Ireland and stating that Britain was not in principle opposed to it, but stressing that the people of the North and South should exercise their right of self-determination separately – thus giving the unionist majority a veto – the declaration hoped to entice the IRA away from violence, while at the same time reassuring Ulster's anxious Protestants. But many key questions about the nature of a possible settlement remained unanswered.

To address them, even as the Downing Street Declaration was unveiled, Boyle and Hadden were jointly writing a new book, with the goal, as Hadden noted, of 'pulling together all the stuff we had been working on'. They called the book *Northern Ireland: The Choice*. Begun in late 1992, it would come out in the spring of 1994, amid continuing uncertainty about the intentions of the IRA and the prospects for peace. Using census data, public opinions polls, findings from the Opsahl Commission and insights from their own large network of contacts, they sought to identify and clarify the choices facing Northern Ireland, Britain and the Irish Republic. The most critical one, they argued, was between 'separation and sharing'. They posed a provocative question:

> whether the different communities can go on living together or whether it would be more realistic to accept that the forces of communal separation are irresistible and should be altered accordingly to provide for a deliberate move towards developing structures for separation?[16]

While spelling out the practical steps that would be involved in formalizing separation – and thus sounding a warning about the consequences of a no peace deal – they made clear this was not their preferred choice. Moreover, from their research, they concluded that in large sections of both communities 'there is a greater willingness to compromise than among their political leaders'.[17] This, they said, was a source of hope for a possible settlement, and it led them to a detailed analysis of various models for a workable political, constitutional and social structure – what they dubbed a 'structure for sharing'. They explored the dilemma created by the competing definitions of self-determination, with nationalists asserting that it referred to all the people in the island of Ireland, and unionists insisting that the people of Northern Ireland had their own separate right. They noted that in international law 'both major communities in Northern Ireland – or in Ireland – have an arguable case for treatment either as a people [with a right to self-determination] or as a minority [with a right to protection]'.

But they argued that 'it ought to be possible to find an acceptable form of words based on the formulation of the Downing Street Declaration and relevant international documents which would meet the claims of both communities. This could then be incorporated into a bill of rights.'[18] This was just one of many arguments they made in support of a Bill of Rights as an essential foundation for peace. Building on their earlier work on the subject, they also proposed that any such document, which would be based on the European Convention of Human Rights, could also contain additional provisions that took into account the particular circumstances of Northern Ireland. These, they said, could include protection for communal as well as individual rights, new constraints on the government's power to introduce emergency laws – a source of so much bitterness in earlier years

– and guarantees to ensure that the bill could not be easily repealed. They also offered detailed language that the Irish government could use to amend its constitutional claim to Northern Ireland, something that had long been a source of unionist anger.

In their 255-page book, Boyle and Hadden did not pretend to have all the answers. But they hoped that by examining what they saw as the crucial questions, they could help 'those involved in the peace process … understand the realities of the situation [and] pursue policies that will produce a lasting peace and so avoid the dangers of a descent into even greater chaos, of the kind which has been produced in Bosnia'.[19]

As with their earlier work, Boyle and Hadden sent copies of the book to the Northern Ireland Office, members of the British and Irish governments, including the taoiseach in Dublin and the prime minister in London, and to influential figures in the media. The response was overwhelmingly positive. Under the headline 'The Way to the Future', a reviewer in *The Irish Times* wrote that 'this valuable book articulately and objectively' outlined pathways out of the conflict.[20] *Human Rights Quarterly* described it as a 'primer for peace',[21] while an official in Britain's Northern Ireland Office sent a letter to Hadden saying 'your latest production is first class, even by your and Prof. Boyle's own high standards'.[22] The official went on, 'we found the book highly relevant, both in terms of material and argument, and our conclusion is that you will be doing all Northern Ireland watchers a great service in so thoroughly ventilating so many of the options and their pros and cons.'[23]

Nineteen ninety-four was a strange time in Northern Ireland. For all the talk of peace, the violence continued unabated. In the first eight months of the year, sixty-five people were killed, yet the Downing Street Declaration had boxed in the Provisionals. If the British government, as the document said, was prepared to accept a united Ireland if achieved through democratic means, then what was the logic of the IRA's campaign of violence? For those like Gerry Adams and Martin McGuinness, who had been pushing to abandon the gun and fully embrace politics, it was a compelling argument. And it led, on 31 August, to the IRA announcing a 'complete cessation of military operations'. Six weeks later, the main loyalist paramilitaries, the UVF and the UDA, followed suit. Among the supporters of the loyalist ceasefire was convicted UVF killer Billy Hutchinson, whose prison correspondence with Boyle in the mid-1980s provided one of the earliest indications that the views of some extreme loyalists were changing. Like Sinn Féin, the UVF now established a political wing and saw the potential of electoral politics.

With the guns silent, the army's presence on the streets of Northern Ireland was dramatically reduced, and something close to normal life began to re-emerge. Meanwhile, the Irish government moved to implement one of its pledges in the Downing Street Declaration: the establishment of a 'Forum on Peace and Reconciliation'. Modelled on the New Ireland Forum, the goal of this new consultative body was to draw Sinn Féin into a post-ceasefire political dialogue, and to facilitate broader discussions among all the parties in conflict about how to move forward. Walter Kirwan was appointed secretary general of the new body, which held its first meeting in October 1994. Because of Sinn Féin's willingness to participate, all Northern Ireland's unionist parties, predictably, refused to attend.

Nonetheless, the exercise went ahead, and Kirwan asked Boyle and Hadden to serve as consultants and produce a study entitled 'The Protection of Human Rights in the Context of Peace and Reconciliation'. As they began their work, however, Sinn Féin objected, whether, as Kirwan later observed, 'because of the moderate cast of their writings or because of Tom's unionist background or because Kevin was not considered nationalist enough'[24] and demanded a third person be assigned to the project. Colm Campbell, a law professor at Queen's University and a former student of Hadden's, who was viewed by Sinn Féin as a more committed nationalist, was brought in to the project. It was not the only time during the Forum when, in the words of Opsahl Commission originator Robin Wilson, Sinn Féin treated the Forum 'as a platform for rehearsing fundamentalist positions with dogmatic certainty, frequently to the frustration of the constitutional-nationalist parties'.[25]

Sinn Féin's biggest complaint was how Boyle and Hadden, who both believed that the citizens of Northern Ireland had a separate right to decide if they wanted to be part of a united Ireland, sought to frame the issue of self-determination. Although personally cordial, the dealings among the three academics were complicated. 'Kevin and I were slightly suspicious of Colm,' Hadden recalled. 'The impression I got is that when I sent drafts to Colm and Kevin, Colm went and discussed it with people in Sinn Féin.' Boyle and Hadden became increasingly cautious in their exchanges when Campbell was involved, but in the end, in order to keep Sinn Féin engaged in the process, and in response to Campbell's argument that this was a 'political matter to be negotiated', they agreed to tone down their language on the self-determination issue.

Nonetheless, when the paper was presented to the Forum in Dublin in November 1995 it was widely praised, with one SDLP participant – no friend of Sinn Féin – describing it as a 'masterly document' and 'everyman's guide to human rights'.[26] The paper stressed the fact that both Ireland and the UK were signatories to the key international human rights conventions, and were thus obligated to uphold them. It called for the establishment of human rights commissions in the North and the Republic, as well as for European and UN involvement in monitoring implementation. More broadly, they called for the creation of a 'culture of human rights' in all institutions of government, in law enforcement, and in civil society.

Undermined by Sinn Féin's grandstanding, as well as by the absence of the unionist parties, the Boyle-Hadden-Campbell paper was one of the highlights of what had become a messy and frustrating process. In February 1996 the IRA, angered by what it viewed as the lack of a substantive British response to its 1994 ceasefire, resumed its campaign of violence, and bombed the Canary Wharf district of London, killing two men and causing some £70 million-worth of damage. The Forum for Peace and Reconciliation basically collapsed. Nonetheless, a decision was made to publish the human rights paper, which was distributed widely by Forum organizers to the media, political parties in the North and South, and senior officials in the British and Irish governments – yet another instance where Boyle and Hadden's ideas made their way to the desks of policy-makers. The violence, meanwhile, continued.

But in May 1997, the political landscape was transformed by a historic British general election. The Labour Party ousted the Conservatives after eighteen years in power, and Tony Blair became the new prime minister. Eager to revive the peace process, he announced a willingness to include Sinn Féin in multi-party talks if there was a new ceasefire, and outlined an ambitious deadline of 9 April 1998 – the day before Good Friday – to achieve an agreement. In July 1997 the Provisionals restored the ceasefire. By that autumn, for the first time since the negotiations that led to Ireland's independence in 1921, representatives of the IRA's political wing were negotiating directly and openly with the British government. Seven other Northern Irish parties, including the unionists, as well as the Irish government, also participated, although the unionists refused to talk directly with Sinn Féin.

Against a backdrop of murders and bombings by republican and loyalist splinter groups seeking to torpedo the talks, the parties struggled to find common ground. In the first week of April 1998, all the delegates were sequestered near the old Northern Ireland parliament at Stormont as Blair, President Bill Clinton's Special Envoy, George Mitchell, and Ireland's new taoiseach, Bertie Ahern, sought to broker a deal. At the last minute Blair asked Clinton to personally intervene by telephoning key figures, including Ulster Unionist leader David Trimble and Gerry Adams. Just before dawn on April 10, an agreement was reached.

The fundamental principle of the Belfast Agreement (known widely as the Good Friday Agreement) was that Northern Ireland could remain in the UK until such time as a majority of people – in both the North and the Republic – voted to create a united Ireland. To assuage unionist anxiety, the Irish Republic dropped its constitutional claim to Northern Ireland. A new legislature was to be established at Stormont with a series of structures to compel representatives of the two communities to govern together, although the British government would for the time being remain in charge of sensitive matters, including security and justice. In a gesture to nationalists, a North-South ministerial council was created to promote cooperation across the border. An explicit and robust endorsement of human rights underpinned these specific steps. The British and Irish governments agreed to incorporate the European Convention on Human Rights into their domestic law.

Both pledged to establish Human Rights Commissions. The British side declared that the Northern Ireland Human Rights Commission would be authorized to define rights supplementary to the European Convention 'to reflect the particular circumstances of Northern Ireland'.[27] Together, the agreement said, all these rights would 'reflect the principles of mutual respect for the identity and ethos of both communities and parity of esteem, and – taken together with the ECHR – constitute a Bill of Rights for Northern Ireland.'[28] Given the controversial history of policing in Northern Ireland – including many issues in which Boyle had been deeply involved, such as allegations of a 'shoot to kill' policy, the use of plastic bullets and the mistreatment of detainees – the agreement called for an independent commission to examine how the police force could be improved.

Although hardly alone in their views, it was striking how the human rights aspects of the agreement reflected positions Boyle and Hadden had articulated and lobbied for over many years. This included the principle of consent, recognition of the legitimacy of both traditions in a Northern Ireland context, the incorporation of the European Convention of Human Rights into domestic law, the drafting of a Bill of Rights, amending one element of the Irish constitution, and reforming the Northern Irish police. Predictably, neither Boyle nor Hadden ever sought public credit for the influence of their ideas. 'They were sort of catalytic people,' observed Maurice Hayes. 'They were not being noticed that much, but they were changing things. They were important.'

According to Walter Kirwan, Boyle and Hadden 'definitely did influence concepts in the Good Friday Agreement. And of course Kevin was very big on the idea that you didn't have to go looking for new norms for human rights. They were already laid out in the European Convention, and what you should be doing is applying them.' Queen's University law professor Brice Dickson, who in 1999 would become the first Chief Commissioner of the Northern Ireland Human Rights Commission, observed that the human rights elements of the Good Friday Agreement were to a significant degree 'based on the ideas that Boyle and Hadden had, and they were persistent in pushing them in a non-judgmental and academically rigorous way'. For his part, the always modest Hadden recalled that, sometime later, Boyle

> told me that one of his contacts in the Irish team said they were struggling to find something to say about a Bill of Rights in the Good Friday Agreement, and they simply adopted what we'd been saying, which was incorporation of the European Convention and then what we used to call the 'add-ons' to reflect the particular circumstances in Northern Ireland. And that's exactly what it says in the agreement. The formulation they used for the construction of a Bill of Rights in Northern Ireland was effectively our formulation.

Shortly after the signing of the agreement, the British government appointed Chris Patten, the last colonial governor of Hong Kong, to chair the Independent Commission for Policing in Northern Ireland. Over the next fifteen months, the Commission, which included Maurice Hayes, held a thousand public meetings and received 450 written submissions. One of them was from Boyle and Ralph Crawshaw, a former British police chief superintendent and visiting fellow at the University of Essex Human Rights Centre whose special interest was the relationship between human rights and policing. The submission focused on the importance of incorporating the protection of human rights into basic police training. This was a view echoed by other submissions, including one from the Committee on the Administration of Justice, long Northern Ireland's most important NGO for the promotion of human rights protections. In September 1999 Patten issued his report, producing a blueprint to change the Royal Ulster Constabulary beyond recognition – not least by changing its name. Gone were 'Royal' and 'Ulster' – terms offensive to many nationalists. In its place would be the Police Service of Northern Ireland. Moreover, Patten wrote that in the report, 'we consider the purpose of policing, which we define as the protection of human rights, and we make proposals to reorient policing in Northern Ireland onto an approach based on upholding human rights and respecting human dignity. This approach underlies the whole of our report.'[29]

'The Patten report is actually founded on human rights,' observed Maurice Hayes, 'partly because it was the right thing to do, but also because it would have been very difficult for people to mount a sustained objection to the invocation of human rights.' To Hayes, the role of Boyle and Hadden in laying the intellectual foundation for such an approach was crucial. 'I think the contribution they made was that they helped give us the language. That was important.'

There is no written record of Boyle's emotional reaction to the dramatic moves that would effectively bring the Troubles to an end. For all his intellectual engagement, it had been two decades since he had left Belfast and a dozen years since moving to England from Galway, and he had deliberately sought to involve himself in other places and other human rights issues. 'Northern Ireland wasn't his central preoccupation,' his son Mark recalled. 'There was some kind of distance.' But according to Joan Boyle, Kevin was unquestionably 'pleased, relieved and hopeful' about the peace deal, although, she said, 'he wondered about so many lives lost up to that point – and for what?' Now, however, with the Troubles effectively ending, Boyle was about to be pulled back to one of its most distressing episodes – Bloody Sunday.

Three months before the Good Friday Agreement, Tony Blair had announced a new inquiry into the killing of fourteen civilians by British troops in Derry during a civil rights march on 30 January 1972. Friends and relatives of the victims had long pushed for such a step and Blair – new in office, and eager to improve the climate for the still-sputtering peace process – decided the time was right. He named Mark Saville, a senior judge and member of the House of Lords, to head the inquiry. There had been a previous investigation, conducted in the immediate aftermath of the killings by Britain's Lord Chief Justice at the time, Lord Widgery, but it met for just a few weeks, interviewed barely a hundred people, and produced a 120-page report, which blamed the Northern Ireland Civil Rights Association, where Boyle had been the press officer, for organizing the march. The Widgery report also claimed that some of the victims had been in contact with fire-arms, and that soldiers had used force only after being fired upon. Many in Northern Ireland, especially in the nationalist community and among supporters of the civil rights movement, saw the report as a whitewash, which smeared the reputations of innocent victims of army brutality. Among them was Boyle, who, on behalf of NICRA, wrote a scathing critique in April 1972. 'The description of the report as whitewash,' Boyle had argued then, 'comes from the manner in which Widgery abused his apparently limited terms of reference to put the best face on the Army's version of Bloody Sunday.'[30]

The Saville Inquiry would be different. After a dozen years and the processing of 2500 statements, in 2010 the Inquiry published a 5000-page report with a dramatically different conclusion, exonerating the victims and pinning responsibility for the killings on the army. Boyle was among those called to give evidence. As he prepared his testimony, his old friend and colleague Francis Keenan, then still working as a lawyer in Belfast, was brought in to advise NICRA. At Keenan's instigation, Boyle joined several other surviving members of the NICRA leadership for a series of meetings in Belfast to discuss how to depict the organization's role in relation to Bloody Sunday. 'The group was assembled by Francis Keenan and we met at a Belfast hotel,' Boyle recalled in an interview some years later. 'I swear, after a half-hour's discussion, I think most people had forgotten it had been thirty years. It seemed natural that the process of meeting should be as if it was a NICRA executive meeting. It was surreal re-living it. It was an extraordinary experience.'[31]

It was becoming clear that lawyers for the soldiers who had carried out the killings would, as Widgery did, attempt to pin the blame on NICRA as the march organizers as well as on the IRA. In addition to their individual statements, the former NICRA leaders agreed that a document should be submitted to the Saville Inquiry on behalf of the organization, detailing its history, attitudes and actions. Keenan was given access to the NICRA archives and compiled an initial draft, which he then shared with Boyle. As Keenan recalled, trying to depict 'the makeup of NICRA, how it was set up, and what its ideas were, was a joint effort', which included Keenan making a number of trips to Colchester to go over material with Boyle.

In one memo to Keenan, Boyle outlined what he felt was at stake. 'The Saville Inquiry is writing history,' he noted. 'There will be no further opportunity, ever, to assess NICRA's role in the events of that day. What is the key issue for NICRA? It is whether the Saville Inquiry will use us, as did Widgery, as a scapegoat for the killings that occurred? That is how the historical record could read.'[32] To avoid such an outcome, the thoroughly documented submission painted a history of NICRA, in Keenan's words, as a 'non-party political movement, a constitutional movement which recognized we were British citizens and we wanted British rights'. Based on his research, Keenan was convinced the document would show that accusations that NICRA had been infiltrated by violence-prone republicans was nonsense. To Keenan, this collaboration with Boyle was among 'the finest pieces of work' the two had ever done.

On 11 June 2001 Boyle finally gave his evidence in Derry. The inquiry was being held in Derry's Guildhall; the place which, in 1972, the civil rights marchers had hoped to reach before being blocked and attacked by the troops. The Guildhall was a neo-Gothic building with high ceilings and stained-glass windows. In the main hall, Lord Saville and his two fellow justices, one a Canadian, the other an Australian, sat on one side, next to a box for witnesses, which faced a giant television screen on which evidence could be projected. Across from them was space for the many lawyers representing the victims as well as the soldiers. Boyle's testimony took the best part of a day. As expected, he was repeatedly challenged by lawyers for some of the soldiers about NICRA's peaceful intentions, whether the organization was secretly controlled by the official IRA, and whether its decision to hold the Derry march was a reckless one. Boyle repeatedly stressed NICRA's non-violent nature, the wide range of personalities and organizations represented in its leadership, and, above all, the burning sense of injustice – fuelled by Northern Ireland's history of sectarian discrimination and then by the implementation of internment without trial – which was driving people onto the streets.

Not all the lawyers were antagonistic. At one point Boyle was questioned by Eilis McDermott, with whom he had been romantically involved at the time of Bloody Sunday. McDermott had gone on to become a prominent and successful lawyer in Belfast, and was now representing the family of Patrick Doherty, one of the fourteen people who had been shot and killed that day. It was Boyle's first encounter with McDermott in decades. There was no hint of their previous relationship: their exchanges were cool and professional. But, in seeking to show that her client was an innocent victim, McDermott asked Boyle a series of questions that gave him an opportunity to forcefully rebut claims that NICRA was an IRA front or had been seeking to provoke violence. Explaining the context, he noted that

> there had been large-scale detention centres. There had been torture. There had been numerous cases of ill treatment in the streets by the soldiers and the police. It was a circumstance which justified, we felt, what we did, but we were never involved or sought to precipitate or in any way engaged in or used violence against anyone.[33]

Boyle found the experience of revisiting such a traumatic period both unusual and stressful. 'There have been inquiries in the past where the person is in the dock and you are trying to think what happened thirty years ago,' he said some years later. 'But to actually have to sit down and try to present to the tribunal your concept of what this organization was, and how it came into existence, and how it wasn't controlled by the Republicans – I never thought I'd have to deal with that.'[34]

Joan Boyle's sense was that 'it felt like something from another life, given how much time had elapsed and how many other things he had been involved in.' To Francis Keenan, Boyle acknowledged that it 'was a little uncomfortable'[35] to be questioned about his opinions and actions from so long ago. Indeed, he wrote to Keenan, 'The only positive aspect of recalling the events of 1972 has been our friendship and efforts together to help.'[36] It would take another decade, but eventually the Saville Inquiry would vindicate NICRA, ensuring that at least history would record that Boyle and his colleagues, even though they organized the demonstration, did not bear responsibility for the deaths that bitterly cold January day so many years ago.

[23]

Crimes Against Humanity

IN EARLY JUNE 2001, the phone rang at Boyle's university office. It was Mary Robinson, the former Irish president and a long-time friend. Robinson had been asked by UN Secretary General Kofi Annan to extend her original four-year tenure as High Commissioner for Human Rights for another twelve months. Was Boyle willing to accept a one-year position as her chief advisor and speech-writer in Geneva? He later wrote: 'If during one of those ordinary days of teaching, shuffling paper and worrying about deadlines, you get a telephone call asking if you would like to take a year's leave from the university to practise what you teach inside the UN, well, you don't hesitate.'[1] According to Robinson, 'it was a complete surprise and shock to him'. But Boyle was thrilled. 'I said yes on the spot, and only later asked what it entailed, and even later cleared my appointment with a supportive Vice-Chancellor and colleagues.'[2]

In the treacherous political minefield of the UN, Robinson valued Boyle for his intellect, legal acumen and long record of defending human rights – his 'good brain', as she called it – but also because 'there is nothing more important than having somebody close to you as a special advisor who also minds your back'. But nothing prepared Boyle for what was to come.

Kevin and Joan packed up and set off, enjoying a drive through the French countryside en route to Geneva. His first day at the Palais Wilson, the sandstone building on the shores of Lake Geneva, which had been the original headquarters of the League of Nations in the 1920s and was now the office of the UN High Commissioner for Human Rights, was to be 11 September 2001.

As Boyle filled in forms and inspected his new office that Tuesday afternoon, Robinson was on a boat off the west coast of Ireland taking a much-needed holiday. The boatman had been listening to the radio. 'Commissioner,' he said, 'I have bad news for you. Planes have just hit the Twin Towers in New York and they are heading for the White House.' Robinson recalled that 'we'd had some beers during a picnic lunch, and I thought he'd had too many beers'. In Geneva, just hours into his job, with Robinson temporarily unreachable, it fell to Boyle to begin crafting a human rights response to the attacks. He later wrote, 'There was no prepared script as to how to respond to the atrocity. As a fledgling international official, I was out of my depth, but then so was just about everyone else.'[3]

Boyle quickly huddled with his new colleagues: Mona Rishmawi, a Palestinian lawyer and a legal advisor, Stefanie Grant, a British woman who was director of research, Frenchman Eric Tistounet, Robinson's special assistant, and others. He was helped by Nuala Ní Mhuircheartaigh, a young Irish lawyer who had just joined the Commissioner's office after working for the European Union on human rights in China. 'The challenge was: how do you apply human rights to what was happening?' Ní Mhuircheartaigh noted. 'How do you apply it to the aftermath? What language do you use? What body of law even do you use? It's hard to think about it in some ways because even that basic question – of what body of law are we looking at – had to be figured out.' Boyle immediately contacted his Essex colleagues Françoise Hampson, Nigel Rodley and Geoff Gilbert asking for advice from a legal point of view about what to say. 'Everything had to have a proper legal foundation,' Gilbert recalled. 'That's an incredibly difficult job, because if you get the law wrong, you undermine your boss.' With Robinson having emerged as the UN's second most prominent public figure after Secretary General Annan, the stakes were high. It was, as Joan Boyle observed, 'a baptism by fire'.

Robinson was quickly in touch by telephone, and that evening a brief statement, which Boyle was involved in drafting, was issued in her name. It expressed 'revulsion' at the attacks, which were described as 'crimes' that 'strike at the fundamental human rights of every person'.[4] But even in this first comment she called for calm 'to ensure that justice, and not revenge, is served'.[5] It was an early expression of the analysis that Boyle and Robinson would begin to develop in the coming days, one that would underpin their approach to dealing with 11 September and its aftermath – and would put them on a collision course with the American government.

As the scale of the tragedy emerged, Boyle later wrote, 'The priority became that of how to answer terrorism.'[6] A series of intense meetings and discussions with Robinson and her key advisors followed as Boyle worked to craft an analysis that would insert a human rights perspective into the impassioned international discussion over how to deal with the attacks. The pressure was extreme.

With input from his Essex colleagues and the help of Mona Rishmawi, just over a week after the attacks Boyle presented Robinson with a paper called 'A Human Rights Approach to the September 11 Terrorist Attacks'. Its central argument was that 'under international criminal law, the ... attacks can be characterized as a crime against humanity', creating 'a duty in all states to assist in bringing the culprits to justice'.[7] The paper called for those behind the attacks to be identified, found and punished, and for action to be taken against terrorist organizations and networks. But, clearly foreseeing the danger posed to human rights by the possibility of an excessive reaction, it reminded governments that 'the search for those responsible for the U.S. attacks must be pursued within the law and under the guidance of the international norms of international human rights and humanitarian law'.[8]

Along with the paper was a joint statement Boyle helped to draft, signed by a half-dozen UN agencies, including the Human Rights Commission, the Office of Humanitarian Affairs, the UN High Commission of Refugees, the World Food Programme, the UN Development Programme and UNICEF. It warned of a looming humanitarian disaster in Afghanistan, and called for 'any form of military action which might occur to be in strict conformity with international human rights and humanitarian law'.[9] But even with the memo, significant differences remained among the various

UN bodies. The issue was not so much about the content, because there was broad agreement about the balance between seeking justice and protecting human rights. Rather, the concern was about the timing. According to Eric Tistounet, 'there were those who were thinking we should keep a low profile and not oppose the US administration at the time, and wait and see how this would unfold. Otherwise, the US would take it extremely badly.' However, in Tistounet's words, Boyle and Robinson argued 'there was a moral responsibility from the office to react and immediately anticipate what might come later'. As Robinson observed, 'it was the difference between the principled humanitarian approach and the more political compromising, especially when the US was so heavily involved.'

Boyle's paper was issued as a 'Note from the United Nations High Commissioner for Human Rights'. On the same day that it and the joint appeal from the various agencies were distributed within the UN system, President George W. Bush addressed an emergency joint session of the US Congress. He used an entirely different formulation. The US was engaged in a 'war on terror', he declared, making clear that military action against Al-Qaeda and its Taliban backers in Afghanistan was imminent. He made no reference to international law or human rights.

Robinson and Boyle did not question the legitimacy of attacking Al-Qaeda and the Taliban, but both believed Bush's notion of a war on terror was fundamentally flawed. 'It was a war on an abstraction,' Robinson said, increasing the possibility of human rights abuses and having the potential to undermine the broad international support the United States currently enjoyed. 'We were quite adamant that we had to try to persuade President Bush that it was wrong to go the terrorism route, that these were crimes against humanity, that the whole world had been with the United States in the aftermath, and that was something to build on.' Indeed, with the goal of strengthening international anti-terrorism cooperation, Boyle's paper also proposed that the Security Council consider establishing an international tribunal to prosecute and try those responsible. This was more than just an academic debate, 'Part of the challenge was to put the response to 9/11 in an international legal framework that had existing substance,' noted Nuala Ní Mhuircheartaigh, 'where there were already clearly understood rules and restrictions. This structure might ensure that important lines, particularly in relation to human rights, were not crossed.'

The argument resonated in many quarters. 'The "war on terror" was a kind of meaningless and very dangerous expression,' said Edward Mortimer, a former British journalist who was then serving as Kofi Annan's spokesman:

> You never know whether you've won the war or how long it might go on, whereas to treat it as a crime would have been a much more sensible way to go about it. I was far from alone in having that view. I don't think there was any disagreement between Kofi and Mary on these issues. He would have certainly endorsed what she said on that.

In Washington, however, such concerns were quickly dismissed. According to Sir Jeremy Greenstock, then British ambassador to the UN, 'when the Americans were gung-ho, quite rightly, in their response in Afghanistan, I think Mary became quite concerned that the Americans were going to cross a line in response to 9/11. They began to find her very difficult. The Bush administration found she got in their way.' Richard Boucher, who was then the State Department spokesman, recalled that 'the administration was firm in opposition to her, because they thought she was overstepping her boundaries and sticking her nose into things that didn't have a big human rights element'.

At the end of September, with CIA teams already on the ground in northern Afghanistan and the US preparing for large-scale military action, the UN Security Council passed Resolution 1373. Adopted under Chapter VII of the UN Charter, which made it binding on all member states, the resolution was intended to be a key pillar in a new international legal framework to combat terrorism. It required all the UN's 191 member nations to adopt a series of anti-terrorism measures, including targeting terrorist funding, freezing the assets of terrorist organizations, denying safe haven to terrorists, tightening border controls and changing domestic laws to ensure that terrorists were 'brought to justice'. To monitor implementation, the Security Council established a Counter-Terrorism Committee chaired by Sir Jeremy Greenstock. The resolution called on all states to report to the committee within ninety days.

On 7 October 2011, nine days after the passage of Resolution 1373, the US began Operation Enduring Freedom in Afghanistan, officially launching its war on terror. The intensive bombing campaign was directed at Taliban targets and Al-Qaeda training camps while supporting the anti-Taliban

Afghan factions known as the Northern Alliance who were seeking to take power in Kabul. But the military campaign exacerbated an already severe humanitarian crisis in Afghanistan, adding to the large number of internally displaced people, raising fears of widespread famine, and killing many innocent civilians. In Geneva, Robinson, working closely with Boyle and in concert with other UN bodies and international aid agencies, sought to establish a humanitarian corridor to get desperately needed supplies to the beleaguered populace before the harsh Afghan winter set in.

Apart from the UN's internal deliberations, Robinson also sought to influence public opinion with a constant stream of media interviews. As her chief advisor, Boyle was in charge of crafting key points for her to emphasize with the press. In the fevered media climate after 9/11, finding the right balance between support for combating terrorism and human rights and humanitarian concerns was not easy. 'Talking to the media on this was extremely delicate,' Eric Tistounet remembered. 'Mary was really trying to make a distinction between these two sets of issues but was constantly misheard and misinterpreted.'

On 12 October, for example, Robinson did an interview with Irish radio. In it, she referred to press reports that if the Taliban handed over Osama bin Laden, Bush might be willing to suspend the air campaign. Robinson said she hoped that would happen because it would provide an opportunity to deliver badly needed relief supplies. Several news agencies, including Reuters, Agence France Press and Germany's DPA, picked up the story, but portrayed Robinson's comment as an explicit call to end the bombing, angering the US and upsetting Kofi Annan. Boyle immediately had to email Annan's chief of staff, Iqbal Riza, with a clarification. 'In fact, the High Commissioner did not call for an end to the campaign,' he wrote, asking that Riza distribute his note to senior UN officials. Robinson herself then sent the transcript of the interview directly to Annan.[10] It was not the only occasion when Boyle would have to scramble to contain the fallout from reports of Robinson's public remarks.

American officials, in particular, did not hide their irritation with Robinson. Boyle made a habit of walking to the office very early in the morning, becoming a familiar face to the Geneva street-walkers finishing their night's work, who invariably offered him cheery greetings, before he arrived at the Palais Wilson. On many mornings his phone would ring and someone from the US mission to the UN in Geneva would launch into a bitter tirade about something Robinson had said or done.

At a Spanish national day reception that October, Boyle was cornered by an American and a British diplomat who both berated him for the positions Robinson was taking. Boyle, a gentle soul struggling to cope with the intense pressure of the job, was deeply upset by the viciousness of the politics. 'There was an incredibly high degree of political tension, and increasing polarization,'[11] he later noted. He described the pressure as 'incredible'.[12] Joan Boyle recalled that 'sometimes, it seemed like he would be about to burst into tears'.

The personal stress did not undermine his close personal and professional relationship with Mary Robinson. Most Saturdays when she was in Geneva, Kevin and Joan would go to her flat. While Joan and Nick Robinson would open a bottle of wine and gossip, Kevin and Mary would sit at her kitchen table discussing strategy, issues and her upcoming speeches.

As the Security Council's Counter-Terrorism Committee waited for the reports mandated from all 191 UN member states, Boyle and Robinson grew increasingly concerned that protection of human rights was not being taken into account in the battle against terrorism. Robinson said at the time that 'there was no logic in discarding the very values that – in principle – they are fighting to ensure'. With the goal of convincing the committee to take human rights seriously, Boyle put together a detailed memo, which Robinson sent to the chair, Sir Jeremy Greenstock. In it, Boyle laid out a series of key legal principles – necessity, proportionality, non-discrimination and due process – and the international legal framework that underpinned them. He then posed twenty-one questions, which he urged the committee to consider in assessing the performance of governments. They included whether any new anti-terrorist legislation could be used to curb peaceful activity protected by international human rights laws; what measures were in place to prevent torture and other abuses and ensure that information obtained through mistreatment would not be admitted as evidence; whether counterterrorism measures could lead to discrimination on the basis of race or religion; and what provisions existed to ensure that claims of asylum were not rejected based on unfounded allegations of terrorist activities. He also raised a question that would soon become a new point of contention with the US: 'Do your counter-terrorism measures allow for the trial of civilians on terrorism-related charges by special or military courts? How does this comport with the requirement of human rights law that everyone is entitled to a fair and public hearing by a competent, independent and impartial tribunal established by law?'[13]

Indeed, around the same time that Robinson sent Boyle's memo to the Security Council, President Bush issued an executive order authorizing the creation of military tribunals for the detention and trial of non-American citizens suspected of involvement in terrorism. The order, promulgated with no warning or public consultation, in effect created a parallel structure where the US could detain and try people outside the American criminal justice system. The move set off alarm bells. Boyle drafted a note to Robinson outlining its dangerous provisions: detainees could be held indefinitely; they did not have to be told the reason for their arrest or of the charges against them; they were not guaranteed legal representation or the right of appeal. The executive order, Boyle concluded, posed

a direct threat to fundamental rights ... [and] will not only occasion lasting damage to the ability of the U.S. to champion human rights and the rule of law around the world, but it will also undermine the human rights standards that underpin the collective efforts currently being deployed by the international community to define and distinguish acts of terrorism from legally permissible conduct.[14]

Boyle urged Robinson to make a 'strong appeal' to Bush to rescind or at least modify the order. But the appeal fell on deaf ears. Hundreds of people were caught up in the new US system, held at secret detention sites in Afghanistan and, starting in January 2002, at the US military base at Guantánamo Bay in Cuba. In the months that followed, reports emerged of brutality and torture, as well as detained suspected terrorists being sent to other countries with well-established records for torture like Egypt and Morocco.

Meanwhile, although Kofi Annan publicly endorsed the importance of protecting human rights while fighting terrorism, Sir Jeremy Greenstock, juggling the differing interests of the fifteen Security Council member states who made up the committee and the entire UN membership who were supposed to be submitting reports, was reluctant to formally incorporate human rights considerations into the committee's work. 'The human rights area was contentious at the UN,' he acknowledged:

Mary Robinson was anxious to make sure that human rights factors were taken into account, but it became no more than a friendly undertaking from me to keep those factors in play. I cannot remember those factors coming into the difficult areas of implementation of the precise wording of 1373 because that did not have any human rights language in it.

Some of Boyle's questions were unofficially communicated to UN member states, but Robinson's request that the entire document be distributed was rebuffed, as was her request that the committee appoint a human rights advisor.

'We were very isolated,' recalled Eric Tistounet. 'There was a deep sense of frustration, that there were victims of the [Bush] administration's activities and priorities – a feeling that everything was going wrong and you couldn't do much.'

However stressed and drained Boyle was by the constant political infighting, the response to 9/11 was only one part of his job. As the world's most visible voice on human rights, Mary Robinson was constantly travelling, attending conferences, giving interviews and delivering speeches. It was Boyle's responsibility not only to craft the language but to help her refine the vision of human rights she was seeking to articulate. It was a vision that went well beyond conventional notions of civil or political rights. 'The international human rights agenda', Robinson wrote in her autobiography, 'must also include economic, social, and cultural rights: to food, safe water, health and sanitation, and education.' Yet these rights were often marginalized and seen by many Western countries as merely vague aspirations. 'I advanced the argument that extreme poverty it itself a human rights violation.'[15] Aware of the impact of her words, Boyle and Robinson regularly brainstormed about what her speeches should say. In Mona Rishmawi's recollection, 'Kevin would talk to a lot of people who had expertise on the issues, do his own research, and synthesize what he thought was the right policy line to be taken.' Robinson said that 'he would do a draft. I would then tweak it, but not much. He would be the main drafter.'

These were not simple projects. Most of the speeches Boyle drafted ran to thousands of words, and dealt with complex intellectual, political, moral and legal issues. As Stefanie Grant, who had written some speeches for Robinson before Boyle's arrival, observed, 'the scope was absolutely huge. What does it mean to ensure the right to education or the right to health?

How do you protect social and economic rights?' The titles for some of the speeches Boyle drafted convey a sense of the scope of the topics he had to cover: 'Bridging the Gap Between Human Rights and Development'; 'A Human Rights Approach to Poverty Reduction'; 'Ethics, Human Rights and Globalization'; 'Women's Rights are Human Rights'; 'Challenges to Human Rights and Development in Africa'; 'Human Rights Education in Primary and Secondary Schools'; 'Human Rights and Corporate Citizenship'. And this did not include the more substantive addresses on current policy issues that Robinson regularly gave within the UN. However influential, throughout this process, though, Boyle deliberately kept a low public profile. 'He was the invisible man,' recalled Stefanie Grant. 'The words were Kevin's. The articulation was Mary's.'

The situation in Afghanistan remained crucially important. Following the successful US military campaign to topple the Taliban in November 2001, Robinson's office worked closely with the new Afghan authorities to promote women's rights, human rights education and the creation of the Afghan Independent Human Rights Commission, with Boyle drafting several speeches Robinson gave to a national human rights workshop in Kabul. The Commission was established in June 2002, with a mandate to monitor human rights abuses throughout the country. For Boyle, 'it was a signal experience to be even peripherally involved in shaping the UN's advice on human rights protection in the new Afghanistan, in particular the liberation of Afghan women'.[16]

Overshadowing such signs of progress, however, was the battle to ensure that protection of human rights was not lost amid the continuing war on terror. Robinson and Boyle remained deeply concerned not only about the American administration's behaviour, but by the fact that, in many countries, cracking down on terror was being used as an excuse to erode civil liberties, curb peaceful dissent and imprison political dissidents. In late February 2002 Boyle worked with Robinson to draft a long document for the UN's Human Rights Commission called *Human Rights: A Uniting Framework*.

The document reiterated the argument that the 9/11 attacks should be seen as a crime against humanity, and maintained that 'an effective strategy to counter terror should use human rights as unifying framework'.[17] It called on all states to implement the anti-terror steps spelled out in the Security Council's Resolution 1373 'in a manner consistent with human rights', and concluded by directly challenging the view that some rights might need to be curtailed to combat terrorism. It stated:

> In the immediate aftermath of 11 September, some suggested that human rights could be set aside while security was being achieved. Now, however, there is wide recognition that ensuring respect for human rights and dignity throughout the world is the best long-term guarantor of security. Such an approach focuses attention on the elimination of the root causes of violence and therefore isolates terrorists. These values are the international community's best answer to terrorism.[18]

To reinforce the point, Boyle's list of twenty-one questions was inserted as an annex to the formal text of Robinson's speech. Described as 'proposal for further guidance' for nations submitting their required reports to the Counter-Terrorism Committee, it was a clever bureaucratic move. 'It made the checklist an official UN document,' observed Nuala Ní Mhuircheartaigh. 'It could be cited. It could be sourced. It helped to get out the clear guidance on what human rights law does and does not allow. It was very practical.'

But the document also further angered the Bush administration. Given the crisis created by 11 September, Robinson had told Kofi Annan she was prepared to stay on for a second full four-year term instead of the one year that had originally been agreed. But by the spring of 2002 it became clear the US was determined to force her out. During a visit to Washington with Boyle, she recalled one 'very uncomfortable meeting' with a State Department official. 'They browbeat me. They gave me every reason to believe that they knew what we were talking about in my private office in Geneva. The inference was it was bugged. They also made it clear to me they would never support me continuing' as High Commissioner. Robinson was, in her words, 'upset and saddened'[19] that Kofi Annan, under intense US pressure, had agreed not to back her for a full second term:

> Of course, I was very conscious of the pressures he was under. But, perhaps naively, I thought this was all the more reason for extending my term, as I would not flinch from speaking out against any policy, Western or otherwise, wherever I took the view that it was contrary to the international human rights agenda.[20]

But the decision had been made. For Kevin Boyle, who by this time had hit his stride, figured out how to operate in the UN system and was, as Joan recalled, 'really enjoying his job and working really well with Mary' – and was prepared to stay on if she did – her forced departure was a bitter disappointment. As Joan put it, 'Mary was sidelined by her friend Kofi to placate the Americans.'

In his remaining weeks as Robinson's chief advisor, Boyle devoted his energies not only to the continuing controversies about fighting terrorism: he was deeply involved in the launch of a new 'Forum for Indigenous Issues', designed to give a voice at the UN to aboriginals, Native Americans and other indigenous peoples. He oversaw the design of a new, reader-friendly publication aimed at explaining the work of the High Commissioner for Human Rights to a broader audience. And in the summer of 2002, a new opportunity arose. The UN was looking to appoint a new Special Rapporteur on freedom of religion and belief, a position created in 1986 to monitor and defend freedom of religion around the world. It was an issue in which Boyle had a long-standing interest, from his early days as a civil rights activist in Northern Ireland to the global survey of freedom of religion he had edited in the late 1990s. With the support of Mary Robinson and the Irish mission to the United Nations, he applied. 'I was trying to support him strongly,' Robinson recalled. 'He would have been great.'

But Boyle was a white, middle-aged Western man in a UN system consciously promoting diversity. In July the job was offered to Asma Jahangir, a prominent Pakistani human rights lawyer. Boyle saw the logic of appointing a Muslim woman to the post, but he was nonetheless, in Joan's words, 'absolutely devastated. I rarely saw Kevin cry, but he wept a tear the day he didn't get that job'. Still, when Jahangir called him soon after, he went out of his way to offer her advice and suggestions.

Kevin Boyle and Mary Robinson's last day was 11 September 2002. Her final event was to be the speaker at a memorial commemoration for 9/11 held at Geneva's main cathedral. She concluded her remarks there by reading 'From the Republic of Conscience', Seamus Heaney's powerful poem, which stressed that the duty to speak out against injustice never ceases. Kevin and Joan were in the audience, Boyle likely remembering that he had given Robinson a framed copy of the poem when she took the job five years earlier, and that it had remained mounted on the wall behind her desk throughout her tumultuous tenure as High Commissioner.

[24]

I Have Always Been a Fighter

AFTER THE MOST intense, demanding, stressful and professionally exhilarating year of his life, Boyle found the adjustment to the routine existence of a college professor a difficult one. 'Kevin was very unsettled on his return to Essex,' Joan Boyle remembered. 'It was hard to come down to earth after the pressure and excitement of Geneva.' The lack of success he and Mary Robinson had achieved in their efforts to blunt the worst excesses of the US war on terror added to Boyle's glum frame of mind, as did his failure to be appointed as UN Special Rapporteur. 'Kevin would have been great for the job,' said his Essex colleague Nigel Rodley, who had himself served as UN Special Rapporteur on torture. 'He seemed to lose heart after that.'

Boyle's frustration, however, did not deter him from continuing engagement with the office of the High Commissioner for Human Rights. In 2003 he was hired as a consultant for a project to develop educational material for teachers and students on eliminating racial prejudice and fostering tolerance. Boyle returned to Geneva to attend a workshop where a dozen papers were presented on topics, such as the impact of racism on health, employment, migration, the media and the administration of justice. He then edited the papers and wrote an introduction to a book the High Commissioner's office published entitled *Dimensions of Racism*, which he described as a 'resource' for the struggle against racism. His conclusion was that 'the main antidote to the persistence of racism' was 'the acceptance of universal standards of human rights and fundamental freedoms'.[1] He challenged student readers to conduct further research on the issue so they could answer the question 'what can you do to combat racism?'[2]

The project was followed by a dialogue between Boyle and Louise Arbour, a Canadian lawyer who had been appointed the new High Commissioner in 2004 after Mary Robinson's immediate successor, Brazilian Sérgio Vieira de Mello, was killed in a 2003 bomb attack on UN headquarters in Baghdad following the US invasion of Iraq. Boyle's close friend from Geneva, Mona Rishmawi, barely survived the bombing. In a meeting and subsequent correspondence with Arbour, Boyle was asked for his advice about a new plan of action that had been drafted for the High Commissioner. He was impressed, but urged Arbour to 'spell out more fully the nexus between human rights, security, and development. That trinity of goals and aims, which is really about recovery of the original interconnectedness of the Charter's purpose, could be explored and explained in your statements and speeches.'[3]

This suggestion reflected Boyle's strong view, which he had refined in drafting speeches for Mary Robinson, that human rights encompassed more than traditional political freedom. For Boyle, economic, social and cultural rights were equally important, as was 'mainstreaming' an appreciation of human rights into all facets of policy-making and behaviour. Indeed, Boyle taught the first courses at Essex focusing on these rights, as well as a new course he created on the right to development. He would often challenge new students at their official welcoming session by asking them to respond to a question: if you had to leave earth and could take only three human rights with you, what would they be? One Brazilian student recalled concluding that it was not possible to bring only three human rights; it was necessary to bring all of them – to which Boyle replied, 'That is the correct answer.' To Kevin, human rights were multifaceted and inseparable.

To further promote this concept of human rights, Boyle collaborated with Mary Robinson to assemble and edit a collection of the speeches she had given during her time as High Commissioner. He grouped the speeches, many of which he had written, thematically – the overall vision, the role of the High Commissioner, building human rights protections, and future challenges – and wrote a long introduction to provide background and context. The book, with a foreword by Kofi Annan, was entitled *A Vision for Human Rights* and was well received. One review noted that it 'succeeds in documenting the legacy of the most prominent world leader in human rights',[4] while another wrote that

> Kevin Boyle, its editor, has done a marvellous job in providing everything the reader might desire from this type of publication, be it the abundance of informative annotations, and introductory commentary, the comprehensive index and appendices, or simply the thematic organization which provides a fascinating and accessible overview of the multiple dimensions of UN human rights work.[5]

Despite his continuing outside activities, Boyle remained deeply committed to his students: none more so than a group of Brazilians. Brazil was emerging from two decades of authoritarian misrule, and Boyle recruited a steady stream of young Brazilian lawyers and activists to come to Essex. 'We used to say we have a Brazilian professor at Essex,' said Lelio Bentes, a labour lawyer who did the LLM degree. 'He was so nice and warm. He always said how much he loved Brazil, how he felt at home there.' As Joan Boyle recalled, 'We both took greatly to Kevin's Brazilian students and felt they had many similarities to the Irish – very friendly and open, always ready to party, and generous.'

The connection was more than personal. 'There was a conceptual identification,' observed Denise Dora, a lawyer who ran a human rights programme for the Ford Foundation in Rio de Janeiro after receiving her Essex degree. 'We were activists and lawyers doing progressive litigation. This was very similar to Kevin's way of thinking.' Indeed, Boyle may well have seen something of his youthful self in the way his students returned to Brazil and took up the cause, and was eager to support them. In the years following his stint with Mary Robinson in Geneva, he made numerous trips to Brazil, attending conferences, giving talks, and, above all, providing advice and support for the setting up of academic human rights centres there. 'Kevin was a source of inspiration for us in building a human rights infrastructure within Brazilian universities,' said Dora. Eugenio Aragon, who studied with Boyle and later became the country's Minister of Justice, said 'Kevin was the brains behind all these projects.'

In 2005 he was invited to become a member of the board of Minority Rights Group (MRG) International, one of the oldest human rights NGOs. Founded in the late 1960s and based in London, it was designed, in the words of its then executive director, Mark Lattimer, 'to do for peoples what Amnesty International did for oppressed individuals', campaigning in dozens of countries on behalf of ethnic, religious and linguistic minorities and indigenous peoples such as the Roma in Europe, Christians in Iraq and the Untouchables in India. For Lattimer and his colleagues, 'Boyle was a thought leader in the human rights world, a kind of elder statesman, so that was very important for us.'

As Hurst Hannum, recruited by Boyle to join him on the MRG board, recalled, 'Kevin helped to revitalize the organization. He brought an energy and sense of optimism that they could do things in a different way.' When Boyle joined the board, Lattimer was shifting the focus of the organization towards a greater emphasis on religious minorities, the result in part of the demonization of Muslims in the wake of the September 11 attacks and the war on terror. 'We had to face this major new challenge of religious persecution, and we had to make sure that people acted to prevent it before it really took over whole communities,' Lattimer recalled. 'Kevin understood very quickly how dangerous mobilization on the basis of religion was. He helped us to think through some of the really big challenges that came from the fact that religious persecution became a global phenomenon.'

Lattimer was also seeking to introduce a new element to MRG's work – 'strategic litigation' – to protect minority rights and produce broader changes in the legal landscape. With his vast experience of cases in Strasbourg, Boyle was a valuable asset. 'This was something new for MRG,' Hurst Hannum noted, 'but Kevin had been successful in this kind of work. He really encouraged them.'

One landmark case involved an effort to overturn a law that made Jews and Roma ineligible to hold the office of president or be a member of the upper house of parliament in Bosnia. The law was a result of the 1995 Dayton Accords, which ended the war in Bosnia and the former Yugoslavia but restricted the highest offices of state to members of Bosnia's three main ethnic and religious groups: the Serbs, Croats and Bosnian Muslims.

Appealing to Strasbourg on behalf of Jakob Finci, a prominent Jew who had sought to run for president but had been barred from doing so, the MRG won a major victory.

The European Court ruled that the Bosnian policy constituted unlawful discrimination, declaring 'that the authorities must use all available means to combat racism, thereby reinforcing democracy's vision of a society in which diversity is not perceived as a threat but as a source of enrichment'.[6] While Boyle did not himself argue the case, he played an important role as an advisor to the MRG team that did. 'As we were trying to build the case, it was great to have the support of someone who had been in the trenches building so much case law himself,' recalled Cynthia Morel, a young Canadian lawyer who had gone to work at MRG after obtaining a degree from Essex. 'He was able to make these things, which seem so intimidating, seem possible.' Boyle played a similar role in another case, this one against the government of Kenya, which had evicted members of the Endorois people from their ancestral lands in the Rift Valley to create a game reserve for tourism – a move that the African Commission on Human and Peoples' Rights ordered should be reversed in response to an MRG legal case. In 2007 Lattimer asked Boyle to become the chair of MRG. Boyle, with his long record of building organizations to fight for human rights, was thrilled.

The mid-2000s also saw Boyle's first sustained engagement with China, as he participated in several conferences bringing Chinese and European academics together to discuss human rights. 'It was the period after China joined the World Trade Organization in 2001 and before the Beijing Olympics of 2008,' noted Yan Mei Ning, a Hong Kong journalist who did a PhD with Kevin at Essex. 'There was a lot of hope. People were thinking China would open further.' However, the difficulty of engaging China on human rights became evident when Boyle was invited to act as a rapporteur at a conference on freedom of expression in the Cambodian city of Siem Reap in 2007. The event was organized by the Asia-Europe Foundation and attended by scholars, lawyers, NGOs and government officials from around the region. Before the gathering, Boyle and his fellow rapporteur, Cherian George, a Singaporean academic of Indian descent, wrote an essay to distribute to participants. To make the document more accessible to Asian readers, George added a couple of pages about Asian concepts of freedom of expression, including a reference to the Buddhist teachings of the Tibetan spiritual leader, the Dalai Lama.

When they arrived in Siem Reap, the European organizers said the Chinese delegation had demanded that the reference to the Dalai Lama, viewed by Beijing as a symbol of Tibetan independence, be deleted. 'We were told this was non-negotiable,' George recalled, 'and that the Chinese were threatening to walk out if they didn't get their way.' But Boyle and George stuck to their guns, insisting that censorship was especially inappropriate at a conference on freedom of expression. To avoid a Chinese walkout, the anxious organizers decided simply not to print the essay, and the conference went ahead. However, since Chinese officials had complained about the document being available only while the conference was underway, the essay was simply printed and distributed after it ended.

Despite this clash, for Boyle the discussions in Siem Reap and his interactions with audiences during a subsequent lecture tour with Cherian George to Singapore, Malaysia, Thailand, Indonesia and Laos, demonstrated 'the bankruptcy of the notion of an Asian–Western divide over the principle of freedom of expression. Instead, there is a clear convergence.'[7] In an article published in a Thai newspaper, he and George wrote that 'there are some key ideas that cut across national boundaries. Freedom of expression is not only an individual right but also an essential ingredient for societal progress. Our interactions across the region have convinced us that people everywhere believe passionately in the right to speak their minds.'[8]

In 2008 Boyle finally made it to China as the keynote speaker at a conference on human rights law. As Boyle's former student Yan Mei Ning, who by then was teaching at a university in southern China, observed, 'during that time period, for Chinese academics, there was no problem talking about human rights education. There was not even a problem offering courses on human rights education.' In two long talks, he covered the UN's human rights system, various international human rights treaties and 'the international human rights agenda for the future, linking development, security and human rights'. His emphasis on the right to development, health and education was consistent with the way China defined human rights – even as Beijing ignored international covenants on civil and political rights. But Boyle also told the Chinese academics that the UN recognized civil society organizations, which the Chinese Communist Party viewed with deep suspicion, as a 'vital force'. Above all, he argued that international law guaranteed people the basic right of freedom of expression and belief. Boyle made similar points in lectures at the Chinese Academy of Social Sciences and two leading universities, including the Peking University law school. And he fulfilled a lifelong ambition to visit the Great Wall of China.

That same year, Boyle marked his sixty-fifth birthday, and his thoughts began to turn to retirement. He planned to leave the University of Essex in the summer of 2010, and decided his major post-retirement endeavour would be to write what he hoped would be his magnum opus: a definitive study of freedom of expression, an issue that had been central to his entire career as an academic, advocate and activist. He raised the idea with Finola O'Sullivan, a commissioning editor at Cambridge University Press and a friend from her days working for Butterworth law publishers in Dublin in the early 1980s.

O'Sullivan viewed Boyle as a 'pioneering figure' in the world of human rights, but when they met, she felt Kevin looked weary, as if 'he had worn himself out' with his constant travel and an astonishing number of projects and commitments. In talking about his book idea, however, he was enthusiastic. 'We discussed his hope to draw together the strands of his life in human rights into a single book,' she recalled:

> Freedom of expression would be its focus [because] this lay at the heart of all the struggles he'd witnessed and participated in. Despite the weariness I sensed across the table from me, there was no doubting his wish to clarify his thinking, and set out a future agenda for those coming after us.

The year 2008 was also the fortieth anniversary of the civil rights movement in Northern Ireland, and the tenth anniversary of the signing of the Good Friday Agreement, which had effectively brought the Troubles to an end. To mark the occasion, a series of events was held throughout Northern Ireland, including a conference at Queen's University called '1968: Civil Rights – Then and Now'. It took place in early October – the same month in which, forty years earlier, the police had attacked a civil rights march in Derry, sparking the protests at Queen's, which led to the formation of People's Democracy and set the course for Kevin Boyle's life. He joined a number of his comrades from those early days – Michael Farrell, now a lawyer in Dublin, Paul Bew and Paul Arthur, both academics, Anne Devlin, who became a successful playwright, and others – for the day-long session.

Tom Hadden and other academics and journalists also attended. They gathered at a moment when the streets of Northern Ireland were peaceful. Daily life had more or less returned to normal. The Good Friday Agreement had enshrined guarantees of human rights that would have been unthinkable in the 1960s. Even more astonishing, in 2007 the Democratic Unionist Party (DUP) had entered into a power-sharing arrangement with Sinn Féin, with DUP leader Ian Paisley forging a remarkable political and personal relationship with Martin McGuinness, the former IRA commander who had then become a top Sinn Féin spokesman. As Anne Devlin noted, 2008 'was a very optimistic time'.

And yet, many of the civil rights veterans still carried the burden of wondering whether – however well intentioned – their actions, especially the march from Belfast to Derry in January 1969, might have been responsible for sparking the bloodshed that would go on to claim so many lives. It was an issue Boyle had long wrestled with. In 2006 he had told a British academic: 'That is something I don't look back on with a great deal of pride. It was a mistake. If we'd known the results, to go ahead couldn't have been justified.'[9] Indeed, Colin Harvey, a law professor at Queen's who was a member of the Northern Ireland Human Rights Commission and helped organize the conference, recalled that the event was 'a day of deep and profound personal reflection about the events of the 1960s and the violent conflict that followed'. As Michael Farrell observed, 'the meeting was fairly contentious. Were we right to cause trouble at all? Were we right to have the Burntollet march?'

Speaking on a panel at the final event of the conference, Boyle sought to put the demands of the civil rights movement in the broader context of the international norms and principles that now underpinned his view of human rights. In the notes for his presentation, he wrote, '"one man, one house" was in effect an economic and social right demand, but it was not understood as such. "One man, one vote" … no consciousness of feminist thinking.'[10] He talked about how, with the passage of time, a deepening knowledge of international law, including human rights, gave him 'an external and objective framework within which to develop ideas for peaceful options'.[11]

Boyle noted that his work with Tom Hadden over the years

was a more or less conscious effort to inject the international discourse of human rights into the search for peaceful ways through the Northern

Ireland conflict. I did not abandon the activist critique of the 1960s, but rather incorporated it into a new ideology – that of universal human rights.[12]

He also tackled what had become a frequent criticism of the civil rights movement – that it should have used the courts to help resolve their grievances, rather than taking to the streets. Michael Farrell noted 'that was a fairly important argument, because there were some people who tried to argue that there was no need for a civil rights movement. And Kevin would certainly not have welcomed that.' Indeed, Boyle maintained that

> the truth was that the Courts and the legal profession, indeed the entire political culture of the UK at that time, was one in which the judicial system was marginalized and wholly unresponsive to the structural injustices which existed. The legal profession was untutored in human rights. The legal culture was one which had little conception of human rights.[13]

Boyle was not alone in his view that, under such circumstances, it was understandable that marching in the streets seemed the only sensible option.

Summing up, he painted a mixed picture: 'There has been clearly a transformation in formal protections of rights since the events of 1968. The legal system has been overhauled and human rights institutions established. A local legislature has been constructed operating under enforced power-sharing.'[14] To Anne Devlin, such a conclusion was comforting. 'There was a feeling that if we did contribute to this [triggering the violence], then, as things were somewhat better, we could put that burden down.' But in critical ways, Boyle noted that Northern Ireland remained deeply polarized. 'It is still a divided society in class and ethno-religious terms, and in schooling and housing it is perhaps even more divided.'[15]

As Robin Wilson, the journalist who helped to organize the Opsahl Commission in the 1990s, observed, 'we are a more polarized society than when we started out with the civil rights movement. You couldn't imagine now a coalition like the civil rights movement getting together, with progressive Catholics, Protestant trade unionists and communists, and making that work. It just wouldn't be feasible now.' To Colin Harvey, 'there was a real sense that, although there had been progress in areas like human rights and equality, some of the promises of the peace process had not been achieved.' One indication of how much remained to be done was the failure of the government to adopt a Bill of Rights, even though the peace deal contained an explicit commitment to do so. Later that day, Boyle discussed the issue over coffee with Harvey, who, as a member of the province's Human Rights Commission, was involved in drafting documents for the British government on how to move forward. But the efforts of Harvey and others who were pushing the notion of a Bill of Rights were in vain. As of this writing, it still has not been enacted.

A little over a year later, in March 2010, Boyle was back in Northern Ireland, this time with Joan, Mark and Stephen, The occasion was the seventieth birthday party of his sister Anne. They also went to Belfast, the first such visit as a family since Mark and Stephen were little. They went to the Queen's campus, the Crumlin Road law courts where Kevin had argued so many cases, and the house on Marlborough Park where Kevin and Joan had first lived. They also took one of Belfast's famous 'black taxi' tours – a drive through the areas most associated with the Troubles, with a local driver providing explanation and commentary. The drive covered the Falls Road, the Shankill Road, and the 'peace wall' that still separated the two communities, a visible symbol that the Good Friday Agreement had not healed the North's sectarian divisions. Mark and Stephen, whom Kevin and Joan had consciously sought to insulate from the baggage of Northern Ireland, were, in Joan's words, 'absorbing it with amazement'.

As they took in the sights, Stephen remembered his father 'being a bit quiet and detached. I don't know what he was going through visiting Belfast.' Unsure whether the driver was a Protestant or a Catholic, Joan said 'Kevin was anxious not to let the driver know who he was.' Indeed, passing one location after another, scenes of events in which Boyle had played a central role, Kevin said very little. 'I actually think he deliberately held back,' Mark said. 'I am sure there was a lot going on behind the surface.' But what those feelings may have been – guilt, sentimentality, taking stock of the progress or lack of it, awareness of lost youth and the passage of time, memories of friends and colleagues who had died – we do not know. After the taxi tour the family went to the Ulster Museum, located just next to Queen's University, where a new gallery devoted to the Troubles had just been opened. Wandering through it, they came upon a large blow-up of the photograph of Kevin speaking through a bullhorn at a People's Democracy demonstration outside Belfast's City Hall in October 1968. It had become one of the iconic images of the Troubles. As they looked at it, Boyle said little, but, seeing the photo for the first time, Stephen remembered feeling 'very proud'.

Throughout the winter of 2010, Boyle had been feverishly working on plans for an ambitious conference that would consider the UN and freedom of expression. The Essex Human Rights Centre was in partnership with the University of Amsterdam, which agreed to host the event. Its main expert on the issue was Tarlach McGonagle, the son of Boyle's former Galway student and then-colleague Marie McGonagle. Tarlach had studied with Boyle at Essex, and then moved to Amsterdam where he specialized in international and European human rights law. 'The idea was to map out all the international perspectives on freedom of expression,' he said, 'by getting experts from each of the UN committees that dealt with the issue. The UN was looking to revamp its standards. Kevin saw the conference as a way to influence the process.' Marie McGonagle had seen Kevin a few months earlier. 'I was struck by the fact that he had lost a lot of weight,' she recalled. 'There was something different about him.' On a visit to Amsterdam that winter to discuss the upcoming event, Tarlach noticed that Kevin had been struggling with a chronic chest infection. Puffing away on his pipe, Boyle, predictably, just carried on.

The conference was due to begin on Friday 23 April. Five days earlier, on Sunday 18 April, Boyle collapsed at Joan's feet on the floor of their kitchen in Colchester. Throughout his life, family, friends and colleagues had marvelled at Kevin's iron constitution. He was rarely ill. The constant pressure and travel seemed not to bother him, and his ability to success-fully juggle many highly complex and demanding projects had become almost legendary. But he was rarely without his pipe, which he began to smoke as a university student because, ironically, his father had said it was less hazardous to his health than cigarettes. Boyle was rushed to the Colchester General Hospital and placed in intensive care. The doctors diagnosed lung cancer, and, soon after, he had a lung removed. Initially, he made good progress, grading papers in his hospital bed, emailing colleagues about numerous projects and looking forward to a full recovery. Indeed, by the early summer he had returned home, and when Nigel Rodley invited him for dinner one evening, he was able to walk unassisted to Rodley's house. 'For a time, he seemed to have a second life,' Joan recalled. 'We were all happy.'

In July the university planned to hold its graduation ceremony, an occasion that would also mark Boyle's formal retirement. His colleagues, especially Françoise Hampson and John Packer, who had taken over as the new head of the Human Rights Centre, proposed that he be given an honorary Master's Degree in the Theory and Practice of Human Rights – the degree Boyle had created and which was the foundation of the human rights programme. 'This was unprecedented,' Hampson recalled:

> They had no problem about giving him something. Their objection was to giving him an honorary MA, because the MA is a degree you can earn, and you should never get in honorary form a degree you can earn. I don't think we realized quite what we were taking on. But John Packer and I would not budge. We wanted Kevin to be given the degree which he had created and which was so closely associated with him.

Ten days before the ceremony, the university finally agreed.

Meanwhile, Boyle had begun suffering severe leg pains. Amid fear that the cancer had returned, he attended the graduation ceremony on 23 July. He was too weak to speak, so Hampson spoke instead. 'It turned out it really mattered to the students,' she said, 'because he was getting the same degree as an awful lot of those who were graduating in front of him.' When Boyle was handed the degree, he received a standing ovation. The last time the students had done so at a graduation ceremony was in 1997, when Nelson Mandela appeared as his partner, Graça Machel, received an honorary degree. Despite his illness, Boyle immediately decided to join the Essex Human Rights Alumni Association, which he had helped to create in 2008, the twenty-fifth anniversary of the Human Rights Centre.

On 7 September, to celebrate his long career, Boyle's colleagues gave him a festschrift. The book was entitled *Strategic Visions for Human Rights*, and was edited by Hampson, Geoff Gilbert and Clara Sandoval-Villalba. 'We gave it that title,' recalled Geoff Gilbert, 'because Kevin had a strategic vision. He could always see the big picture.' The book contained contributions by former students, as well as scholars involved in different stages of his life and the various causes he had championed, from an essay by Tom Hadden on Northern Ireland, to discussions of the war on terror, freedom of religion, and the future of the European Court of Human Rights. A reception was held at the Human Rights Centre, but by this time Boyle's condition had significantly deteriorated, and he was back in hospital. However, fortified with painkillers, he received the doctor's permission to attend. As he sat in a wheelchair, Françoise Hampson presented him with the book. Boyle was deeply moved. That night, he struggled into his hospital bed clutching the festschrift as a child might hold a stuffed animal. To Joan, he said that receiving this honour from his colleagues had been the best day of his life.

Around the same time, Ralph Crawshaw, the former police officer who had in 1999 with Boyle co-written a submission to the Patten Commission on police reform in Northern Ireland, attended a poetry reading by Seamus Heaney. The Nobel Prize-winning poet, an old friend of Boyle's, had just published a new book of verse. Entitled *Human Chain*, it was a reflection on death, loss, regret and memory, built around the image of a human chain linking the generations. Crawshaw told Heaney of Boyle's illness, and asked him to sign a copy. The poet wrote, 'Dear Kevin, You are a strong link in the chain.' The next day Crawshaw gave the book to Boyle. Kevin was, in Joan's recollection, 'quite poorly that day'. When he received the book, Boyle was so moved that he cried.

Just days later, the doctors told Boyle that his condition was terminal. There was nothing more they could do but make him as comfortable as possible. Hearing the news, Clara Sandoval-Villalba raced to the hospital. 'He was crying,' she recalled. 'He was devastated.' There were other patients nearby facing the same diagnosis. Sitting with Boyle, she recalled that 'there was a guy who was even more upset than Kevin, so Kevin, despite his condition, was trying to calm this guy down, saying – don't worry'. Indeed, despite the grim prognosis, Boyle was not ready to give up. He continued to communicate with students and colleagues, reading papers, sending emails, staying engaged. To his old student Gerard Quinn, now one of the world's leading authorities on rights for the disabled, he wrote, 'I have lung cancer but am fighting it. I think I always have been a fighter and am certainly keeping positive and optimistic.'[16]

In October he was allowed to return home. Joan looked after him. 'It was very hard for her,' Mark Boyle recalled. Occasionally, she would get away for a brief break, with Mark or Stephen coming to stay. 'I really treasure the fact that I got to stay with him and look after him a couple of times during his illness,' Stephen said. 'That was important to me.' Meanwhile, a steady stream of friends came to see Kevin. 'Having visitors very definitely buoyed him up,' Mark observed:

> Sitting in the front room and talking to people, seeing people he hadn't seen in a while. That was hugely positive and helped him get through it. You just think someone in a different situation wouldn't have had that vast cast of people coming through the door and coming from various countries and different times of his life. That's what you get if you have lived a good and interesting life that has been populated by interesting characters.

Hurst Hannum visited with a bottle of Armagnac. Despite doctor's orders for Kevin not to have any alcohol, the two shared a drink as they reminisced. Orlando Delogu from the University of Maine, one of Boyle's closest friends, also arrived. 'We sat in his front room. He was thin and wan. I think he knew that there was only a month or two left. He knew he was nearing the end.' With Delogu, Boyle talked about something that was increasingly on his mind – whether things might have gone differently in Northern Ireland. 'He was just parsing out – if we'd done this, if we'd done that – there could have been a resolution of the Troubles. It's just human nature for people to wonder if they'd done enough.' Indeed, in a note to Gerard Quinn, Boyle wondered if 'we might have had a more measured response'. Perhaps, he felt, that would have helped avoid or reduce the violence.[17]

On 20 November a large group of Boyle's former students gathered in a London office to pay tribute. Kevin joined them via Skype. He had just returned home from the hospital. It was clear that both he and they knew it would their last encounter. For half an hour, one Essex graduate after another told him how important he had been to their life and work. 'It was very emotional,' recalled Corrine Lennox, a Canadian who had worked with Boyle at the Minority Rights Group after receiving her Essex degree. 'In talks with him, I knew that he never fully realized how much he was loved and valued for his role in teaching and mentorship and how extremely important this was among his many legacies. There was so much love in the room for him. But it was also melancholic.'

Observing Kevin, Joan recalled that 'he was exhilarated and very touched. He was very buoyed up by the events of that afternoon. He had all his dearest former students in one room.' However, Boyle had not lost his self-deprecating sense of humour. 'I wonder if I can gather all these compliments up, and maybe I will look for another job,' he joked, as his students burst into laughter. Then Corrine Lennox asked Kevin whether he would accept the position of honorary president of the Essex Human Rights Alumni Association, now that he had his LLM degree. 'We wanted to show him what we had achieved with the association and as alumni,' said Lennox. 'We represented another facet of his legacy – a room full of alumni who had learned from him and become experts in their field as a result.' Boyle, beaming, formally accepted the position, and then turned serious, urging continued networking to strengthen the human rights endeavour in which they were all engaged. As for the compliments, he said in a strong voice, 'They mean a lot to me. They will mean a lot to me. There's a lot of love going on. And there's a lot of love from this side. I love you all as well.' His image then slowly faded from the screen.

On Christmas Day 2010, with Joan, Mark and Stephen by his side, Kevin Boyle died at a hospice in Colchester. He was sixty-seven years old. On his gravestone at Colchester Cemetery, below his name, Joan had arranged for the words of Seamus Heaney's tribute to be engraved: 'A Strong Link in the Chain'.

Afterword

THE COURSE of Kevin Boyle's life reflected the turbulent progress of the international human rights movement. From its modern manifestations in the late 1960s to its emergence as a powerful force helping to shape the international agenda in the 1990s and 2000s, Boyle was at the forefront of a struggle, based, as he put it, on the 'extraordinary appeal of the concept of common humanity and the belief in universal rights and freedoms to be enjoyed by all'.[1] With the 1948 Universal Declaration of Human Rights – a document Boyle revered – as its foundation, he devoted his energies as an activist, advocate and academic to the establishment of a legal framework for a global order based on human rights.[2] It put him at the cutting edge of issues that today remain a source of controversy and conflict around the world: freedom of the press and expression; state-sanctioned killing and torture; coping with terrorism; the clash between liberal values and the forces of Islamic fundamentalism and extreme nationalism; the rights of women, gays and minorities; the struggle to build a robust international system to protect human rights in challenging times.

Moreover, in his final years, he presciently identified a series of emerging new challenges. At the conference marking the fortieth anniversary of the civil rights movement in Belfast in 2008, he noted that 'the use of technology to effectively eliminate the right to privacy' – a fundamental right for people to be able live in dignity and security – was becoming 'a distinctive human rights issue of the current era of global terrorism and counter-terrorism'.[3] He also warned that 'the enormous accumulation of storage of information by private corporations' could have 'long-term worrying effects on personal freedom'⁴ – a decade before concerns over the political manipulation of Facebook, YouTube and social media became a burning international issue.

In the years since Boyle's death, an increasingly toxic combination of terrorist attacks and counterterrorist abuses, anti-immigrant sentiment fuelled by economic inequality and waves of migration, often of people fleeing violence, poverty and persecution, discrimination against Muslims and other minorities, the rise of far-right political parties and leaders, and the abuse of the tools of technology has led to a significant weakening of some of the human rights safeguards Boyle fought so hard to establish. In Turkey, President Recep Tayyip Erdoğan has undermined democratic institutions, imprisoned opponents and intensified attacks on the Kurds whose rights Boyle sought to protect. The relative tolerance of the China that Boyle visited in 2008 has been replaced by a more severe crackdown on dissent, civil society and openness under the autocratic rule of President Xi Jinping, who pioneered the use of artificial intelligence to monitor and control the population. The thuggish thievery of Vladimir Putin and the emergence of extreme nationalist governments in Hungary and Poland has eroded the promise of a more liberal order in the former Soviet Union and eastern Europe. From Donald Trump to Rodrigo Duterte in the Philippines to Brazil's far-right president, Jair Bolsonaro, to Brexit, populism and intolerance have become politically fashionable again. And the UK's decision to leave the European Union, with its robust human rights protections, has threatened the delicate political framework that brought peace to Northern Ireland. Amid alarming headlines like 'The End of Human Rights' some analysts have warned that 'the human rights movement is facing the greatest test it has confronted since its emergence in the 1970s as a major participant in the international order'.⁵

With so many setbacks, it would be easy to conclude that Kevin Boyle spent much of his life in a losing battle. But that would be wrong. He had many triumphs in his long and colourful career. His contributions to international human rights law on issues like discrimination, press freedom and torture, from the historic gay rights case of Jeffrey Dudgeon to the Kurds, for whom he obtained a measure of justice, to the many journalists and writers he helped to free and protect – as well as his crucial contribution to the peace process in Northern Ireland – constitute an enduring legacy.

Beyond that are the countless people he trained and inspired who today continue to work on human rights issues around the world, and who will, in turn, train and inspire others.

More broadly, Kevin Boyle had been steeled by the political struggles on the streets of Northern Ireland and the intense courtroom battles of later decades. For all his idealism, he was a hard-headed realist. He was well aware, as he wrote in 2008, that the 'ambition of universal human rights as a whole is clearly an ambition that has not been realized. The majority of mankind does not enjoy the promise of full human rights.'[6] Unlike some others, Boyle recognized that human rights can never be taken for granted. With the threat to existing human rights standards in the UK posed by Brexit, the erosion of civil liberties in the US amid the Trump administration's retreat from the traditional American role as a champion of democracy and multilateralism, Boyle's belief that human rights have to be fought for over and over, despite the likelihood of setbacks, seems more relevant today. For him, as Hurst Hannum observed, 'it was not always about winning the battle. It was making sure you haven't lost the war – that you were still on the field.' Boyle's style of fighting was low-key, but he was dogged in pursuit of justice, and passionate about providing the tools and structures for others to do the same. He recognized that establishing legal norms was just one step, although of crucial importance. He learned from his early experiences in Northern Ireland that to implement such changes also requires political engagement. While he would undoubtedly find much of what has happened in the years since his death to be depressing, Boyle would likely have been thrilled by such emerging movements as #MeToo, Black Lives Matter, the American high school students mobilizing against guns, public demands to combat climate change, the huge demonstrations against the emergence of authoritarian leaders in eastern Europe, and the dogged determination and remarkable courage of the journalists, lawyers and civil society activists fighting, often against daunting odds, in places like the Philippines, China and the Middle East.

Moreover, in the words of Françoise Hampson, 'as far as the newer challenge to a rules-based international order is concerned, the old Kevin would have done something about it'. As he did in the case of Salman Rushdie, it is not hard to imagine Boyle seeking to build a coalition to fight back, using the same combination of analytical, legal and political skills he brought to his work on human rights. 'You need international relations experts, historians, philosophers, political scientists, politicians, NGOS,' Hampson observed. 'They need to be organized and coordinated from outside universities, but include academics [and] need to form part of an overall campaign. Kevin would have been ideally placed to play a key role. He had excellent contacts and was used to working in that kind of group.'

Boyle saw himself, and the human rights movement, engaged in a never-ending struggle, one that required frequent adjustments of strategy and tactics without losing sight of the long-term goal. In January 2001, while awaiting the European Court to rule on the Banković case involving the NATO bombing of the Serbian television headquarters in Belgrade which left sixteen civilians dead, Boyle told his students, 'we see this case as just one modest step on the long road to the rule of international law. Even if we fail, ultimately someone will build on it.'[7] This kind of clear-eyed, under-stated, but committed view underpinned Kevin Boyle's approach to human rights, as did his refusal to lose hope or give up. As Mary Robinson declared in her farewell speech as UN High Commissioner for Human Rights on 11 September 2002, using words Boyle may well have crafted and certainly agreed with, 'human rights are not expendable. It is time for those who believe in human rights to keep their nerve.'[8] That was true then, as the world reeled from the fallout of the 9/11 attacks a year earlier. It remains equally true today.

Acknowledgments

I WOULD LIKE to express my profound gratitude to Joan Boyle. She not only shared countless details and insights about Kevin and their life together, but also provided access to private papers and other material not available in the Boyle archive at the National University of Ireland, Galway. In addition, she helped put me in touch with dozens of Kevin's colleagues, students, friends, relatives and others who played in a role in, or were influenced by, his life and work. Joan understood that, as a journalist and historian, I would approach telling Kevin's story in my own way, and I am deeply grateful for her trust and kindness. Other members of the Boyle family – his sons Mark and Stephen, and especially his brother Louis – were unstinting in their support and assistance.

I owe particular thanks to those who read all or parts of the manuscript: Geoff Budlender, my sons Dan and Ben Chinoy, my sister Clara Mora Chinoy, Tony Fisher, Tom Hadden, Françoise Hampson, Hurst Hannum, Francis Keenan, Jo Lusby, Michael O'Boyle, Phil Revzin and Leon Sigal. This book is far better because of their corrections and suggestions. Francis Keenan, in particular, provided crucial guidance. Tony, Francis, Françoise, Tom, Hurst and Michael, along with Nuala Ní Mhuircheartaigh, also helped me to make sense of the complexities of international law and of bodies such as the European Court of Human Rights, giving me a much deeper understanding of Kevin Boyle's work and world.

My agent, Jonathan Williams, has been a strong supporter of this project from the very beginning, offering encouragement and advice, and meticulously editing the manuscript. He not only elevated my prose, but saved me from more than a few small but critical mistakes. Special thanks to my old friend Conor O'Clery for his initial enthusiasm and for connecting me with Jonathan.

From our first meeting, Antony Farrell saw the promise in this story. He and his colleagues at The Lilliput Press, especially Ruth Hallinan, copy editor Djinn von Noorden and indexer Jane Rogers, have provided a congenial home for the book, and I am proud to be associated with them.

The essential resource for learning about Kevin Boyle's life is the remarkable archive of his papers in the James Hardiman Library at the National University of Ireland, Galway. Heartfelt thanks to Barry Houlihan and his colleagues Kieran Hoare, Geraldine Curtin, Margo Donohue, Mary O'Leary, Marie Boran, Aisling Keane and Brendan Duffy for hosting me during the many weeks I spent exploring the archive, and for being so willing to help me navigate the thousands of documents it contains. I also consulted the records of the National Archives of Ireland in Dublin and the Public Record Office of Northern Ireland in Belfast. At PRONI, special thanks to Lorraine Bourke and Desmond McCabe.

I would also like to express my gratitude to Donncha O'Connell, both for his insights and suggestions, and, along with John Cox, for helping to arrange financial support from NUI Galway to conduct research.

Simon Prince, whose book *Northern Ireland's '68* is one of the most important contributions to understanding the origin of the Troubles, provided me with four hours of audio from a 2006 interview he conducted with Boyle. It was an essential resource, and I am very grateful for his generosity.

Marie McGonagle, who was a student, colleague and close friend of Kevin Boyle, was an invaluable source, as was her son Tarlagh, who, a generation after Marie, also studied with Boyle.

Aoife Duffy, Niall Ó Dochartaigh, Lelia Doolan, Brice Dickson and Paul O'Connor provided valuable assistance as well.

In Northern Ireland, Peter Taggart provided crucial help in tracking down contacts, digging up material, and helping me find my way around.

Special thanks as well to Siobhán Mullaly of the Irish Centre for Human Rights and Lorna McGregor and Clara Sandoval-Villalba of the Human Rights Centre at the University of Essex. I am especially grateful to all those who contributed to the Lilliput Press effort to raise funds to promote the book.

By inviting me to join her 2016 summer programme on 'Religion, Conflict and Human Rights' that involved bringing a group of American students to Northern Ireland, Lyn Boyd Judson, my colleague from the University of Southern California, became the catalyst for my decision to begin work on this book. Of the students I met in that summer programme, Gita Howard proved to be a first-class research assistant, and she and Mary Cate Hickman, Milena Margaryan and Anastasia Najarian helped transcribe interviews. So did Hannah Hughes, who wrote her undergraduate thesis at NUI Galway on the Boyle archive.

For intellectual and emotional support during the nearly four years it has taken to complete this project, I want to thank my sister Clara, my sons Dan and Ben, my cousin, the writer John Krich, my niece Nandi, Woodrow and Unit Two. Finally, my biggest thanks go to my wife, Inez Ho. A native of Hong Kong, she knew little about Northern Ireland when I began this book – but not only did she accompany me to Belfast and Derry on my first research trip, in the years that followed she displayed remarkable tolerance in putting up with what must at times have seemed like an all-consuming project. I am forever grateful for her love and support.

Interviewees

Alston, Philip – 10 December 2018
Aragon, Eugenio – 20 December 2018
Arnold, Tom – 22 February 2018
Arthur, Paul – 26 February 2018
Beetham, David – 27 June 2018
Bentes, Lelio – 12 December 2018
Bew, Paul – 19 July 2016
Boucher, Richard – 27 November 2018
Boyle, Eugene – 1 August 2017
Boyle, Joan – multiple interviews 2016, 2017, 2019
Boyle, Louis – multiple interviews 2016, 2017, 2018, 2019
Boyle, Mark – 20 October 2018
Boyle, Stephen – 14 July 2018
Brady, Conor – 1 August 2016
Bratza, Nicolas – 18 October 2016
Browne, Vincent – 24 February 2018
Budlender, Geoff – 4 May 2018
Byrne, Iain – 25 October 2018
Carson, Kit – 1 June 2018
Coleman, Audrey – 18 August 2018
Coulter, Paddy – 17 May 2018
Crewe, Ivor – 10 October 2018
D'Souza, Frances – 14 July 2017
Delogu, Orlando – 9 March 2018
Devlin, Anne – 25 February 2016; 24 June 2018
Dickson, Brice – 1 August 2017
Dora, Denise – 18 December 2018

Doran, Bernadette – 9 July 2016

Doran, Paul – 9 July 2019

Dudgeon, Jeffrey – 29 July 2017

Dugard, John – 29 May 2018

Edwards, Ruth Dudley – 21 January 2018

Elsner, Richard – 2 May 2018

Emmerson, Michael – 30 January 2017

Fairleigh, John – 31 August 2017

Farrell, Michael – 1 December 2016; 15 June 2018

Fisher, Tony – 26 June 2018

Fujita, Sanae – 18 September 2016

Gearty, Conor – 31 August 2017

George, Cherian – 18 December 2018

Gilbert, Geoff – 25 July 2017

Glazebrook, Peter – 9 January 2018

Grant, Stefanie – 19 April 2018

Gray, John – 15 February 2017

Greenstock, Sir Jeremy – 27 September 2018

Griffith, Liz – July 2017

Guelke, Adrian – 18 November 2018

Hadden, Tom – multiple interviews 2016, 2017, 2018

Hampson, Françoise – 24 July 2017

Hannum, Hurst – 25 May 2016; 11 November 2016; 3 August 2017

Harvey, Colin – 26 November 2018

Hayes, Maurice – 15 September 2017

Higgins, Michael D. – 21 November 2017

Hillyard, Paddy – 29 November 2016

Hughes, Thomas – 17 May 2018

Hutchinson, Billy – 26 October 2017

Jersild, Jens Olaf – 24 September 2018

Kearney, Brandon – 7 August 2017

Keenan, Francis – 30 July 2016; 12 August 2017

Kelly, Mary – 29 January 2018

Keyes, Gerard – 17 August 2017

Kiernan, Joan – 4 February 2017

Kirchner, Emile – 28 June 2018

Kirwan, Walter – 30 July 2016; 2 December 2016; 22 February 2018

Kruger, Hans – 9 November 2018

Lattimer, Mark – 26 June 2018

Lennox, Corrine – 26 June 2018

Levin, Leah – 17 July 2016

Lindblom, Lance – 29 January 2018

Lockwood, Bert – 2 April 2018

Logue, Hugh – 22 February 2018

Maia, Luciano – 23 December 2018

Manning, Maurice – 22 February 2018

Marcus, Gilbert – 31 July 2018

Matchett, Albert – September 2017

Mei Ning, Yan – 20 December 2018

McAleese, Mary – 3 May 2017

McAliskey, Bernadette Devlin – 29 November 2016

McCann, Eamonn – 30 November 2016

McGonagle, Marie – multiple interviews, 2016, 2017, 2018

McGonagle, Tarlach – 7 August 2017; 18 February 2018

McGuffin, Judith – 15 February 2017

McKittrick, David – 12 September 2017

McShane, Rory – 27 February 2017

Moloney, Ed – 4 February 2017

Morel, Cynthia – 13 February 2018

Mortimer, Edward – 24 September 2018

Naughton Jones, Anne – 1 October 2018

Neier, Aryeh – 2 October 2017

Ní Mhuircheartaigh, Nuala – 24 September 2018; 2 December 2018

O'Boyle, Michael – multiple interviews 2016, 2017, 2018, 2019

O'Connell, Donncha – 3 August 2016; 23 November 2017

O'Connor, Fionnuala – 23 June 2018

Ó Dochartaigh, Niall – 27 July 2016

O'Hara, Joe – 21 November 2016

O'Sullivan, Finola – 11 December 2018

Oud, Malin – 21 January 2019

Petranov, Borislav – 13 June 2018

Phillips, Andrew – 27 June 2018

Phillips, John – 29 September 2017

Piette, Luisa – 7 September 2017

Piette, Matthew – 7 September 2017

Pollak, Andy – 16 November 2018

Purcell, Betty – 21 February 2018

Quinn, Gerard – 8 March 2018

Ragg, Nicholas – 15 June 2017

Reidy, Aisling – 7 July 2017; 23 July 2017

INTERVIEWEES

Rishmawi, Mona – 17 April 2018

Robinson, Mary – 19 April 2018

Rodley, Nigel – 19 September 2016

Ryan, Richard – October 2018

Sandoval-Villalba, Clara – 19 September 2016; 25 June 2018

Schabas, William – 11 November 2018

Shawcross, William – 28 October 2017

Sheen, Juliet – 9 June 2018

Silke, Leonard – 5 August 2017

Slowgrove, Anne – 26 July 2017

Smart, Malcolm – 14 July 2017

Taylor, Peter – 13 June 2017

Tistounet, Eric – 4 December 2018

Trier, Tyge – 27 September 2018

Twining, Penelope – 20 July 2016

Twining, William – 20 July 2016

Ward, Jim – 17 August 2017

Weir, Stuart – 8 September 2018

Wilson, Robin – 18 November 2018

Wolland, Steingrim – 30 September 2018

Yates, David – 10 January 2018

Bibliography

BOOKS

Arthur, Paul, *The People's Democracy* (Belfast 1974)

Article 19, *Fiction, Fact, and the Fatwa: A Chronology of Censorship* (London 1992)

Bardon, Jonathan, *A History of Ulster* (Belfast 1992)

Bates, Ed, *The Evolution of the European Convention on Human Rights* (Oxford 2010)

Beetham, David and Kevin Boyle, *Introducing Democracy: 80 Questions and Answers* (Paris 1995)

Boyle, Kevin, *Article 19, World Report 1988, Information, Freedom and Censorship* (New York 1988)

Boyle, Kevin and Tom Hadden, *Ireland: A Positive Proposal* (London 1985); *Northern Ireland: The Choice* (London 1994)

Boyle, Kevin and Juliet Sheen, *Freedom of Religion and Belief: A World Report* (London 1997)

Boyle, Kevin, Tom Hadden and Paddy Hillyard, *Law and State: The Case of Northern Ireland* (London 1975); *Ten Years On in Northern Ireland: The Legal Control of Political Violence* (London 1980)

Boyle, Kevin, Colm Campbell and Tom Hadden, *The Protection of Human Rights in the Context of Peace and Reconciliation in Ireland* (Dublin 1996)

Boyle, Louis, *Standing Alone*, unpublished memoir

Conroy, John, *Belfast Diary: War as a Way of Life* (Boston, Mass. 1987)

Devlin, Bernadette, *The Price of My Soul* (New York 1969)

Dickson, Brice, *The European Convention on Human Rights and the Conflict in Northern Ireland* (Oxford 2010)

Dunne, Derek and Gene Kerrigan, *Round Up the Usual Suspects: The Cosgrave Coalition and Nicky Kelly* (Dublin 1984)

Egan, Bowes and Vincent McCormack, *Burntollet* (Cork 1969)

Farrell, Michael (ed.), *Twenty Years On* (Dingle 1988); *Northern Ireland: The Orange State* (London 1980)

Feeney, Brian, Seamus Kelters, David McKittrick and Chris Thornton, *Lost Lives: The Stories of the Men, Women and Children Who Died as a Result of the Northern Ireland Troubles* (Edinburgh 2004)

Fenton, Siobhán, *The Good Friday Agreement* (London 2018)

Fisk, Robert, *The Point of No Return: The Strike Which Broke the British in Ulster* (London 1975)

FitzGerald, Garret, *Just Garret* (Dublin 2011)

Fraser, Ronald (ed.), *1968: A Student Generation in Revolt* (New York 1988)

Gilbert, Geoff, Françoise Hampson and Clara Sandoval (eds), *Strategic Visions for Human Rights: Essays in Honour of Professor Kevin Boyle* (London 2011)

Goldhaber, Michael, *A People's History of the European Court of Human Rights* (New Brunswick 2007)

Harris, David, *The White Tribe of Africa* (Berkeley 1981)

Hastings, Max, *Barricades in Belfast: The Fight for Civil Rights in Northern Ireland* (London 1970)

Hayes, Maurice, *Minority Verdict* (Belfast 1995)

Heaney, Seamus, *From the Republic of Conscience*, Amnesty International, 1985; *Human Chain* (London 2010)

Hennessey, Thomas, *Hunger Strike* (Dublin 2014); *The Evolution of the Troubles*, 1970–72 (Dublin 2007)

Holland, Jack, *Hope Against History: The Course of the Conflict in Northern Ireland* (London 1999)

Hope, Ann, 'From civil rights to guerrilla war: The Northern Ireland Civil Rights Association struggle for democracy 1969–1972' (unpublished thesis, Ruskin College, 1976)

Human Rights Watch, *Human Rights in Northern Ireland*, 1991

McCafferty, Nell, *Nell* (Dublin 2004)

McCann, Eamonn, *War and an Irish Town* (London 1993)

McGuffin, John, *Internment* (Dublin 1973)

McKittrick, David and David McVea, *Making Sense of the Troubles* (New York 2002)

Moloney, Ed, *A Secret History of the IRA* (London 2002); *Voices from the Grave: Two Men's War in Ireland* (London 2011)

Moloney, Ed and Andy Pollak, *Paisley* (Dublin 1986)

Moore, Charles, *Margaret Thatcher. At Her Zenith: In London, Washington and Moscow* (London 2016)

Murray, Douglas, *Bloody Sunday: Truth, Lies and the Saville Inquiry* (London 2011)

Myers, Kevin, *Watching the Door: A Memoir 1971–1978* (Dublin 2006)

NICRA, 'We Shall Overcome: The History of the Struggle for Civil Rights in Northern Ireland 1968–1978'

Novosel, Tony, *Northern Ireland's Lost Opportunity: The Frustrated Promise of Political Loyalism* (London 2013)

Ó Dochartaigh, Niall, *From Civil Rights to Armalites: Derry and the Birth of the Irish Troubles* (Cork 1997)

O'Doherty, Malachi, *Gerry Adams: An Unauthorised Life* (London 2017)

O'Rawe Richard, *Blanketmen: An Untold Story of the H-Block Hunger Strike* (Dublin 2005); *Afterlives: The Hunger Strike and the Secret Offer that Changed Irish History* (Dublin 2010)

Pipes, Daniel, *The Rushdie Affair* (London 2017)

Pollak, Andy (ed.), *A Citizen's Inquiry: The Opsahl Report on Northern Ireland* (Dublin 1992)

Prince, Simon, *Northern Ireland's '68: Civil Rights, Global Revolt and the Origin of the Troubles* (Dublin 2007)

Prince, Simon and Geoffrey Warner, *Belfast and Derry in Revolt* (Dublin 2012)

Purcell, Betty, *Inside RTÉ* (Dublin 2014)

Purdie, Bob, *Politics in the Streets: The Origins of the Civil Rights Movement in Northern Ireland* (Belfast 1990)

Richtarik, Marilynn, *Stewart Parker: A Life* (Oxford 2012)

Robinson, Mary, *A Voice for Human Rights* (Philadelphia 2006); *Everybody Matters* (London 2013)

Rose, Richard, *Governing Without Consensus* (London 1971)

Sandbrook, Dominic, *State of Emergency* (London 2011); *White Heat: A History of Britain in the Swinging Sixties* (London 2009)

Sumner, Finola, *Double the Boys* (Cork 1990)

Sunday Times, *Northern Ireland: A Report on the Conflict* (London 1972)

Taylor, Peter, *Loyalists* (London 2000); *Provos: The IRA and Sinn Féin* (London 1998); *Beating the Terrorists* (London 1980)

Toolis, Kevin, *Rebel Hearts: Journeys within the IRA's Soul* (New York 1995)

Van Voris, William, *Violence in Ulster: An Oral Documentary* (Amherst 1975)

Wilford, Rick and Robin Wilson, *The Trouble with Northern Ireland: The Belfast Agreement and Democratic Governance* (Dublin 2006)

Winchester, Simon, *In Holy Terror* (London 1975)

BIBLIOGRAPHY

NEWSPAPERS, MAGAZINES AND MEDIA

BBC
Belfast Telegraph
Bernadette: Notes on a Political Journey, Lelia Doolan (director), documentary, 2011
Chicago Tribune
Daily Mail
Fortnight
Irish Echo
Irish Independent
Life Magazine
National Public Radio
News Letter
Portland Press Herald
RTÉ
The Atlantic
The Daily Telegraph
The Gown
The Guardian
The Independent
The Irish Times
The Nation
The New York Times
The New Yorker
The Observer
The Day the Troubles Began, Michael Fanning (director), BBC documentary, 2008
The Times
The Wall Street Journal
The Washington Post
Vanity Fair
Village Magazine

JOURNALS

A New Beginning: Policing in Northern Ireland: The Report of the Independent Commission on Policing in Northern Ireland, September 1999

African Affairs

American Journal of International Law

Asia Pacific Law Review

Australian Journal of Law and Society

Essex Human Rights Review

Études Irlandaises

Higher Education and Research Opportunities in the United Kingdom, 1 July 2003

How to Read the New Ireland Forum, Kevin Boyle and Tom Hadden, 1984

Human Rights Quarterly

International and Comparative Law Quarterly

International Human Rights Review

International Journal of Human Rights Foreign Policy

Netherlands Quarterly of Human Rights

New Hibernia Review

New Left Review

Report of the Bloody Sunday Inquiry, June 2010

The Honest Ulsterman

The Modern Law Review

The Western Law Gazette

Violence and Civil Disturbances in Northern Ireland in 1969: Report of Tribunal of Inquiry, April 1972

We Shall Overcome: The History of the Struggle for Civil Rights in Northern Ireland, 1968–1978, Northern Ireland Civil Rights Association

Wyvern

Notes

PROLOGUE

1 Louis Boyle, remarks at Kevin Boyle funeral, 17 January 2011.
2 Borislav Petranov, 'In Memoriam; Kevin Boyle, Strong Link in the Chain', *International Journal of Human Rights*, December 2010.
3 Nigel Ridley, remarks at Kevin Boyle funeral, 17 January 2011.
4 Françoise Hampson, remarks at Kevin Boyle funeral, 17 January 2011.
5 'Obituary: Kevin Boyle – Inspirational Figure Behind Original Civil Rights Movement', *Belfast Telegraph*, 31 December 2010.
6 'Kevin Boyle', *Irish Independent*, 2 January 2011.
7 Letter to Joan Boyle from Albert Matchett, 6 January 2011.
8 Françoise Hampson, remarks at Kevin Boyle funeral, 17 January 2001.
9 Donncha O'Connell, letter to Joan Boyle, 17 August 2011.
10 Condolence note to Joan Boyle from Urgur Erdal, 15 January 2011.
11 Condolence note to Joan Boyle from Zolomphi Nkowani, 15 January 2011.
12 Condolence note to Joan Boyle from Pia Jennings, 15 January 2011.

CHAPTER 1

1 Finola Sumner, *Double the Boys* (Cork 1990), p. 12.
2 ibid. p. 17.
3 Kevin Boyle, interview transcript in William Van Voris, *Violence in Ulster: An Oral Documentary* (Amherst 1975), p. 24.
4 Sumner, *Double the Boys*, p. 17.
5 'The Brothers Grim', *The Guardian*, 18 November 2009.
6 Sumner, *Double the Boys*, pp. 7–8.
7 ibid. pp. 7–8.

8 ibid. p. 72.

9 Van Voris, *Violence in Ulster*, p. 24.

10 ibid. p. 26.

11 Summer, *Double the Boys*, p. 26.

12 Van Voris, *Violence in Ulster*, p. 24.

13 Jack Holland, *Hope Against History: The Course of the Conflict in Northern Ireland* (London 1999), p. 21.

14 Max Hastings, *Barricades in Belfast: The Fight for Civil Rights in Northern Ireland* (London 1970), p. 29.

15 Reported in Parliamentary Debates, Northern Ireland House of Commons, vol. XVI, cols 1091–5. Quoted in Jonathan Bardon, *A History of Ulster* (Belfast 1992), pp. 538–9.

16 Van Voris, *Violence in Ulster*, p. 23.

17 ibid. pp. 23–4.

18 Kevin Boyle, interview with Simon Prince, 21 October 2006.

19 Van Voris, *Violence in Ulster*, pp. 28–9.

20 ibid. p. 28.

21 Van Voris, *Violence in Ulster*, p. 23.

22 ibid. p. 23.

23 Damien Daley, email to Joan Boyle, 17 September 2016.

24 ibid.

25 Van Voris, *Violence in Ulster*, p. 61.

26 ibid. p. 62.

27 ibid. pp. 61–2.

28 ibid. p. 29.

29 ibid. p. 29.

30 ibid. p. 30.

31 ibid. p. 30.

32 'Calm and Cheerful Ulster Militant', *The New York Times*, 6 February 1972.

CHAPTER 2

1 Seamus Heaney interview, 1996, RTÉ Archives.

2 Van Voris, *Violence in Ulster*, p. 59.

3 ibid. p. 30.

4 ibid. p. 30.

5 Quoted in *Australian Journal of Law and Society*, vol. 5, 1985/11, p. 102.

6 Van Voris, *Violence in Ulster*, p. 30.

7 ibid. p. 31.

8 Marilynn Richtarik, *Stewart Parker: A Life* (Oxford 2012), p. 17.

9 Kevin Boyle, interview with Simon Prince, 21 October 2006.

10 Van Voris, *Violence in Ulster*, p. 26.

11 Kevin Boyle, interview with Simon Prince, 21 October 2006.

12 Kevin Boyle, *The Gown*, 12 October 1962, courtesy Special Collections, Queen's University Belfast.

13 Kevin Boyle diary, 1965.

14 Letter from Elizabeth Boyle to Kevin Boyle, 22 August [year not clear].

15 Louis Boyle, funeral talk for Anne Boyle.

16 Letter to Kevin Boyle from Lesley [former girlfriend], 10 November 1964.

17 Kevin Boyle diary, 1965.

18 ibid.

19 Van Voris, *Violence in Ulster*, p. 59.

20 Quoted from the *Belfast Telegraph*, 5 May 1969, and cited in Michael Farrell, *Northern Ireland: The Orange State*, p. 256.

21 Ed Moloney and Andy Pollak, *Paisley* (Dublin 1986), p. 201.

22 Van Voris, *Violence in Ulster*, p. 59–60.

23 Kevin Boyle, 'Belfast and its Sundays', undated university essay.

24 Van Voris, *Violence in Ulster*, p. 60.

25 ibid. p. 60.

26 Simon Prince, *Northern Ireland's '68* (Dublin 2007), p. 64.

27 Nell McCafferty, *Nell* (Dublin 2004), p. 81.

28 Eamonn McCann interview with Eamonn Mallie, 20 February 2012.

29 McCafferty, *Nell*, p. 74.

30 Van Voris, *Violence in Ulster*, p. 62.

31 ibid. p. 60.

32 Kevin Boyle, interview with Simon Prince, 21 October 2006.

33 ibid.

34 ibid.

35 Van Voris, *Violence in Ulster*, p. 61.

36 Holland, *Hope Against History*, p. 28.

37 Michael Farrell (ed.), *Twenty Years On* (Dingle 1988), p. 19.

38 Gerry Fitt, maiden speech at House of Commons, Westminster, 25 April 1966.

39 Hastings, *Barricades in Belfast*, p. 30.

40 Kevin Boyle, Tom Hadden, Paddy Hillyard, *Law and State: The Case of Northern Ireland* (London 1975), p. 7.

41 Van Voris, *Violence in Ulster*, p. 62.

42 ibid. p. 61.

43 ibid. p. 60.

CHAPTER 3

1 Hastings, *Barricades in Belfast*, p. 71.
2 Kevin Boyle journal, 1969.
3 Kevin Boyle diary, 1967.
4 Kevin Boyle, Queen's University promotion application, 1969.
5 Michael Farrell, *Northern Ireland: The Orange State* (London 1980), p. 245.
6 Kevin Boyle, testimony before the Saville Inquiry, 11 June 2001.
7 Kevin Boyle, 'Politics and Personalities, 1968–70: Personal Notes on the C.R. Campaign', 1971.
8 ibid.
9 Kevin Boyle, interview with Simon Prince, 21 October 2006.
10 Anthony Coughlan, 'Recalling the North's Civil Rights Movement', *Village Magazine*, 6 February 2017.
11 ibid.
12 Louis Boyle, *Standing Alone*, unpublished memoir, p. 9.
13 Kevin Boyle, interview with Simon Prince, 21 October 2006.
14 Van Voris, *Violence in Ulster*, p. 63.
15 Kevin Boyle, interview with Simon Prince, 21 October 2006.
16 Boyle et al., *Law and State: The Case of Northern Ireland*, p. 15.
17 Kevin Boyle interview, Talkback Radio, 5 October 1988.
18 Paul Arthur, *The People's Democracy* (Belfast 1974), p. 27.
19 Eamonn McCann, *War and an Irish Town* (London 1993), p. 98.
20 Bernadette Devlin, *The Price of My Soul* (New York 1969), p. 97.
21 Hastings, *Barricades in Belfast*, p. 57.
22 Kevin Boyle, interview with Simon Prince, 21 October 2006.
23 Devlin, *The Price of My Soul*, p. 99.
24 Eilis McDermott 'Law and Order' in Michael Farrell (ed.), *Twenty Years On*, p. 148.
25 Bob Purdie, *Politics in the Streets: The Origins of the Civil Rights Movement in Northern Ireland* (Belfast 1990), p. 206.
26 Kevin Boyle, interview with Simon Prince, 21 October 2006.
27 McDermott in *Twenty Years On*, p. 149.
28 Kevin Boyle, interview with Simon Prince, 21 October 2006.
29 Kevin Boyle journal, January 1969.
30 Devlin, *The Price of My Soul*, pp. 100–1.
31 Van Voris, *Violence in Ulster*, p. 73.
32 Devlin, *The Price of My Soul*, p. 101.
33 McDermott in *Twenty Years On*, p. 149.

34 Kevin Boyle, interview with Simon Prince, 21 October 2006.

35 Kevin Boyle journal, January 1969.

36 Van Voris, *Violence in Ulster*, pp. 73–4.

37 ibid. p. 74.

38 ibid. pp. 74–5.

39 *The Irish Times*, 'Restraint by QUB Students Praised', 14 October 1968.

40 Ronald Fraser (ed.), *1968: A Student Generation in Revolt* (New York 1988), p. 235.

41 *The Irish Times*, 'University March Achieves Object', 17 October 1968.

42 Speeches made at meeting of People's Democracy at Belfast City Hall, 16 October 1968, Public Records Office of Northern Ireland (PRONI).

43 *The Irish Times*, 'The People's Democracy', 27 November 1968.

44 ibid.

45 ibid.

46 Kevin Boyle, interview with Simon Prince, 21 October 2006.

47 Kevin Boyle, statement to the Saville Commission Inquiry, 4 August 2000.

48 Kevin Boyle, interview with Simon Prince, 21 October 2006.

49 Kevin Boyle, 'Politics and Personalities, 1968–70: Personal Notes on the C.R. Campaign', 1971.

50 Van Voris, *Violence in Ulster*, p. 74.

51 Devlin, *The Price of My Soul*, p. 110.

52 Kevin Boyle interview, Talkback Radio, 5 October 1988.

53 Hastings, *Barricades in Belfast*, p. 68.

54 Sunday Times, *Northern Ireland: A Report on the Conflict* (London 1972), p. 60.

55 Hastings, *Barricades in Belfast*, p. 74.

56 Kevin Boyle, testimony before the Scarman Tribunal, 30 April 1971, p. 5.

57 *Northern Ireland: A Report on the Conflict*, p. 61.

58 ibid. p. 62.

59 Text of O'Neill speech, Government of Northern Ireland Press Office, 9 December 1968.

60 Louis Boyle, *Standing Alone*, p. 80.

61 Kevin Boyle, interview with Simon Prince, 21 October 2006.

62 McDermott in *Twenty Years On*, p. 150.

CHAPTER 4

1 Devlin, *The Price of My Soul*, p. 126.

2 Police memo: 'Civil Rights March through Co. Antrim on 1/2 January'.

3 ibid.

4 ibid.

5 Devlin, *The Price of My Soul*, p. 129.

6 Police memo: 'Civil Rights March through Co. Antrim on 1/2 January'.

7 Hastings, *Barricades in Belfast*, p. 82.

8 Devlin, *The Price of My Soul*, p. 132.

9 *Northern Ireland: A Report on the Conflict*, p. 64.

10 Devlin, *The Price of My Soul*, p. 133.

11 Fraser (ed.), *1968: A Student Generation in Revolt*, p. 239.

12 RUC report, 'People's Democracy March from Belfast to Londonderry from 1st January–4th January'.

13 Devlin, *The Price of My Soul*, p. 134.

14 Van Voris, *Violence in Ulster*, p. 86.

15 Kevin Boyle, interview with Simon Prince, 21 October 2006.

16 Van Voris, *Violence in Ulster*, p. 85.

17 RUC report, 'People's Democracy March from Belfast to Londonderry from 1st January–4th January'.

18 Van Voris, *Violence in Ulster*, p. 87.

19 RUC report, 'People's Democracy March from Belfast to Londonderry from 1st January–4th January'.

20 Van Voris, *Violence in Ulster*, p. 88.

21 ibid. p. 88.

22 Devlin, *The Price of My Soul*, p. 137.

23 Bowes Egan and Vincent McCormack, *Burntollet* (Cork 1969), p. 22.

24 ibid. p. 22.

25 The Belfast *News Letter*, 6 January 1969, quoted in Egan and McCormack, *Burntollet*, p. 24.

26 In his 1972 interviews with US scholar William Van Voris, Kevin says he did go into Derry. In a 2006 interview with British scholar Simon Prince, he says he did not. But both interviews make clear that he met with John Hume that night.

27 Purdie, *Politics in the Streets*, p. 190.

28 Van Voris, *Violence in Ulster*, p. 89.

29 ibid. p. 89.

30 Kevin Boyle, interview with Simon Prince, 21 October 2006.

31 Van Voris, *Violence in Ulster* p. 89.

32 ibid. p. 89.

33 ibid. p. 89.

34 Michael Farrell, speaking in RTÉ video clip.

35 Kevin Boyle, interview with Simon Prince, 21 October 2006.

36 Devlin, *The Price of My Soul*, p. 137.

37 ibid. p. 138.

38 Van Voris, *Violence in Ulster*, p. 91.

39 Devlin, *The Price of My Soul*, p. 139.

40 Van Voris, *Violence in Ulster*, p. 91.

41 *The Irish Times*, 'Battling Through to Derry', 6 January 1969.

42 Egan and McCormick, *Burntollet*, p. 33.

43 Devlin, *The Price of My Soul*, p. 139.

44 *The Irish Times*, 'Battling Through to Derry', 6 January 1969.

45 Van Voris, *Violence in Ulster*, p. 91.

46 ibid. p. 92.

47 ibid. p. 92.

48 ibid. p. 92.

49 ibid. p. 93.

50 ibid. p. 93.

51 ibid. p. 93.

52 ibid. p. 93.

53 ibid. p. 93.

54 *The Irish Times*, 'Battling Through to Derry', 6 January 1969.

55 ibid.

56 McDermott in *Twenty Years After*, p. 151.

57 *The Irish Times*, 'From Violence to Peace', 6 January 1969.

58 *The Irish Times*, 'Battling Through to Derry', 6 January 1969.

59 Van Voris, *Violence in Ulster*, pp. 96–7.

60 Cameron Commission, quoted in Sunday Times, *Northern Ireland: A Report on the Conflict*, p. 68.

61 *The Irish Times*, 'O'Neill May Call Up Special Police', 6 January 1969.

62 Hastings, *Barricades in Belfast*, p. 89.

63 Van Voris, *Violence in Ulster* p. 97.

64 Louis Boyle, *Standing Alone*, p. 88.

65 ibid. pp. 89–90.

66 *The Irish Times*, 'Newry Attacks End in Baton Charge', 13 January 1969.

67 Kevin Boyle, notes for Newry speech, PRONI Archive, D3297/1/6.

68 ibid.

69 Van Voris, *Violence in Ulster* pp. 97–8.

70 Quoted in Sunday Times, *Northern Ireland; A Report on the Conflict*, p. 69.

71 Ed Moloney, *A Secret History of the IRA* (London 2002).

72 Kevin Boyle, People's Democracy thoughts, PRNI 03297/1/6.

73 ibid.

74 ibid.

75 Devlin, *The Price of My Soul*, p. 117.

76 Kevin Boyle, interview with Simon Prince, 21 October 2006.

77 Eamonn McCann, 'People's Democracy: A Discussion on Strategy', *New Left Review*, 20 April 1969.

78 Kevin Boyle, interview with Simon Prince, 21 October 2006.

79 ibid.

80 Kevin Boyle interview, Talkback Radio, 5 October 1988.

81 Kevin Boyle, interview with Simon Prince, 21 October 2006.

CHAPTER 5

1   William Van Voris, *Violence in Ulster*, p. 103.

2   Kevin Boyle, PD election strategy notes in PRONI document 3297/1/1/16.

3   Devlin, *The Price of My Soul*, p. 149.

4   Kevin Boyle, PD election strategy notes in PRONI document 3297/1/1/16.

5   Devlin, *The Price of My Soul*, p. 149.

6   Kevin Boyle, interview with Simon Prince, 21 October 2006.

7   Louis Boyle, *Standing Alone*, p. 95.

8   ibid. p. 96.

9   Van Voris, *Violence in Ulster*, p. 108.

10 Louis Boyle, *Standing Alone*, p. 103.

11 ibid. p. 104.

12 ibid. p. 104.

13 Van Voris, *Violence in Ulster*, p. 108.

14 ibid. p. 108.

15 *The Irish Times*, 'Final Votes Show a Radical Trend', 26 February 1969.

16 Ann Hope, 'From civil rights to guerrilla war: The Northern Ireland Civil Rights Association struggle for democracy 1969–1972' (unpublished thesis, Ruskin College, 1976), p. 54.

17 NICRA, 'We Shall Overcome: The History of the Struggle for Civil Rights in Northern Ireland, 1968–1978'.

18 Ann Hope, 'From civil rights to guerrilla war', p. 56.

19 Devlin, *The Price of My Soul*, p. 154.

20 ibid. p. 159.

21 Arthur, *The People's Democracy*, p. 56.

22 Van Voris, *Violence in Ulster*, pp. 116–17.

23 ibid. p. 115.

24 Devlin, *The Price of My Soul*, p. 171.

25 ibid. p. 173.

26 Van Voris, *Violence in Ulster*, p. 116.

27 Hastings, *Barricades in Belfast*, p. 103.

28 Dominic Sandbrook, *White Heat: A History of Britain in the Swinging Sixties*

(London 2009), p. 747, quoting from *Hansard*, 22 April 1969.

29 Quoted in Ronald Fraser (ed.), *1968*, p. 243.

30 Kevin Boyle, interview with Simon Prince, 21 October 2006.

31 *The Observer*, 'Cassandra in a Mini-Skirt', 27 April 1969.

32 ibid.

33 Hastings, *Barricades in Belfast*, p. 117.

34 Van Voris, *Violence in Ulster*, p. 133.

35 Ann Hope, 'From civil rights to guerrilla war', p. 63.

36 Kevin Boyle, statement to the Scarman Tribunal, 13 October 1969.

37 Van Voris, *Violence in Ulster*, p. 122.

38 Kevin Boyle, testimony before the Scarman Tribunal, 30 April 1971.

39 ibid.

40 Van Voris, *Violence in Ulster*, p. 122.

41 ibid. p. 123.

42 ibid. p. 123.

43 Hastings, *Barricades in Belfast*, p. 126.

44 Van Voris, *Violence in Ulster*, p. 134.

45 Sunday Times, *Northern Ireland: A Report on the Conflict*, p. 116.

46 Hastings, *Barricades in Belfast*, p. 134.

47 Devlin, *The Price of My Soul*, p. 202.

48 ibid. p. 9.

49 Kevin Boyle, Statement to the Scarman Tribunal, 11 October 1969.

50 Van Voris, *Violence in Ulster*, p. 134.

51 ibid. p. 135.

52 Kevin Boyle, testimony to the Scarman Tribunal, 30 April 1971.

53 *The Irish Times*, 'Porter Bans All Parades for Month', 14 August 1969.

54 Van Voris, *Violence in Ulster*, p. 135.

55 Kevin Boyle, testimony to the Scarman Tribunal, 11 October 1969.

56 ibid.

57 ibid.

58 ibid.

59 Van Voris, *Violence in Ulster*, p. 137.

60 Kevin Boyle, Statement to the Scarman Tribunal, 11 October 1969.

61 Van Voris, *Violence in Ulster*, p. 137.

62 ibid. p. 138.

63 ibid. p. 138.

64 Sunday Times, *Northern Ireland: A Report on the Conflict*, p. 129.

65 Van Voris, *Violence in Ulster*, p. 139.

66 ibid. p. 140.

67 ibid. p. 139.

68 McDermott in *Twenty Years On*, p. 152.

69 Kevin Boyle, interview with Simon Prince, 21 October 2006.
70 Kevin Boyle, testimony to the Scarman Tribunal, 30 April 1971.
71 Sandbrook, *White Heat,* p. 754.

CHAPTER 6

1   David McKittrick and David McVea, *Making Sense of the Troubles* (New York 2002), p. 56.
2   McDermott in *Twenty Years On,* p. 152.
3   Van Voris, *Violence in Ulster,* p. 174.
4   Kevin Boyle, notes at People's Democracy Conference, October 1969.
5   Hastings, *Barricades in Belfast*, p. 186.
6   Eilis McDermott, speech to the National Association of Irish Justice, November 1969.
7   McDermott in *Twenty Years On,* p. 153.
8   *The Irish Times*, 'Boyle Replies to Communist Charge', 19 November 1969.
9   The *Irish Times*, 'PD Not to Contest NICRA Election', 14 February 1970.
10 Van Voris, *Violence in Ulster*, p. 179.
11 Kevin Boyle, letter to Maureen Burke, 7 April 1970.
12 Van Voris, *Violence in Ulster*, p. 182.
13 *The Irish Times*, 'Estate Youths Meet Over Grievances', 13 April 1970.
14 *The Irish Times*, 'Politics, Not Stones, Needed in North', 11 July 1970.
15 Van Voris, *Violence in Ulster*, p. 181.
16 ibid. p. 182.
17 ibid. p. 179.
18 ibid. p. 158.
19 *The New York Times*, 'Calm and Cheerful Ulster Militant', 6 February 1972.
20 Tom Hadden, 'Working with Kevin – A Personal Reminiscence', 2011.
21 Boyle et al., *Law and State,* p. 12.
22 *The Irish Times*, '28 Priests in N.I. Law Protest', 26 April 1971.
23 ibid.
24 Boyle, Scarman testimony, 30 April 1971.
25 *The Irish Times*, 'No campaign of riots was planned either by the IRA or any Protestant organisation', 7 April 1972.
26 Van Voris, *Violence in Ulster,* p. 158.

CHAPTER 7

1   Sunday Times, *Northern Ireland: A Report on the Conflict*, p. 260.
2   Sandbrook, *State of Emergency* (London 2011), p. 242.

3 Moloney, *A Secret History of the IRA*, p. 360.
4 Simon Winchester, *In Holy Terror* (London 1975), p. 163.
5 Sandbrook, *State of Emergency*, p. 245.
6 Van Voris, *Violence in Ulster*, p. 222.
7 Kevin Boyle, interview with Simon Prince, 21 October 2006.
8 ibid. p. 222.
9 ibid. p. 223.
10 ibid. p. 224.
11 McKittrick and McVea, *Making Sense of the Troubles*, p. 72.
12 Kevin Boyle, testimony before the Saville Commission, 11 June 2001.
13 Van Voris, *Violence in Ulster*, p. 225.
14 Kevin Boyle, interview with Simon Prince, 21 October 2006.
15 Van Voris, *Violence in Ulster*, p. 227.
16 Kevin Boyle, testimony to the Saville Commission, 11 June 2001.
17 Van Voris, *Violence in Ulster* p. 229.
18 Notes of an interview with Kevin Boyle by John Barry, *The Sunday Times*, presented as evidence to the Saville Commission.
19 ibid.
20 Kevin Boyle, testimony to the Saville Commission, 11 June 2001.
21 Notes of an interview with Kevin Boyle by John Barry, *The Sunday Times*, presented as evidence to the Saville Commission.
22 Kevin Boyle, testimony to the Saville Commission, 11 June 2001.
23 Winchester, *In Holy Terror*, p. 188.
24 Kevin Boyle, testimony to the Saville Commission, 11 June 2001.
25 ibid.
26 Notes of an interview with Kevin Boyle by John Barry, *The Sunday Times*, presented as evidence to the Saville Commission.
27 Kevin Boyle, testimony to the Saville Commission, 11 June 2001.
28 *The Irish Times*, 'CR Outlines Peace Programme', 21 December 1971.
29 *The Irish Times*, '5000 Defy North's Ban on Marches', 3 January 1972.
30 Kevin Boyle, letter to J.A. Paul, Department of Education, Queen's University, 24 January 1972.
31 ibid.
32 Van Voris, *Violence in Ulster*, p. 239.
33 Notes of an interview with Kevin Boyle by John Barry, *The Sunday Times*, presented as evidence to the Saville Commission.
34 Van Voris, *Violence in Ulster*, p. 239.
35 Sandbrook, *State of Emergency*, p. 481.
36 Saville Commission, 'Principal Conclusions and Overall Assessment of the Bloody Sunday Inquiry, vol. X, p. 58.

37 *The Irish Times*, 'Security Forces Plan to Seal Off Newry', 4 February 1972.
38 Van Voris, *Violence in Ulster*, p. 246.
39 ibid. p. 245.
40 ibid. p. 246.
41 Kevin Boyle, testimony to Saville Commission, 11 June 2001.
42 *The Irish Times*, 'CRA Hopes to Avoid Newry Clashes', 4 February 1972.
43 Van Voris, *Violence in Ulster*, p. 246.
44 ibid. p. 247.
45 Kevin Boyle, interview with Simon Prince, 21 October 2006.
46 ibid.

CHAPTER 8

1   McKittrick and McVea, *Making Sense of the Troubles*, p. 83.
2   Kevin Boyle, interview with Simon Prince, 21 October 2006.
3   Statement of Gerard Donnelly for case before European Commission of Human Rights, 20 April 1972.
4   'Final Observations on the Merits Submitted by the Applicants in the Case of Application Nos. 5577/72–5583/72, Gerard Donnelly, Gerard Bradley, Edward Duffy, John Carlin, Francis McBride, Anthony Kelly, Thomas Kearns versus the Government of the United Kingdom of Great Britain and Northern Ireland'.
5   'Individual Applications Under the European Convention of Human Rights and the Concept of Administrative Practice: The Donnelly Case', *American Journal of International Law*, vol. 68, no. 3 (July, 1974), pp. 440–53.
6   Emergency Application, Gerard Donnelly, Gerard Bradley, Edward Duffy, John Carlin, Francis McBride, Anthony Kelly, Thomas Kearns versus the Government of the United Kingdom of Great Britain and Northern Ireland, 27 May 1972.
7   Kevin Boyle, letter to Professor R. Haughton, 17 January 1972.
8   Edwina Stewart, letter to Kevin Boyle, 5 September 1972.
9   Kevin Boyle, letter to Judge Turlough O'Donnell, 16 April 1973.
10 Kevin Boyle, journal of his time at Yale University, 1973.
11 Letter from Anne Boyle, 25 October 1972.
12 Kevin Boyle, journal of his time at Yale University, 1973.
13 ibid.
14 Claire Palley, letter to Kevin Boyle, 2 March 1973.
15 Donnelly and others vs United Kingdom, Admissibility Decision, 05/04/1973 application number 5577/72; 5583/72.
16 European Commission of Human Rights, verbatim record of the hearing of the parties on admissibility held in Strasbourg on 3, 4 and 5 April 1973, p. 42.

17 Donnelly and others vs United Kingdom, Admissibility Decision, 05/04/1973 application number 5577/72; 5583/72.
18 ibid.
19 ibid.
20 ibid.
21 ibid.
22 ibid.
23 ibid.
24 ibid.
25 *The Irish Times*, 'N.I. "Torture" Claims to be Investigated', 7 April 1973.
26 Kevin Boyle, letter to Judge Turlough O'Donnell, 16 April 1973.

CHAPTER 9

1 Letter to Kevin Boyle from Eileen, December 1973.
2 Letter to Kevin Boyle from Judith, May 1972.
3 Kevin Boyle, letter to Paul Arthur, 1 June 1973.
4 Kevin Boyle, letter to Mike Chinoy, 21 January 1974.
5 ibid.
6 Kevin Boyle et al., *Law and State*, p. 93.
7 ibid. p. 148.
8 ibid. p. 97.
9 Kevin Boyle, Tom Hadden, Paddy Hillyard, 'The Facts on Internment', *Fortnight*, 29 November 1974.
10 ibid.
11 ibid.
12 'Final Observation on the Merits Submitted by the Applicants in the Case of Gerard Donnelly, Gerard Bradley, Edward Duffy, John Carlin, Francis McBride, Anthony Kelly, Thomas Kearns versus the Government of the United Kingdom of Great Britain and Northern Ireland', September 1975, pp. 4–6.
13 ibid. p. 6.
14 ibid. p. 41.
15 Kevin Boyle, letter to Paul O'Higgins, 20 July 1975.
16 ibid.
17 *The Irish Times*, 'European Judges Visit Long Kesh', 24 June 1975.
18 'Final Observation on the Merits Submitted by the Applicants in the Case of Gerard Donnelly, Gerard Bradley, Edward Duffy, John Carlin, Francis McBride, Anthony Kelly, Thomas Kearns versus the Government of the United Kingdom of Great Britain and Northern Ireland', September 1975, p. 22.

19 Counter-Memorial of the Government of the United Kingdom, 19 January 1974, cited in Final Observations. p. 30.

20 'Final Observation on the Merits Submitted by the Applicants in the Case of Gerard Donnelly, Gerard Bradley, Edward Duffy, John Carlin, Francis McBride, Anthony Kelly, Thomas Kearns versus the Government of the United Kingdom of Great Britain and Northern Ireland', September 1975, p. 6.

21 ibid. p. 11.

22 ibid. p. 24.

23 ibid. p. 43.

24 ibid. p. 24.

25 ibid. pp. 51–2.

26 ibid. p. 4.

27 European Commission of Human Rights, Decision, 'Gerard Donnelly and six others against the United Kingdom', 15 December 1975, p. 87.

28 ibid. p. 85.

29 Kevin Boyle letter to Hurst Hannum, 21 June 1976.

30 *American Journal of International Law*, vol. 71, no. 2, April 1977.

31 Kevin Boyle, letter to Dan Charles, 6 March 1975.

32 Kevin Boyle, letter to Hurst Hannum, 21 June 1976.

CHAPTER 10

1 Kevin Boyle, 'The Role of Law, Past and Present, in Ireland', presentation at conference organized by the Committee for an Irish Forum, August 1975.

2 ibid.

3 ibid.

4 ibid.

5 ibid.

6 Moloney, *A Secret History of the IRA*, p. 145.

7 Kevin Boyle, letter to Laurie Taylor, 16 March 1977.

8 ibid.

9 *The Irish Times*, 'Search Continues for UDA Men', 10 April 1975.

10 'In Her Majesty's Court of Criminal Appeal in Northern Ireland, R. vs John Noel Deery', 13 May 1977.

11 Kevin Boyle, letter to Seán MacBride, 11 October 1977.

12 Kevin Boyle, letter to Laurie Taylor, 16 March 1977.

13 Kevin Boyle, interview with Simon Prince, 21 October 2006.

14 'The Case for Reform', Kevin Boyle and Patricia Maynes, *The Honest Ulsterman*, February 1969, pp. 2–3.

15 Jeffrey Dudgeon, letter to Kevin Boyle, 30 October 1975.

16 Kevin Boyle, letter to Jeffrey Dudgeon, 31 October 1975.

17 Kevin Boyle, letter to Michael O'Boyle, 7 November 1975.

18 ibid.

19 ibid.

20 'Initial Observations of the Applicant X against United Kingdom', European Commission of Human Rights, 3 March 1978.

21 Kevin Boyle, handwritten notes on homosexual law issues, undated.

22 ibid.

23 ibid.

24 ibid.

25 'Initial Observations of the Applicant X against United Kingdom', European Commission of Human Rights, 3 March 1978.

26 ibid.

27 ibid.

28 ibid.

29 Kevin Myers, *Watching the Door* (Dublin 2009), p. 148.

30 Herbert McCabe obituary, *The Daily Telegraph*, 20 August 2001.

31 Kevin Boyle, letter to William Twining, 15 October 1976.

32 ibid.

CHAPTER 11

1 Holland, *Hope Against History*, pp. 121–3.

2 *The Irish Times*, 'Professor Says Uncooperative NI Catholics Get Heavier Sentences', 10 August 1977.

3 Peter Taylor, *Beating the Terrorists* (London 1980), p. 221.

4 ibid. p. 222.

5 Amnesty International, *Report of an Amnesty International mission to Northern Ireland*, London, June 1978.

6 Taylor, *Beating the Terrorists*, pp. 332–3.

7 Observations by the applicant on the Observations by the Government of the United Kingdom on the Admissibility of Application No. 7525/76 lodged by Jeffrey Dudgeon, 22 February 1977.

8 ibid.

9 ibid.

10 European Commission of Human Rights, Decision of the Commission as to the Admissibility of Application 7525/76, 3 March 1978.

11 Observations by the applicant on the Observations by the Government of the United Kingdom on the Admissibility of Application No. 7525/76 lodged by Jeffrey Dudgeon, 7 April 1977.

12 European Commission of Human Rights, Decision of the Commission as to the Admissibility of Application 7525/76, March 3, 1978.

13 Observations by the applicant on the Observations by the Government of the United Kingdom on Admissibility of Application No. 7525/76 lodged by Jeffrey Dudgeon, 7 April 1977.

14 ibid.

15 ibid.

16 European Commission of Human Rights, Decision of the Commission as to the Admissibility of Application 7525/76, 3 March 1978.

17 Michael D. Goldhaber, *A People's History of the European Court of Human Rights* (New Brunswick 2009), p. 37.

18 Kevin Boyle, letter to David Norris, 4 August 1977.

19 Francis Keenan, letter to Theo Gruber, Acting Secretary to the European Commission of Human Rights, 22 September 1977.

20 ibid.

21 Peter Glazebrook, letter to Kevin Boyle, 20 May 1977.

22 Kevin Boyle, letter to Colm Ó hEocha, 20 July 1977.

23 Peter Glazebrook, letter to Kevin Boyle, 25 June 1977.

24 Kevin Boyle, letter to Seán Donlon, 8 December 1978.

25 ibid.

26 Kevin Boyle, letter to Seán Donlon, 8 December 1978.

27 'Legal Studies at UCG: A Prospectus', May 1980.

28 ibid.

29 Kevin Boyle, letter to Seán Donlon, 8 December 1978.

30 'Legal Studies at UCG: A Prospectus', May 1980.

31 ibid.

32 Kevin Boyle, letter to Justice Costello, 13 November 1979.

33 ibid.

34 Kevin Boyle, letter to Hurst Hannum, undated but likely autumn 1979.

35 ibid.

CHAPTER 12

1 Ed Bates, *The Evolution of the European Convention on Human Rights* (Oxford 2010), p. 14.

2 Council of Europe, *European Yearbook, 1975,* p. 529.

3 European Commission of Human Rights, 'Decision as to the Admission, Application 7525/76 by Jeffrey Dudgeon against the United Kingdom', 3 March 1978, p. 15.

4 Dudgeon v. the Government of the United Kingdom of Great Britain and Northern Ireland, Applicant's Observations on the Merits, 26 August 1978.

5 Observations by the applicant of the Government of the United Kingdom on the Merits of Application No.7525/76 lodged by Jeffrey Dudgeon, 20 March 1979.

6 ibid.

7 European Commission of Human Rights, Application No. 7525/76, Jeffrey Dudgeon v. the United Kingdom, Verbatim Record of the Hearing on the Merits held in Strasbourg on 6 July 1979, pp. 3–4.

8 ibid. p. 4.

9 ibid.

10 ibid.

11 ibid. p. 6.

12 ibid. p. 10.

13 ibid.

14 ibid. p. 13.

15 ibid. p. 14.

16 ibid. p. 21.

17 ibid. p. 20.

18 ibid. p. 21.

19 ibid. p. 22.

20 ibid. p. 23.

21 ibid.

22 ibid. p. 27.

23 ibid.

24 ibid. p. 28.

25 ibid. p. 35.

26 ibid. p. 42.

27 ibid.

28 ibid. p. 45.

29 ibid. p. 46.

30 ibid. p. 49.

31 European Commission of Human Rights, Application No. 7525/76, Jeffrey Dudgeon v. the United Kingdom, Report of the Commission, 13 March 1980, p. 36.

32 ibid. p. 30.

33 ibid. p. 35.

34 ibid. p. 38.

35 Letters from Jeffrey Dudgeon to Kevin Boyle and Francis Keenan, 1 July 1980.

36 ibid.

37 Kevin Boyle, letter to Jeffrey Dudgeon, 30 March 1981.

38 ibid.

39 European Court of Human Rights, Case of Dudgeon v. the United Kingdom, Judgment, 22 October 1981, p. 14.
40 ibid. p. 19.
41 Goldhaber, *A People's History of the European Court of Human Rights*, p. 412.

CHAPTER 13

1   Kevin Boyle, letter to Hurst Hannum, 7 September 1978.
2   European Commission of Human Rights, Application 8317/78, Thomas McFeeley et al. v. the United Kingdom, 15 May 1980, p. 67.
3   ibid. p. 77.
4   ibid. p 68.
5   Kevin Boyle, letter to Hurst Hannum, 7 September 1978.
6   *The Irish Times,* 'H-Block Men to Seek New Code', 9 August 1978.
7   Thomas Hennessey, *Hunger Strike* (Dublin 2014), p. 31.
8   Kevin Boyle, letter to Hurst Hannum, mid-1979.
9   ibid.
10 Kevin Boyle, Tom Hadden and Paddy Hillyard, *Ten Years On in Northern Ireland: The Legal Control of Political Violence* (London 1980), p. 96.
11 ibid.
12 ibid.
13 ibid. p. 97.
14 Kevin Boyle, letter to David Nelligan, 1 September 1979.
15 ibid. p. 44.
16 ibid. p. 86.
17 ibid. p. 90.
18 ibid. p. 86.
19 ibid.
20 Brice Dickson, *The European Convention on Human Rights and the Conflict in Northern Ireland* (Oxford 2010), p. 282.
21 Hennessey, *Hunger Strike*, p. 226.
22 Michael Farrell, letter to Kevin Boyle, 29 October 1980.
23 McKittrick and McVea, *Making Sense of the Troubles*, p. 143.
24 Hennessey, *Hunger Strike*, p. 253.
25 Former IRA prisoner Richard O'Rawe contended that, in order to reap the political benefits, Adams deliberately rejected a deal that would have ended the hunger strike and saved the lives of several of those involved. See Richard O'Rawe, *Blanketmen: An Untold Story of the H-Block Hunger Strike* (Dublin 2005).
26 Kevin Boyle, interview with Simon Prince, 21 October 2006.

27 Kevin Boyle, letter to Orlando Delogu, 21 July 1981.

28 Kevin Boyle, letter to Garret FitzGerald, 26 August 1981.

29 *Portland Maine Press Herald*, 'Irish Lawyer says Situation Misunderstood in the U.S.', 23 September 1981.

CHAPTER 14

1 Kevin Boyle, letter to Lord Lowry, 18 December 1981.

2 Kevin Boyle, letter to Orlando Delogu, 15 February 1982.

3 Conor Gearty, 'Doing Human Rights: Three Lessons From the Field' in G. Gilbert, F. Hampson and C. Sandoval (eds), *Strategic Visions for Human Rights: Essays in Honour of Professor Kevin Boyle*, (London 2011), p. 52.

4 Kevin Boyle, letter to Declan Costello, 11 January 1983.

5 Kevin Boyle, letter to Bert Lockwood, 5 February 1983.

6 Kevin Boyle handwritten notes, undated.

7 *The Irish Times*, 'Itinerant Rights Set Out in New Charter', 11 June 1984.

8 Kevin Boyle, 'Human Rights Perspectives: What We have Learned So Far', *Essex Human Rights Review*, vol. 5, no. 1, July 2008, p. 10.

9 'A Short History of the Plastic Bullet', *Fortnight*, July/August 1981.

10 Kevin Boyle, letter to Hurst Hannum, 26 October 1982.

11 Kevin Boyle, 'The Use of Plastic Bullets (or Baton Rounds) – The Legal Position', submission to the International Tribunal of Inquiry into Deaths and Serious Injuries caused by Plastic Bullets in Northern Ireland, 2 August 1981.

12 ibid.

13 ibid.

14 ibid.

15 ibid.

16 Kevin Boyle, letter to Hurst Hannum, 26 October 1982.

17 'Applicant's Observations on the Admissibility and Merits of Application No. 9013/80, Olive Farrell v. the United Kingdom', January 1982.

18 ibid.

19 ibid.

20 Kevin Boyle, letter to Leonard Leigh, 6 October 1982.

21 *The Irish Times*, 'Strasbourg Hearing on Three Deaths', 15 December 1982.

22 Hust Hannum, letter to Kevin Boyle, 20 June 1983.

23 Kevin Boyle, letter to Richard Ferguson QC, 27 September 1983.

24 ibid.

25 Report of the Commission, Olive Farrell v. the United Kingdom, 2 October 1984.

26 Kevin Boyle, letter to Richard Ferguson QC, 7 September 1982.

CHAPTER 15

1 Quoted in Holland, *Hope Against History*, p. 159.
2 Garret FitzGerald, *Just Garret* (Dublin 2011), p. 383.
3 Kevin Boyle, handwritten notes for a talk on the New Ireland Forum, undated but likely 1984.
4 Kevin Boyle, letter to Colm Ó hEocha, 13 January 1984.
5 Kevin Boyle and Tom Hadden, Submission to the New Ireland Forum, 25 November 1983.
6 ibid.
7 ibid.
8 ibid.
9 Geraldine Smyth, letter to Orlando Delogu, 21 February 1984.
10 Kevin Boyle, 'Document Two', undated.
11 Walter Kirwan, note, 30 December 1983.
12 *New Ireland Forum Report*, Chapter 5, paragraph 7, 2 May 1984.
13 FitzGerald, *Just Garret*, p. 387.
14 *New Ireland Forum Report*, Chapter 5, paragraph 10, 2 May 1984.
15 Walter Kirwan, 'Kevin Boyle: His Role in Promoting a Political Settlement and Shaping its Human Rights Dimension', address for Commemorative Conference for Kevin Boyle, 11 June 2011.
16 Kevin Boyle and Tom Hadden, 'How to Read the New Ireland Forum Report: Searching Between the Lines for a Realistic Framework for Action', June 1984.
17 ibid.
18 ibid.
19 ibid.
20 ibid.
21 ibid.
22 *The Irish Times*, 'Recognition of Northern Ireland Included in Peace Plan', 24 September 1984.
23 ibid.
24 Letter from D.A. Hill, Private Secretary to the Secretary of State for Northern Ireland to John Coles, Private Secretary for Foreign and Defence Affairs to the Prime Minister, 13 March 1984.
25 Copy of Kevin Boyle and Tom Hadden submission to the New Ireland Forum with underlined sections accompanying letter from D.A. Hill, Private Secretary to the Secretary of State for Northern Ireland to John Coles, Private Secretary for Foreign and Defence Affairs to the Prime Minister, 13 March 1984.

26 ibid.

27 *The Irish Times*, 'Another Conspiracy Theory Takes Root', 10 November 1984.

28 Tom Hadden, 'Mining the Kevin Boyle Archive', 28 November 2014.

29 ibid.

30 'Note for the Record', Anglo-Irish Summit, first evening, 19 November 1984.

31 FitzGerald, *Just Garret*, p. 387.

32 ibid. p. 390.

33 Transcript, Margaret Thatcher press conference, 19 November 1984.

34 ibid.

35 *The Irish Times*, text of Chequers communiqué, 20 November 1984.

36 Tom Hadden 'Mining the Kevin Boyle Archive', 28 November 2014.

37 Email from Tom Hadden, 10 April 2018.

38 Agreement between the Government of Ireland and the Government of the United Kingdom, 15 November 1985.

39 Kevin Boyle and Tom Hadden, *Ireland: A Positive Proposal* (London 1985), p. 47.

40 Walter Kirwan, 'Kevin Boyle: His Role in Promoting a Political Settlement and Shaping its Human Rights Dimension', address for Commemorative Conference for Kevin Boyle, 11 June 2011.

CHAPTER 16

1 *The Washington Post*, 'S. African Panel Urges Overhaul of Courts', 9 April 1984.

2 Michael Savage, 'The Imposition of the Pass Laws on the African Population of South Africa, 1916–1984', *African Affairs*, Oxford Academic Press, vol. 85, issue 339, 1986, p. 181.

3 David Harris, *The White Tribe of Africa* (Berkeley 1981), p. 256.

4 Geoff Budlender interview, Legal Resources Centre Oral History Project, 14 December 2007.

5 Kevin Boyle, 'South Africa: Imprisonment Under the Pass Laws', Amnesty International Report, January 1986, p. 5.3.

6 ibid. p. 6.5.

7 ibid. p. 3.3.

8 ibid. p. 5.8.

9 ibid. p. 5.3.

10 ibid. p. 6.8.

11 ibid. p. 6.5.

12 ibid. p. 6.10.

13 ibid. p. 6.10.

14 ibid. p. 5.8.

15 ibid. p. 6.4.

16 ibid. p. 6.12.

17 ibid. pp. 7.7–7.10.

18 Kevin Boyle, letter to Joan Boyle, 26 May 1985.

19 ibid.

20 ibid.

21 *The Washington Post*, 'S. African Panel Urges Overhaul of Courts', 9 April 1984.

22 Kevin Boyle, letter to Joan Boyle, 26 May 1985.

23 Kevin Boyle, letter to Joan Boyle, 21 May 1985.

24 Kevin Boyle, 'South Africa: Imprisonment Under the Pass Laws', Amnesty International Report, January 1986, pp. 6.13–6.14.

25 Kevin Boyle, letter to Joan Boyle, 26 May 1985.

26 Kevin Boyle, 'South Africa: Imprisonment Under the Pass Laws', 1986, p. 9.1.

CHAPTER 17

1 *The Irish Times*, 'Wrongly Jailed for Train Heist', 18 October 2014.

2 Derek Dunne and Gene Kerrigan, *Round Up the Usual Suspects* (Magill 1994), p. 224.

3 'Petition of Eamonn Nick Kelly to the European Commission of Human Rights, filed on his behalf by Professor K. Boyle, Barrister at Law and Mary Robinson, Senior Counsel', 7 June 1983.

4 Kevin Boyle, letter to Nicky Kelly, 16 June 1983.

5 Letter from H. Kruger, Secretary to the European Commission of Human Rights, to Garrett Sheehan, 19 July 1983.

6 'Observations of the Government of Ireland, Application 10416/83, Eamonn N. Kelly v. Ireland', p. 31, undated but likely late 1983.

7 ibid. p. 18.

8 Kevin Boyle, letter to Nicky Kelly, 4 January 1984.

9 Eamonn N. Kelly v. Ireland, Application 10416/83, Applicant's Replies to Government's Observations, February 1984, p. 19.

10 Kevin Boyle and Mary Robinson, 'Confidential Memorandum to the Irish Government', 29 May 1984.

11 ibid.

12 ibid.

13 *The Irish Times*, 'Very Difficult to Defend Stance', 19 July 1984.

14 'Quinn v. Ireland, Judgment, European Court of Human Rights', 21 December 2000.

15 Billy Hutchinson, letter to Kevin Boyle, 4 December 1984.

16 Kevin Boyle, letter to Billy Hutchinson, 18 December 1984.

17 'Special Category Life Sentence Prisoners', memo sent from Billy Hutchinson to Kevin Boyle, undated but likely December 1984.

18 ibid.
19 ibid.
20 Kevin Boyle, letter to Billy Hutchinson, 15 February 1985.
21 Bernadette McAliskey, letter to Kevin Boyle, 20 August 1985.
22 Mary McGlinchey, letter to Kevin Boyle, August 1985.
23 Bernadette McAliskey, letter to Kevin Boyle, 20 August 1985.
24 Kevin Boyle, letter to Bernadette McAliskey, 9 September 1985.
25 Kevin Boyle, letter to Seamus Ó Cathail, 4 May 1988.
26 Kevin Boyle, letter to Judy Hayes, 8 July 1987.
27 Kevin Boyle, letter to Kit Carson, 23 November 1985.

CHAPTER 18

1 Statement by Zwelakhe Sisulu on the Occasion of the 20th Anniversary of the Founding of Article 19, 11 December 2008.
2 Kevin Boyle, 'The Plight of Zwelakhe Sisulu', Index on Censorship, 5/87.
3 Kevin Boyle, letter to Ben Hooberman, 16 December 1986.
4 Kevin Boyle, letter to David Goodhall, 9 September 1986.
5 Kevin Boyle, 'Article 19: Origins and Achievements', Article 19, July 2008.
6 Kevin Boyle, 'Freedom of Information and the Press', speech at the International Institute of Human Rights, 31 July 1992.
7 UN General Assembly Resolution 59(1), 14 December 1946.
8 Kevin Boyle, letter to B. Dembitzer, 6 May 1986.
9 ibid.
10 ibid.
11 ibid.
12 Kevin Boyle, letter to David Goodhall, 9 September 1986.
13 Kevin Boyle, 'Article 19: Origins and Achievements', Article 19, July 2008.
14 Kevin Boyle, interview with National Public Radio, undated but likely 1988.
15 ibid.
16 ibid.
17 Kevin Boyle, 'Article 19: Origins and Achievements', Article 19, July 2008.
18 ibid.
19 ibid.
20 *Article 19 Bulletin*, August–September, 1987.
21 *Article 19, World Report 1988, Information, Freedom and Censorship* (New York 1988), Kevin Boyle introduction, p. 10.
22 ibid. p. 11.
23 Kevin Boyle, letter to Seamus Ó Cathail, 4 May 1988.
24 Kevin Boyle, letter to Judy Hayes, 8 July 1987.

25 Kevin Boyle, letter to Seamus Ó Cathail, 4 May 1988.

26 Statement by Zwelakhe Sisulu on the Occasion of the 20th Anniversary of the Founding of Article 19, 11 December 2008.

27 Salman Rushdie, 'The Disappeared', *The New Yorker,* 17 September 2012.

28 Daniel Pipes, *The Rushdie Affair* (London 2017), p. 27.

29 Christopher Hitchens, 'Assassins of the Mind', *Vanity Fair,* February 2009.

30 Rushdie, *The New Yorker,* 17 September 2012.

31 *Fact, Fiction, and the Fatwa: A Chronology of Censorship,* Article 19 (London 1992), p. 7.

32 Kevin Boyle personal notes, undated.

33 *The Times Literary Supplement,* 3–9 March 1989.

34 ibid.

35 ibid.

36 ibid.

37 *The Irish Times,* 'Literary World in Rushdie Campaign', 2 March 1989.

38 Kevin Boyle personal notes, undated.

39 'The Crime of Blasphemy – Why It Should Be Abolished', The International Committee for the Defence of Salman Rushdie and his Publishers, May 1989.

40 *Fact, Fiction, and the Fatwa,* p. 29.

41 Email from Salman Rushdie via his agent, 2 May 2018.

CHAPTER 19

1 'Somalia: Report on an Amnesty International Visit and Current Human Rights Concerns', London, 25 January 1990.

2 Kevin Boyle, letter to Lance Lindblom, 9 October 1989.

3 Kevin Boyle, 'Twenty-Five Years of Human Rights at Essex', *Essex Human Rights Review,* vol. 5, no. 1, July 2008, p. 14.

4 Kevin Boyle talk, 'Indivisibility of Human Rights, Social Justice, and Article 18 of the Universal Declaration', 1998.

5 Geoffrey Robertson and Ivor Crewe, Sir Nigel Rodley obituary, *The Guardian,* 2 February 2017.

6 Kevin Boyle, *Essex Human Rights Review,* vol. 5, no. 1, July 2008, p. 16.

7 International Human Rights Law class, final examination 1997–8, MA in the Theory and Practice of Human Rights, University of Essex.

8 Kevin Boyle, *Essex Human Rights Review,* vol. 5, no. 1, July 2008, p. 11.

9 ibid. p. 10.

10 ibid. p. 11.

11 'British Democracy – How Healthy is It?' *Wyvern,* 22 May 1991.

12 For an example of a more recent audit, see 'How Democratic is the UK? The 2012 Audit', Democratic Audit, 2012.

13 Kevin Boyle talk, 'Indivisibility of Human Rights, Social Justice, and Article 18 of the Universal Declaration', 1998.

14 ibid.

CHAPTER 20

1 Kevin Boyle, 'Speech for the Applicant', European Court of Human Rights, 20 April 1994.

2 Memo from Kevin Boyle to law colleagues, 24 April 1994.

3 European Commission of Human Rights, 'Decision of the Commission as to the Admissibility of Application 1580/89 by Jens Olaf Jersild Against Denmark', 8 September 1992, p. 3.

4 Kevin Boyle memo, 'About Jersild', undated but likely 1989.

5 Kevin Boyle, 'Jersild and Jensen v. Denmark, Case Filed With the European Commission of Human Rights', August 1989.

6 'Application No. 15890/89, Jersild v. Denmark, Written observations of the Government of Denmark on the admissibility and merits of the case', 20 December 1991, p. 6.

7 European Court of Human Rights, 'Case of Jersild v. Denmark, Judgment', 23 September 1994, p. 14.

8 Application No. 15890/89, Jersild v. Denmark, Applicant's written observations in response to the observations of the Danish government', 17 February 1992, p. 6.

9 ibid. p. 2.

10 ibid. p. 5.

11 ibid.

12 ibid. p. 6.

13 ibid. p. 11.

14 ibid. p. 16.

15 ibid. p. 26.

16 ibid. p. 18.

17 ibid. pp. 18 and 19.

18 ibid. p. 51.

19 European Commission of Human Rights, 'Application No. 15890/89, Jens Olaf Jersild v. Denmark, report of the Commission', 8 July 1993, p. 21.

20 Audio transcript of hearing before the European Court of Human Rights, Jersild v. Denmark, 20 April 1994.

21 ibid.

22 ibid.

23 European Court of Human Rights, 'Case of Jersild v. Denmark, Judgment', 23 September 1994, p. 20.

24 ibid. p. 21.

25 ibid.

26 *The Western Law Gazette*, 'In Conversation with Professor Kevin Boyle', Spring 1995, p. 17.

27 Draft of Betty Purcell application to the European Commission of Human Rights, July 1989.

28 ibid.

29 ibid.

30 ibid.

31 European Commission of Human Rights, 'As to the admissibility of Application No. 15404/89 by Betty Purcell et al. against Ireland', 16 April 1991, p. 13.

32 ibid. p. 11.

33 *The Irish Times*, 'Section 31', 18 December 1993.

34 *The Irish Times*, 'American Writers in Adams Protest', 8 August 1993.

35 *The Independent*, 'Let us hear what they say: Dublin's draconian political censorship is at last looking vulnerable', 21 October 1993.

36 *The Irish Times*, 'Let in the Light', 12 January 1994.

37 European Commission of Human Rights, '*Bladet Tromsø* and Stensas v. Norway, Report of the Commission', 9 July 1998, p. 6.

38 ibid. p. 45.

39 ibid. p. 27.

40 European Commission of Human Rights, 'Decision as to the Admissibility of Application 21980/93, *Bladet Tromsø* and Pal Stensas v. Norway', 26 May 1997, p. 14.

41 European Commission of Human Rights, '*Bladet Tromsø* and Stensas v. Norway, Report of the Commission', 9 July 1998, pp. 27, 28.

42 European Court of Human Rights, 'Case of *Bladet Tromsø* and Stensas v. Norway, Application 21980/93, Verbatim record of hearing', 27 January 1999, p. 11.

43 ibid. p. 12.

44 ibid. p. 13.

45 ibid. p. 18.

46 ibid. p. 18.

47 ibid. p. 15.

48 ibid.

49 ibid. pp. 24 and 25.

50 ibid. p. 27.

51 European Court of Human Rights, 'Case of *Bladet Tromsø* and Stensas v. Norway, Application No. 21980/93, Judgment', 20 May 1999, p. 35.

52 ibid. p. 34.

CHAPTER 21

1 Kevin Boyle, publishing proposal for Cambridge University Press, 'Litigating Gross Violations of Human Rights: The case of Turkey', 23 July 1998.
2 Kevin Boyle, letter to Mary Robinson, 13 September 1994.
3 ibid.
4 Hüseyin Akdivar and Others v. Turkey, Application No. 2893/93, Applicants' Memorial on the Merits, 23 June 1995.
5 Goldhaber, *A People's History of the European Court of Human Rights*, pp. 125–6.
6 European Commission of Human Rights Application No. 21893/93, Hüseyin Akdivar, Abdurrahman Akdivar, Ahmet Akdivar, Ali Akdivar, Zülfükar Çiçek, Ahmet Çiçek, Abdurrahman Aktas, Mehmet Karabulut, against Turkey, Report of the Commission, 26 October 1995, p. 4.
7 ibid. p. 17.
8 Hüseyin Akdivar and Others v. Turkey, Application No. 2893/93, Applicants' Memorial on the Merits, 23 June 1995.
9 ibid.
10 ibid.
11 ibid.
12 European Commission of Human Rights, Application No. 21987/93, Zeki Aksoy against Turkey, Report of the Commission, 23 October 1995, p. 11.
13 ibid. p. 13.
14 ibid. p. 14.
15 ibid. p. 13.
16 Human Rights Watch, 'Displaced and Disregarded: Turkey's Failing Village Return Program', October 2002.
17 Hüseyin Akdivar and Others v. Turkey, Application No. 2893/93, Applicants' Memorial on the Merits, 23 June 1995.
18 European Court of Human Rights, Case of Akdivar and Others v. Turkey, Application 21893/93, Judgment, 19 September 1995, p. 22.
19 European Court of Human Rights, Case of Aksoy v. Turkey (100/1995/606/ 694), Judgment, 1 December 1996, p. 3.
20 'Gross Violations of Human Rights: Invoking the European Convention on Human Rights in the Case of Turkey', Aisling Reidy, Françoise Hampson and Kevin Boyle, *Netherlands Quarterly of Human Rights*, vol. 15/2, 161–73, 1997.
21 Dr Onder Bakircioglu and Prof. Brice Dickson, 'The European Convention in Conflicted Societies: The Experience of Northern Ireland and Turkey', *International and Comparative Law Quarterly*, 2017, 66(2), p. 22.
22 Goldhaber, *A People's History of the European Court of Human Rights*, pp. 137–8.

23 European Commission of Human Rights, Application No. 23178/94 Sukran Aydin v. Turkey, Report of the Commission, 7 March 1996.

24 European Court of Human Rights, Case of Aydin v. Turkey 57/1996/676/866, Judgment, 25 September 1997.

25 Goldhaber, *A People's History of the European Court of Human Rights*, p. 136.

26 Dilek Kurban, 'Strasbourg Court Jurisprudence and Human Rights in Turkey: An Overview of Litigation, Implementation, and Domestic Reform', Report prepared for the JURISTRAS project funded by the European Commission, January 2007, pp. 23–4.

CHAPTER 22

1 Kevin Boyle and Tom Hadden, *Northern Ireland: The Choice* (London 1994), p. 2.

2 'Analysis: A Place Apart', BBC News, 26 November 1992.

3 Andy Pollak, (ed.), *A Citizen's Inquiry: The Opsahl Report on Northern Ireland* (Dublin 1992), p. 391.

4 Kevin Boyle, 'Reactions to TH Draft', 3 January 1993.

5 ibid.

6 Tom Hadden and Kevin Boyle, 'Northern Ireland: Building a Democratic Future, A Submission to the Opsahl Commission', February 1993.

7 Pollak, *A Citizen's Inquiry: The Opsahl Report on Northern Ireland*, p. 219.

8 Garret FitzGerald, 'A Welcome Antidote to the Politics of Despair', *The Irish Times*, 12 June 1993.

9 Kevin Boyle, letter to Northern Ireland Standing Advisory Committee on Human Rights, 23 December 1992.

10 ibid.

11 Moloney, *A Secret History of the IRA*, p. 278.

12 The Downing Street Declaration, 15 December 1993.

13 ibid.

14 ibid.

15 Walter Kirwan, 'Address for Commemorative Conference for Kevin Boyle', 11 June 2011.

16 Boyle and Hadden, *Northern Ireland: The Choice*, pp. 2–3.

17 Kevin Boyle and Tom Hadden, 'Separation or Sharing', draft essay, undated but likely spring 1994.

18 Boyle and Hadden, *Northern Ireland: The Choice*, pp. 212–13.

19 ibid. p. xiv.

20 *The Irish Times*, 'The Way to the Future', 10 September 1994.

21 *Human Rights Quarterly*, vol. 16, no. 3 (August 1994), p. 591.

22 Letter to Tom Hadden from Peter Bell, 6 April 1994.

23 ibid.

24 Kirwan, 'Address for Commemorative Conference for Kevin Boyle'.

25 Robin Wilson, 'Forum or Farce: The Failure of Political Dialogue in Northern Ireland', *Études Irlandaises*, 1992, p. 189.

26 Kirwan, 'Address for Commemorative Conference for Kevin Boyle'.

27 The Belfast Agreement, 10 April 1998.

28 ibid.

29 'A New Beginning: Policing in Northern Ireland', The Report of the Independent Commission on Policing in Northern Ireland, September 1999, p. 11.

30 Kevin Boyle, *Widgery: A Critique*, April 1972.

31 Kevin Boyle, interview with Simon Prince, 21 October 2006.

32 Kevin Boyle note, 'Bloody Sunday Inquiry – Meeting with Counsel', undated but likely 2000.

33 Kevin Boyle, testimony before the Saville Commission, 11 June 2001.

34 Kevin Boyle, interview with Simon Prince, 21 October 2006.

35 Kevin Boyle, letter to Francis Keenan, 1 August 2000.

36 ibid.

CHAPTER 23

1 Kevin Boyle, 'My Year with the UN', *Higher Education and Research Opportunities in the United Kingdom*, 1 July 2003.

2 ibid.

3 ibid.

4 Mary Robinson statement, 11 September 2001.

5 ibid.

6 Kevin Boyle, 'My Year with the UN'.

7 Note from the United Nations High Commissioner for Human Rights, 'A Human Rights Perspective on the September 11 Terrorist Attacks in the United States', 20 September 2001.

8 ibid.

9 Draft Joint Statement by OHCHR, UNHCR, UNICEF, UNDP, OCHA and WFP, 19 September 2001.

10 Kevin Boyle, email to Iqbal Riza, 12 October 2001.

11 'Championing Human Rights in a Year of International Conflict', University of Essex news release, 28 October 2002.

12 ibid.

13 Note to the Chair of the Counter-Terrorism Committee: 'A Human Rights Perspective on Counter-Terrorist Measures', December 2001.

14 Kevin Boyle memo to Mary Robinson, 'A Comment on the Presidential Decree of 13 November, 2001: Military Order on the Detention, Treatment

and Trial of Certain Non-U.S. Citizens in the War Against Terrorism', November 2001.

15 Mary Robinson, *Everybody Matters* (London 2013), p. 207.

16 Kevin Boyle, 'My Year with the UN'.

17 Mary Robinson, 'Human Rights: A Uniting Framework, Report of the High Commissioner submitted pursuant to General Assembly resolution 48/141', 27 February 2002.

18 ibid.

19 Robinson, *Everybody Matters*, p. 271.

20 ibid.

CHAPTER 24

1 *Dimensions of Racism*, Proceedings of a Workshop to Commemorate the End of the United Nations Third Decade to Combat Racism and Racial Discrimination, Paris, 19–20 February 2003, United Nations, 2005, p. 9.

2 ibid. p. 11.

3 Kevin Boyle, letter to Louise Arbour, 8 June 2005.

4 Stephen Marks, 'International Law and the "War on Terrorism": Post 9/11 Responses by the United States and Asia Pacific Countries', *Asia Pacific Law Review*, vol. 14, no. 2, 2006.

5 Florian Hoffman, '*A Voice for Human Rights* edited by Kevin Boyle', book review, *International Human Rights Review*, June 2006.

6 Case of Sejdić and Finci v. Bosnia and Herzegovina (Applications 27996/06 and 34836/06), Judgment, Strasbourg, 22 December 2009.

7 Kevin Boyle and Cherian George, 'Freedom of Speech: The Emerging Global Consensus', *The Nation*, 26 November 2008.

8 ibid.

9 Kevin Boyle, interview with Simon Prince, 21 October 2006.

10 Kevin Boyle talk notes, 'QUB – Civil Rights 1968 – Then and Now 3–4 October 2008'.

11 ibid.

12 ibid.

13 ibid.

14 ibid.

15 ibid.

16 Kevin Boyle, email to Gerard Quinn, 8 November 2010.

17 ibid.

AFTERWORD

1 Kevin Boyle, '25 Years of Human Rights at Essex', 2008, p. 2.
2 ibid.
3 Kevin Boyle talk notes, 'QUB – Civil Rights 1968 – Then and Now 3–4 October 2008'.
4 ibid.
5 David Rieff, 'The End of Human Rights?' *Foreign Policy*, 9 April 2018.
6 Boyle, '25 Years of Human Rights at Essex', p. 2.
7 Kevin Boyle, 'Text of Talk to Essex University Graduate Human Rights Students', 22 January 2001.
8 Mary Robinson, *A Voice for Human Rights* (Philadelphia 2006), p. 350.

Index